Antiques MAGAZINE

The indispensable weekly guide to buying & selling antiques

The full-colour weekly magazine offering a combination of News, Views and Specialist Articles for lovers of antiques, including Exhibitions coverage, up-to-date Auction Reports, the unique Art Prices Index and comprehensive Fairs and Auction Calendars.

et the
perts

pione

Preview
The Spring Olympia Fair

Scottish Barometers

Around the Saplerooms

TV & Radio Selection

Auction & Fairs Calendars Pull-out

News on the Net

1 year's subscription is £52 weekly UK (48 issues),
Europe £72.00, USA/Canada £92.00, Australia/New Zealand £132.00
To Subscribe please contact:
The Subscriptions Department, Antiques Magazine,
2 Hampton Court Road, Harborne, Birmingham, B17 9AE
Telephone: 0121 681 8017 Fax: 0121 681 8005

Website: http://www.antiquesbulletin.com

MILLER'S
Ceramics
BUYER'S GUIDE

MILLER'S
Ceramics
BUYER'S GUIDE

Consultant Editor

Christopher Spencer

Project Editor

Jo Wood

MILLER'S CERAMICS BUYER'S GUIDE

Created and designed by
Miller's
The Cellars, High Street
Tenterden, Kent, TN30 6BN
Tel: 01580 766411
Fax: 01580 766100

Consultant Editor Christopher Spencer
Project Editor Jo Wood
Editorial Assistants Carol Gillings, Lalage Johnstone
Production Assistants Catherine Carson-Parker, Gillian Charles, Léonie Sidgwick
Advertising Executive Elizabeth Smith
Advertising Assistant Melinda Williams
Designers Kari Reeves, Philip Hannath
Advertisement Designer Simon Cook
Indexer Hilary Bird
Additional Photographers Ian Booth, Roy Farthing, Robin Saker

First published in Great Britain in 2000
by Miller's, a division of Mitchell Beazley,
imprints of Octopus Publishing Group Ltd,
2–4 Heron Quays, London E14 4JP

© 2000 Octopus Publishing Group Ltd

A CIP catalogue record for this book is
available from the British Library

ISBN 1-84000-267-0

Film output by CK Litho, Whitstable, Kent
Colour origination by CK Litho, Whitstable, Kent
Printed and bound by Toppan Printing Co (HK) Ltd, China

Front cover illustrations:
from top left: A Worcester bell-shaped cup, with wishbone handle, c1758, 2¼in (5.5cm) high. **£280–300 JUP**
A Sadler's teapot, in the form of a coach, 1930s, 8in (20.5cm) long. **£350–400 Bev**
A Goebel wall mask, c1930, 8in (20.5cm) high. **£45–50 HEW**
An Arcadian figure, Miss Holland, 1920–30, 5in (12.5cm) high. **£150–170 MGC**
A Poole Pottery vase, painted by Hilda Trim, c1925, 9in (23cm) high. **£450–500 HarC**
A Clarice Cliff milk jug, with Red Roofs design, 1931, 3½in (9cm) high. **£400–450 HEW**
A Beswick Sunflower six-piece sandwich set, 1930s, plate 7in (18cm) wide. **£180–200 ChA**
A Ridgways British Scenery series platter, c1820, 14in (35.5cm) wide. **£300–350 GN**

Miller's is a registered trademark of
Octopus Publishing Group Ltd

Contents

Acknowledgements

The publisher would like to acknowledge the great assistance given by the following consultants:

CHRISTOPHER SPENCER began his interest in antiques and paintings during his teenage years while helping his father in the family antiques business. Chris realized his vocation lay in lecturing and writing about antiques rather than buying and selling, and after qualifying as a teacher he continued to lecture and write, mainly about ceramics and Cornish painters. Chris now works full time in the antiques trade as a valuer, as an 'expert' on the *Antiques Roadshow* and a consultant to Millers Publications.

LES BAMBRIDGE, of Church Street Antiques, Godalming, Surrey, has specialized in Art Deco ceramics for 15 years.

BEVERLEY started collecting ceramics in 1958 and began dealing in Portobello Road, one of London's most popular areas for antique collectors and dealers. Since 1983, she has owned a shop in the north-west of London, specializing in ceramics and glass from 1850 to 1950.

MIKE BROWN and his wife, Carol, are fascinated by the 1930s, and have been collectors and part-time dealers of Clarice Cliff for nearly 20 years. Mike also writes books on 20th-century history.

MARILYNN AND SHEILA BRASS run their antiques business in Boston, Massachussetts, specializing in interior design consultation. Their collection of antique food moulds and kitchenware is considered to be one of the finest in the US.

MERVYN CAREY joined Harrods auction galleries in London in 1964. In 1971 he set up the Fine Art Department for Geering & Colyer, Kent, building it up to be one of the leading auctioneers in the south-east of England. In 1991 he set up his own practice, holding regular fine art auctions in Tenterden, Kent.

GEOFFREY CROFTS is an Associate of the ISVA, and after five years with Russell, Baldwin & Bright worked for La Barre Antiques exporting to the USA. Having had his own shop from 1986 to 1991, he rejoined Russell, Baldwin & Bright in their Fine Art Department.

ANDREW DAVIES is Manager of the Ceramics Department at Hamptons International Auctioneers and Valuers in Godalming, Surrey. He is particularly interested in the development of techniques used in the manufacture of ceramics, and is an avid collector.

LEONARD GRIFFIN founded the Clarice Cliff Collectors' Club in 1982. His research led to five books, including *Bizarre Affair* and *Fantastic Flowers of Clarice Cliff*. He was consultant for the Wedgwood Museum's Centenary exhibition in 1999, which was linked to his book *The Art of Bizarre*. He lectures widely throughout Britain, Australia, New Zealand and North America.

ANDREW HILTON joined Phillips Auctioneers in 1973, taking over the Pot Lid Department in 1975. In 1992, he set up Special Auction Services, specializing in the auction of traditional collectables such as Pot Lids, Fairings, Commemoratives, Doulton, Baxter prints and Stevengraphs.

MARK LAW has been interested in ceramics since he was a small child. He joined Dreweatt Neate, in Newbury, Berkshire, in 1984 and became their youngest partner in 1997. Mark particularly specializes in English pottery and porcelain, and often speaks and writes on the subject.

JUDY MALING began her interest in antiques in the 1940s, progressed to researching and buying items for other dealers, and finally opened her own antiques shop in Burwash, East Sussex.

GILLIAN NEALE developed an interest in blue and white ware having inherited a collection from her grandparents. She now runs a large and successful business in Aylesbury, Buckinghamshire, is a member of BADA and exhibits at leading antiques fairs all over the country.

JANICE PAULL is a specialist dealer in English Ironstone, having been in the trade for 35 years. She has been involved in every aspect of art and antiques from the organizing of fairs and advisory boards to retailing. She is a member of BADA, LAPADA and CINOA, and exhibits at major fairs in the UK and America.

LYNDA J. PINE began her interest in Goss and Crested China 20 years ago. She now runs the Goss & Crested China Club and museum at Horndean, Hampshire, to explain and illustrate how the Goss souvenir industry began and was made. Together with a professional team, she produces a monthly catalogue on the subject.

VICTORIA DE RIN, of Rogers de Rin in London, began her interest in Wemyss ware after buying a piece in Bermondsey market many years ago. In 1976, David Battie asked her to mount a selling exhibition of Wemyss at Sotheby's Belgravia, after which she produced the definitive book on the subject and went on to become a renowned specialist in Wemyss ware.

ISLWYN WATKINS specializes in ceramics and country antiques at his shop in Knighton, Powys, Wales, and has a special interest in the products of country workshops. He is also a painter and sculptor.

How to Use this Book

I t is our aim to make this Guide easy to use. In order to find a particular item, consult the contents list on page 5 to find the main heading, for example, Pottery. Having located your area of interest, you will find that larger sections have been sub-divided. If you are looking for a particular factory, designer or craftsman, consult the index which starts on page 380.

A Staffordshire blue and white salt-glazed tavern pot, damaged, c1750, 5in (13.5cm) high.
£120–150 IW

A creamware mug, painted in underglaze blue with a Chinese figure holding a parasol, with an ear-shaped strap handle, crack to base, c1770, 6¼in (16cm) high.
£550–600 WW

▶ A child's transfer-printed mug, 1920s, 2in (7cm) high.
£5–10 OD

A Bovey Tracey Mocha ware pint tankard, c1850, 4¾in (12cm) high.
£80–100 IW

A Scottish pearlware mug, with 2 leaf scroll handles, picked out in puce, blue, green and brown, c1840, 6in (16cm) high.
£650–750 DN

A brown and buff hunting mug, probably Mortlake, late 18thC, 8in (20.5cm) high.
£675–750 OCH

A pearlware mug, painted in colours and with copper lustre, c1830, 5in (13.5cm) high.
£85–95 OCH

A Liverpool delft puzzle jug, c1760, 8in (20.5cm) high.
£1,000–1,200 JHo

A mug, entitled 'John Gilpin', c1828, 2in (6.5cm) high.
£85–95 OCH

Further Reading
Miller's Antiques Price Guide 2000, Miller's Publications, 1999

A frog mug, painted with roses in relief, small chip, c1850, 4in (10cm) high.
£150–180 GLN

A Mocha ware mug, the green ground decorated with a blue stripe and applied excise stamp 'Quart', 1820, 6in (15cm) high.
£120–140 RYA

Old Bill
Old Bill, a walrus-moustached, disillusioned Cockney soldier from WW1, was created by artist and journalist Captain Bruce Bairnsfather (1888–1959). Bairnsfather served in France during the 1914–18 war and became famous for his cartoons. Old Bill's sidekick was his pal Bert, gormless and grousing and with a cigarette dangling from his lip. The most famous depiction of the pair shows them stuck in a shell hole, with the caption 'Well if you knows of a better 'ole, go to it'.

102 **POTTERY • Mugs & Jugs**

Price Guide
these are worked out by a team of trade and auction house experts, and are based on actual prices realised. Remember that Miller's is a price guide not a price list and prices are affected by many variables such as location, condition, desirability and so on. Don't forget that if you are selling it is quite likely you will be offered less than the price range. Price ranges for items sold at auction tend to include the buyer's premium and VAT if applicable.

Further Reading
directs the reader towards additional sources of information.

Caption
provides a brief description of the item including the maker's name, medium, year it was made and in some cases condition.

Information Box
covers relevant collecting information on factories, makers, care and restoration, fakes and alterations.

Source Code
refers to the Key to Illustrations on page 376 that lists the details of where the item was photographed.

General Information

The term 'ceramics' refers to anything that is shaped from wet clay and then fired in a kiln to make it hard. Different consistencies and colours of clay, mixed with a variety of other ingredients, produce different types of finished ceramic body, from coarse-grained, porous earthenware and the harder stoneware, both referred to as pottery, to the finest porcelain.

THE BODY

Earthenware: To make it waterproof, earthenware has to be coated with a glaze. Earthenware clays come in many colours, which can often only be seen if the object has a chip, and the colour can give a clue as to its origins. For example, Torquay and Watcombe earthenwares contain the rusty orange of the iron-rich Devon clays. Creamware, a form of earthenware, was developed in Staffordshire in the mid-18th century using good-quality white Devon clay, and was a cheap alternative to porcelain. It can be fired at a higher temperature than other earthenwares, and has been used consistently for everyday crockery.

Stoneware: Harder than earthenware, stoneware is also finer-textured and non-porous even if left unglazed, and could be fired at a higher temperature. Fine white stoneware was developed by Staffordshire potters in the early 18th century to compete with imported Chinese porcelain. The white, strong clay could be potted very thinly to produce a cream-coloured body. Other fine stonewares include black basalt and jasper ware.

Porcelain: First developed in China over a thousand years ago, porcelain can be white, grey or cream. Objects are strong but delicate and often translucent – hollow pieces usually resonate when tapped. Its development came from experiments in adding materials such as ground glass, quartz, flint and bones to the clay base. Soft-paste porcelain was made in Europe from the 16th century onwards, and was fired at a lower temperature than hard-paste porcelain. Hard-paste porcelain originated in China and is watertight even if left unglazed. It consisted of a mixture of china clay, or kaolin, and a ground felspar mineral called china stone, or petuntse, and the resulting shiny surface is difficult to scratch. A true porcelain similar to this but creamier was made at Meissen in Germany by Böttger c1708, and was first produced in Britain in 1768, using china clay and china stone from Cornwall.

THE GLAZE

Glaze is a glassy film, usually made from powered minerals mixed with water, washed over the ceramic body to which it fuses during firing. Glazes are used either to make a piece waterproof, as in the case of earthenware, or for decoration. They can be matte or shiny, soft or hard, coloured or colourless. Earthenware glazes were commonly based on either tin or lead, while European hard-paste porcelain used glazes based on ground felspar. A colourless lead glaze was used on early soft-paste porcelain, but later a mixture of crushed flint and/or glass was used, known as frit. The three principal glazes are:

Lead glaze – transparent, glassy, used on most European earthenware. It can also be coloured by adding metal oxides. Creamware, developed by Josiah Wedgwood in the 18th century, is covered in a thin, lead glaze.

Tin glaze – contains tin oxide, giving the glaze an opaque white finish that could be left plain or decorated with colours.

Salt-glaze – formed by throwing salt into the kiln at about 1,300ºC during the firing of stoneware. The sodium in the salt combined with silicates in the body to form a thick glassy glaze. English salt-glaze from the mid-18th century is light buff in colour with a dimpled 'orange peel' surface.

THE SURFACE

The surface of pottery often features distinctive characteristics:

Crackling – the surface of lead-glazed wares often features a network pattern, owing to the fact that the glaze does not form a natural bond with the body and also has cooled at a different rate, thus causing a cracking of the surface.

Iridescence – the structure of lead glaze is prone to break down over time into layers, giving an iridescent or 'rainbow' effect.

Pinholes – minute air bubbles sometimes produce small holes in the glaze. This effect can also be caused by variations in the thickness of the glaze.

DECORATION

It is sometimes hard to distinguish between transfer-printing and painting on ceramics, but after close examination and a little experience it becomes easier to recognise the difference. For instance, shading that has been painted on to an object will be colour-washed, while on a transfer-print taken from a copperplate engraving it will be crosshatched. Vertical lines on a printed image are consistently straight, whereas an artist will create a different impression with freehand brushstokes. Although few pieces would be signed by an artist, some factories added a code to their own mark to indicate who painted the item. If a signature of a renowned artist appears on a piece, it indicates a transfer-print as they would not have painted commercial porcelain themselves.

Underglaze colours, known as high temperature colours, are able to withstand a temperature of 1,300ºC. The colours are usually antimony (yellow), iron (brown), manganese (purple) and copper (green).

Overglaze enamels, fired at a lower temperature of up to 950ºC, give a much greater range. Enamel colours were made by adding metallic oxides to molten glass and reducing the cooled mixture to a fine power. This was then mixed with an oily base, painted on to the surface and fused by firing.

Slip decoration:

1.   Sgraffito: a sharp pointed tool is used to cut through a layer of slip (liquid clay with a creamy consistency, applied using a nozzle), to the pottery body underneath. Used throughout Europe on earthenware and stoneware, this technique was also used in the United States.
2.   Slip combing: two colours of slip are combed over one another to give a feathered effect.
3.   Slip trailing: the body is trailed with slip in a colour contrasting to the ground colour of the piece.
4.   Sprigging: relief decoration moulded from slip is added to the surface of a piece before firing.
5.   Stamping: a pad of contrasting clay is applied to the body and a design stamped on to it. The excess clay is removed when dry.
6.   Piercing: the unfired body is marked with a design that is then cut out using a knife.
7.   Metallic lustre: shiny, metallic decoration with the appearance of copper or silver.
8.   Sponging: the piece is daubed with a sponge giving a mottled effect after firing. Popular in the United States from about 1825 to 1850, pottery with this type of decoration was known as spatterware.
9.   Low relief: decoration that is slightly raised from the surface of the object.
10. Incised decoration: made by cutting or engraving into the body.

MOULDING & CASTING

Most ceramic figures were reproduced in quantities ranging from tens to thousands, using moulds made from an original model. Clay pressed into the mould was left to harden before the figure was freed and fired. To make more complex forms with bold or undercut detail, parts of the figure or vessel would be made in separate moulds and then stuck together with slip. Heavy, almost solid pieces were produced by this method.

Many factories used moulds made from plaster of Paris from c1720. Liquid clay was poured into these moulds and left to stand; the water was absorbed into the plaster leaving a layer of clay to harden on the mould's inner surface. Excess slip was poured off and after drying the hardened clay could be removed. Called slip-casting, this method allowed finer detail to be used.

HANDLING CERAMICS

An essential part of learning about ceramics is handling them. Damage can occur very easily, and with a little care pitfuls can be avoided. Firstly, when picking up an object that has a lid, always remove the lid first, preferably not by the knop which may be insecure. Secondly, lift hollow objects by supporting the body gently with two hands. Handles are often weakened by use, so it is best not to use these to hold an item. After examining an object, replace it carefully, well away from any other objects on the surface. Try to avoid touching gilding as it is easily rubbed and worn through handling.

CARE & RESTORATION

The investment value of old pottery and porcelain will be reduced considerably by damage, except in the case of very early and rare earthenware where a certain amount of damage is inevitable. However, a buyer may wish to build up a dinner service from a certain pattern and may find items with some damage that will not affect its practical use.

Different types of ceramic bodies need to be cleaned in various ways. Despite its fragile appearance, hard-paste porcelain and high-fired stoneware can safely be washed by hand in warm water with a little detergent added. Unglazed ceramics are porous and washing them may cause the dirt to soak into the body causing discolouration. Soft-paste porcelain and low-fired earthenwares may also be discoloured and damaged by washing, but can usually be wiped gently with a damp cloth. If in doubt about how to deal with a certain type of ceramic do not be afraid to consult a specialist dealer or restorer for advice.

As the main problem with handling ceramics is breakage, it is advisable to have repairs carried out by a specialist. Everyday crockery of little or no monetary value can be mended at home using special resin, but it is essential that the surfaces to be joined are clean and dry before the glue is applied. Any excess adhesive that seeps out from the join must be wiped off immediately before it sets, otherwise it will be impossible to remove when it dries. Broken parts of figures etc can be remodelled with plastic resins or ceramic pastes, but this would be a job for a qualified restorer who will also know how to retouch the paint and glaze to disguise the repair.

Always check for rivets and signs of poor repair when purchasing an old piece pottery. If the object is inexpensive and attractive, you can have the rivets removed and any poor restoration can probably be improved upon by a professional restorer.

Pottery

Collectors of pottery have an incredibly diverse range of wares and types from which to choose their collecting field. Almost inevitably the pottery collector is as concerned with social history as with the decorative quality of their collection – and what fascinating fields of study are available. From 17th- and 18th-century delftwares, through 18th-century stonewares and creamwares to the huge range of 18th-century ironstones and earthenwares, each presenting opportunities to understand something of the struggles, not only of the potters, but of the ordinary people for whom these wares were made.

Minor damage to pottery seems less disfiguring than on porcelain. Pottery also responds well to modern restoration techniques, perhaps because its appeal is based more on its robustness and social links than the purely decorative appeal of some porcelains.

Pottery collectors are active in almost all areas of collecting and we have seen the return to very high prices for early Staffordshire wares, majolica, delftware, creamware and Yorkshire Prattwares. Even areas that have shown little movement over the past few years, such as Pot Lids, (see page 289) are showing signs of recovery. In almost every case it is the publication of a new book or the appearance of a specialist collection that stimulates the market.

Collections of Staffordshire figures are particularly interesting. For the original owner they encapsulated the memory of an event in the way that a photograph might do today – figures of actors brought home as a memento of a visit to a play, a pair of boxers to remind one of a visit to a prize fight, or a horse in memory of a prized animal. Some figures were bought to be instructional, others as reminders of national events or to celebrate heroes.

A Staffordshire collection not only looks good, but provides years of fun researching the events they depict and the factories who made them. A word of warning here – the moulds from which these figures were made were extensively copied, and moulds from one factory were often transferred to another. It is extremely difficult to attribute figures with any certainty, unless an exact comparison is found with one that has the maker's name on the mould. Fakes also abound. These can be very convincing, particularly if they have been coated with grime. Watch out for Staffordshire figures, including watchholders, with deeply recessed bases. These are brand new and fresh from the Far East. Most country auctions seem to throw up one or two examples, and it is easy to be fooled, given the excitement of a possible bargain! In spite of the risk of buying a fake, or an over-restored piece, this is an exciting collecting area, and there are plenty of items for the new collector, many for under £100 if damaged.

The market for rare figures is especially strong at the moment, as a recent sale at Dreweatt Neate in Berkshire proved. Collectors from both sides of the Atlantic were very active and prices were generally well above estimate. As with other collecting areas, it was rare, perfect pieces that were most keenly contested and provenance created a premium, in some cases almost double the price of similar items from recent non-specialist sales. New collectors would do well to study the many comprehensive books on figures, as rarities can occasionally turn up in general sales and non-specialist antique shops.

Two other types of ware fascinate me – ironstone and majolica. I have managed to acquire a small collection of Mason's and other ironstone over the past 20 years. The sheer volume of factories engaged in ironstone production is exciting – the inventive names, the florid backstamps and the copying of shapes and patterns, as one factory responded to the popularity of another's output. This ware encapsulates the energy of 19th-century industrial production and is well worth the search for interesting pieces. There are not too many pitfalls for the new collector. Fakes do exist but their quality is poor and one mistake is usually enough to educate the eye.

Majolica holds a different appeal for me. In common with most collectors, I am especially drawn to Minton and George Jones. These factories used particularly strong colours, and produced a range of naturalistic models that I find charming. Now their popularity has soared, so have prices, but there is no doubt that a majolica collection looks fantastic. As new collectors could pay large sums of money if majolica was to be the chosen collecting area, it is advisable that they learn to detect restoration, as it can be especially difficult to spot and, while a small amount is acceptable, it should be reflected in the price.

There are so many potential collecting areas that it is impossible to cover them all here. Some are well-founded and have long-established clubs that add the opportunity of potential friendships to the joys of collecting (see page 372). It is well worth spending some time visiting museums, specialist dealers and attending specialist auctions. But, be warned – whatever area is chosen, pottery collecting becomes both a passion and an obsession, albeit one which provides unlimited interest and new, similarly obsessed, friends. **Chris Spencer**

ANIMALS

A tin-glazed model of a lion, probably Liverpool, decorated in manganese and red, with hollow body and glazed inside, mid-18thC, 8in (20.5cm) high.
£4,500–5,000 JHo

A Staffordshire creamware model of a recumbent goat, with manganese horns, the naturalistically modelled ground splashed with brown and green glazes, horns restuck, c1790, 7in (18cm) wide.
£1,300–1,500 CNY

A Dutch Delft model of a recumbent cow, decorated in blue, with floral garlands, the horns painted in yellow, slight restoration, marked, 18thC, 11½in (29cm) wide.
£460–500 S(Am)

▶ A pair of Staffordshire animals, modelled as a deer and a doe, c1795, 5½in (14cm) high.
£800–1,000 JHo

A Staffordshire model of a water buffalo, possibly Whieldon, c1760, 7½in (19cm) high.
£1,000–1,200 JHo

A Staffordshire Prattware model of a deer, under-glazed in shades of fawn and green, c1790, 6in (15cm) wide.
£600–650 JRe

A Staffordshire pottery model of a recumbent doe, with sponged ochre details, on a green oval base, late 18thC, 6in (15cm) wide.
£450–500 RBB

Items in the Pottery section have been arranged in date order within each sub-section.

A Ralph Wood-type creamware model of a fox, splashed in brown, on a mound base, damaged, c1780, 3in (8cm) high.
£300–350 DN

A creamware model of a dog, with enamel decoration over the glaze, c1790, 8in (20.5cm) long.
£900–1,000 JRe

A model of a squirrel eating a nut, with translucent green glaze, c1790, 10in (25.5cm) high.
£3,000–3,300 HOW

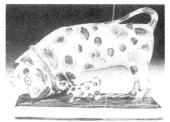

A Staffordshire or Yorkshire pearlware bull baiting group, both animals splashed in light brown, on a green base, restored, c1790, 12in (30.5cm) wide.
£1,500–1,800 C

A pair of Staffordshire creamware models of recumbent leopards, with black markings, each on a green-glazed mound base, damaged, c1790, 3½in (9cm) wide.
£1,000–1,200 DN

A Staffordshire model of a lion, standing with a front leg resting on a yellow ball, raised on a moulded and enamel-painted oval base, c1800, 7in (18cm) wide.
£850–950 CGC

A Staffordshire model of a show horse, with docked tail, sponged in dark grey and wearing a blue and yellow saddlecloth, standing on a green washed waisted base, c1800, 6¼in (15.5cm) high.
£1,700–1,900 CGC

A Prattware model of a lion, underglaze-decorated with green and blue glazed base, c1800, 12¼in (31cm) wide.
£4,500–5,000 JRe

A Staffordshire model of a fox carrying a goose, c1800, 6in (15cm) high.
£700–900 JHo

A Staffordshire model of a lion, late 18thC, 7in (18cm) high.
£4,000–4,500 JHo

A pair of Staffordshire models of greyhounds, one with a hare in its mouth, the other with a hare at its feet, each standing on an oval base, 19thC, 10in (25.5cm) high.
£440–480 DN

A Staffordshire creamware model of a stag, repairs to antlers, c1800, 6in (15cm) high.
£500–600 RA

A Prattware bear group, c1800, 8¼in (21cm) wide.
£3,000–3,500 JHo

A Staffordshire pottery model of an eagle, decorated in yellow on a black and green base with a pink and white flower, c1810, 7¾in (19.5cm) high.
£700–800 DAN

◄ A Staffordshire pearlware model of a lion, its front paw resting on a ball, decorated in brown, on a base with stiff leaf moulded band, marbled in blue, brown, yellow and orange, damaged, c1810, 12½in (32cm) wide.
£600–675 DN

A Staffordshire pearlware model of a recumbent hound, picked out in brown, the green ground base modelled with an ochre flowerhead, damaged, and repaired, c1810, 3½in (9cm) high.
£450–500 DN

A Staffordshire pearlware bull-baiting group, the bull and hound splashed in black, on green-glazed oval mound base, repaired, c1810, 5¼in (13.5cm) high.
£260–320 DN

A Yorkshire model of a rabbit, c1810, 5in (12.5cm) high.
£600–700 JHo

A Prattware coloured model of a lion, c1810, 7in (17.5cm) wide.
£1,250–1,450 HOW

A Staffordshire game spill vase, c1815, 8¾in (22cm) high.
£220–275 DAN

A Staffordshire group of a ewe and a lamb, on a rustic base, c1810, 5½in (14cm) high.
£200–250 RBB

A Yorkshire group of a cow, calf and a milkmaid, c1820, 5½in (14cm) high.
£1,100–1,200 JHo

A Yorkshire model of a cow and her calf, decorated with black and orange, early 19thC, 7in (18cm) wide.
£600–700 JHo

A Staffordshire model of a dog, grey with brown markings, on a green and brown rocky base, early 19thC, 6¼in (15.5cm) wide.
£600–680 JHo

A Bovey Tracy model of a cat, decorated with orange and black, cracked, early 19thC, 4¼in (11cm) high.
£350–400 JHo

A pair of Staffordshire models of lions, c1820, 2½in (6.5cm) high.
£1,400–1,600 JHo

A pair of Staffordshire models of lions with curly white manes, each with a lamb before them, on a shaped and gilded base, early 19thC, 4¼in (11cm) high.
£3,300–3,600 DA

A Staffordshire model of a greyhound, on a brown and green rocky base, early 19thC, 6¼in (15.5cm) wide.
£600–700 JHo

A Staffordshire model of a sheep, with orange decoration, bocage behind, c1820, 4¾in (12cm) high.
£160–180 OCH

A Staffordshire Enoch Wood pearlware model of a greyhound, overglaze enamel-decorated, c1820, 4in (10cm) high.
£700–800 JRe

A Staffordshire model of a pug, enamel-painted over a pearl glaze, c1820, 3½in (9cm) high.
£400–500 JRe

A Staffordshire Enoch Wood pearlware model of a pointer, overglaze decorated, c1820, 3¾in (9.5cm) high.
£550–650 JRe

A pearlware model of a lion, enriched in shades of brown, the globe in pink, the base painted green above a black marbled section, some damage, repair and overpainting, c1820, 11¾in (30cm) wide.
£1,600–1,800 CSK

A pair of Staffordshire models of spaniels, one chipped, 19thC, 6in (15cm) wide.
£380–450 LT

A pair of Sherratt-type pearlware models of cows, with flowering bocage, naturalistically painted in colours, each base painted with rainbow colours, restored, c1820, 7½in (19cm) high.
£850–1,000 CSK

A Staffordshire model of a deer, with bocage, c1820, 7in (18cm) high.
£400–440 JHo

A pair of John Walton enamelled models of a ram and a ewe, moulded banner marks 'Walton', 1818–35, 7in (18cm) high.
£1,400–1,600 Bon

Bocage

- Vegetation forming the background to many ceramic animals and figures.
- The leaves often resemble hawthorn, and are arranged in groups often with coloured flowers at the centre.

A Staffordshire model of a red and white deer, with bocage behind, on a brown and green base, c1820, 4in (10cm) high.
£400–450 JHo

A Staffordshire model of a black and white setter, on a green, red and brown base, c1820, 7½in (19cm) high.
£1,000–1,200 JHo

A pair of enamelled pearlware models of lions, each looking back to a snake emerging from a leafy tree, with scroll-moulded bases picked out in blue, restored, c1820, 8in (20.5cm) high.
£1,800–2,200 Bon

A Staffordshire pearlware model of a lion, with one front paw resting on a ball, the green-glazed base picked out in blue, yellow, puce and red, some damage, c1825, 6in (15cm) high.
£750–850 DN(H)

A pearlware model of a swan, c1825, 6½in (16.5cm) high.
£900–1,100 DAN

A Staffordshire model of a peacock, c1830, 4in (10cm) high.
£600–700 RWB

A Brampton salt-glazed model of a spaniel, decorated in brown, c1830, 3in (7.5cm) high.
£340–380 SPU

A salt-glazed stoneware model of a lion, c1830, 5in (12.5cm) high.
£500–600 JRe

A pair of Derbyshire Brampton salt-glazed models of spaniels, with incised brown decoration, c1830, 14in (35.5cm) high.
£3,400–3,800 SPU

A Staffordshire hound's head stirrup cup, picked out in black and brown, on a bright cream ground, c1830, 6¾in (17cm) wide.
£800–880 DN

A Staffordshire model of a hound, decorated in brown and wearing a gilt collar, standing on a gilt-decorated mound base, c1830–40, 5in (12.5cm) high.
£200–250 DN

A salt-glazed stoneware model of a spaniel, seated on a hollow cushion base, c1830, 8in (20.5cm) high.
£360–400 CGC

A Staffordshire model of a cow and calf, c1830, 5in (12.5cm) high.
£300–350 MSA

A Staffordshire model of a sheep, its front feet resting on a basket of flowers, c1830, 2in (5cm) wide.
£300–330 JO

A Yorkshire treacle-glazed earthenware model of a stag, c1830, 5in (12.5cm) high.
£160–180 SER

A pair of Staffordshire stoneware models of dogs, with brown decoration, c1830, 8in (20.5cm) high.
£800–880 JO

A Staffordshire model of a rabbit, repaired, early 19thC, 2½in (6cm) high.
£450–550 JHo

A Staffordshire model of a cow and calf, standing before floral bocage, c1830, 5½in (14cm) high.
£300–350 MSA

An enamelled pearlware model of a hunting dog, wearing a yellow collar, restored, c1830, 6½in (16.5cm) high.
£1,000–1,200 Bon

A Staffordshire pearlware model of a sheep, standing before floral bocage, c1830, 3½in (9cm) high.
£300–350 MSA

A pair of Staffordshire models of sheep, highlighted with gilt lines, restored, c1830, 4½in (11.5cm) high.
£270–320 SER

A Yorkshire model of a horse, damaged, early 19thC, 6in (15cm) high.
£2,000–2,500 JHo

◄ A pair of Staffordshire models of cats, one with a kitten, c1835, 2¾in (7cm) high.
£600–700 JO

► A Staffordshire Pratt-type eagle, c1830, 10in (25.5cm) high.
£1,000–1,200 JHo

A pearlware model of a setter, sponged in black, with floral bocage, the mound base titled in black beneath a puce scroll band, restored, c1830, 6in (15cm) high.
£700–800 DN

A Staffordshire group of 2 sheep beneath a tree with multi-coloured flowers for leaves, c1835, 3in (7.5cm) wide.
£300–360 JO

A Staffordshire model of a spaniel, with a rust-coloured coat, seated on a gilt-enriched tasselled cushion base, c1840, 4¾in (12cm) high.
£380–420 CGC

A Staffordshire model of a leopard and a cub, on a shaped plinth base, c1840, 5in (12.5cm) wide.
£460–500 RBB

A pair of Staffordshire porcellaneous models of spaniels, decorated with dark red/brown markings, c1840, 3¼in (8.5cm) high.
£300–360 RWB

A Staffordshire model of a leopard, yellow with black markings, on a light blue-washed rocky and gilt-lined base, c1840, 7½in (19cm) high.
£1,100–1,300 CGC

A Staffordshire earthenware model of a brown and white cow, with a milkmaid, c1840, 7½in (19cm) high.
£350–400 SER

A Staffordshire model of a spaniel, with yellow eyes, gold locket and chain and black coat, free-standing front legs, c1840, 12in (30.5cm) high.
£450–500 CGC

A glazed stoneware model of a lion, possibly Yorkshire, c1840, 7½in (19cm) wide.
£140–160 IW

Fakes & Reproductions

Staffordshire models that have been faked or reproduced are often pure white and stained to simulate age. A network of small cracks or veins, known as crazing, is present in the glaze in most old examples, and modern manufacturers can go to great lengths to reproduce the effect. This can result in crazing that appears too regular and pronounced to be convincing.

A pair of Staffordshire models of seated poodles, each wearing a gilt collar, with granatic decoration, one restored, c1850, 5½in (14cm) high.
£200–250 DN

A Staffordshire group of a whippet and a spaniel, 'Elegance and Patience', restored, c1845, 5½in (14cm) high.
£200–250 SER

A Staffordshire model of a
greyhound with a rabbit, c1850,
11in (28cm) high.
£160–180 SER

A Staffordshire clock face group
of a poodle and spaniels, c1850,
9¾in (24.5cm) high.
£450–500 RWB

A Staffordshire swan group,
decorated in green, yellow and red,
c1850, 4½in (11.5cm) high.
£130–150 SER

A pair of Staffordshire models of recumbent lambs,
c1850, 3½in (9cm) high.
£100–125 SER

A pair of Staffordshire models of greyhounds
with hares, c1850, 10½in (26.5cm) high.
£450–550 RWB

A life-sized model of a pug dog,
mid-19thC, 24in (61cm) long.
£700–800 AAV

A Staffordshire model
of a dog and puppy,
c1855, 5½in (14cm) high.
£750–850 BHA

A pair of Staffordshire models of spaniels,
holding flower baskets in their mouths,
c1850, 9in (23cm) high.
£1,000–1,200 RWB

A Staffordshire model of a cat,
sponge-decorated in brown and
black, mid-19thC, 5½in (14cm) high.
£200–220 SER

A Staffordshire model
of a greyhound, c1850,
8in (20.5cm) high.
£150–180 AnE

A Staffordshire group
of a sheep and lamb,
c1850, 5¼in (13cm) high.
£150–180 JO

A Staffordshire model
of a dalmation, 19thC,
3½in (9cm) high.
£90–110 ACA

▶ A Staffordshire watch holder, modelled as 2 whippets chasing a hare, c1855, 8¾in (22cm) high.
£340–380 RWB

A Staffordshire spill vase group, modelled as a cow and calf, on an oval base, c1860, 7in (18cm) high.
£200–250 MR

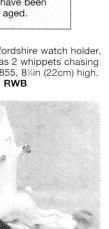

A pair of Staffordshire spill vases, with gold and brown lions and cubs on a white ground, the interior coloured orange, c1860, 11½in (29cm) high.
£1,200–1,400 BHA

A spill vase, modelled as a horse and snake, restored, mid-19thC, 9½in (24cm) high.
£300–350 SER

A Staffordshire spill vase, modelled as a stag and hound, 19thC, 7½in (19cm) high.
£150–180 RWB

◀ Two Staffordshire flatback spill vases, modelled and enamelled as a lion and elephant before trees, c1850, 7in (18cm) high.
£1,000–1,200 CSK

▶ Two spill vases, modelled as elephants, on gilt-lined bases, slight wear, 19thC, 6in (15cm) high.
£1,700–2,000 CSK

◀ A Staffordshire spill vase, modelled as a family of swans in their nest, on a white base, c1860, 4¾in (12cm) high.
£100–120 JO

A pair of Staffordshire groups of red spaniels with barrels, c1850, 4in (10cm) high.
£200–220 SER

A pair of Scottish models of seated spaniels, each sponged in black and wearing an ochre collar, 19thC, 9¼in (23.5cm) high.
£300–350 DN

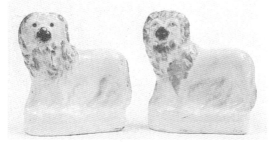

A pair of Staffordshire miniature models of lions, c1850, 3½in (9cm) high.
£250–300 SER

◄ A Staffordshire lustre model of a hen on a nest, c1860, 5½in (14cm) high.
£120–180 SER

A pair of Staffordshire models of spaniels, standing on leaf-capped green and rustic arched pink bases, 19thC, 8in (20.5cm) high.
£2,400–2,800 AH

A pair of Staffordshire models of cockerels, c1850, 4½in (11.5cm) high.
£100–125 SER

These models were recovered from a ship that was wrecked in the mid-19thC.

A Staffordshire model of a rabbit, picked out in black, on green-glazed oval mound base, c1860, 3¼in (8.5cm) wide.
£220–250 DN

A Staffordshire model of a poodle, on a blue and white base, c1860, 3¾in (9.5cm) wide.
£50–55 OCH

A pair of Staffordshire cow and calf groups, decorated with brown and black, c1860, 5½in (14cm) wide.
£550–650 DAN

A pair of Staffordshire lop-eared rabbits, each eating a leaf, one damaged, c1860, 3¾in (9.5cm) high.
£800–1,000 TMA

A model of a seated tortoiseshell cat, stamped 'John Mortlock Pottery Galleries, London', 19thC, 11¾in (30cm) high.
£800–900 AG

A Staffordshire model of a spaniel, sponged in black and white, c1860, 10in (25.5cm) high.
£75–95 SER

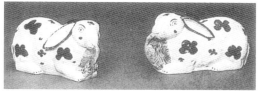

A pair of Staffordshire pearlware models of recumbent rabbits, each splashed in black and eating a lettuce leaf, cracked, 19thC, 9½in (24cm) wide.
£3,000–3,500 DN

A pair of Staffordshire models of greyhounds, with hares in their mouths, 19thC, 7¾in (19.5cm) high.
£200–220 ACA

A Staffordshire copper lustre model of a spaniel, c1860, 9½in (24cm) high.
£60–70 SER

A pair of Staffordshire models of spaniels, with flower baskets in their mouths, c1860, 7½in (19cm) high.
£750–850 RWB

A pair of Staffordshire brown-glazed models of greyhounds, late 19thC, 2½in (6.5cm) high.
£100–130 SPU

A Staffordshire stirrup cup, in the form of a fox's mask, with black snout, 19thC, 5in (12.5cm) wide.
£200–250 P(O)

A pair of Staffordshire models of cockerels, each with facial features detailed in red and black, 19thC, 11¾in (30cm) high.
£800–900 P(B)

A pair of Staffordshire pottery models of zebras, each on a green oval foliage-encrusted base, 19thC, 5in (12.5cm) high.
£250–300 HCH

Stirrup Cups

Earthenware examples dating from c1770 in the shape of foxes' masks are attributed to Whieldon. A wide variety of fox's-head stirrup cups were made by the Staffordshire potters during the late 18th and early 19thC, but examples are rarely marked. Hound's-head stirrup cups were also made by many of the Staffordshire potters and were almost as popular as the fox's-head variety.

A pair of Staffordshire models of red and white spaniels, each with collar and padlock, slight damage, 19thC, 8in (20.5cm) high.
£240–280 TMA

A pair of Staffordshire quill stands, modelled as two dalmations with yellow collars, on blue bases, mid-19thC, 6in (15cm) high.
£150–200 CaC

◄ A pair of Staffordshire models of bearded collies, c1860, 6¼in (16cm) high.
£650–800 JO

A Staffordshire greyhound pen holder, mustard yellow on a blue base, 19thC, 6in (15cm) wide.
£120–150 DAC

A Staffordshire group of a cherub and spaniel, 19thC, 6¼in (16cm) high.
£200–225 ACA

A Staffordshire model of a spaniel, with fan tail, 19thC, 12½in (32cm) high.
£145–165 ACA

A Staffordshire model of a stag, bocage restored, 19thC, 5½in (14cm) high.
£150–200 ACA

A Staffordshire group, of a spaniel with kennel, c1860, 4in (10cm) high.
£130–150 JO

A Yorkshire model of a horse, damaged, c1860, 6in (15cm) high.
£1,600–1,800 JHo

A pair of Staffordshire models of spaniels, one seated on a barrel, c1860, 8½in (21cm) high.
£200–250 AnE

◄ A pair of Staffordshire models of dogs and puppies, on blue bases, c1865, 6in (15cm) high.
£450–500 JO

A pair of Staffordshire models of sheep, c1880, 2½in (6.5cm) high.
£200–225 JO

A Continental earthenware model of a parakeet, painted in brightly coloured glazes, orange glass inset eyes, damaged, black painted monogram to underside, late 19thC, 16in (40.5cm) high.
£120–150 MJB

Staffordshire Animals

As well as producing models of farmyard animals and domestic pets, the opening of the first zoological gardens in the 19thC and the popularitiy of travelling circuses increased the demand for models of exotic beasts. The favourite subject of all, however, was the dog, in particular the King Charles spaniel.

► A pair of Staffordshire models of black spaniels, with traces of gilding and with glass eyes, c1880, 13¼in (33.5cm) high.
£220–260 EL

A Staffordshire model of an elephant, on a yellow base, late 19thC, 5¾in (14.5cm) high.
£1,000–1,200 DAN

A pair of Staffordshire models of Indian elephants, shaded in tones of brown, the bases edged with gilt lines, damaged, late 19thC, 10in (25.5cm) high.
£1,500–1,800 S

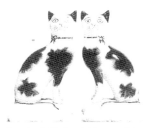

A pair of Staffordshire models of cats, c1900, 4in (10cm) high.
£250–300 ACA

A Gallé faïence model of a seated cat, decorated with yellow and white hearts and circles on a dark blue ground, with inset blue glass eyes, signed 'E. Gallé, Nancy', c1900, 13in (33cm) high.
£1,200–1,400 Bea

A Quimper vase, in the form of a goose, decorated in green, yellow, blue and red, c1883, 10in (25.5cm) high.
£580–640 VH

An Austrian terracotta model of a dog, with black head and ears, 1890–1910, 5½in (14cm) high.
£220–250 INC

A Sarreguemines model of a penguin, No. 3527, c1900, 10½in (26.5cm) high.
£150–175 PC

Quimper

Faïence was produced in Quimper in France from the late 17thC, and by the mid-19thC was one of the few towns in the country where faïence was still produced.

Items from Quimper are known for their decoration featuring Breton peasants and simple landscapes. The painting techniques featured single brush strokes, using soft blue, yellow, green and pink.

Chief among the producers was the Henriot factory, from which earlier examples were marked 'HB' and 'HR'. Later examples from 1922 onwards are marked 'Henriot'.

The factory is active today, and even modern pieces are becoming collectable.

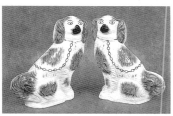

A pair of Staffordshire models of brown and white King Charles spaniels, late 19thC, 11in (28cm) high.
£200–250 SER

◀ A pair of Staffordshire models of elephants, each with seated figures and tigers, possibly Kent & Co, c1900, 9in (23cm) high.
£2,000–2,500 HOW

A Martin Brothers salt-glazed stoneware bird, with removable head, glazed in white, brown, blue, black and ochre, incised, dated '1906', 9in (23cm) high.
£4,500–5,000 S(NY)

A Wedgwood black basalt model of a squirrel, by E. W. Light, with glass eyes, impressed mark, c1913, 5¼in (13.5cm) high.
£450–500 SK

A Denby pig money box, restored, 1920s, 6in (15cm) wide.
£120–140 KES

A lustre model of a white dog with a puppy, with brown markings, c1920, 3¼in (8cm) high.
£15–20 JMC

Two German white bisque dogs, lustre-glazed, with red collars, by Gebrüder Heubach, impressed on the base with a sunburst, c1920, 7in (18cm) high.
£200–250 YC

A lustre model of a peacock, with yellow neck and head, pink breast and silver tail, 1930s, 4¼in (11.5cm) high.
£8–10 JMC

A Wedgwood pottery trial group, designed by John Skeaping, with straw-coloured glaze, marked, 1927, 8in (20.5cm) high.
£1,100–1,300 P

An Adnet pottery group of doves, with crackleware glaze, indistinct monogram, c1930, 17¾in (45cm) wide.
£120–150 P(B)

A Denby model of a giraffe, with green markings, c1930, 10in (25.5cm) high.
£250–300 KES

A SylvaC model of a rabbit, coloured in yellow and orange, No. 305, c1930, 5½in (14cm) high.
£55–65 TAC

A Royal Doulton model of a white bull terrier, HN 1133, model No. 959B, 1930s, 7in (18cm) wide.
£800–900 PGA

A SylvaC pink rabbit, No. 1027, 1930s, 9in (23cm) high.
£275–300 TAC

SylvaC

- Founded in Stoke-on-Trent by William Shaw and William Copestake in 1894, and first used the name SylvaC in the mid-1930s.
- Produced tableware as well as models of animals, wall decorations and ornaments such as vases, posy holders, ashtrays and eggcups.
- Most SylvaC pieces are impressed on the base with the company name, the model number and 'England'.
- Many examples were matte green in colour, but other colours, particularly blue, have become highly sought after.

▶ A set of 5 models of grey Larry the Lambs, designed by Nancy Great-Rex, c1930, largest 8½in (21.5cm) high.
£25–100 each AND

A SylvaC model of chipmunk, white with black eyes, No 5105, c1930, 6½in (16.5cm) high.
£35–40 TAC

A Wedgwood black basalt model of an elephant, with glass eyes and painted tusks, impressed marks, c1930, 5¾in (14.5cm) high.
£400–450 Bon

A Midwinter model of Peggy the Calf, c1930, 5in (12.5cm) high.
£60–70 AND

A Midwinter model of Larry the Lamb, c1930, 3½in (9cm) high.
£35–40 AND

A SylvaC model of a brown camel, No. 5230, c1934, 5in (12.5cm) wide.
£40–45 TAC

A SylvaC model of a yellow giraffe, No. 5234, c1934, 6in (15cm) high.
£38–43 TAC

A SylvaC model of a dog, with a bow, red glaze, No. 1119, c1930, 3½in (9cm) high.
£70–80 PC

A Beswick model of a colt, first version, 1939–71, 5in (12.5cm) high.
£45–50 MAC

A SylvaC model of Puss in Boot, coloured in yellow with green cats, No. 4977, c1934, 5in (12.5cm) high.
£35–40 TAC

A Beswick model of a grey Shire horse, 1940–present, 7in (18cm) high.
£60–80 MEG

Beswick

- The factory was started by James Wright Beswick in 1894 in Longton, Staffordshire, making tablewares, figures, flowerpots and pedestals and other domestic ware.
- By the late 19thC, two more factories had been opened.
- After Beswick died in 1921, his son John took over the business and modernized the designs.
- In the 1930s, over 50 women were employed in the factory to meet the demand for the company's Art Deco styles.
- The authenticity of their animal models played an important part in Beswick's success, particularly when producing horses.

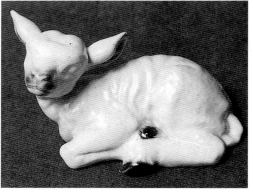

A Poole Pottery model of a recumbent lamb, modelled by Marjorie Drawbell, 1940s, 5in (12.5cm) long.
£75–90 HarC

A Beswick model of a light brown dog, with white tip to its tail, c1950, 4in (10cm) high.
£45–55 PAC

A Midwinter stylized model of a fawn, c1950, 5in (12.5cm) high.
£50–60 AND

A Beswick model of a bull, decorated in orange and black, by Colin Melbourne, 1950s, 5in (12.5cm) high.
£100–120 PAC

A Beswick model of a bay pony, 1945–89, 4in (10cm) high.
£25–30 MAC

A Midwinter model of a swan, c1950, 2½in (6.5cm) high.
£40–45 AND

BASKETS

A pearlware basket and stand, moulded with basketwork panels, the basket with flared sides linked by scroll bands, and picked out in underglaze blue, c1790, 12in (30.5cm) wide.
£350–400 DN

A pair of Spode pearlware baskets, with transfer-printed underglaze blue border, overglaze decoration and gilding, with a central floral spray, c1820, 8in (20.5cm) wide.
£500–600 DAN

A pearlware basket and stand, printed in underglaze blue and white with figures among classical columns, floral and diaper borders, lattice piercing and moulded lug handles, printed title 'Ancient Rome' in underglaze blue, c1820, 10¾in (27.5cm) wide.
£300–350 Hal

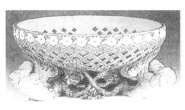

A Minton majolica bowl, shape No. 874, pierced with a trellis pattern below a moulded band of flowerheads above oak leaves issuing from branches, supported by 3 doves, enriched in colours, damaged and repaired, impressed marks, date code for 1867, 12¾in (32.5cm) diam.
£1,500–2,000 CSK

A Rye Pottery green basket, c1900, 8¾in (22cm) diam.
£100–120 NCA

LOCATE THE SOURCE
The source of each illustration in Miller's can be found by checking the code letters below each caption with the Key to Illustrations, pages 376–379.

A Royal Winton basket, decorated with Tartan pattern, 1930s, 4in (10cm) wide.
£30–40 BET

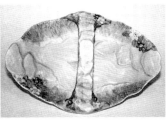

A Royal Winton basket, decorated with Woodland Stream pattern in shades of green and beige with red and blue flowers, c1930, 8in (20.5cm) long.
£50–60 CSA

A Royal Winton basket, decorated with Marion pattern, 1930s, 5¼in (13cm) wide.
£150–160 BEV

A Quimper basket, decorated with a blue rim, 1920s, 4¾in (12cm) wide.
£120–135 VH

A Crown Ducal basket, designed by Charlotte Rhead, decorated with Persian Rose pattern, with a green handle, c1935, 5½in (14cm) high.
£75–100 HEA

A Royal Winton basket, decorated with Marguerite pattern, 1930s, 4in (10cm) diam.
£70–80 BEV

A Shorter petal-shaped basket, in shades of red and green, c1950, 5in (12.5cm) high.
£25–30 CSA

BISCUIT BARRELS

A Moorcroft square two-handled biscuit box and cover, tube-lined with Claremont pattern, in red, purple and white on a green ground restored, impressed and signed in blue, c1910, 6in (15cm) high.
£600–700 DN

A Carlton Ware biscuit barrel, with silver-plated lid, decorated with lithographic transfer of peonies on a blush ground, black crown mark, early 20thC, 5¼in (13.5cm) diam.
£40–60 StC

A Carlton Ware biscuit barrel, with silver-plated mounts and stand, decorated in blue with white classical figures, blue crown mark, early 20thC, 9¾in (25cm) high.
£120–150 StC

A Carlton Ware biscuit barrel, in the form of a thatched cottage, No. 778973, 1920s, 8¾in (22cm) high.
£65–80 PC

A Beswick biscuit box, No. 249, 1920s, 7½in (19cm) high.
£60–70 PC

A biscuit barrel, retailed by Price of Kensington 1930s, 7½in (19cm) high.
£40–50 PC

A SylvaC biscuit barrel, in the form of a thatched cottage, with original label, 1920s, 5in (12.5cm) wide.
£40–50 LA

A Crown Devon biscuit barrel, 'Patch', c1930, 11in (28cm) high.
£150–200 BEV

A Paramount Pottery biscuit barrel, in the form of a cottage, chipped, 1930s, 7½in (19cm) high.
£20–30 LA

A Price Bros biscuit barrel, in the form of a cottage, 1930s, 7in (18cm) high.
£25–30 WAB

A Japanese biscuit barrel, in the form of a twin-gabled house with a blue roof, 1930s, 6½in (16.5cm) wide.
£40–50 PC

◄ A Burlington Devon Cob biscuit box, 1920s, 6in (15cm) wide.
£30–40 PC

BOWLS

An English delft blue and white bowl, c1750, 12in (30.5cm) diam.
£2,500–3,000 JHo

A creamware monteith, possibly Staffordshire, c1775, 13½in (34.5cm) long.
£1,750–2,000 JHo

A monteith is a bowl for cooling or rinsing wine glasses.

A pearlware bowl, printed in blue with portrait of Amdiral Lord Nelson and sailing ships within a border inscribed with Nelson's signal and name, flanked by verse and naval trophies, the rim with flowers and butterflies, lined in brown, minor damage, early 19thC, 8in (20.5cm) diam.
£600–700 SAS

A spongeware bowl, c1840, 4in (10cm) high.
£80–100 RYA

An English delft punch bowl, painted in blue with chinoiserie landscapes, damaged and repaired, mid-18thC, 13½in (34.5cm) diam.
£250–300 Bon

A pearlware bowl, printed in black with a picture of Mary Bewley attended by Charlotte and Leopold, 1816, 6¼in (16cm) diam.
£200–250 SAS

Mary (called Goody) Bewley lived in a small cottage within the grounds of Claremont, the residence of Princess Charlotte and her husband Prince Leopold, who were her frequent visitors, Goody Bewley used to read a fine-print Bible, and the Princess is seen here presenting her with an edition with large print.

A yellow-ground pottery bowl, painted in bright enamel colours, possibly Staffordshire, c1824, 6in (15cm) diam.
£240–280 HOW

Spongeware

By dabbing the surface of pottery with a sponge or roll of rags dipped in colour a stippled effect was created. Sponged decoration was mostly used on table ware.

A Staffordshire glazed and gilded bowl, c1765, 5½in (14cm) diam.
£600–660 JHo

A pearlware bowl, printed in blue with a central medallion surmounted by a crown with brown line rim, restored, c1793, 10¼in (26cm) diam.
£300–350 SAS

A creamware bowl, the interior painted with ships, the exterior decorated with transfer-printed hunting scenes, impressed 'Wedgwood', c1785, 12½in (32cm) diam.
£1,800–2,000 JHo

A Minton majolica four-tiered stand, the bowls formed as oyster shells, with metal mechanism, shape No. 636, damaged and restored, impressed marks and date code for 1872, 10½in (26.5cm) high.
£2,500–3,000 CSK

A spongeware bowl, decorated with red flowers and green leaves, late 19thC, 8½in (21.5cm) diam.
£60–70 SWN

A Wedgwood yellow jasper dip salad bowl and servers, with black relief of grapevine festoons terminating at lions' masks, silver-plated rim and utensils, impressed mark to bowl, 19thC, 8½in (21.5cm) diam.
£400–450 SK(B)

A majolica bowl, by Richard Ginori, painted with a band of masks, birds and flowers, on 4 mermaid, mask and scroll feet, slight damage, painted mark, late 19thC, 13in (33cm) wide.
£440–480 HOLL

A Doulton Lambeth stoneware bowl, decorated with a band of flowers and leaves in blue and white by Frances E. Lee, beneath a silver-mounted rim, Birmingham 1881, printed mark and impressed '1881', 9in (23cm) diam.
£300–350 Oli

A Wedgwood majolica Argenta ware salad comport, decorated with a fork and spoon, slight rim crack, impressed mark, c1877, 10¼in (26cm) diam.
£600–675 SK

▶ A Doulton Lambeth blue and cream salad bowl and servers, by Florence E. Barlow, with silver rim, c1880, 12in (30.5cm) diam.
£1,400–1,600 POW

A Brannam double bowl, with fish supports, c1890, 5½in (14cm) high.
£150–200 NCA

A Moorcroft MacIntyre salad bowl, with silver-plated rim, tube-lined with a band of growing anemonies and leaves picked out in blue, green and brown, on a cream ground, printed mark in brown and registration No. 401753 and green painted signature, c1903, 10¼in (26cm) diam.
£700–800 DN

◀ A Moorcroft MacIntyre Florian ware trough-shaped bowl, decorated with Poppy pattern, in shades of blue and green on a white ground, c1903, 13in (33cm) long.
£1,000–1,250 NP

A John Marshall & Co, Scotland, earthenware basin, decorated in black with Canadian Sports pattern, c1880, 14in (35.5cm) diam.
£1,400–1,600 RIT

A William de Morgan ruby lustre bowl, decorated with fish among leaves and scrolls, c1890, 13¼in (33.5cm) diam.
£700–800 P(G)

A Rye Pottery cut-out bowl, decorated with coiled grass snakes, c1900, 6in (15cm) diam.
£500–575 NCA

A spongeware bowl, c1900, 6in (15cm) diam.
£40–50 IW

A Royal Doulton bowl,
by Florrie Jones, 1905,
7in (18cm) diam.
£180–200 PSA

A Moorcroft bowl, painted and
piped with red-capped fungi on
a blue-green ground, signed,
c1910, 9in (23cm) diam.
£580–650 L

A Royal Doulton bowl, the rim
decorated with flowers, c1910,
7½in (19cm) diam.
£85–95 RAC

An Arts and Crafts bowl, by Bernard
Moore, c1910, 10in (25.5cm) diam.
£400–450 SHa

A Moorcroft bowl, decorated with
Pomegranate pattern on a dark
blue ground, on a Tudric pewter
base, c1912, 10¼in (26cm) diam.
£750–850 P(B)

A Dorset sugar bowl, inscribed
'elp theezel to the sugar', c1915,
3in (7.5cm) high.
£20–30 PC

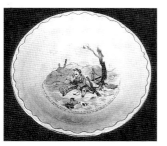

A pottery bowl, printed in sepia,
inscribed 'Here with a loaf
of bread...', c1918,
10in (25.5cm) diam.
£60–70 SAS

A Gouda twin-handled pottery bowl,
painted with flowers and stylized foliage
against white, c1918, 12in (30.5cm) wide.
£400–450 OO

A pottery bowl, printed in sepia,
inscribed 'Well if you knows of
a better 'ole, go to it', with wavy
black and gilt-lined border, c1918,
9¾in (25cm) diam.
£50–60 SAS

A St Ives stoneware bowl, by Shoji
Hamada, the thick olive-green glaze
incised with chrysanthemum
decoration, impressed marks,
c1923, 6¼in (16cm) diam.
£1,600–1,800 Bon

A Rye Pottery green and white
miniature posy bowl, c1920,
1½in (3.5cm) high.
£35–45 NCA

A Torquay bowl, decorated with
a kingfisher in shades of blue,
orange and green on a blue
ground, c1920, 6½in (16.5cm) diam.
£40–45 DSG

◄ A Myott fruit bowl, decorated with
a central flower and leafy branches,
1920–30, 12in (30.5cm) diam.
£85–95 BEV

► A Watcombe bowl, decorated
with yellow bearded irises on a green
ground, c1920, 3½in (9cm) diam.
£15–20 TPCS

An Art Deco Phoenix ware bowl, decorated in muted greens, brown and amber tones with stylized pendant foliage and slender stems, with separate stand, c1925, 11in (28cm) diam.
£40–50 DSG

A William Moorcroft bowl and cover, decorated with fish and plants under salt glaze, c1930, 6½in (16cm) diam.
£650–750 HEA

A Poole Pottery covered bowl, designed by Dora Batty, decorated with 2 children playing and birds in flight above, c1934, 4in (10cm) high.
£75–100 RDG

A Barton sugar bowl, decorated with a sailing boat in black on a blue ground, inscribed 'Ryde', 1922–38, 3½in (9cm) wide.
£10–15 PC

A Wedgwood pottery bowl, designed by Keith Murray, with horizontal ribbing beneath a crackled white glaze, on a spreading circular foot, 1930s, 10in (25.5cm) diam.
£160–180 AAV

A Maling ware lustre bowl, with floral decoration on a dark blue ground, No. 6190, 1920–30s, 8½in (21.5cm) diam.
£150–180 MAR

A Burleigh Ware Avon bowl, designed by Charlotte Rhead, decorated with Garland pattern, No. 4101/A, c1928, 10in (25.5cm) diam.
£200–250 PC

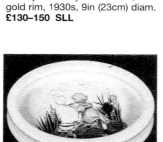

A Gray's Pottery lustre bowl, with gold rim, 1930s, 9in (23cm) diam.
£130–150 SLL

A Daison Art Pottery bowl, decorated with a pixie on a mushroom in shades of green and blue, 1928–32, 5in (13cm) diam.
£25–30 PC

A SylvaC bowl, decorated with an elf and a rabbit in orange, green and pink, No. 1614, c1930, 7½in (19cm) wide.
£50–60 TAC

A Grimwades child's plate, decorated with Bubbles pattern 1930s, 8in (20.5cm) wide.
£32–38 WAB

A SylvaC yellow bowl, decorated with a harvest mouse, No. 5250, c1934, 4in (10cm) high.
£25–30 TAC

► A Derbyshire salt-glazed pouring bowl, c1840, 8in (20.5cm) wide.
£40–50 IW

Further Reading
Miller's Twentieth-Century Ceramics, Miller's Publications, 1999

◄ A Carlton Ware leaf and lobster bowl, the leaf pattern supported on 3 lobster feet, together with a pair of servers with pincer terminals, c1939, 9½in (24cm) diam.
£50–60 P(B)

A Maling lustre bowl, with blue band and decorated with flowers, 1940s, 6¼in (16cm) wide.
£100–120 SLL

A Bursley Ware bowl, designed by Charlotte Rhead, second period, decorated in shades of blue, yellow and brown with turquoise rim, pattern No. TL2, 1940s, 9in (23cm) diam.
£120–150 PC

A Royal Winton three-bowl dish, decorated with Marguerite pattern, c1950, 8in (20.5cm) diam.
£60–70 PAC

A Quimper bowl, decorated with stylized flowers and leaves in shades of orange and green with a blue rim, 1950s, 7in (18cm) diam.
£25–30 RAC

A Crowan Pottery (Harry & May Davis) celadon stoneware bowl, c1950, 6¼in (16cm) diam.
£40–45 SnA

A Quimper bowl, decorated with blue and orange abstract pattern on a cream ground, 1950s, 5in (12.5cm) diam.
£12–15 RAC

A Rye Pottery bowl, decorated with a grey and white pattern, 1950s, 10in (25.5cm) high.
£110–130 NCA

An Eileen Lewenstein bowl, decorated with thick drip glaze, supported on a double knop stem and circular base, stamped 'EL' seal, c1950, 10¼in (26cm) high.
£90–120 P(B)

A Denby bowl, designed by Glyn Colledge, c1950, 8¾in (22cm) diam.
£65–75 PC

A celadon glazed bowl, by James Walford, c1950, 5¾in (14.5cm) diam.
£90–100 IW

► A Denby two-handled bowl, designed by Glyn Colledge, c1950, 8in (20.5cm) diam.
£75–85 PC

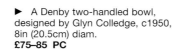

◄ A Rye Pottery bowl, decorated with a white, black, yellow and red pattern, c1950s, 4in (10cm) high.
£35–45 NCA

BUILDINGS

A pair of Staffordshire pearlware cottages, 1820, 3½in (9cm) high.
£250–280 JHo

A Staffordshire model of a castle, c1820, 5in (12.5cm) high.
£200–220 JO

A Staffordshire pastille burner, modelled as a cottage, c1820, 4in (10cm) high.
£150–180 JO

A Staffordshire pastille burner, modelled as a cottage, c1820, 5in (12.5cm) high.
£150–200 JO

A Yorkshire pearlware cottage with a blue roof, base restored, c1820, 6in (15cm) high.
£450–500 JHo

A Dixon, Austin & Co watch stand, modelled as a grandfather clock, decorated in Pratt colours, with 2 classical figures leaning against plinths on either side, slight damage, impressed mark, c1820, 11in (28cm) high.
£520–580 P

A Staffordshire pastille burner, c1835, 3¾in (9.5cm) high.
£120–140 JO

A Staffordshire cottage group, c1830, 8in (20.5cm) high.
£550–620 JO

A Staffordshire two-piece pastille burner, modelled as a cottage, with flowered borders, c1835, 4¾in (12cm) high.
£220–280 DAN

A Staffordshire pastille burner, c1840, 6in (15cm) high.
£200–225 JO

Pastille burners

Originating in Elizabethan times, pastille burners were a popular way of disguising unpleasant smells. Earlier examples were made of silver or bronze but in the 19th century they were frequently made of pottery or porcelain, and modelled as cottages or houses. The scented smoke from the burning pastille or taper escaped through the chimneys and windows.

A pottery longcase clock money box, by J. Emerey, Mexborough, with a dog in front of the clock, on a green base, painted orange, green, black and blue under a pearl glaze, restored, c1838, 9in (23cm) high.
£250–300 SER

A Scottish pottery cottage money box, slight restoration, c1840, 5in (12.5cm) wide.
£420–500 DAN

A Staffordshire lilac pastille burner, modelled as a castle, c1840, 5¾in (14.5cm) high.
£200–225 JO

A Brampton type stoneware cottage-shaped box and cover, c1840, 5in (12.5cm) high.
£100–120 OCH

A Pratt-type pottery money box, with 3 money slots to the roof and chimneys, damaged, inscribed 'Salley Harper Hougate, March 16th, 1845', 7in (18cm) high.
£700–850 CSK

A Staffordshire clock tower spill vase, decorated in green, pink and brown, c1850, 9½in (24cm) high.
£240–280 GAZE

A Staffordshire pastille burner, modelled as a folly, c1840, 6½in (16.5cm) high.
£130–150 JO

A Staffordshire pastille burner, 19thC, 4in (10cm) high.
£220–260 JHo

A Staffordshire spill holder, modelled as a castle, 19thC, 5¼in (13cm) high.
£80–95 JO

LOCATE THE SOURCE
The source of each illustration in Miller's can be found by checking the code letters below each caption with the Key to Illustrations, pages 376–379.

► A Staffordshire model of Potash Farm, c1849, 5½in (14cm) wide.
£170–190 RWB

Potash Farm was the location of a notorious Victorian murder, and many variations of the model were made.

A Staffordshire pastille burner, modelled as a cottage, c1845, 4½in (11.5cm) high.
£100–125 JO

A Staffordshire souvenir money box, modelled as a house, inscribed 'A Present from Scarborough', c1850, 5in (12.5cm) wide.
£150–170 RWB

A Staffordshire model of a cottage, c1850, 7in (17.5cm) high.
£200–225 JO

A Staffordshire pastille burner, modelled as a cottage scene, 19thC, 6in (15cm) high.
£145–165 ACA

A Staffordshire pastille burner, modelled as a castle, c1855, 10¼in (26cm) high.
£200–220 JO

A Staffordshire model of a mansion, c1860, 7¼in (18.5cm) high.
£100–120 JO

A Staffordshire pastille burner, c1860, 8¼in (21cm) high.
£220–250 TVM

A Staffordshire pastille burner, depicting Swan Cottage, c1860, 6¾in (17cm) high.
£80–95 JO

A Staffordshire pastille burner, modelled as a folly, c1860, 5in (12.5cm) high.
£100–125 JO

◄ A Staffordshire model of a castle, with green and rust decoration on a tan ground, c1860, 8½in (21.5cm) high.
£135–150 EL

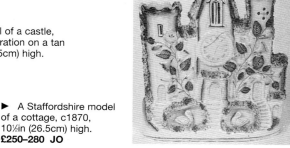

► A Staffordshire model of a cottage, c1870, 10½in (26.5cm) high.
£250–280 JO

BUSTS

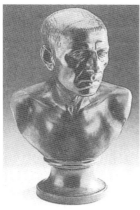

A Wedgwood black basalt bust of Cicero, slight damage, marked, c1790, 20in (51cm) high.
£1,800–2,200 C

A Staffordshire bust of the Earl of St Vincent, c1795, 8in (20.5cm) high.
£500–600 JHo

A Staffordshire pearlware bust of Queen Charlotte, her hair in brown ringlets on her forehead and tied in a spiral bun, raised on a square purple sponged base, slight chip, c1800, 5½in (14cm) high.
£400–450 Hal

A Staffordshire pearlware bust of Zingara, enamel-decorated, possibly by Enoch Wood, 1800, 10½in (26.5cm) high.
£800–900 JRe

A Leeds bust of Shakespeare, c1815, 9½in (24cm) high.
£200–250 SER

A Staffordshire bust of young Napoleon, possibly pearlware, c1800, 9½in (24cm) high.
£1,000–1,200 MSA

A Wedgwood black basalt bust of Mercury, restored, marked, c1840, 17¾in (45cm) high.
£900–1,100 SK

A Wedgwood black basalt bust of Venus, marked, late 19thC, 13½in (34.5cm) high.
£400–450 Bon

A Wedgwood black basalt library bust of Lord Byron, impressed 'Wedgwood' and with title, c1900, 15in (38cm) high.
£850–950 Bon

CANDLESTICKS & CANDLE EXTINGUISHERS

A Wiesbaden rococo scroll-moulded candlestick, painted *en camaieu vert* with flower-sprays, damage to nozzle and restuck, rim chips, c1770, 9in (23cm) high.
£2,200–2,800 C

A Dutch Delft candlestick, after a silver example, decorated in enamel colours with scrolling foliage and scaled bands, slight damage, etched 'C' to base, mid 18thC, 6in (15cm) high.
£4,200–4,600 S(Am)

A pair of three-light candelabra, in the form of a cobbler and his wife, decorated in coloured enamels, damaged, mark in blue, c1895, 10in (25.5cm) high.
£500–600 DN

► A pair of Doulton Lambeth candlesticks, incised and moulded with strapwork decoration in blue and gold, c1890, 8in (20.5cm) high.
£250–350 BWA

A candle extinguisher and tray, decorated with lilac blossom and gold trim, c1900, 4in (10cm) high.
£200–250 TH

A pair of moss ware candlesticks, c1860, 4½in (11.5cm) high.
£30–36 OCH

A pair of Wedgwood lustre candlesticks, mid 19thC, 6in (15cm) high.
£500–550 JHo

Did you know?

Candle extinguishers became decorative items from c1840, when the new 'snuffless' candle was introduced, which could be blown out easily. Many 19thC extinguishers caricatured popular characters of the time.

A Torquay candle holder, decorated with a cockerel, inscribed 'From Kirkby Lonsdale', 1915–28, 4in (10cm) wide.
£25–35 BEV

A Carlton Ware chamber stick, marked, 1930s, 5½in (14cm) diam.
£300–350 YY

A pair of Gouda pottery Crocus design candlesticks, c1927, 10½in (26cm) high.
£250–300 OO

◄ A Poole Pottery off-white three-piece candlestick set, designed by John Adams, 1930s, dish 11in (28cm) wide.
£75–85 WAC

CHEESE DISHES

A George Jones majolica cheese dish and cover, modelled as a cylindrical tower, with banner finial, naturalistically coloured, the interior in pale blue, slight damage, impressed factory and registration mark for 1873, 12¾in (32.5cm) wide.
£1,800–2,200 CSK

A cheese dish, in the form of a water mill, 1920s, 7½in (19cm) wide.
£40–50 LA

◄ A cheese dish and cover, moulded and painted with flowers and foliage, within gilt borders, on cream ground, late 19thC, 9½in (24cm) diam.
£350–400 GAK

A Burleigh Ware cheese dish, with sloping cover, decorated with the Briar pattern, printed marks, c1900, 9in (23cm) wide.
£100–120 GAK

A Marutomo ware cheese dish, in the form of a house, Japanese, 1920s, 6¾in (17cm) wide.
£40–50 PC

A smear-glazed stoneware Stilton cheese dish and cover, with blue ground, late 19thC, 11in (28cm) diam.
£200–250 PCh

◄ A majolica cheese dome, decorated in brown, pink and green, c1880, 15in (38cm) high.
£750–850 JBL

A spongeware cheese dish, decorated with brown, green and yellow, c1900, 7½in (19cm) wide.
£120–150 Ber

A Crown Devon cheese dish and cover, 1920–30, 3¼in (8cm) high.
£70–80 MEG

A Radford thatched cottage cheese dish, 1920s, 9in (23cm) wide.
£50–60 PC

A Carlton Ware cheese dish and cover, with embossed Blackberry design, registered Australian design mark, 1930s, 3in (7.5cm) high.
£60–70 StC

A cheese dish, in the form of an inn, 1920s, 7½in (19cm) wide.
£25–30 PC

A pearlware cow creamer, depicting a cow and suckling calf, with coloured sponged decoration, c1780, 4¼in (11cm) high.
£700–800 BHa

A Prattware-type cow creamer, patched in ochre and green against a powdered blue ground, horns chipped, late 18thC, 6in (15cm) high.
£300–400 Bon

A cow creamer, with a milkmaid, sponged in black with a green-lined base, the tail forming a handle, north country, early 19thC, 5½in (14cm) wide.
£440–520 HYD

A Yorkshire cow creamer, with honey-coloured sponged decoration, original lid, c1800, 5¾in (14.5cm) high.
£650–750 BHa

A cow creamer and cover, sponged with multi-coloured glazes on a green moulded base, probably north country, early 19thC, 5½in (14cm) long.
£420–500 HYD

A Prattware cow creamer, restored, c1800, 5½in (14cm) wide.
£700–800 DAN

A cow creamer, decorated in Prattware colours, c1810, 5in (12.5cm) high.
£400–450 SWN

An earthenware cow creamer and cover, modelled with a milkmaid, the cow sponged in pale blue and brown colours on a buff ground, c1800, 5in (12.5cm) wide.
£550–600 HYD

A pearlware cow creamer, on a green-lined slab base, sponged in red and black glazes on a cream ground, c1800, 5½in (14cm) wide.
£320–380 HYD

Did you know?

Small jugs modelled as cows were first produced in the mid-18thC, particularly in the north of England. Their popularity lasted about 100 years, until it was thought that they might be unhygienic to use as it was difficult to clean inside them.

A Swansea cow creamer, with naturalistic colouring, c1830, 7in (17.5cm) wide.
£350–450 RP

A cow creamer, decorated with red, slight restoration, possibly Swansea, c1830, 5½in (14cm) wide.
£320–380 DAN

A Staffordshire cow creamer, decorated in red and white on a green moulded base, 19thC, 7in (18cm) long.
£120–150 HCH

CRUET SETS

Two Linthorpe salt cellars, shape No. 305, designed by Christopher Dresser, c1880, 3in (7.5cm) diam.
£100–120 each NCA

A Beswick three-piece cruet set on a stand, in the form of Tudor houses, 1920s, 7in (18cm) wide.
£60–70 PC

A Price of Kensington condiment set in the form of twin houses, 1920s, 7in (18cm) wide.
£70–80 LA

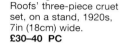

A Burlington 'Thatched Roofs' three-piece cruet set, on a stand, 1920s, 7in (18cm) wide.
£30–40 PC

A Shorter & Son three-piece cruet set on a tray, 1920s, 4½in (11.5cm) wide.
£50–60 LA

A Carlton Ware cruet set, 1920s, 6in (15cm) wide.
£70–85 PC

A Price of Kensington three-piece cruet set on a stand, 1920s, 5in (12.5cm) wide.
£50–60 PC

A three-piece cruet set on a tray, in the form of a teapot, milk jug and sugar basin, 1920s, 6in (15cm) wide.
£30–40 LA

A three-piece cruet set on a stand, in the form of houses and foliage, 1920s, 5in (12.5cm) wide.
£40–50 LA

A Royal Winton cruet set, decorated with Sweet Pea pattern, 1930s, 5in (12.5cm) wide.
£120–140 BEV

A Royal Winton Chintz ware cruet set, decorated with English Rose pattern, with pink and blue flowers on a cream ground, c1940, 5in (12.5cm) wide.
£60–70 CSA

Items in the Pottery section have been arranged in date order within each sub-section.

A Rye Pottery black candy-striped cruet set, 1950s, 3in (7.5cm) high.
£18–22 JR

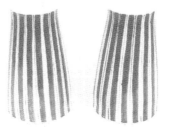

A Rye Pottery cruet set, 1950s, 6½in (16.5cm) high.
£30–35 each NCA

A Midwinter condiment set, Riviera design by Sir Hugh Casson, c1954, dish 8½in (21.5cm) wide.
£20–30 DgC

CUPS & SAUCERS

◄ Two creamware bell-shaped cups, with reeded loop handles, each decorated in coloured enamels, with an iron-red line rim, c1770, 2½in (6.5cm) high.
£300–350 DN

A Wedgwood encaustic decorated cup and stand, painted in white and terracotta with anthemion and bead borders, cup impressed upper case 'WEDGWOOD', c1775, saucer 5½in (14cm) diam.
£450–500 Bon

Davenport

John Davenport founded the porcelain and earthenware factory at Longport, Staffordshire in 1794, producing high-quality stone china for dinner and dessert services. He adapted Oriental patterns for decoration, and also painted landscapes, flowers, fruit and birds, often lavishly gilded. Production declined from the 1870s, and the factory closed in 1887.

A creamware feeding cup, c1800, 6½in (16.5cm) wide.
£50–70 IW

A Davenport buff earthenware coffee can and saucer, c1805, saucer 4¼in (11cm) diam.
£200–220 DN

A Wedgwood coffee can and saucer, sprigged in white with of flowers and fruit suspended from rams' masks between lilac oval cameos and trophies, on a green jasper dip ground, slight damage, marked, early 19thC, saucer 4in (10cm) diam.
£650–720 S(S)

A miniature pearlware cup and saucer, hand-painted with floral sprays and brown rims, c1820, saucer 3¾in (9.5cm) diam.
£100–120 DAN

A cup and saucer, with chinoiserie decoration, c1830, saucer 6in (15cm) diam.
£40–45 OD

A lustre ware cup and saucer, chipped, c1830, saucer 5½in (14cm) diam.
£15–20 OD

◄ A pair of Wedgwood *rosso antico* cups and stands, impressed in upper case 'WEDGWOOD' and other marks, mid-19thC, saucer 3¾in (9.5cm) diam.
£700–800 Bon

A Scottish pottery hound's-head stirrup cup, decorated in black and puce, with green and black bands, hair crack, c1840, 5in (12.5cm) long.
£300–400 DN

A George Jones majolica teacup and saucer, with raised floral and foliate decoration on turquoise blue ground with pink interior, the handle in the form of a lily, c1875, saucer 4in (10cm) wide.
£380–420 AG

A Victorian cup and saucer, inscribed 'Present from the Isle of Man', saucer 4½in (11.5cm) diam.
£10–15 OD

◄ A Burleigh Ware nursery trio, decorated with ducks, c1930, plate 6½in (16.5cm) diam.
£40–50 BKK

◄ A Burleigh Ware cup and saucer, decorated with Bunny pattern, 1930s, 3in (7.5cm) high.
£65–70 BUR

▶ A Burleigh Ware Zenith shape coffee cup and saucer, decorated with Dawn Breckland pattern, 1930s, cup 2½in (6.5cm) high.
£35–45 BUR

▶ A Quimper cup and saucer, marked 'HR', c1885, saucer 4¾in (12cm) diam.
£180–200 VH

A Moorcroft Florian Ware cup and saucer, c1902, saucer 4in (10cm) diam.
£400–500 RUM

A Radford trio, decorated with pink and yellow flowers on a cream ground, c1935, cup 2½in (6.5cm) high.
£20–30 CSA

◄ A William Moorcroft coffee can and saucer, decorated with Pomegranate pattern in shades of orange on a green ground, c1928, cup 2½in ((6.5cm) high.
£375–425 NP

A Susie Cooper geometric cup and saucer, c1930, cup 2½in (6.5cm) high.
£100–120 SCA

A Royal Winton cup and saucer, decorated with Somerset pattern, 1930s, saucer 5½in (14cm) diam.
£60–65 BEV

A Wedgwood Queensware Windsor grey cup and saucer, from the Travel series, with Balloon design by Eric Ravilious, c1936, 2½in (6.5cm) high.
£70–80 YY

A Royal Winton cup and sandwich saucer, decorated with Eleanor pattern, 1930s, saucer 7¾in (20cm) diam.
£55–60 BEV

A Burleigh Ware Zenith shape trio, decorated with Orange Tree pattern, 1930s, cup 3in (7.5cm) high.
£35–45 BUR

A Myott cup and saucer, c1935, cup 2in (5cm) high.
£38–45 BKK

◄ Two Royal Winton miniature cups and saucers, decorated with Rosina pattern, 1930s, saucer 2in (5cm) diam.
£105–115 each BET

A Kelsboro Ware cup and saucer, decoreated in black and white, 1950s, saucer 6in (15cm) diam.
£12–15 GIN

Further Reading
Miller's Collecting Pottery & Porcelain,
Miller's Publications, 1997

A Rye Pottery cup and saucer, c1950, cup 3in (7.5cm) high.
£40–45 NCA

A Midwinter Stylecraft coffee cup and saucer, decorated with Spruce design by Jessie Tait, c1953, cup 3in (7.5cm) high.
£18–25 AND

A Midwinter trio, decorated with Red Domino pattern, c1953, cup 3½in (9cm) high.
£15–20 RAT

A Midwinter Stylecraft coffee cup and saucer, with Riviera design by Sir Hugh Casson, c1954, cup 3in (7.5cm) high.
£35–40 AND

► A Midwinter Stylecraft cup, saucer and side plate, decorated with Nature Study pattern in black and white, designed by Sir Terence Conran, c1955, plate 6½in (16.5cm) diam.
£40–50 P(B)

DISHES

An English delft dish, painted in blue with a cottage within a chainlink border and stylized flower rim, 18thC, 13in (33cm) diam.
£260–330 BR

A Wedgwood argenta strawberry dish, with loop handle, moulded in relief with a sunburst mask, on turquoise ground, within blue-ground flowerhead moulded borders, cracked, impressed marks, c1870, 15¾in (40cm) wide.
£700–800 DN

A George Jones majolica cheese bell and stand, moulded in relief with insects and foliage, impressed mark, pattern No. 3432, c1870, 13½in (34cm) high.
£1,500–1,700 S(S)

A Victorian jasperware blue and white cheese dish and cover, probably Adams, the cover with a continuous frieze of winged figures and trees, with oak and acorn borders, c1885, 10in (25.5cm) high.
£100–120 Hal

A lustre dish, with pink design depicting the zodiac sign Gemini, c1880, 7½in (19cm) diam.
£70–80 SLL

Two majolica oyster dishes, c1900, largest 13in (33cm) diam.
l. £80–100
r. £30–40 MLL

◀ An earthenware dish, printed with 'The Sailor's Farewell' within lustre borders, c1880, 10in (25.5cm) wide.
£50–60 Ber

▶ A majolica leaf-shaped dish, decorated in green, brown and cream, c1880, 10½in (26.5cm) wide.
£55–65 Ber

◀ A Royal Winton butter dish, decorated with Summertime pattern, 1930s, 5¾in (14.5cm) square.
£130–150 BEV

A Buckley brown pottery dish, c1890, 13¾in (35cm) wide.
£150–180 IW

A Rye Pottery dish, decorated with hops, c1910, 4½in (11.5cm) diam.
£70–85 NCA

Two Quimper dishes, in the shape of leaves, one decorated with a lady and coloured in blue and yellow, the other with a man, coloured green, mustard and orange, c1910, 10in (25.5cm) wide.
£90–100 PSA

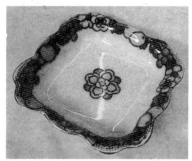

A Losol dish, decorated with Suntrae pattern, c1925, 8¾in (22cm) wide.
£25–30 CSA

A Carlton Ware Rouge Royale dish, signed, stamped mark, c1930, 8½in (21.5cm) wide.
£50–60 WN

A majolica two-handled dish, c1900, 14in (35.5cm) wide.
£200–250 MofC

A spongeware dish, decorated with flags and crowns, inscribed 'Are we Downhearted? No!', 1914–18, 6¾in (17cm) diam.
£85–95 Ber

A Maling ware dish, decorated with pink and yellow flowers on a blue ground, c1928, 7½in (19cm) wide.
£70–80 CSA

A Burleigh Ware dish, designed by Charlotte Rhead, pattern No. S606, c1930, 10½in (27cm) diam.
£90–110 BKK

◄ A Royal Doulton dish, c1910, 17¾in (45cm) wide.
£30–40 PSA

A Bursley Ware Amstel dish, designed by Frederick Rhead, decorated in shades of blue, red and black, 1920s, 4½in (11.5cm) diam.
£40–50 BDA

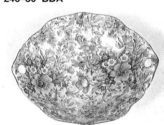

A Royal Winton Chintz ware dish, decorated with Sunshire pattern, in shades of pink, green and orange on a white ground, 1930s, 5½in (14cm) wide.
£50–55 BEV

A Falcon ware dish, decorated with flowers in red, yellow, green and blue on a white ground, c1930, 12in (30.5cm) diam.
£90–110 LUC

Crown Ducal

In 1915, the firm of A. G. Richardson was established at the Gordon Pottery, Tunstall, Staffordshire, to make useful and ornamental lines and novelties under the Crown Ducal trade name. The firm also produced a series of pieces decorated with tube-lined slip filled with coloured glazes.

By 1921, transfer-printed ware and tea ware decorated in plain colours applied by aerograph were being produced.

The most popular Crown Ducal wares are those with decoration designed by Charlotte Rhead.

A Crown Ducal dish, decorated with Rose and Peony pattern, 1930s, 14in (35.5cm) wide.
£125–150 BEV

A Susie Cooper hand-painted hors d'oeuvres dish, 1930s, 9in (23cm) diam.
£90–120 SCA

A Royal Winton butter dish, decorated with Nantwich pattern, 1930s, 6½in (16.5cm) wide.
£150–175 BEV

A Royal Winton dish, decorated with Estelle pattern, 1930s, 9¼in (24cm) wide.
£70–80 BEV

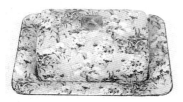

A Shelley butter dish, decorated with Melody pattern, 1930s, 7in (18cm) wide.
£80–90 BEV

A Losol dish, decorated with Waterlily pattern, c1930, 8¼in (21cm) wide.
£15–20 CSA

A Royal Winton dish, decorated with Sweet Pea pattern, 1930s, 7in (18cm) wide.
£70–80 BEV

A Royal Winton butter pat, decorated with Summertime pattern, 1930s, 3½in (8cm) diam.
£20–30 BET

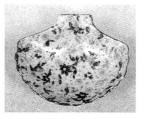

A Royal Winton shell-shaped butter pat, decorated with Eleanor pattern, 1930s, 3¼in (8.5cm) diam.
£20–30 BET

A Carlton Ware dish, with blackberry design, c1930, 8¾in (22cm) wide.
£40–50 CSA

A Carlton Ware dish, c1935, 11¾in (30cm) long.
£40–50 CSA

A Crown Devon dish, with tube line decoration and flowers, c1935, 9in (23cm) long.
£20–30 CSA

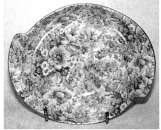

A Royal Winton dish, decorated with Sunshine pattern, c1935, 5½in (14cm) wide.
£30–40 CSA

A Carlton Ware dish, decorated with New Poppy design, c1935, 8in (20.5cm) wide.
£40–50 CSA

► A Royal Winton Chintz ware dish, decorated with Sweet Pea pattern, in shades of yellow, pink and blue flowers, c1935, 10in (25.5cm) wide.
£60–70 CSA

A Susie Cooper hors d'oeuvres set, painted with scroll motif on a cream ground, painted mark '2226', c1930s, largest 6in (15cm) wide.
£80–100 HYD

A Royal Winton comport, decorated with a white rose, 1930s, 10½in (26.5cm) wide.
£15–18 PSA

A Royal Winton Chintz ware dish, decorated with Estelle pattern in shades of pink and yellow flowers on a cream ground, c1935, 10in (25.5cm) wide.
£50–60 CSA

A New Hall lustre dish, by Lucien Boullemier, 1935, 12½in (32cm) wide.
£50–60 CSA

A Royal Winton Chintz ware dish, decorated with Old Cottage pattern, with pink and blue flowers on a grey ground, c1935, 5in (12.5cm) wide.
£20–30 CSA

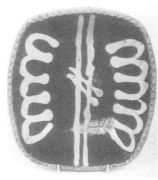

A Winchcombe Pottery slipware dish, c1940, 10in (25.5cm) wide.
£90–100 IW

A pottery dish, by Stig Lingberg for Gustavesberg, Sweden, c1940, 10½in (26.5cm) wide.
£40–45 RCh

▶ A Shorter dish, decorated with 2 large flowers, c1940, 13½in (34.5cm) wide.
£20–30 CSA

A James Kent jam dish, decorated with Florita pattern, c1940, 4½in (11.5cm) long.
£30–40 CSA

A Crown Ducal dish, designed by Charlotte Rhead, with pink flowers on a mottled brown ground, shape No. 9, 1940s, 7in (18cm) wide.
£60–70 PC

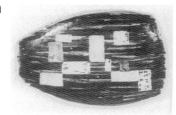

A Carlton Ware soap dish, the exterior painted with black stripes on a white ground, late 1940s, 6in (15cm) long.
£12–15 CHU

▶ A Rye Pottery dish, decorated with a yellow, white and green pattern, c1950, 9in (23cm) wide.
£70–75 NCA

◀ A Shorter petal-shaped dish, with green and red petals, c1950, 7in (18cm) wide.
£10–12 CSA

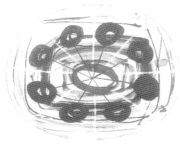

A Rye Pottery avocado dish,
1950s, 5¾in (14.5cm) wide.
£40–45 NCA

A Rye Pottery dish, decorated with
a green and white pattern, c1950,
9in (23cm) wide.
£80–90 NCA

A Rye Pottery dish, c1950,
8½in (21.5cm) wide.
£90–100 NCA

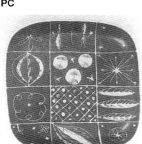

A Grimwades Royal Winton dish,
1950s, 10in (25.5cm) wide.
£35–45 PC

A Denby hand-painted dish,
Glyn Colledge painted signature,
c1950, 9½in (24cm) diam.
£125–150 PGA

▶ A Denby Cheviot dish,
decorated with patterns in square
sections, c1955, 8in (20.5cm) wide.
£25–30 PC

A Rye Pottery butter dish,
decorated in yellow, red
and grey bands and blue
zig-zag pattern, c1950,
5in (12.5cm) diam.
£22–26 NCA

**These dishes were made
specially to hold the individual
post-war butter ration.**

EGG CUPS

A majolica egg holder set, with
central chick in an eggshell, c1900,
3in (7.5cm) high.
£130–150 MLL

A Savill & Co yellow egg
cup, retailer's mark,
c1880, 2¼in (5.5cm) high.
£35–40 AMH

A Carlton Ware tinted faience
all-in-one egg cup and stand,
with pepper and salt wells, ribbon
mark, pattern No. 600, 1890–94,
3¾in (9.5cm) diam.
£30–40 StC

Four Rye Pottery egg cups, c1950,
2in (5cm) high.
£45–50 DSG

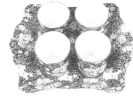

▶ A Royal Winton egg cup set,
decorated with Hazel pattern, 1930s,
tray 7in (18cm) wide.
£200–225 BEV

A Wedgwood creamware
egg cup, internally
decorated with a red
rosebud and green leaves,
1940, 2in (5cm) high.
£8–10 AnS

FIGURES

A Staffordshire figure
of a woman, in a brown
and cream robe, c1770,
8½in (21.5cm) high.
£500–550 JHo

A pair of Pratt-type
pearlware figures of a hunter
and companion, a spotted
dog pawing at the man
standing with a gun under
one arm, the companion
holding a bird and spotted
bag, both hollow figures
picked out in greens, ochre
and brown, late 18thC,
7in (18cm) high.
£1,000–1,200 Bon

A Staffordshire pearlware
group of a shepherd and
shepherdess, a hound
and 2 lambs at their feet,
decorated in coloured
enamels, entitled 'Shepherd'
in black, 1790–1800,
12½in (32cm) high.
£700–800 DN

A Prattware figure
of Mercury, c1790,
8in (20.5cm) high.
£250–280 TVM

A Niderviller faïence figure
of a huntswoman, painted
in *petit feu* enamels, minor
chips, Custine period, c1780,
6¼in (16cm) high.
£350–450 S

A pearlware figure of recumbent
Antony, his head raised, wearing
a cuirass and cape, above a rocky
moulded mound base, painted in
colours, damaged, painted number,
c1790, 12in (30.5cm) wide.
£350–400 CSK

A Ralph Wood spill vase,
depicting a rural couple and a
lamb, c1810, 10½in (26.5cm) high.
£1,200–1,400 MSA

A Prattware figure
of Charity, c1800,
9½in (24cm) high.
£225–255 SER

A Staffordshire cream-
ware figure, decorated
in shades of yellow
and green, c1795,
7½in (19cm) high.
£240–280 IW

A Staffordshire spill vase,
depicting a Guardian
Angel watching over
2 sleeping children, and
a bird on a tree, c18430,
9in (23cm) high.
£145–160 SER

A Staffordshire fiure of
Milton, restored, c1800,
15in (38cm) high.
£320–380 OD

A Staffordshire figure of a reclining lady, decorated in green, yellow and pink, slight damage, c1800, 3½in (9cm) high.
£130–150 SER

A Staffordshire figure of a Scotsman, on an orange base, early 19thC, 9¼in (23.5cm) high.
£850–950 JHo

◀ A Staffordshire figure of Neptune, with his foot on a dolphin, early 19thC, 10½in (26.5cm) high.
£450–520 TVM

A pair of Staffordshire pearlware figures of putti, each holding a basket of flowers, early 19thC, 4½in (11.5cm) high.
£350–400 JHo

A pair of Staffordshire figures, 'Tenderness' and 'Friendship', c1800, 6½in (16cm) high.
£800–1,000 JHo

A Staffordshire figure of Diana, carrying a bowl in her right hand and quiver of arrows in her left, early 19thC, 12in (30.5cm) high.
£200–220 GAK

A Staffordshire figure of Charity, slight damage, 1800–15, 7½in (19cm) high.
£230–280 SER

A Prattware figure of a woman in a brown coat, carrying a basket, c1800, 4in (10cm) high.
£200–250 ALB

A Staffordshire figure group, entitled 'Rural Pastime', enamelled in colours, on a square base, c1800, 7½in (19cm) high.
£600–650 JRe

A Staffordshire figure of a boy, c1810, 5½in (14cm) high.
£360–400 JHo

A Staffordshire group, modelled as a flautist and his female companion, seated beside a waterfall with lambs and swans, with bocage, painted in overglaze enamel colours, on a rustic sprigged base, early 19thC, 8½in (21.5cm) high.
£280–330 HYD

A Staffordshire Walton figure of a lady gardener, dressed in pink, on a green base, slight damage, 1815–25, 5½in (14cm) high.
£200–250 SER

A Staffordshire pearlware reclining figure of Cleopatra, her dress painted in blue and iron-red with flowers and leaves, the green-glazed mound base moulded with flowers and leaves, slight damage, 1790–1800, 11½in (29cm) long.
£360–400 DN

Two pearlware figures of pugilists, comprising a figure of Tom Cribb, standing with fists raised beside a post, damaged, the other in similar pose, painted in colours, early 19thC, 8in (20.5cm) high.
£2,000–2,200 CSK

A pearlware group of a musician and companion, a monkey at their feet, on a plinth base, restored, c1810, 8in (20.5cm) high.
£800–1,000 DN

A Prattware figure of a young girl, kneeling with her head resting on a cushioned pedestal, decorated with orange, blue, pink and yellow, c1810, 2½in (6.5cm) high.
£450–550 RA

A Staffordshire figure of a woman holding a bird, with painted decoration, standing on a square base, c1810, 4in (10cm) high.
£75–85 RBB

An enamelled pearlware group, entitled 'Widow and Orphan', the young woman gathering kindling with the help of 2 children, a baby on her back, wearing a headdress, green cape and patterned iron-red dress, titled rustic base, c1810, 10½in (27cm) high.
£450–500 Bon

A Staffordshire figure, entitled 'The Poor Laborer', early 19thC, 6in (15cm) high.
£250–300 JHo

A Staffordshire group, entitled 'Return', the sailor wearing a blue jacket and trousers and black hat, his companion wearing a white dress and white hat with black band, restored, c1825, 9in (23cm) high.
£250–300 SER

Miller's is a price GUIDE not a price LIST

A Staffordshire group, early 19thC, 7½in (19cm) high.
£300–350 JHo

A Staffordshire group, entitled 'Peter Restoring the Lame Man', c1820, 8in (20.5cm) high.
£750–850 JHo

A group attributed to Obadiah Sherratt, entitled 'The Baptism of Mary', one figure missing, c1820, 9½in (24cm) high.
£1,000–1,200 JBL

Cross Reference
See Colour Review

◄ A Walton figure of a lady seated reading with a cat, under an arbour, 1820, 5½in (14cm) high.
£700–800 BHa

► A pair of Staffordshire figures, entitled 'Gardners', with bocage, c1820, 5¼in (13.5cm) high.
£600–660 JHo

A pair of Staffordshire pearlware figures of young women, emblematic of Summer and Winter, each in contemporary costume and with a child at their side, decorated in green, blue, yellow and ochre, on oval scroll and shell-moulded mound bases, restored, c1825, 9in (23cm) high.
£1,200–1,400 DN

A Staffordshire figure group, entitled 'Charity', c1820, 9in (23cm) high.
£450–500 MSA

A Staffordshire pearlware figure of a young girl, wearing a yellow and blue dress, holding a flower and an umbrella, seated before floral bocage, on a green-glazed square base with black sponged border, restored, c1825, 10in (25.5cm) high.
£700–800 DN

A Staffordshire pearlware figure, entitled 'Elijah', by John Walton, enamelled in colours, impressed strap mark, 1820, 12in (30.5cm) high.
£320–350 JRe

A Staffordshire figure of a girl at a pump, c1820, 6in (15cm) high.
£750–850 JHo

A Yorkshire figure of a man on a horse, restored, early 19thC, 10½in (26.5cm) high.
£3,000–3,300 JHo

In the early 19thC, the Yorkshire factories mainly produced models of cows and horses. Figures on horseback, however, are extremely rare.

A Staffordshire group of a woman and child riding a dog, early 19thC, 8in (20.5cm) high.
£550–650 JHo

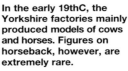

A pair of Staffordshire pearlware figures, entitled 'Sheperd' and 'Sheperdess', early 19thC, 5½in (14cm) high.
£600–700 TVM

A pair of pearlware figures, entitled 'Gardners', he with a spade and she with a watering can, each decorated in coloured enamels and standing before floral bocage, on titled mound bases, restored, c1825, 5in (13cm) high.
£350–400 DN

◄ A set of 4 enamelled pearlware figures, entitled 'The Four Apostles', each standing before bocage, wearing predominantly orange coloured dress, on green rustic bases reserved with titles picked out in black, restored, c1830, 10in (25.5cm) high.
£1,400–1,600 Bon

A St Peter's Pottery, Thomas Fell figure of Apollo, painted with sprigs of flowers, damaged, impressed mark, c1820, 13½in (34cm) high.
£400–500 CSK

◄ A Staffordshire figure, entitled 'Fire', holding a magnifying glass and burning branch, wearing green trousers, a white jacket with brown edging and a black hat with yellow flower, c1825, 6in (15cm) high.
£170–200 SER

A Staffordshire pearlware group, of a Savoyard with a dancing bear and a lion, c1830, 9in (23cm) high.
£2,700–3,000 MSA

A Staffordshire pottery Walton-type group, entitled 'Rualere', modelled as a rustic male musician and his female companion, painted in enamel colours, c1820, 7in (18cm) high.
£320–350 HYD

A pair of Staffordshire figure groups, c1830, 7½in (19cm) high.
£1,000–1,200 JHo

A pair of Staffordshire figures of a shepherd and shepherdess, possibly Lloyd of Shelton, c1835, 7¼in (18.5cm) high.
£350–400 JO

A Staffordshire figure of Jim Crow, c1836, 6¼in (16cm) high.
£400–450 RWB

A Staffordshire pearlware group, entitled 'Rural Pastimes', c1830, 9in (23cm) high.
£700–800 MSA

A Staffordshire group, early 19thC, 9in (23cm) high.
£600–700 JHo

A Staffordshire pearlware figure of a boy with a dog, decorated in green and yellow, c1830, 7in (18cm) high.
£350–400 JRe

A pair of figures of Robert Burns and Highland Mary, he wearing a plumed hat, turquoise jacket and tartan sash, his foot resting above a fountain, she wearing a simple dress, on oval gilt-lined bases, painted in colours and gilt, damaged, 19thC, 14½in (37cm) high.
£400–500 CSK

A pair of Staffordshire figures, entitled 'Old Cobbler and His Wife', 1840–60, 13in (33cm) high.
£250–300 AnE

A Staffordshire figure of a reclining drummer boy, 19thC, 7in (18cm) high.
£280–320 AnE

Figures • POTTERY   55

A Staffordshire figure of the Fat Sailor, with pink shirt and blue trousers, repaired, c1840, 13½in (34.5cm) high.
£100–120 Ber

A Staffordshire figure of Napoleon, with cannon and cannonballs, c1830–40, 12½in (32cm) high.
£750–850 TVM

A Staffordshire group, entitled 'Death of Nelson', depicting the Admiral supported by 2 officers, c1840, 8in (20.5cm) high.
£750–850 TVM

A Staffordshire figure of Nelson, in blue jacket with yellow sash, blue hat and green trousers, 1840s, 8in (20.5cm) high.
£250–300 TVM

A Staffordshire figure, depicting a clock seller in a brown overcoat and cream-coloured suit, on a cream base, c1840, 7½in (19cm) high.
£180–230 GEM

A Staffordshire white figure of a child in a gown with a poodle, c1840, 6in (15cm) high.
£120–150 SER

A figure of a girl in a pink dress, holding a ball, mid-19thC, 5¾in (14.5cm) high.
£40–50 MEG

A Staffordshire group, featuring an egg vendor clutching a basket of eggs, painted in colours with naturalistic faces, c1840–50, 13in (33cm) high.
£160–180 GAK

A Staffordshire figure of Robinson Crusoe, in grey coat with a yellow hat, c1840, 6in (15cm) high.
£160–200 RWB

▶ A pair of Staffordshire porcellaneous figures of a shepherd and shepherdess, in the style of James Dudson, c1845, 6¾in (17cm) high.
£320–380 JO

Pugh numbers

The cataloguing system used by P. D. Gordon Pugh in his book *Staffordshire Portrait Figures*, published by Antique Collectors' Club, 1970, refers to identified portrait figures and allied subjects of the Victorian period.

A pair of Staffordshire figures, based on the story *John Gilpin's Ride*, c1845, 8in (20.5cm) high.
£600–700 RWB

A Staffordshire portrait figure of Jemmy Wood, c1845, 7½in (19cm) high.
£220–250 RWB

Jemmy Wood was a Gloucester draper whose disputed will was the subject of intense public interest.

A Staffordshire figure of a Guardian Angel, possibly watching over The Princess Royal and Prince of Wales, c1845, 9in (23cm) high.
£130–160 SER

Two equestrian figures of Napoleon Bonaparte, wearing blue capes and military uniform on piebald mounts, above rocky mounds applied with foliage on gilt-lined bases, painted in colours and gilt, worn, c1845, 6in (15cm) high.
£450–500 CSK

Three Staffordshire figures of Napoleon, c1845, largest 8¾in (22.5cm) high.
£200–300 each JO

A Staffordshire clock face group, portraying Mrs Siddons as Lady Macbeth, and John Philip Kemble as Hamlet, c1845, 8in (20.5cm) high.
£200–250 RWB

A Staffordshire figure, depicting a lady archer, 19thC, 6¼in (16cm) high.
£130–150 ACA

A Staffordshire spill holder, modelled as a shepherd and shepherdess, with a dog and a sheep, c1850, 9¾in (25cm) high.
£170–190 RWB

A Staffordshire candlestick, modelled as Queen Victoria and Prince Albert, with the Prince of Wales sculling in a boat, c1848, 9½in (24cm) high.
£350–400 RWB

A pair of Staffordshire figures of the Prince of Wales and Princess Royal, c1846, 7in (18cm) high.
£420–480 JO

Fakes and copies

Staffordshire figures have been extensively copied, faked and even reproduced using original moulds. Fakes are usually artificially aged with smears of an oily substance, beware any obviously dirty figures but also those showing no sign of wear. Later examples are usually lighter in weight than the originals.

A Staffordshire figure, entitled 'Sloth', possibly by Ralph Wood, 19thC, 7¾in (20cm) high.
£125–150 ACA

A Staffordshire figure, depicting Prince Albert, restored, 19thC, 11½in (29cm) high.
£125–150 ACA

A Staffordshire quill holder, in the form of a girl with goat, in shades of pink, brown, beige and green, c1850, 5in (12.5cm) high.
£100–125 SER

A figure of a cobbler by A. G. Popov, with high gloss glaze finish, undermarked, 1850–80, 6in (15cm) high.
£350–400 PC

A Staffordshire figure, entitled 'Nightwatchman', 19thC, 9in (23cm) high.
£200–250 ACA

A Staffordshire figure of a Turkish soldier, wearing a plumed hat and holding a flag, 1850–60, 15in (38cm) high.
£270–300 SER

A pair of Staffordshire theatrical figures, depicting T. P. Cook as Ben Backstay, and companion, c1850, 9¼in (23.5cm) high.
£275–300 RWB

Two Staffordshire Astley's Circus figures, seated in a boat before bocage, on a wavy base, c1850, 10½in (27cm) high.
£200–240 SER

► A Staffordshire figure, depicting Winter, 19thC, 7¼in (18.5cm) high.
£145–165 ACA

A pair of Staffordshire figures of a girl and boy holding flags, sitting on stags, c1850, 15in (38cm) high.
£275–325 SER

A pair of Staffordshire figures of Chelsea Pensioners, c1850, 8½in (21.5cm) high.
£800–900 RWB

Production of Staffordshire Figures

A clay figure was made from which a plaster mould was taken in two parts, front and back. The two halves were bound together and a liquid clay poured in and after a carefully judged period, the excess was poured off. When the clay was dry the mould was opened. In some cases a plastic clay was pressed into the mould instead of a poured slip. As more and more moulds were made from the original, quality deteriorated. Flatback figures, intended to be placed against a wall, were only painted on the front. Bright colours were popular, particularly cobalt blue, and Victorian figures often had well-detailed hair and eyebrows – features that tend to be missing from later copies.

A Staffordshire spillvase, with children playing, c1850, 11½in (29cm) high.
£160–180 JO

A set of Staffordshire figures, entitled 'Spring', 'Summer', 'Autum' and 'Winter', 3 figures dressed in blue coats, c1850, 8in (20.5cm) high.
£750–900 JBL

A Staffordshire group, firing crack, c1850, 10in (25.5cm) high.
£120–150 AnE

◀ A Staffordshire theatrical figure of William Charles Macready as Rob Roy MacGregor, c1850, 14in (36cm) high.
£250–300 RWB

Miller's is a price GUIDE not a price LIST

▶ A Staffordshire figure of Aunt Chloe, by Thomas Parr, c1852, 6½in (16.5cm) high.
£300–350 JNic

A Staffordshire figure of a sailor, on a gilt-lined base, c1850, 9in (23cm) high.
£240–280 CGC

▶ A Staffordshire figure of the Duke of Cambridge, decorated in black, pink, mauve, green and orange, c1854, 14¼in (36cm) high.
£230–260 TVM

A Staffordshire figure of Napoleon, wearing a blue jacket, c1854, 16in (40.5cm) high.
£300–330 SER

A Staffordshire group, entitled 'Queen & King of Sardinia', c1855, 13¾in (35cm) high.
£225–250 SER

A Staffordshire figure of
Louis Napoleon of France,
with navy blue jacket,
c1854, 16in (40.5cm) high.
£300–350 RWB

**Louis Napoleon was
President of the 2nd
Republic of Franc from
1848 until 1852, when
he became Emperor
Napoleon III.**

A Staffordshire group,
entitled 'Turkey, England
and France', portraying
Abd-ul-Medjid, Queen
Victoria and Napoleon III,
restored, c1854,
11in (28cm) high.
£400–450 SER

A Staffordshire clock
face group, depicting
Queen Victoria and
Victor Emmanuel II,
c1854, 9in (23cm) high.
£300–350 RWB

A Staffordshire figure of
the Reverend Charles
Spurgeon, c1856,
11½in (29.5cm) high.
£250–300 SER

A Staffordshire group,
entitled 'Dog Tray',
the man wearing a green
cape, the dog with red
spots, restored, c1860,
12¼in (31cm) high.
£75–85 EL

A Staffordshire group,
entitled 'Robin Hood',
c1860–80, 14¾in
(37.5cm) high.
£75–85 EL

A Staffordshire circus
group, depicting
Mazeppa bound naked
to his horse being
pursued by wolves,
with a spill vase
behind, c1860,
9½in (24cm) high.
£650–750 TVM

A Staffordshire spill vase
group, depicting a boy,
a girl and a dog, c1860,
8¼in (21.5cm) high.
£120–150 DAN

◄ A Staffordshire figure,
entitled 'Liberté', depicting
a soldier in an orange tunic
holding a banner, on a leaf
and scroll decorated base,
mid-19thC, 9in (23cm) high.
£180–220 AH

A Staffordshire model of
Jessica and Lorenzo, from
The Merchant of Venice,
with green bocage, c1860,
10in (25.5cm) high.
£160–175 JO

A Staffordshire figure,
entitled 'Louis Kossuth',
wearing a black hat with
pink plume and blue
frock coat, on a titled
base, mid-19thC,
10¾in (27.5cm) high.
£320–360 AH

Cross Reference
See Colour Review

A Staffordshire figure of
a jockey, wearing pink
jacket with black polka
dots, yellow stockings
and green hat, 1850–60,
9in (23cm) high.
£185–225 RWB

A Staffordshire spill vase, modelled as a shepherdess and sheep, c1850, 6in (15cm) high.
£120–140 JO

A Staffordshire gypsy group spill vase, c1850, 8in (20.5cm) high.
£160–200 AnE

A Staffordshire figure, entitled 'The Soldier's Dream', from a poem by Thomas Campbell, c1854, 10¼in (26cm) high.
£150–180 SER

A Staffordshire spill vase, depicting gypsies around a fire with a cooking pot, c1855, 9½in (24cm) high.
£160–180 JO

A Staffordshire spill vase, depicting a boy and a sheep, c1830, 7in (18cm) high.
£600–700 MSA

A Staffordshire figure of a female musician on a couch, c1860, 8¾in (22cm) high.
£150–180 SER

A pair of Staffordshire spill vases, depicting Highland children, c1860, 9in (23cm) high.
£450–550 MSA

A Staffordshire figure of Red Riding Hood and the Wolf, c1860, 9½in (24cm) high.
£200–250 SER

A Staffordshire figure of Charity Girl, by Kent and Parr, c1880, 7in (18cm) high.
£120–150 SER

◄ A Staffordshire spill vase, depicting a zebra with a man in a blue coat, c1865, 7in (18cm) high.
£125–150 JO

Staffordshire

In the late 17th century, London was the centre of the British pottery industry, but by 1710 Staffordshire rivalled and soon overtook London as the hotbed of ceramic inspiration. The five main towns in Staffordshire that form the area known as the Potteries are Stoke-on-Trent, Burslem, Hanley, Longton and Tunstall, with Cobridge, Fenton, Longport, Shelton and Lane Delph nearby. The first products of note to come from this area were the Elers brothers' stoneware and Thomas Tofts's slipware.

A pair of Staffordshire figures of Victoria and Albert, c1850, 11in (28cm) high.
£300–350 P(E)

A Staffordshire figure of a female gardener, c1850, 8in (20.5cm) high.
£250–300 SER

A Staffordshire figure, of the Duke of Wellington on horseback, wearing a black cocked hat, black robe and iron-red jacket, painted throughout in colours, on a green and iron-red washed base, restored, 19thC, 12in (30.5cm) high.
£200–230 GAK

A pair of Minton majolica figures, in the form of a hawker and fish-wife, decorated in blue, purple, brown and green, repaired, impressed marks, c1865, largest 13¾in (35cm) high.
£900–1,000 P

A Staffordshire figure of the King of Sardinia, c1854, 13in (33cm) high.
£700–800 RWB

A Staffordshire figure of Eugénie, Empress of France, c1854, 11½in (29cm) high.
£130–160 SER

A pair of Staffordshire threatrical figures, some restoration, c1860, 8in (20.5cm) high.
£180–220 OD

◄ A Staffordshire group entitled 'Highland Jessye', c1857, 14in (35.5cm) high.
£650–700 RWB

A pair of Staffordshire figures of Harlequin and Columbine, attributed to Thomas Parr, c1855, 6in (15cm) high.
£600–700 HOW

A pair of Staffordshire figures, Sancho Panza and Don Quixote, c1870, 9½in (24cm) high.
£450–500 MSA

A Staffordshire figure of a music hall star, c1870, 13¾in (35cm) high.
£130–160 SER

A Staffordshire figure of a girl in a blue, pink and green dress, standing next to a pump, c1870, 3¾in (9.5cm) high.
£40–50 SER

A pair of Staffordshire figures of horsemen, c1870, 7½in (19cm) high.
£450–500 MSA

A pair of Staffordshire figures, William III and Mary II, white and gilt, c1870, 9½in (24cm) high.
£300–330 SER

A Staffordshire figure of William I, King of Prussia, sparsely coloured, with gilt script, by Sampson Smith, c1870, 17in (43cm) high.
£200–250 SER

A Staffordshire figure of Daniel O'Connell, wearing a black coat and white trousers, coloured and gilt, indistinctly titled in gilt 'Dan O'Connell', c1875, 18in (46cm) high.
£360–400 CSK

A pair of Continental figures of musicians, the girl holding a lute, the man holding a violin, possibly Sarreguemines, late 19thC, 19¼in (49cm) high.
£300–350 TRL

A Staffordshire figure of a reclining man, c1880, 8in (20.5cm) high.
£300–350 AnE

Further Reading
Miller's Pottery Antiques Checklist, Miller's Publications, 1995

A Staffordshire figure of General Roberts, by William Kent, c1900, 14in (35cm) high.
£180–220 SER

A Continental pottery figure of the Trusty Servant, c1890, 7½in (19cm) high.
£55–65 SAS

A Victorian Staffordshire figure of William Shakespeare, leaning on a pile of books on a pillar, 18½in (47cm) high.
£220–240 WilP

A Royal Doulton stoneware figure of Admiral Lord Nelson, on a square base, impressed and incised marks, c1905, 8in (20.5cm) high.
£400–450 DN(H)

A Quimper handbell, in the form of a lady, her leg acting as the bell clapper, marked, c1920, 5in (12.5cm) high.
£180–200 VH

A pair of figures, depicting a boy and a girl, each with a cow, probably German, restored, c1900, 2¾in (7cm) high.
£100–120 MEG

A figure of a maiden, her head buried in her arms, and leaning on a tree, on a square base, stamped '1031', early 20thC, 46½in (118cm) high.
£1,200–1,500 P

A Staffordshire figure, by William Kent of Burslem, entitled 'Garibaldi', standing with his horse on a rocky base, c1920, 13in (33cm) high.
£600–650 JBL

A Dulevo figure of a mother washing children, marked, 1930–40s, 8¾in (22cm) high.
£200–250 SRC

A Doulton Lambeth figure, depicting a farmer with a scythe, by L. Harradine, c1920, 6in (15cm) high.
£300–350 P

Two Wade figures of Sam and Sarah, designed by Mable Lucie Attwell, 1930s, 3¼in (8.5cm) high.
£375–425 PGA

A Wade figure, entitled 'Sunshine', with sprayed cellulose decoration, 1930s, 8in (20.5cm) high.
£150–160 PAC

A Wade figure, entitled 'Barbara', with sprayed cellulose decoration, green ribbons and a pink and yellow dress, 1930s, 9in (23cm) high.
£180–200 PAC

A pair of Staffordshire figures of a shepherd and shepherdess, each standing with a dog, she wearing a striped dress, he wearing yellow breeches and a brown jacket, with bocage, on green and brown mound bases, c1820, 5¼in (13.5cm) high.
£520–580 TVM

A Staffordshire figure of a Scottish gamekeeper, wearing a kilt, standing with his dog, c1820, 8in (20.5cm) high.
£3,300–3,650 JHo

A Staffordshire figure of Minerva, on an inscribed square base, c1790, 12in (30.5cm) high.
£550–600 TVM

A Staffordshire figure, entitled 'William Tell', restored, c1850, 10½in (26.5cm) high.
£165–185 SER

A Staffordshire figure of Lord Byron, base inscribed, c1845, 7½in (19cm) high.
£300–350 RWB

A Staffordshire figure of a female gardener, seated on a branch holding a watering can, c1850, 7½in (19cm) high.
£120–150 SER

A Staffordshire figure of Andromache, standing beside an urn, bocage missing, c1820, 9½in (24cm) high.
£250–300 DAN

A Staffordshire group, with 2 figures seated in an arbour, possibly depicting Jessica and Lorenzo, mid-19thC, 9in (23cm) high.
£300–340 TVM

A Staffordshire figure of a shepherd, leaning on a tree, wearing a blue coat and a tricorn hat, with a sheep at his feet, c1860, 13½in (34.5cm) high.
£220–280 DAN

A Staffordshire group, depicting of Princess Alice and Prince Louis of Hess, on an oval base, c1862, 14in (35.5cm) high.
£450–500 RWB

A Dutch Delft figural gin bottle, restored, 18thC, 14¾in (37.5cm) high.
£5,200–5,800 S(Am)

A pair of Staffordshire figures, entitled 'Age', c1810, 6in (15cm) high.
£350–400 JO

A pair of Staffordshire figures, restored, c1820, 9in (23cm) high.
£350–400 SER

A Staffordshire figure, entitled 'The Rape of Lucretia', c1820, 13in (33cm) wide.
£1,500–1,650 JHo

A Staffordshire figure, c1825, 8in (20.5cm) high.
£400–450 JRe

A Staffordshire group, damaged, c1825, 6½in (16.5cm) high.
£350–400 DAN

A pair of Staffordshire figures of gardeners, c1820, 6in (15cm) high.
£400–450 TVM

A Staffordshire group, entitled 'Tee Total', c1830, 8½in (21.5cm) high.
£3,000–3,300 JHo

A Staffordshire group, entitled 'The Rural Harvest', c1880, 13in (33cm) high.
£80–100 JO

A Staffordshire figure, c1855, 16in (40.5cm) high.
£250–280 RWB

A Royal Dux Bohemia group, c1900, 17½in (44.5cm) high.
£1,000–1,200 HCC

◄ A Royal Dux pottery figure of a fisherman carrying nets, applied pink triangle mark, impressed numerals '1371', c1900, 21in (53.5cm) high.
£600–650 HCC

A Staffordshire figure group, entitled 'Courtship', c1820, 7in (17.5cm) high.
£2,000–2,200 JHo

A creamware group of St. George and the Dragon, restored, impressed 'Ra. Wood, Burslem', c1770, 11in (28cm) high.
£1,200–1,400 Bon

A Tittensor cow creamer, with calf, on a mound base, with bocage, c1820, 6½in (16.5cm) high.
£1,000–1,200 BHA

A pair of Staffordshire pearlware figures of a stag and hind, on oval mound bases, restored, c1800, 6in (15cm) high.
£800–1,000 DN

A Quimper swan-shaped vase, c1920, 8in (20.5cm) high.
£300–375 MofC

A Staffordshire pearlware group of Sacred and Profane Love, c1810, 17in (43cm) high.
£1,000–1,200 CNY

Further Reading

Miller's Pottery Antiques Checklist, Miller's Publications, 1995

A pair of Staffordshire models of Dalmations, wearing gilt-painted collars, on turquoise floral encrusted bases, c1850, 7in (18cm) wide.
£1,500–1,800 HOW

A Staffordshire shell and floral piece, repaired, early 19thC, 7¼in (18.5cm) high.
£1,000–1,250 JHo

A Staffordshire creamware model of a baby deer, with bocage, c1820, 4in (10cm) high.
£250–300 BHa

A pearlware model of a performing lion, decorated in underglaze colours, on a square base, probably Staffordshire, c1800, 7in (18cm) wide.
£4,000–5,000 JHo

A Staffordshire stirrup cup, c1800, 6in (15cm) wide.
£1,300–1,500 JHo

A Yorkshire pearlware model of a horse, wearing a saddlecloth and bridle, on a green base, restored, c1800, 6in (15cm) wide.
£2,000–2,500 BHa

A pair of Staffordshire models of black and white spaniels, with maroon collars and chains, one restored, c1840, 10in (25.5cm) high.
£200–220 SER

A Staffordshire model of a parrot, on a tree stump base, c1855, 9in (23cm) high.
£200–250 RWB

A Yorkshire Prattware model of a cow, calf and farmer, c1800, 6in (15cm) high.
£1,100–1,300 RWB

A Yorkshire pottery cow creamer, sponged and decorated in Prattware colours, c1800, 7¼in (18.5cm) wide.
£800–900 BHa

A north country cow creamer, with milkmaid, sponged and decorated in colours, c1810, 5½in (14cm) high.
£550–600 RWB

A Scottish pearlware dog and pups, decorated in overglaze enamel colours, c1845, 3¾in (9.5cm) high.
£500–600 JRe

A pair of Staffordshire figures of Queen Victoria and Prince Albert, both standing on grey rock base, 19thC, largest 18½in (47cm) high.
£1,300–1,500 MSW

A Staffordshire Obadiah Sherratt tithe pig group, with bocage, c1835, 8½in (21.5cm) high.
£1,000–1,200 JO

A Staffordshire Obadiah Sherratt group, depicting Dr Syntax playing cards, c1820, 7½in (19cm) high.
£2,000–2,500 BHa

A pair of Staffordshire figures, depicting the Princess Royal and the Prince of Wales, c1855, 6½in (16.5cm) high.
£700–750 HOW

A Staffordshire figure, entitled 'Princess', c1850, 8in (20.5cm) high.
£400–450 RWB

A Staffordshire pearlware figure of William III as a Roman emperor, c1810, 8¾in (22cm) high.
£3,600–4,200 JRe

A pair of Staffordshire figures, by Kent, The Cobbler and his Wife, on square bases, slight damage, c1880, 12in (30.5cm) high.
£160–190 SER

A Staffordshire figure of a skater, depicting 'Winter', c1800, 8in (20.5cm) high.
£200–250 SER

A pair of Staffordshire figures, Betsy Trott and Mr Dick, from *David Copperfield*, c1845, 6¾in (17cm) high.
£500–550 JO

A Staffordshire mustard, pepper, and oil or vinegar pot, c1860, largest 6in (15cm) high.
£70–80 each JO

A pair of Staffordshire Obadiah Sherratt ale bench groups, c1820, 8in (20.5cm) high.
£7,000–8,000 BHa

A Staffordshire salt-glazed teapot, c1765, 4¼in (11cm) high.
£1,350–1,550 JHo

A Yorkshire creamware teapot, some damage, c1750, 4in (10cm) high.
£240–280 IW

A Staffordshire spill vase, depicting Red Riding Hood with the wolf, c1850, 10½in (26.5cm) high.
£100–135 SER

A Staffordshire spill vase, early 19thC, 4¾in (12cm) high.
£500–550 JHo

A Staffordshire model of a Scottish castle keep, c1820, 5½in (14cm) high.
£350–400 JO

A Staffordshire model of Fantasy Castle, c1860, 11¾in (30cm) high.
£160–185 SER

A Desvres faïence basket, supported by 2 figures, old repairs, c1860, 8¾in (22cm) wide.
£120–140 IW

A Wedgwood Fairyland lustre vase, designed by Daisy Makeig-Jones, painted with Imps on a Bridge pattern, c1920, 12in (30.5cm) high
£3,500–4,000 S

A Minton majolica game pie dish and cover, repaired, impressed marks for 1876, 15½in (39.5cm) high.
£11,000–12,000 DN

A pottery hand warmer, made in the form of 2 books, with a hole at one end for hot water, c1660, 5¼in (13.5cm) long.
£25,000–30,000 JHo

A pair of Le Nove maiolica bottle vases, comet mark in blue, c1900, 19¼in (49cm) high.
£1,800–2,000 Bon

A Minton majolica game pie dish and cover, damaged, c1880, 18in (45.5cm) wide.
£32,500–34,000 S

A pottery model of a cow, decorated in underglaze colours, possibly Bovey Tracey, horns restored, c1770, 8in (20.5cm) wide.
£2,300–2,600 JHo

A Prattware model of a lion, painted in ochre, with acanthus leaves around the base, c1800, 7½in (19cm) wide.
£3,000–3,300 JHo

A Prattware model of a ram, restored, c1800, 6½in (16.5cm) wide.
£1,000–1,200 DAN

A pair of Staffordshire models of zebras, with separate and raised legs, flowing manes and wearing bridles, on gilt-lined bases, c1850, 8in (20.5cm) wide.
£750–850 TVM

Two Staffordshire models, depicting a lion and a unicorn, marks for John Walton, some restoration, c1820, 6½in (16.5cm) wide.
£4,000–4,400 JHo

A Staffordshire model of a seated cat, wearing a collar, c1860, 3½in (9cm) wide.
£200–250 DAN

A pearlware cow creamer, sponged in blue/grey on a cream ground, with a milkmaid, c1800, 5½in (14cm) wide.
£460–500 HYD

A creamware cow creamer and cover, sponged in ochre and brown, c1800, 6in (15cm) wide.
£350–400 HYD

A Staffordshire pearlware model of a lion, c1810, 5½in (14cm) wide.
£850–950 JRe

A Wemyss blue-glazed cat, c1900, 13in (33cm) high.
£13,000–14,000 S

A cow creamer and cover, early 19thC, 5½in (14cm) wide.
£350–400 HYD

A Staffordshire pottery model of a water buffalo, restored, c1760, 8in (20.5cm) high.
£8,500–9,500 JHo

A Staffordshire agateware cow creamer and calf, stopper renewed, c1775, 7½in (19cm) wide.
£1,500–1,750 JHo

A Staffordshire military group, early 19thC, 10¼in (26cm) wide.
£3,000–3,300 JHo

A Staffordshire pearlware model of a deer, with bocage, c1820, 6in (15cm) high.
£300–350 OCH

A Staffordshire cow creamer and cover, with a milkmaid, c1830, 6in (15cm) high.
£380–420 JO

A Staffordshire cow creamer and cover, c1835, 5in (12.5cm) high.
£550–600 JO

A Staffordshire model of a poodle, on an oval base decorated with sea shells, c1840, 3½in (9cm) high.
£330–360 JO

A Staffordshire group, possibly portraying the Prince of Wales, c1850, 9½in (24cm) high.
£400–450 RWB

A Staffordshire treacle-glazed lion, on an oval base, c1860, 14in (35.5cm) wide.
£800–900 ANT

A pair of Staffordshire models of seated spaniels, each with russet markings and gilt collars, mid-19thC, 8in (20.5cm) high.
£180–200 AAV

A pair of Staffordshire models of dogs, each picked out in brown on a white ground, restoration to one foot, c1885, 14in (35.5 cm) wide.
£250–300 SER

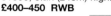

A Bristol delft plate, decorated with a peacock, c1730, 7¾in (19.5cm) diam.
£1,200–1,350 JHo

An English delft plate, decorated with an Oriental landscape, mid-18thC, 11¾in (30cm) diam.
£600–700 BIG

A pair of Dutch Delft plates, decorated with geometric and floral pattern, c1740, 12in (30.5cm) diam.
£600–675 ANT

A Dutch Delft polychrome dish, 18thC, 13¾in (35cm) diam.
£400–450 OCH

A slipware dish, with a piecrust rim, damaged and repaired, 18thC, 13½in (34.5cm) diam.
£4,500–5,000 P

A Mason's dessert plate, with transfer-printed decoration, c1813, 8in (20.5cm) diam.
£100–110 JP

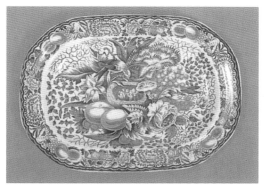

A blue and white platter, decorated with Bird's Nest pattern, c1820, 20in (51cm) wide.
£875–975 OCH

An Austrian dish, by Ernst Wahliss, in the form of a leaf with nuts and biscuits, on a green ground, c1900, 12½in (32cm) wide.
£300–360 BRT

A set of 6 Longchamps asparagus plates, c1880, 11in (28cm) diam.
£350–400 MLL

A Wemyss plate, painted with carnations, with a green line border, c1895, 5½in (14cm) diam.
£250–275 RdeR

An Italian maiolica charger, with a central figure on horseback, late 19thC, 25in (63.5cm) diam.
£340–380 SWO

A Dutch Delft doré basket, with double scroll handles, the base decorated with a courting couple, 18thC, 9½in (24cm) wide.
£6,000–7,000 S(Am)

A pottery basket and stand, decorated with Piping Shepherd pattern, c1820, 10in (25.5cm) wide.
£350–450 GN

A Davenport footed bowl, decorated with Heron pattern and gilding, c1810, 10½in (26.5cm) diam.
£450–500 JP

A Dutch Delft dish, with a building and a tree, mid-18thC, 11¼in (28.5cm) wide.
£1,500–1,800 S(Am)

A George Jones majolica punchbowl, the holly-moulded bowl supported by a figure of Mr Punch, cracked and rim chipped, marked, c1872, 13¾in (35cm) diam.
£4,800–5,300 DN

A spongeware bowl, with polychrome decoration, c1870, 13in (33cm) diam.
£180–200 RYA

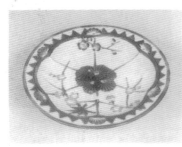

◄ A Mason's Ironstone pot pourri bowl, with 2 covers, painted with enamel and gilt sprays on a lilac ground, one cover restored, marked, c1820, 14¾in (37.5cm) diam.
£500–600 Bon

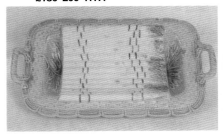

A French majolica asparagus cradle, late 19thC, 16in (40.5cm) wide.
£130–150 SSW

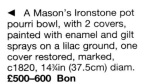

A Wedgwood majolica comport, from a dessert service, c1880, 9in (23cm) diam.
£100–120 SSW

A Mason's Ashworth punchbowl, decorated with Flying Bird pattern, marked, c1880, 18½in (47cm) diam.
£1,300–1,600 JP

A Wemyss Audley bowl, painted by James Sharp, c1900, 7in (18cm) diam.
£650–700 RdeR

A Mason's dessert dish, decorated with Scroll pattern and relief gilding, marked, c1814, 11in (28cm) wide.
£330–360 JP

A Wemyss quaiche, decorated with strawberries, c1900, 7½in (19cm) diam.
£250–300 RdeR

A Carlton Ware Hydrangea pattern hors d'oeuvres dish, c1930, 13in (33cm) diam.
£100–120 CSA

A Staffordshire creamware teapot, of Whieldon type, cover restored, c1760, 3½in (9cm) high.
£400–450 IW

A Staffordshire teapot, decorated with an Oriental pattern, c1765, 6in (15cm) high.
£6,000–6,500 JHo

A Staffordshire teapot, impressed 'Wedgwood', c1770, 6¼in (16cm) high.
£2,700–3,000 JHo

A Sunderland earthenware tea cup and saucer, with lustre borders, c1880, cup 2¾in (7cm) high.
£45–50 Ber

A Staffordshire teapot and sugar bowl, by Enoch Wood & Sons, depicting Wadsworth Towers, c1818, teapot 8½in (21.5cm) high.
£750–850 A&A

A Staffordshire earthenware coffee pot and cover, with floral decoration on a buff ground, c1755, 8in (20.5cm) high.
£6,000–7,000 S(NY)

A Staffordshire salt-glazed cup, c1735, 2¾in (7cm) high.
£3,300–3,600 JHo

A child's pottery 17-piece teaset, c1840, teapot 4½in (11.5cm) high.
£180–200 TMA

A Mason's Ironstone Table and Flowerpots pattern jug, c1815, 6¾in (17cm) high.
£200–225 VH

A Staffordshire agateware tea canister, c1755, 5in (12.5cm) high.
£4,500–5,000 JHo

A copper lustre beaker, c1830, 4½in (11.5cm) high.
£40–50 SER

A lustre goblet, c1840, 4½in (11.5cm) high.
£50–55 BRU

A blue and white transfer-printed loving cup, c1830, 5in (12.5cm) high.
£260–300 Nor

A Staffordshire Toby jug, c1885, 10½in (26.5cm) high.
£120–140 JO

A Victorian stoneware vase, 10¼in (26cm) high.
£165–185 HEI

An English delft blue and white flower brick, c1760, 9¼in (23.5cm) wide.
£900–1,000 JHo

A Wemyss vase, early 20thC, 21in (53.5cm) high.
£3,500–4,000 S

A Wemyss vase, c1920, 13in (33cm) high.
£350–400 MSW

A garniture of 5 Dutch Delft vases, with angel knops, damaged and repaired, mid-18thC, largest 19½in (49.5cm) high.
£7,000–8,000 S

A pair of Mason's Ironstone vases, impressed marks, one repaired, c1815, 10in (25.5cm) high.
£1,100–1,200 VH

A pair of Royal Doulton stoneware three-handled vases, commemorating the coronation of 1911, 6½in (16.5cm) high.
£90–100 SAS

A Quimper vase, depicting a view of Quimper, marked, c1895, 20in (51cm) high.
£900–1,000 VH

A creamware part dinner service, comprising 109 pieces, each piece painted with a named specimen flower, perhaps Staffordshire, some damage, c1805.
£35,000–40,000 C

A set of 6 St. Clément plates, c1900, 8½in (21.5cm) diam.
£250–285 MofC

A Pratt-type commemorative flask, with moulded portraits of George III and Queen Charlotte, c1780, 5in (12.5cm) high.
£300–350 Bon

A double-faced St. Clément jug, with impressed mark, c1900, 9in (23cm) high.
£80–120 MofC

A Lambeth delft Persian blue posset pot, glaze chips, late 17thC, 4½in (11.5cm) high.
£12,000–15,000 Bea

An asparagus plate, c1890, 9½in (24cm) diam.
£40–60 MofC

A pair of Staffordshire salt-glazed stoneware marriage mugs, mid-18thC, largest 6½in (16.5cm) high.
£1,300–1,500 DN

A majolica Neptune vase, c1885, 17in (43cm) high.
£450–500 MofC

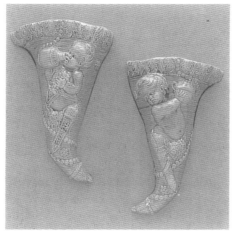

A Prattware tea caddy, probably by Gordon's Pottery, Prestonpans, late 18thC, 8in (20.5cm) high.
£250–350 RA

A pair of Staffordshire Ralph Wood-type creamware wall pockets, emblematic of Autumn and Winter, gilding worn, c1780, 9½in (24cm) high.
£1,500–2,000 CNY

A Delft charger, painted in shades of blue and yellow, Bristol or London, c1700, 13½in (34.5cm) diam.
£3,000–3,300 JHo

A Thun pottery charger, Switzerland, c1885, 14¾in (37.5cm) diam.
£300–350 DSG

A Martin Brothers stoneware vase, incised with comical fish, dated '25.5.79', 10¾in (27cm) high.
£600–700 P

An Art Pottery lustre charger, possibly designed by Walter Crane, c1880, 12¼in (31cm) diam.
£400–450 P(B)

A Burmantofts faïence vase, with twin handles, decorated with florets in roundels, c1885, 8in (20.5cm) high.
£140–160 DSG

A Barnstaple pottery jardinière, possibly by Alex Lauder, c1890, 11½in (29cm) high.
£140–160 P(B)

A William de Morgan vase, decorated by Joe Juster, c1890, 7in (18cm) high.
£3,100–3,500 HAM

A pair of J. Stiff & Sons, Lambeth, stoneware vases, c1890, 5in (12.5cm) high.
£100–120 SnA

A Langley Pottery jardinière, decorated in coloured slips, c1900, 8in (20.5cm) high.
£200–250 DSG

A Della Robbia pottery charger, signed with ship monogram 'DR', c1894, 15in (38cm) diam.
£330–360 P(B)

A Scottish *faix bois* lustre jug, with a pewter lid, c1900, 8in (20.5cm) high.
£30–40 OD

A North Devon Pottery twin-handled vase, by W. L. Baron, c1895, 5½in (14cm) high.
£120–140 DSG

An Art Nouveau pottery jardinière, by Ravissant, coloured in orange and honey glaze, c1900, 8¼in (21cm) high.
£80–100 P(B)

A Weller pottery vase, American, c1915, 8in (20.5cm) high.
£180–200 EKK

A Shelley lustre vase, by Walter Slater, c1920, 15in (38cm) high.
£1,200–1,500 DSG

A Quimper Art Deco style-jardinère, c1920, 6in (15cm) high.
£220–250 MLL

A Bauer ringware pottery jug, c1920, 8in (20.5cm) high.
£130–150 EKK

A pair of Gouda plates, painted with nasturtiums, c1924, 7½in (19cm) diam.
£45–50 OO

A Gouda pottery oviform vase, decorated in colours in batik manner with stylized flowers, c1920, 8¼in (21cm) high.
£150–180 DSG

An Austrian earthenware vase, by Otto Prutscher, c1923, 15in (38cm) high.
£2,500–3,000 DORO

A Rubian baluster vase, with transfer-printed decoration, c1920, 8¼in (21cm) high.
£120–140 DSG

A Gouda Srebo vase, c1920, 7½in (19cm) high.
£120–140 OO

A pottery jug, probably Crown Ducal, decorated by Charlotte Rhead, with tube-lined flowers, 1930s, 8½in (21.5cm) high.
£150–170 PrB

A Susie Cooper Kestrel shape coffee set, decorated with green stars and green and orange banding, pattern No. 1530, c1930, coffee pot 7¼in (18.5cm) high.
£650–750 MAV

Two Susie Cooper horizontally ribbed tankards, with inset handles, decorated in various colours on a cream ground, printed crown works mark, c1930, 5in (12.5cm) high.
£75–85 CDC

A Crown Ducal charger, by Charlotte Rhead, with tube-lined decoration, c1930, 12in (30.5cm) diam.
£280–300 MAV

A Charlotte Rhead dish, tube-lined and painted with stylized foliage, c1930, 12in (30.5cm) wide.
£160–190 PrB

A George Clews Chameleon Ware vase, c1930, 5¾in (14.5cm) high.
£50–60 PrB

A Charlotte Rhead pottery vase, with tube-lined decoration, probably Crown Ducal, c1930, 6in (15cm) diam.
£150–170 PrB

A Crown Ducal Charlotte Rhead pottery vase, decorated with flowers and foliage, c1935, 12½in (32cm) high.
£380–430 DSG

A Rookwood pottery baluster vase, American, c1930, 9in (23cm) high.
£550–600 EKK

A George Clews Chameleon Ware vase, base stamped, c1935, 10¼in (26cm) high.
£140–160 P(B)

A Myott & Sons bowl, decorated with red, brown and green banding and floral sprays, on a stepped base, c1930, 11in (28cm) wide.
£50–60 CSA

A Pilkington Lancastrian monochrome twin-handled vase, covered overall with an orange glaze, 1930s, 5½in (14cm) high.
£55–65 DSG

A Burleigh ware vase, in the form of 2 interlocking lozenge shapes with double angle poised handles, 1930s, 7in (18cm) high.
£350–400 P(B)

A George Clews Chameleon Ware sandwich set, comprising 5 pieces, decorated with stylized blue flowers and foliage, on a beige ground, 1930s, plate 4½in (11.5cm) wide.
£80–100 MRW

A Carlton Ware jug, with a black handle, decorated with orange, yellow, green and red bands, with a black interior, 1930s, 3in (7.5cm) high.
£40–50 MRW

FLASKS & BOTTLES

A Staffordshire salt-glazed bottle, c1760, 8¼in (21cm) high.
£2,200–2,600 JHo

A scallop shell-shaped pearlware flask, c1790, 4½in (11.5cm) wide.
£200–240 IW

◀ A salt-glazed porter bottle, with mid-brown top, lower portion impressed 'W. Hooper Rols, 1814', badly cracked, 9in (23cm) high.
£170–200 BBR

A Bourne's Pottery salt-glazed stoneware spirit flask, incised 'Success to Reform', c1830, 8in (20.5cm) high.
£300–320 TVM

A salt-glazed stoneware spirit flask, in the shape of a fish, c1830, 7in (18cm) long.
£160–180 TVM

A glazed pottery boot flask, c1870, 6½in (16.5cm) high.
£35–40 WAB

A Linthorpe Oriental series moon flask, designed by Christopher Dresser, c1880, 6in (15cm) high.
£700–800 NCA

A salt-glazed bottle, with impressed mark 'Hubaudière Quimper', 1885–90, 12½in (32cm) high.
£100–120 VH

A stoneware bottle, with handle to rear, black transfer-printed 'Wicklow Distillery, Old Irish Whiskey', with an owl perched on a branch, some body speckling, 1920–30s, 7¾in (19.5cm) high.
£80–100 BBR

▶ A pair of Wedgwood green jasper bottles, each decorated with 4 Muses, cracked, impressed mark, c1900, 9in (23cm) high.
£250–300 Bon

A hot water bottle, inscribed 'The Adaptable Hot Water Bottle & Bed Warmer' and 'Old Fulham Pottery', c1910, 8in (20.5cm) diam.
£15–20 JUN

◀ A Rye Pottery bottle, decorated with a white, black, blue and yellow pattern, 1950s, 3in (7.5cm) high.
£40–50 NCA

A stoneware ginger beer bottle, with transfer of a bearded man, inscribed 'Brewed Ginger Beer, R. Stothert & Sons, Atherton', c1900–10, 8in (20.5cm) high.
£100–110 BBR

INKWELLS & PEN HOLDERS

A Liverpool delft inkwell, c1760, 4in (10cm) wide.
£380–420 JHo

A Staffordshire pearlware inkwell, in the form of a shoe, enamel-decorated, c1820, 2½in (6.5cm) long.
£350–380 JRe

An Italian maiolica inkwell, in the form of a winged griffin attendant, late 19thC, 4in (10cm) wide.
£125–140 GAK

> ## Did you know?
> By the 18thC, the inkstand was a fashionable addition to the writing desk. It comprised accessories such as an inkpot with holes for spare quills, a 'sand' box for powdering the paper, a 'wafer' box for seals, a taper-holder and a tray for penknife, pencil etc.

A Staffordshire quill holder, modelled as a parrot, 19thC, 5in (12.5cm) high.
£165–185 ACA

A Staffordshire pen holder, modelled as a stag, c1840, 4in (10cm) high.
£100–125 JO

▶ A Staffordshire group pen holder and inkwell, c1860, 4½in (11.5cm) high.
£60–75 JO

JARDINIÈRES

Two Minton majolica jardinières and stands, decorated with ochre, brown, blue and green glazes, impressed marks, 1860–70, largest 7in (17.5cm) diam.
£300–350 WW

A Minton majolica jardinière, with ribbon-tied laurel wreaths applied to the sides, some restoration to base, c1870, 14¾in (37.5cm) high.
£950–1,100 WW

A Minton majolica jardinière and stand, relief-moulded with strawberry plants on a pink ground, slight damage, impressed mark, 19thC, 9½in (24cm) diam.
£900–1,100 RBB

A Minton majolica jardinière, impressed marks and date code for 1871, 20in (51cm) high.
£3,200–3,500 Bea(E)

◀ A pair of Doulton stoneware jardinières and stands, decorated with Natural Foliage pattern in shades of brown on a mottled grey/green ground some chips, impressed marks, c1880, 29½in (75cm) high.
£800–1,000 S(S)

A Linthorpe jardinière, shape No. 533, designed by Christopher Dresser, c1880, 8in (20.5cm) high.
£500–600 NCA

A Doulton Lambeth stoneware jardinière, by George Tinworth, incised and glazed with a band of seaweed on an ochre ground, with serpent handles, incised monogram, dated '1881', 9¼in (23.5cm) high.
£1,300–1,500 S

A Liberty stoneware jardinière, designed by Archibald Knox, applied with 2 lug handles below a band with incised Celtic knot motifs, impressed Liberty mark, minor restoration, c1890, 19½in (49cm) high.
£1,200–1,500 CSK

A late Victorian cachepot, with floral decoration on a cream and brown ground, beneath a pierced brass rim, on raised base, 14¾in (37.5cm) diam.
£200–250 Gam

A Burmantofts jardinière, incised with 3 pairs of blue dogs wearing yellow collars, running between stylized trees, impressed marks, c1890, 9¾in (25cm) high.
£1,000–1,200 S(S)

A Burmantofts jardinière, decorated with blue and green flowers and leaves, c1890, 12in (30.5cm) diam.
£250–350 ASA

A majolica jardinière, by W. Schiller & Sons, Bodenbach, Bohemia, restored, late 19thC, 8in (20.5cm) high.
£200–220 RIT

An iridescent jardinière, by Clement Massier, with bronze mount, dated '1892', 11¾in (30cm) diam.
£900–1,000 SUC

An Orchies cachepot, late 19thC, 8in (20.5cm) high.
£150–180 MofC

A Barbotine cachepot, c1900, 9in (23cm) high.
£220–250 MofC

A Minton majolica green-glazed jardinière, with ribbon banding, c1900, 12¼in (31cm) high.
£200–240 AH

◄ A Watcombe Pottery jardinière and stand, decorated with yellow daffodils on a green ground, c1900, 42in (106.5cm) high.
£1,200–1,400 PLY

► A Minton jardinière and stand, with patera and ribbon-tied laurel garlands picked out in blue, on a purple ground, damaged, impressed mark and numerals, late 19thC, 40in (101.5cm) high.
£350–400 DN

A Doulton Burslem flower pot, printed in brown with portraits and inscribed 'Australian Federation' and with quotation from Joseph Chamberlain, 1901, 4¾in (12cm) high.
£100–110 SAS

A late Victorian jardinière, painted with bluebirds and blossom, 13in (33cm) diam.
£325–365 PSA

A Moorcroft Florian Ware jardinière, decorated with Poppy pattern, c1902, 2in (30.5cm) diam.
£3,500–4,000 RUM

A Royal Doulton stoneware jardinière, decorated with stylized flowers on a blue ground, early 1900s, 7½in (19cm) high.
£220–250 TMA

A Burmantofts blue jardinière, c1900, 45in (114.5cm) high.
£700–800 PAC

A Crown Ducal planter, designed by Charlotte Rhead, decorated in shades of pink and cream, pattern No. 6778, shape No. 279, c1940, 10½in (27cm) diam.
£150–180 PC

◄ A Minton 'Secessionist' jardinière and stand, decorated in purple and green on a mottled blue ground, slight damage, printed and impressed marks and shape No. 3472/1, 1901–09, 35½in (90cm) high.
£400–450 DN

JARS

Two Dutch Delft tobacco jars and domed brass covers, minor damage, marked 'De Drie Astonnekes', 18thC, 12in (30.5cm) high.
£2,000–2,500 S(Am)

A Derbyshire salt-glazed handled jar, c1800, 6¼in (16cm) high.
£60–70 IW

A North Midlands black-glazed handled jar, c1800, 5½in (14cm) high.
£70–80 IW

◄ A Yorkshire handled jar, with flattened sides, early 19thC, 9½in (24cm) high.
£75–90 IW

► A Penrith Pottery brown and cream tobacco jar, the cover with bird finial, beak missing, c1880, 6in (15cm) high.
£55–70 ANV

A Carlton Ware blue faïence tobacco jar, chipped, crown mark, late 19thC, 4in (10cm) high.
£40–50 StC

An Italian maiolica 16thC-style oviform jar, probably made in the Pesaro workshop of Ferrucio Mengarone, the reverse with a coat-of-arms, initials 'W.W.V.S.' and date 'M.C.XLI' with 'W' below, enclosed by green bands, slight damage, late 19thC, 9½in (24cm) high.
£1,800–2,000 C

A Gouda pottery tobacco jar and cover, decorated with Westland design, c1920, 8in (20.5cm) high.
£300–350 OO

A Quimper jar, by Fougeray, marked 'HB', c1920, 9in (23cm) high.
£140–160 MofC

A Denby green, brown and blue tube-lined tobacco jar, with golf ball finial, c1925, 6in (15cm) high.
£350–400 KES

A Royal Doulton tobacco jar, 'Paddy', D5845, by Harry Fenton, 1939–42, 5½in (14cm) high.
£370–420 BBR

A blue Manchu ginger jar, by Charlotte Rhead, c1940, 7in (17.5cm) high.
£300–350 HEA

A William Moorcroft salt-glazed tobacco jar, decorated with Fish pattern, in shades of blue and green on a cream ground, c1935, 6in (15cm) high.
£300–350 NP

JUGS

A Staffordshire blue and white salt-glazed tavern pot, damaged, c1750, 5¼in (13.5cm) high.
£120–150 IW

A Staffordshire glazed and gilded hot water jug, c1795, 6¼in (16cm) high.
£500–550 JHo

A London delft blue and white tavern pot, impressed mark, c1760, 6½in (16.5cm) high.
£100–120 IW

A Liverpool delft puzzle jug, c1760, 8in (20.5cm) high.
£1,000–1,200 JHo

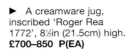

▶ A creamware jug, inscribed 'Roger Rea 1772', 8½in (21.5cm) high.
£700–850 P(EA)

Puzzle Jugs

Made from c1570 to the early 1800s in creamware, delft ware, brown saltglaze, etc, these jugs had a hollow handle leading to a tube round the rim connecting three or more spouts. One aperture had to be stopped up in order to drink from another. To make drinking more difficult, some jugs had openwork decoration round the rug below the spouts.

A Liverpool creamware baluster-shaped jug, with loop handle, inscribed in blue 'Lord Weymouth And Success to the Mines', c1780, 12in (30.5cm) high.
£850–1,000 DN

A tavern jug, in white salt-glaze with scratch blue decoration, late 18thC, 6¼in (16cm) high.
£75–90 SAS

A Ralph Wood-type creamware Bacchus mask jug, with loop handle, picked out in green and brown, on scroll-moulded round base, damaged and repaired, c1780, 4½in (11.5cm) high.
£180–200 HOLL

An earthenware bear jug and cover, probably Staffordshire, applied with shredded clay to simulate its coat, dipped in brown slip, with white clay eyes, paws and teeth, late 18thC, 10¼in (26cm) high.
£7,000–8,000 S

A pearlware baluster-shaped harvest jug, inscribed 'Thomas Massey Heaton Norris 1800' within a foliate cartouche, foliate swags below the rim, cracked, 10in (25cm) high.
£750–900 C

A pearlware jug, decorated in underglaze blue, c1790, 5¾in (14.5cm) high.
£180–200 IW

A Wedgwood jasper jug, with dark blue dip and applied green quatrefoils, damaged, impressed mark, late 18thC, 5½in (14cm) high.
£1,200–1,400 SK

A Wedgwood *rosso antico* jug, with applied basalt decoration, c1800, 5¾in (14.5cm) high.
£380–400 PGA

A transfer-printed jug, decorated with the Duke of York, c1800, 5in (12.5cm) high.
£800–850 JHo

► A pearlware barrel-shaped jug, inscribed 'Richd Cockerman Treburley, Lezant', above a flourish flanked by flowersprays and leaves in blue, green, yellow and ochre, cracked, c1805, 8½in (21.5cm) high.
£200–250 DN

Did you know?

- One of Wedgwood's earliest lines was cream-coloured earthenware, printed or painted, known as Queens ware due to Wedgwood achieving the royal patronage of Queen Charlotte in 1765.
- Wedgwood's famous blue jasper ware was made at his second factory at Etruria – a name derived from the Greek classical pottery excavated at Pompeii and Herculaneum that was at that time thought to be Etruscan.
- *Rosso antico*, or buff creamware with red relief decoration, was a short-lived innovation from the Wedgwood factory.

◄ A Wedgwood felspathic stoneware jug, moulded in relief with figures within blue bordered panels, with angled scroll handle, c1800, 5in (12.5cm) high.
£90–110 TMA

A Prattware jug, decorated with The Sailor's Farewell, c1800, 6in (15cm) high.
£250–300 RP

A pearlware jug, moulded and decorated with a portrait of the Duke of Wellington, early 19thC, 5¼in (13.5cm) high.
£150–165 SWN

A John & William Ridgway stoneware covered jug, decorated with flowers and foliage, printed Ironstone mark, c1814, 7½in (19cm) high.
£250–280 JP

A Bristol jug, painted with red and yellow flowers and green leaves, dated '1815', 6¾in (17cm) high.
£300–350 DAN

A Prattware baluster-shaped jug, decorated with equestrian figures, early 19thC, 5½in (14cm) high.
£200–250 AH

A creamware jug, by Dawson & Co, Low Ford Pottery, Sunderland, with transfer print entitled 'Peace and Plenty', c1810, 8in (20.5cm) high.
£300–350 IW

A white stoneware jug, moulded with a hunting scene, the ground blue-glazed to imitate jasper, c1815, 5½in (14cm) high.
£100–120 DAN

A north Devon slipware cider jug, the amber-glazed baluster body decorated with a stag between giant flowering stems, the back with a panel of verse above the words 'Made for Mrs Felix, Aberayon 1807', 10¼in (26cm) high.
£2,000–2,200 P(G)

A Wedgwood pearlware jug, with loop handle, inscribed in black 'Robt. and Sah. Gould' and dated '1812', the orange ground decorated in green, puce, black and yellow with scrolling flowers and leaves, impressed mark, 9in (23cm) high.
£450–550 DN

A pearlware jug, printed in black with 2 country seats interspersed with a pink rose and bud spray beneath a bright green neck band and handle, impressed numeral '3', c1810, 6¾in (17cm) high.
£450–550 Bon

A lustre ware jug, decorated with leaves and berries, c1815, 5¼in (13.5cm) high.
£130–150 PCh

Three relief-moulded buff-coloured jugs, with white twisted serpent handles and spouts, some restoration, with Brameld pad on base of smallest, early 19thC, largest 6½in (16.5cm) high.
£200–250 MEG

A Staffordshire pearlware mask jug, c1820, 8in (20.5cm) high.
£300–350 W

A Staffordshire 2 gallon tavern jug, the earthenware body printed and hand-coloured, c1825, 12in (30.5cm) high.
£200–220 WL

A Staffordshire Prattware jug, in the form of a cottage, c1820, 3½in (9cm) high.
£100–125 JO

A yellow-ground jug, with coloured enamel decoration, probably Staffordshire, c1820, 4½in (11.5cm) high.
£340–370 HOW

A Staffordshire pearlware harvest jug, decorated with lustre bands, with enamelled transfers of harvest and agricultural attributes, inscribed 'Uriah & Sarah Edge, 1824', 8in (20cm) high.
£500–600 WL

A lustre jug, decorated with 'The Great Australia Clipper-Ship', 'True Love from Hull' and verse, with orange lustre surround, 19thC 9in (23cm) high.
£380–420 RBB

Transfer Printing

Transfer-printing was developed in the 1750s, and enabled British manufacturers to speed up the decoration of their ceramics.
At first, only one colour could be used at a time. Multicolour printing was experimented with in the late 1750s, but was not commercially developed until the 1840s.

◄ A lustre pearlware harvest jug, transfer-printed in black with a view of the Iron Bridge, the reverse with agricultural emblems in a shield with motto, printed marks in black 'J. Philips, Hylton Pottery' and 'Dixon, Austin & Co, Sunderland, c1825, 9in (23cm) high.
£650–750 DN

A pearlware jug, painted in purple lustre with a rural scene, c1820, 6¼in (16cm) high.
£110–125 OCH

A Sunderland pink lustre jug, with loop handle, colour-printed with 'West View of the Castle on Bridge over the River Wear...open'd 9 Aug 1796' and 'Sailor's Farewell', with floral printed upper border, 19thC, 7½in (19cm) high.
£380–420 P(C)

A pink lustre jug, monochrome printed with 'Iron Bridge at Sunderland' and verses with coloured surrounds, 19thC, 8½in (21.5cm) high.
£250–300 RBB

A copper lustre jug, the body hand-painted with trailing yellow berries and blue and white flowerheads, mid-19thC, 5½in (14cm) high.
£150–180 DA

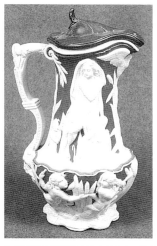

A Charles Meigh jug, with pewter lid, decoratd with blue and white relief moulding in Amphitrite pattern, c1856, 10½in (27cm) high.
£80–100 P(B)

A Campbellfield Pottery jug, decorated in blue, 1870–80, 6½in (16.5cm) high.
£35–40 CSA

A Linthorpe 'camel' jug, shape No. 347, with C. Dresser and H. Tooth marks, c1880, 7in (18cm) high.
£600–700 NCA

A jug, relief-moulded with tree-trunk handle, decorated with a gypsy scene and pink interior, slight damage to rim, late 19thC, 7½in (19cm) high.
£65–80 MEG

A Staffordshire cottage jug, c1860, 5½in (14cm) high.
£50–60 OD

A pottery frog jug, decorated in brown and green, impressed 'Steel', c1875, 8in (20.5cm) high.
£200–250 BRT

A Sunderland lustre jug, printed and painted, inscribed with verse 'The Sailor's Farewell', 19thC, 7½in (19cm) high.
£280–320 GAK

A cream-coloured jug, with brown relief-moulded prunus decoration, damaged and repaired, 19thC, 6½in (16.5cm) high.
£30–40 MEG

An Albion white jug, with hinged pewter cover, moulded with coats-of-arms and Prince of Wales feathers, 1863, 7½in (19cm) high.
£65–75 SAS

A set of 3 Holdcroft majolica bear-shaped jugs, each carrying a drum on its back, glazed in brown, turquoise and yellow, some chips, c1875, 7½ to 9½in (19 to 24cm) high.
£1,800–2,000 S

A black-dip stoneware jug, probably by Samuel Alcock, moulded with a scene, probably the Siege of Acre in 1799, and Sir Sydney Smith, firing cracks, 19thC, 13½in (34.5cm) high.
£550–650 CSK

A Quimper jug, c1875, 5¼in (13.5cm) high.
£100–115 VH

A Mocha ware jug, with inlaid coloured clay borders, banding and trees, early 19thC, 13½in (34.5cm) high.
£320–350 GAZE

A copper lustre and enamel-decorated jug, c1830, 5½in (14cm) high.
£55–70 IW

A Staffordshire Prattware mask jug, decorated in yellow, red and green, c1830, 4½in (11.5cm) high.
£165–185 SER

A buff jug, with pewter cover, decorated with Tam-o'-Shanter and Souter Johnnie, c1830, 9½in (24cm) high.
£180–220 P(B)

Tam-o'-Shanter was the hero of a poem by Robert Burns (1759–96), and also gave his name to the Scottish cap. In the same poem Burns also popularized another figure who was to be turned into a jug, Sir John Barleycorn, a personification of malt liquor.

A blue spongeware jug and basin set, c1830, basin 13¼in (33.5cm) diam.
£240–265 SWN

A red printed earthenware jug, decorated with dogs, c1830, 4¼in (11cm) high.
£120–140 IW

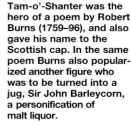

A Minton grey jug, decorated with Silenus pattern, c1831, 7½in (19cm) high.
£90–100 P(B)

A Ridgway buff-coloured jug, with pewter cover, c1835, 9in (23cm) high.
£150–175 ALB

A Staffordshire jug, decorated in brown, yellow and green with a hunting scene, c1830, 6¼in (16cm) high.
£150–200 ALB

Lustre ware

A glazed surface is painted with metallic oxides, mixed with fine ochre and refired at a low temperature, to produce an iridescent metallic surface. Large quantities were produced at Sunderland, Staffordshire, Swansea and Leeds during the 19thC.

A Charles Meigh & Sons buff-coloured jug, decorated with Julius Caesar pattern, c1839, 8in (20.5cm) high.
£120–140 P(B)

A brown salt-glazed puzzle jug, possibly Scottish, with eagle handle, restored, c1840, 8¼in (21.5cm) high.
£120–140 BBR

A Sunderland lustre pink jug, depicting the Iron Bridge, restoration to spout, c1840, 9½in (24cm) high.
£200–250 SER

A Staffordshire copper
lustre clock face jug,
c1840, 9½in (24cm) high.
£150–180 RP

A Bell pottery jug, relief-
moulded with blue, pink and
cream lustre finish, c1840,
8¼in (21cm) high.
£65–80 MEG

A Bovey Tracey creamware jug,
covered in green sparkle slip, painted
with foliage in cream and brown,
inscribed below spout 'J. & S. Gale,
1818', 6½in (16.5cm) high.
£700–800 Bea(E)

**Shards of similar items have been
excavated at the site of the Bovey
Pottery, and are illustrated in
A Potwork in Devonshire by Brian
Adams and Anthony Thomas.**

A green transfer-printed jug,
mid-19thC, 2in (5cm) high.
£30–40 OD

A Derbyshire salt-glazed jug,
c1840, 5¾in (14.5cm) high.
£100–120 IW

A blue and white jug, decorated in
relief with a hunting scene, 1840–50,
7¼in (18.5cm) high.
£120–140 P(B)

A Charles Meigh Minster jug, relief-
moulded with panels depicting religious
figures, c1842, 7½in (19cm) high.
£180–200 MEG

**Charles Meigh produced some of
the finest relief-moulded jugs of the
mid-19thC. A great Gothic designer,
he created many pieces based on
religious and mythological themes.**

A Victorian wine jug, decorated with
flowers, with plated mounts, handle
and cover, 8½in (22cm) high.
£120–150 Gam

An Edward Walley buff jug,
decorated with the Cup Tosser
design, c1841, 9in (23cm) high.
£120–140 P(B)

A Jones & Walley buff-coloured jug,
decorated with Good Samaritan
pattern, c1841, 8¾in (22cm) high.
£90–110 P(B)

A Staffordshire York Minster jug,
with relief-moulded religious
scenes, exhibition mark, 1846,
10in (25.5cm) high.
£125–150 ALB

A Sunderland lustre jug, with inscription
and sailing boat on reverse, spout
restored, c1850, 4¼in (11cm) high.
£130–160 SER

A Minton majolica jug, moulded with reserves of 17thC soldiers drinking, on a deep maroon ground, the neck painted blue, the border and handle ochre, slight damage, c1870, 14¼in (36cm) high.
£1,550–1,700 Bri

A Doulton Lambeth stoneware jug, by Hannah Barlow, with blue trim and incised decoration, c1873, 6¼in (16cm) high.
£500–600 SnA

A Dudson buff stoneware jug, relief-moulded with a beehive set among sprays of flowers, c1870, 10½in (27cm) high.
£125–150 DAN

A Doulton Lambeth brown salt-glazed stoneware jug, in the form of a landlord sitting on a barrel, impressed mark, 1877–80, 10¼in (26cm) high.
£150–180 P(B)

Two Mocha ware jugs, probably by T. & G. Green, c1870, largest 8in (20.5cm) high.
£150–180 SMI

The mossy decoration on Mocha ware was made by dabbing the wet pot with a liquid pigment known as tea, said to contain tobacco juice, urine and manganese, which then fanned out into frond-like patterns when fired. Mocha ware was cheap and utilitarian – in the 19thC such pieces cost under a shilling.

A Minton majolica tower jug, shape No. 1231, moulded in relief with figures dancing, cover missing, impressed marks for 1876, 9½in (24cm) high.
£250–300 DN

A Wedgwood majolica jug, moulded with a design of birds on a blossoming branch between fans, raised registration diamond mark for 1879 and other impressed marks, 6½in (16.5cm) high.
£100–120 Bon

▶ A pair of majolica fish-shaped jugs, with loop handles, each brightly decorated in grey, puce, green and orange, slight damage, late 19thC, 9½in (24cm) high.
£65–80 HOLL

A Royal Doulton stoneware jug, by George Tinworth, with plain silver rim, 1879, 9¼in (23.5cm) high.
£650–750 Bea(E)

A Martin Brothers ewer, decorated with aquatic creatures in shades of buff and green, the base incised 'Martin Bros, London', late 19thC, 5¼in (13.5cm) high.
£850–950 HYD

▶ A majolica jug, in the form of a cob of corn, with leaf scroll handle, late 19thC, 9½in (24cm) high.
£120–150 HOLL

A majolica jug, in the form of a parakeet, late 19thC, 7½in (19cm) high.
£130–150 SSW

A Brannam pottery jug, with
fish-shaped spout, decorated
in blue on a grey ground,
late 19thC, 5½in (14cm) high.
£65–80 MEG

A Staffordshire earthenware
moulded jug, with Celtic-style
design, c1875, 13½in (34.5cm) high.
£85–95 TVM

A Savoie jug, with yellow rim,
c1880, 5in (12.5cm) high.
£40–45 MLL

A majolica jug, modelled as an
owl, c1880, 9in (23cm) high.
£200–220 SSW

A tavern salt-glazed water jug,
with pewter cover, moulded in
relief, c1880, 5in (12.5cm) high.
£35–40 CPA

A Doulton ewer, by Emily Stormer,
decorated with stylized rosettes
and foliage, impressed marks,
dated '1881', 12in (30.5cm) high.
£250–280 GAK

An Alsace jug, decorated
with blue splashes, c1880,
18in (45.5cm) high.
£140–160 MLL

A brown-glazed jug, patent No. 452078,
late 19thC, 5in (12.5cm) high.
£50–65 ANV

A Sarreguemines majolica
jug, marked 'No. 797',
c1890, 9½in (24cm) high.
£200–250 MofC

◄ An Elton Ware
jug, decorated with
applied dot design,
marked, c1890,
13¼in (34cm) high.
£280–300 PGA

► A Minton Celladine
ware jug, with white
decoration on a green
ground, c1890,
6½in (16.5cm) high.
£145–165 PAC

A Doulton Lambeth brown
salt-glazed stoneware jug,
c1890, 5½in (14cm) high.
£45–50 RAC

A Doulton Lambeth stoneware jug, c1890, 4½in (11.5cm) high.
£25–30 CSA

A Sarreguemines penguin jug, No. 3567, c1900, 7in (18cm) high.
£180–200 PC

A Zuid-Holland earthenware jug, painted by J. Th. Stam, in shades of blue, green, yellow and purple on a cream ground, c1899, 5¾in (14.5cm) high.
£330–360 S(Am)

A Brannam jug and basin set, by A. Bamflin, c1895, 7in (18cm) high.
£200–250 NCA

A Doulton Lambeth owl jug, the silver rim with coat-of-arms and engraved initials, c1894, 9½in (24cm) high.
£1,200–1,450 POW

A Doulton Lambeth chiné gilt jug, decorated with blue and white flowers, c1895, 9½in (17cm) high.
£60–70 SnA

Chiné was patented by John Slater. Dampened lace was pressed into the wet clay, the lace was destroyed in the firing and left a pattern behind which was then coloured and gilded.

A majolica jug, decorated with grape pickers, c1900, 9in (23cm) high.
£250–280 MofC

A set of 3 Crown Devon Fieldings jugs, decorated with sprays of flowers, tinted orange with gilt rims, c1900, largest 6½in (16.5cm) high.
£120–140 AAC

A Nimy les Mous majolica jug, c1900, 8½in (21.5cm) high.
£250–280 MofC

A French pottery wine jug, c1900, 7in (18cm) high.
£40–50 MLL

▶ A Martin Brothers double-faced stoneware jug, incised 'R. W. Martin & Bros, London & Southall'. c1900, 6½in (16.5cm) high.
£1,400–1,600 S

A Villeroy & Boch coffee jug, c1900, 9in (23cm) high.
£150–180 SUC

A Cornish earthenware jug, by Lakes Pottery, Truro, c1900, 7½in (19cm) high.
£25–30 IW

Lakes Pottery, in Truro, Cornwall, produced utilitarian wares that were highly regarded by the Studio potters at St Ives.

A Tams patent measure one pint jug, blue with cream handle and spout, c1902, 4½in (11.5cm) high.
£30–40 IW

A Moorcroft MacIntyre jug, decorated with Poppy pattern, c1904, 6½in (16cm) high.
£450–500 HEA

A pottery jug, inscribed in brown on white with 'The Niger, The Last of the Full-Rigged Ships', c1904, 6¾in (17cm) high.
£270–300 A&A

A brown slip-decorated pottery pub jug, probably Halifax, inscribed 'Parr Sept 1906', 3¼in (8.5cm) high.
£65–80 IW

A Losol jug, decorated with Exotic pattern c1910, 6¾in (17cm) high.
£35–40 CSA

A Doulton Burslem blue and white jug, c1910, 9in (23cm) high.
£100–120 CSA

◄ An Elton Ware gilt crackle-ground jug, c1910, 5in (12.5cm) high.
£180–220 NCA

Sir Edmund Elton (1846–1920) devoted his later life to making handmade art pottery. His under-gardener, George Masters, became his chief assistant, and they set up a workshop at Elton's estate at Clevedon, Somerset.

An Onnaing majolica jug, marked '740 Frie', c1920, 7½in (19cm) high.
£120–145 MofC

An Onnaing majolica jug, marked '824 Frie', c1920, 7½in (19cm) high.
£180–200 MofC

An Empire Pottery Tudor design milk jug, 1920s, 7½in (19cm) high.
£30–40 LA

A Burlington Ware Devon cob milk jug, 1920s, 5in (12.5cm) high.
£15–20 PC

A Bernard Leach stoneware jug, in green ash glaze with vertical combed design, with impressed 'BL' and 'St Ives' seals, early 20thC, 7½in (19cm) high.
£500–600 Bon

An Aller Vale jug, decorated with a cockerel, c1925, 5½in (14cm) high.
£30–40 CSA

A Torquay jug, decorated in blue and brown on a cream ground, inscribed 'Say little but think much', 1920–30s, 4in (10cm) high.
£25–30 BEV

A Royal Winton Tudor house milk jug, 1920s, 6in (15cm) wide.
£25–30 LA

Aller Vale

Founded c1887 in Devon, Aller Vale Pottery used local clays to produce terracotta and slip-decorated ware. The company merged with Watcombe Terracotta Co c1900, and by 1904 the merged companies, based in Newton Abbot, were advertising a wide range of decorated grotesque and mottoed ware and artware, all richly-coloured and glazed. Aller Vale also produced wares such as plaques for resting curling tongs. The company continued to make slipware for the tourist market until its closure in 1962.

A Barton milk jug, decorated with a flower in pink, white and green within black lines on a blue ground, 1922–37, 2½in (6.5cm) high.
£15–20 PC

A Myott jug, painted in yellow, orange, brown and green, 1920–30, 9in (23cm) high.
£65–75 BEV

A Myott water jug, painted in red and green, 1920–30, 8¼in (21cm) high.
£30–40 BEV

A Shorter jug, decorated with Iris design, c1935, 11in (28cm) high.
£60–70 CSA

A Doulton Series ware jug, c1935, 5in (12.5cm) high.
£30–40 CSA

A Susie Cooper hand-painted jug, c1928, 7in (18cm) high.
£200–225 WTA

A Bretby jug, decorated in shades of brown, red and green, with incised floral decoration and brown handle, 1920–30, 8in (20.5cm) high.
£85–95 DSG

A Susie Cooper jug, by Gray's Pottery, decorated with orange, yellow and black bands, c1928, 5½in (14cm) high.
£30–40 CSA

A Nelson Ware jug, decorated with Heather pattern, 1930s, 2¼in (5.5cm) high.
£35–40 BEV

A Gray's Pottery Brocade water jug, hand-painted in bright colours, c1930, 4½in (11.5cm) high.
£35–40 RAC

A Royal Winton Chintz ware jug, decorated with Hazel pattern, 1930s, 2½in (6.5cm) high.
£60–70 BEV

A Carter, Stabler & Adams jug, painted in coloured enamels by Ann Hatchard, with a band of stylized tulips and leaves beneath a wave and roundel band, slight damage, impressed and painted marks, c1930, 14½in (37cm) high.
£300–350 DN

A Myott jug, painted in brown, orange and green on a cream ground, c1930, 8in (20.5cm) high.
£30–40 CSA

A Hancock's Ivory ware jug, c1930, 10½in (27cm) high.
£25–30 CSA

A Wadeheath musical jug, moulded with Three Little Pigs and Big Bad Wolf handle, 1930s, 10in (25.5cm) high.
£700–800 SWO

A Myott hand-painted jug, c1930, 7in (18cm) high.
£55–65 WAC

A Burleigh Ware yellow jug, with moulded Grape pattern, c1930, 7in (18cm) high.
£250–300 BEV

A Longpark cream jug, decorated with Crocus pattern in shades of red, yellow, green, mauve and blue, 1930–40, 2½in (6.5cm) high.
£15–20 PC

Potters often 'borrowed' fashionable designs from other factories and this pattern is clearly based on Clarice Cliff's famous crocus pattern.

A set of 3 Adams jugs, with Cries of London scenes, different on each side, c1920s, tallest 6¾in (17cm) high.
£250–300 WN

A Quimper jug, marked 'Henriot Quimper', c1920, 8in (20.5cm) high.
£125–150 MofC

A Gray's Pottery jug, with lustre finish, designed by Susie Cooper, 1920–30s, 4½in (11.5cm) high.
£85–95 YY

A Burleigh lustre jug, c1938, 7¼in (18.5cm) high.
£60–70 CSA

A pair of Myott jugs, painted in yellow, green and black with pink flowers, c1932, 9in (23cm) high.
£220–250 BKK

A Falcon ware jug, 1930s, 6in (15cm) high.
£35–40 COL

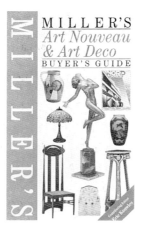

▶ A Honiton jug, decorated with stylized flowers within panels, 1930s, 2¾in (7cm) high.
£30–40 YY

◀ A Myott jug, painted in green and brown, 1931–36, 8in (20.5cm) high.
£120–150 BEV

▶ A Wade musical jug, decorated with and inscribed 'Snow White & The Seven Dwarfs', damaged, c1938, 7½in (19cm) high.
£400–450 WTA

A Burleigh Ware jug, decorated with Garden pattern, 1930s, 7½in (19cm) high.
£200–250 BUR

A Burleigh Ware jug, with moulded Honeycomb pattern, 1930s, 8½in (21.5cm) high.
£300–350 BUR

A Burleigh Ware jug, decorated with Flamingo pattern, c1930, 9in (23cm) high.
£225–250 BEV

A Burleigh Ware green and yellow jug, the handle in the form of a gnome, 1930s, 7in (18cm) high.
£350–400 BEV

A Burleigh Ware jug, decorated with a tube-lined design, by Harold Bennett, 1930s, 9½in (24cm) high.
£180–200 BDA

A Myott jug, hand-painted with orange and brown decoration, inscribed 'ITR', c1930, 6¾in (17cm) high.
£30–40 WAC

A Crown Ducal ewer, designed by Charlotte Rhead, decorated with stylized flowers in orange, black and yellow with gilt detail on a beige speckled ground, printed marks, signed and impressed '145', 1930s, 10in (25.5cm) high.
£230–260 GAK

Burleigh Ware

The firm of Burgess & Leigh was founded in 1851 in Staffordshire, specializing in underglaze-decorated earthenware. Burleigh Ware is the name they gave to their pottery.

In 1927 the company employed Charlotte Rhead, daughter of Frederick Rhead and an accomplished artist, who went on to produce a number of original designs with beautiful underglaze colourings. In the 1930s, the company introduced original and unusual designs, in particular jugs with handles in the form of animals or people. These jugs are popular with collectors today, many of whom concentrate on collecting different versions of one animal or person.

A Doulton jug, decorated with roses, c1930, 3½in (9cm) high.
£15–20 CSA

A Carter, Stabler & Adams jug, designed by Truda Carter, decorated with a geometric pattern in blue, black, beige and lime green, painted by Eileen Prangnell, 1930s, 8in (20.5cm) high.
£300–350 HarC

A Royal Winton jug, depicting a pixie in a red suit, on a brown and green ground, c1930, 3½in (9cm) high.
£20–30 CSA

A Burleigh Ware flower jug, the handle in the form of a Highwayman, c1933, 8in (20.5cm) high.
£250–275 WTA

A Keele Street Pottery Co miniature cream jug and sugar bowl, 1930s, 3in (7.5cm) wide.
£15–20 LA

A Burleigh Ware jug, decorated with The Highwayman, c1933, 7¼in (18.5cm) high.
£200–225 WTA

A Crown Ducal jug, pattern No. 4298, by Charlotte Rhead, c1935, 6½in (16.5cm) high.
£65–80 HEA

A Samford ware jug, decorated in green, yellow and black with Fantasy pattern, 1936–39, 9in (23cm) high.
£30–40 CSA

A Crown Ducal ribbed ewer, designed by Charlotte Rhead, with loop handle, tube-lined with a band of fruits and leaves picked out in green, brown and yellow, on a brown ground, printed mark in green, painted signature and 'No. 5802', c1935, 8in (20.5cm) high.
£170–200 HOLL

A Carlton Ware black and gilt jug, c1935, 7in (18cm) high.
£170–200 CSA

A Royal Winton lustre jug, decorated with flowers on an orange ground, c1935, 12in (30.5cm) high.
£175–200 WTA

◄ A Susie Cooper jug, decorated with Dresden Spray pattern, c1935, 4¾in (12cm) wide.
£30–35 WAC

A James Kent jug, decorated with flowers and leaves on a green ground, c1935, 8in (20.5cm) high.
£30–40 CSA

A Vulcan ware jug, decorated in pink, green, blue and yellow with a flower and fern pattern, c1935, 9in (23cm) high.
£40–50 CSA

A Shelley Melody jug, decorated with flowers on a green ground, c1935, 6½in (16.5cm) high.
£50–60 CSA

A Burleigh Ware jug, the handle formed as a female tennis player, c1935, 7¼in (18.5cm) high.
£500–550 WTA

A Susie Cooper hot water jug, decorated in sgraffito with crescent motifs, c1936, 6in (15cm) high.
£50–55 WAC

A Susie Cooper sgraffito jug, c1938, 9½in (23.5cm) high.
£70–80 CSA

A Bursley Ware pitcher, designed by Charlotte Rhead, decorated in shades of orange, green and blue, pattern No. TL5, 1940s, 9in (23cm) high.
£230–250 BDA

A Moorcroft jug, decorated with a green Art Deco peacock feather pattern, impressed factory mark with facsimile signature and painted signature to base, c1938, 9in (23cm) high.
£300–350 RTo

A Bursley Ware jug, designed by Charlotte Rhead, pattern No. TL14, c1940, 11in (28cm) high.
£160–200 HEA

A Crown Ducal jug, designed by Charlotte Rhead, pattern No. 6822, c1940, 9in (23cm) high.
£100–120 HEA

A Crown Devon jug, enamelled with a butterfly, c1940, 4in (10cm) high.
£25–30 CSA

A Denby jug, designed by Glyn Colledge, c1950, 5in (12.5cm) high.
£70–80 PC

► A Watts pottery jug, decorated in red and green with an apple motif, 1940s, 5½in (14cm) high.
£50–60 MSB

MUGS & TANKARDS

A Staffordshire unglazed redware mug, with pseudo Chinese mark on base, c1750, 3½in (9cm) high.
£500–600 JRe

A Staffordshire brown and cream mug, restored, chips to rim, c1765, 3in (7.5cm) high.
£400–450 JHo

A Bristol salt-glazed stoneware loving cup, 1766, 5¾in (14.5cm) high.
£3,000–3,300 JHo

A creamware mug, painted in underglaze blue with a Chinese figure holding a parasol, with an ear-shaped strap handle, crack to base, c1770, 6¼in (16cm) high.
£550–600 WW

A Yorkshire creamware tankard, c1775, 6½in (16.5cm) high.
£3,300–3,800 JHo

A Staffordshire creamware tankard, probably Wedgwood, 1780, 6in (15cm) high.
£350–400 JHo

A brown and buff hunting mug, probably Mortlake, late 18thC, 8in (20.5cm) high.
£675–750 OCH

A Liverpool mug, with black and white transfer print entitled 'The Gipsy Fortune Teller', c1790, 4½in (11.5cm) high.
£400–450 JHo

A creamware tankard, entitled 'The happy return, Peter & Ann Scott 1797', some restoration, possibly Yorkshire, c1797, 6¼in (16cm) high.
£700–780 JHo

> **Cross Reference**
> See Colour Review

◀ A Derbyshire salt-glazed loving cup, c1800, 5¼in (13.5cm) high.
£160–200 IW

A silver lustre mug, with lily of the valley decoration, c1815, 3¼in (8.5cm) high.
£80–90 SER

A pearlware two-handled mug, the brown and blue banded ground decorated in white slip with garlands, inscribed in black 'W. Rogers, Boiler Maker, Moorfields, Bristol', damaged, c1820, 7½in (19cm) high.
£900–1,000 DN

A pearlware frog mug, with leaf-moulded scroll handle, fluted and basketwork bands, inscribed 'Winchester Measure, Warranted', and picked out in black, green, yellow and iron-red, c1825–30, 4¼in (10.5cm) high.
£270–300 DN

A Scottish pearlware frog mug, with 2 leaf scroll handles, the exterior modelled with monkeys in Turkish costume, picked out in puce, blue, green and brown, inscribed 'Thomas Parkes', the interior modelled with 2 frogs and 2 lizards, picked out in brown, c1840, 6¼in (16cm) high.
£650–750 DN

A Staffordshire mug, decorated with black transfer print depicting Battle Church, c1850, 3in (7.5cm) high.
£10–15 VSt

A pearlware mug, the brown ground decorated in green and ochre with bands, inscribed 'A Trifle for Ann', c1820, 2¾in (7cm) high.
£220–240 HOLL

A mug, entitled 'John Gilpin', c1828, 2⅝in (6.5cm) high.
£85–95 OCH

A two-handled loving cup, by John & Robert Godwin, Cobridge Pottery, printed in brown and coloured with a steeplechase pattern, cracked, c1850, 8in (20.5cm) diam.
£370–400 Hal

A frog mug, painted with roses in relief, small chip, c1850, 4in (10cm) high.
£150–180 GLN

A Mocha ware mug, the green ground decorated with a blue stripe and applied excise stamp 'Quart', 1820, 6in (15cm) high.
£120–140 RYA

A pearlware mug, painted in colours and with copper lustre, c1830, 5¼in (13.5cm) high.
£85–95 OCH

A Bovey Tracey Mocha ware pint tankard, c1850, 4¾in (12cm) high.
£80–100 IW

A Victorian transfer-printed mug, depicting street urchins, inscribed 'How's Business' and 'Slack', 4in (10cm) high.
£50–65 ANV

A two-handled cider mug, with colour transfer-printed decoration, c1850, 5in (12.5cm) high.
£140–160 GLN

A quart mug, decorated with black and blue bands, c1860, 6in (15cm) high.
£60–90 IW

A Staffordshire three-handled tyg, inscribed with 'The Farmers Arms' and verse 'God Speed the Plough', c1860, 5in (12.5cm) high.
£100–120 SER

An Irish mug, decorated with cockerel design, 19thC, 3¼in (8.5cm) high.
£60–70 Byl

An Irish spongeware mug, decorated with brown, red and green flowers, 19thC, 4¼in (11cm) high.
£90–110 Byl

An Irish mug, decorated with brown transfer print, inscribed 'Cattle D L & S' on the base, 19thC, 4¼in (11cm) high.
£90–110 Byl

An Irish mug, decorated with brown transfer print of a rural scene, 19thC, 4¼in (11cm) high.
£90–110 Byl

A copper lustre mug, decorated with central blue stripe, c1860, 2¾in (7cm) high.
£25–30 OCH

A Victorian Staffordshire mug, decorated with black transfer print depicting the Residence of Shakespeare, 3¼in (8.5cm) high.
£20–25 VSt

A yellow and brown earthenware mug, inscribed 'Sup all, eat all and pay nowt', Halifax, 19thC, 5in (12.5cm) high.
£50–55 MTa

An earthenware cider mug, with colour transfer decoration, c1860, 5in (12.5cm) high.
£180–200 GLN

◄ A pair of Doulton pottery beakers, made to simulate leather, with silver rims, c1900, 4¼in (11cm) high.
£100–120 SPU

A Mocha ware mug, with moulded mark, possibly T. & G. Green, c1870, 6in (15cm) high.
£85–100 IW

The firm of T. & G. Green was founded in 1864, and is still active today. Based at Church Gresley, Derbyshire, one of their their marks shows a church above the word 'Gresley'.

A Linthorpe tankard, shape No. 505, with Christopher Dresser and Henry Tooth signatures, the EPNS rim by Hukin & Heath, c1880, 9½in (24cm) high.
£450–550 NCA

A Maling Mocha ware pint mug, late 19thC, 5in (12.5cm) high.
£70–80 IW

A Mocha ware pint mug, possibly Edge, Malkin & Co, c1880, 5¼in (13.5cm) high.
£80–90 IW

An F. Pratt of Fenton coffee can, colour-printed with a rural scene, c1885, 2¾in (7cm) high.
£90–110 PSA

An Elton Ware tyg, the green slip glaze with burgundy decoration of flowers and birds in flight, c1900, 8¼in (21cm) high.
£270–300 WAC

A sgraffito slipware mug, possibly Fremington or Donyatt, c1903, 4in (10cm) high.
£80–120 IW

A Dorset tooth mug, decorated with a landscape scene, c1915, 3½in (9cm) high.
£20–30 TPCS

A Martin Brothers stoneware mug, by Ernest Marsh, incised with spiny fish and an octopus, in shades of brown on a pale blue ground, incised 'Marsh 2–1908 Martin Bros London & Southall EBM', 4½in (11.5cm) high.
£400–500 CSK

A Heath mug, decorated with flowers and leavs, anchor mark, 19thC, 4in (10cm) high.
£75–85 Ber

◄ A Grimwades mug, transfer-printed in brown, inscribed 'Gott Straff, This barbed wire', c1917, 3in (7.5cm) high.
£130–145 LeB

▶ An Adams pottery mug, decorated with a cockerel on a white ground, c1920, 5in (12.5cm) high.
£35–45 Ber

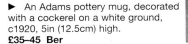

A pottery mug, modelled as Old Bill, decorated in brown on a buff ground, c1918, 4½in (11.5cm) high.
£80–100 SAS

Old Bill

Old Bill, a walrus-moustached, disillusioned Cockney soldier from WW1, was created by artist and journalist Captain Bruce Bairnsfather (1888–1959). Bairnsfather served in France during the 1914–18 war and became famous for his cartoons. Old Bill's sidekick was his pal Bert, gormless and grousing and with a cigarette dangling from his lip. The most famous depiction of the pair shows them stuck in a shell hole, with the caption 'Well if you knows of a better 'ole, go to it'.

A Carlton Ware blue and white transfer-printed mug and cover, black crown mark, early 20thC, 4½in (11.5cm) high.
£100–120 StC

A Susie Cooper mug, decorated with a golfer in black checked trousers, yellow top and black cap, c1920, 4in (10cm) high.
£200–250 PGA

A child's transfer-printed mug, 1920s, 2¾in (7cm) high.
£5–10 OD

A Burgess & Leigh Florentine pattern tankard, c1931, 9½in (24cm) high
£100–130 HEA

A Maling ware chocolate cup, decorated with embossed Peony pattern, c1935, 4½in (11.5cm) high.
£40–50 CSA

A Royal Doulton Pip, Squeak and Wilfred mug, 1930s, 9in (23cm) diam.
£85–95 SnA

Pip, Squeak and Wilfred was a children's cartoon strip appearing in the *Daily Mirror* 1919–46. The characters were a penguin, a dog and a rabbit, and the series also featured Popski, a bearded anarchist. The *Daily Mirror* started a children's fan club, members of which were known as 'The Gugnuncs'. Pip, Squeak and Wilfred also became army slang for three medals of WWI: the 1914–15 Star, the British War medal and the Victory medal.

A Carlton Ware musical tankard, entitled 'Last Drop', c1935, 5¼in (13.5cm) high.
£250–300 CSA

A Crown Ducal tankard, pattern No. 6189, by Charlotte Rhead, c1939, 8in (20.5cm) high.
£140–180 HEA

▶ A Denby mug, designed by Glyn Colledge, slight damage, signed, 1950s, 5¼in (13.5cm) high
£20–25 MAC

◀ Four Denby tankards, designed by Glyn Colledge, c1950, 5in (12.5cm) high.
£40–45 each PC

PLAQUES

A pearlware portrait medallion of Josiah Wedgwood, moulded in relief and decorated in Pratt colours, possibly Yorkshire, damaged, c1796, 5¼in (13.5cm) diam.
£450–500 C

A Prattware plaque, moulded with 'The Sailor's Return' within a rope-twist frame, c1800, 6in (15cm) wide.
£550–600 Bon

A creamware plaque of Paris and Oenone, painted in underglaze blue, c1800, 9in (23cm) high.
£280–320 OD

A Pratt-type plaque, relief moulded with Prometheus and the Eagle, cracked, c1810, 10in (25.5cm) diam.
£180–220 RWB

A North Shields Pottery lustre wall plaque, green with pink rim, impressed 'C. C. & Co', c1830, 6½in (16.5cm) high.
£150–175 IS

A Sunderland lustre plaque, inscribed 'Prepare to meet thy God', c1840, 9¼in (23.5cm) wide.
£120–140 OCH

◄ A Tyneside/Wearside pink lustre wall plaque, decorated with unamed sailing ship, c1850, 8in (20.5cm) wide.
£120–140 IS

Ship plaques are more sought-after if the ship is named.

► A lustre wall plaque, with pink surround, attributed to Dixon & Co, Sunderland Pottery, c1839, 6½in (16.5cm) diam.
£160–180 IS

◄ A ceramic plaque, by Webb & Co, depicting a classical head in profile, c1910, 14¼in (36cm) diam.
£200–240 DAF

A Doulton faïence wall plaque, decorated in coloured enamels, within a brown line rim, impressed marks for 1878 and monogram 'SK', 13¼in (34cm) diam.
£375–425 DN

A majolica plaque, moulded in relief with putti playing musical instruments beneath a tree, on a blue ground, framed, 19thC, 18¾in (47.5cm) wide.
£380–420 HOLL

A Prattware plaque, painted in brown, green and yellow, early 19thC, 11in (28cm) wide.
£500–600 AH

A Tyneside/Wearside orange lustre wall plaque, c1850, 8in (20.5cm) square.
£110–130 IS

Orange lustre is generally not as popular as pink lustre.

A Sunderland lustre plaque with pink and gold border, decorated with 'Sailor's Farewell', c1880, 9¼in (23.5cm) wide.
£120–150 SER

A plaque, moulded in relief with an equestrian portrait of the Duke of Wellington, painted in underglaze pale blue, yellow, brown and green, the reverse impressed 'Elliott', 19thC, 7½in (19cm) wide.
£150–180 SAS

A Midwinter deer's head wall plaque, c1950, 6¼in (16cm) high.
£18–21 AND

◄ A Brannam wall plaque, decorated with fish and seaweed on a pale blue ground, incised marks for 1903 and decorator's monogram for Thomas Liverton, 13¼in (33.5cm) diam.
£400–450 DN

A Continental plaque, painted with the Virgin and Child, signed 'G. Burtini' late 19thC, 8in (20.5cm) high.
£450–500 DN

A pair of Dutch Delft wall plaques, with polychrome decoration, the central panels depicting harbour scenes, in a marbled blue and white fluted border, one riveted, 19thC, 14½in (37cm) high.
£360–400 EH

A set of 3 Wedgwood green jasper plaques, the square panels applied with pairs of putti by a tree, and another with a central panel framing an oval medallion within bay leaves and ribbons, impressed 'WEDGWOOD' marks, 19thC, 7½in (19cm) square.
£450–500 Bon

PLATES

Two London delft farmhouse deep plates, polychrome painted in blue, brown and green, damaged, c1750, 9½in (24cm) diam.
£7,000–8,500 C

Six Holics plates, painted with horses, the borders with puce rococo-scroll cartouches and sprigs of flowers within yellow line rims, chipped and restored, 'H' marks, c1750, 9¼in (23.5cm) diam.
£7,000–8,000 C

Holics is also known as Holitsch.

A Staffordshire agate ware plate, c1755, 6in (15cm) diam.
£2,200–2,500 JHo

An Italian faïence oval-shaped dish, probably Faenza, Ferniani factory, painted in *famille rose* enamels, minor damage, c1760, 15in (38cm) wide.
£1,200–1,500 S

A Liverpool delft plate, decorated in blue, green, orange and yellow with 2 swans, an insect, bamboo and rockwork, within an orange line rim, restored, c1760, 8½in (21.5cm) diam.
£350–400 DN

A Liverpool delft plate, painted in Fazackerley palette with a central spray of flowers and leaves, the rim decorated with scattered flowers, slight damage, c1750, 9¼in (23.5cm) diam.
£500–550 DN

A Staffordshire creamware stand, possibly by Thomas Whieldon, the border decorated with pierced latticework alternating with panels edged with embossed fruit and nuts, sponged decoration in green and manganese, scrolling rim, c1760, 11in (28cm) wide.
£1,100–1,300 S

An English delft blue and white plate, painted in Japanese style with a design of a figure by a pagoda, and a tethered dog barking at a bird flying overhead, mid-18thC, 8½in (21.5cm) diam.
£180–200 Hal

A Bristol delft plate, painted in blue with a fisherman within a *bianco-sopra-bianco* flower border, slight damage, c1760, 9in (23cm) diam.
£220–250 DN

The term *bianco-sopra-bianco* means white-on-white.

English delft

The word 'delft' derives from 'delving' or digging the clay, and has come to be synonymous with tin-glazed earthenware. The first English delft ware was of high quality, made at Aldgate, London from 1571, and potteries at Southwark, Bristol and Lambeth soon followed. Most delft ware was decorated in blue and white until the early 18thC when other colours were introduced, especially at the Bristol potteries. Liverpool and Dublin factories produced a substantial quantity of transfer-printed delft tiles. The production of delft ware declined with the development of creamware towards the end of the 18thC.

A Liverpool delft plate, decorated in Fazackerley palette with buildings, bridges and haystack in a river landscape, damaged, c1760, 8½in (21.5cm) diam.
£300–350 DN

A Liverpool delft plate, decorated in Fazackerly palette with a central spray of flowers and leaves, the rim with 3 similar sprays, damaged, c1760, 9in (23cm) diam.
£270–320 DN

A Staffordshire creamware plates, with rococo scroll border, splashed in green and yellow, on a grey sponged ground, the reverse sponged in brown, damaged, c1770, 14in (36cm) wide.
£250–350 DN

A pair of Liverpool delft octagonal plates, each centrally 'pencilled' with Cupid amid flowers and leaves, the rims with a flowerhead panelled diaper band, damaged, c1765, 12½in (32cm) diam.
£500–600 DN

> **Miller's is a price GUIDE not a price LIST**

▶ A delft polychrome-decorated plate, c1770, 9in (23cm) diam.
£130–150 ALB

A Les Islettes plate, decorated in green, red and yellow with a Chinaman fishing, late 18thC, 9in (23cm) diam.
£200–225 VH

A pair of Wedgwood creamware platters, decorated in red and green with a central floral spray within a floral border, early 19thC, 15in (38cm) diam.
£160–180 SWO

A pottery plate, printed all over in brown with 4 panels, depicting Britannia and Neptune, and Fame mourning at Admiral Lord Nelson's tomb, inscribed 'Nelson 21, 1805' against a background of flowers and foliage, orange-lined rim, restored, 8¼in (21cm) diam.
£180–220 SAS

A Herculaneum creamware plate, printed with a portrait of Admiral Lord Nelson, c1815, 10in (25.5cm) diam.
£650–750 TVM

A pearlware plate, the feather-edged rim finished in underglaze blue, the centre printed in blue with a scene depicting George III presenting a book to a child, above an inscription, 1820, 6¼in (16cm) diam.
£600–650 SAS

Plates such as this were made in memory of George III at the time of his death, and possibly distributed to the pupils of the Lancastrian School of which the King was patron.

Pearlware

In 1779, Wedgwood developed a variation of his creamware to increase its whiteness and porcelain-like appearance. This was called 'pearlware' because of its slightly bluish glaze, which can be seen where it pools around the base of a piece. Pearlware was used by all the major potters in England and Wales until the late 19thC, and pieces were mainly painted or printed with underglaze blue chinoiserie or floral subjects.

A pair of children's plates, decorated in iron-red and green with 'Symptoms of Grave Digging' and 'Symptoms of Angling', c1820, 5½in (14cm) diam.
£190–210 OCH

A child's plate, by Dillwyn, Swansea, decorated with a black transfer-printed rural scene, c1830, 5½in (14cm) diam.
£80–100 RP

A Staffordshire plate, decorated with a black transfer-printed religious scene, c1840, 6½in (16.5cm) diam.
£35–45 SER

A Bristol delft shallow plate, painted in underglaze blue, brown and green enamels, minor damage, mid-18thC, 13½in (34cm) diam.
£1,600–1,800 Bea

A Swansea creamware plate, decorated in sepia by Thomas Pardoe, c1825, 10in (25.5cm) diam.
£180–200 RP

A pearlware plate, painted in pink and purple lustre with a building, the border green, c1830, 8in (20.5cm) diam.
£140–160 OCH

A gilt-decorated plate, decorated with a scene entitled 'The Truant', oak leaf and acorn border, c1860, 9½in (24cm) diam.
£130–150 SAS

A majolica oyster plate, c1860, 9½in (24cm) diam.
£130–150 SSW

▶ An F. Pratt of Fenton plate, No. 319, depicting 2 boys drinking and eating, c1860, 7in (18cm) diam.
£25–35 SER

A Spode New Stone dish, applied with 2 moulded branch handles, decorated in Imari colours with the Oriental pattern, incised marks and pattern No. 3875, c1825, 10½in (26.5cm) wide.
£230–280 GAK

A Staffordshire alphabet plate, the centre decorated with a picture entitled 'The Village Blacksmith', c1840, 7in (18cm) diam.
£25–30 SER

A pottery plate, by Dixon Philips & Co of Sunderland, the border moulded with daisies, the centre printed in mauve with 2 full-length Oriental dancing figures, entitled 'Chinese Polka', 1844, 7¾in (19.5cm) diam.
£240–270 SAS

A set of 6 plates, decorated with asparagus and artichokes, c1880, 9in (23cm) diam.
£250–300 MLL

A child's brown transfer-printed plate, by Whittingham Ford & Riley, decorated with Eureka pattern, marked 'W. F. & R.', c1876–82, 7¾in (20cm) diam.
£22–30 OD

A set of 6 Lunéville majolica asparagus plates, decorated with green and white on a blue ground, c1880, 9in (23cm) diam.
£350–400 MLL

A Lunéville majolica artichoke dish, c1880, 10in (25.5cm) long.
£150–200 MofC

A Lunéville majolica asparagus cradle, c1880, 10in (25.5cm) long.
£220–250 MofC

A Continental majolica plate, c1880, 12in (30.5cm) diam.
£200–250 ARE

Lunéville

The three French factories of Niderviller, Lunéville and St Clément used the fine Lorraine clay to produce a material resembling English creamware, known in France as *faïence fine*.

A set of 8 Cauldon plates, decorated in Imari style with blue, red and gold, 1890s, 10in (25.5cm) diam.
£150–200 MSB

A Société de Faïencerie Salins asparagus dish, c1890, 15in (38.5cm) wide.
£240–280 MofC

A Brown, Westhead & Moore brown transfer-printed plate, c1882, 9in (23cm) diam.
£25–35 OD

A French majolica asparagus plate, c1890, 17in (43.5cm) long.
£200–250 MofC

Six majolica plates, decorated with love birds, marked 'Salins', c1890, 8in (20.5cm) diam.
£250–280 MofC

An Ashworth charger, decorated in brown with a woman's head, c1885, 14in (35.5cm) diam.
£250–300 DSG

A French majolica strawberry plate, c1890, 13in (33cm) wide.
£250–280 MofC

A plate, painted and sponge-decorated with flow blue, c1890, 10in (25.5cm) diam.
£65–80 IW

A Carlton Ware plate, transfer-printed in brown and hand-enamelled with carnations, pattern No. 621, blue crown mark, c1890–94, 8½in (21.5cm) diam.
£80–100 StC

A Rozenburg earthenware wall plate, decorated with thistles in front of a spider's web, in shades of blue, green and brown, painted factory mark and date code 'L', 1894, 10¾in (27.5cm) diam.
£1,100–1,300 S(Am)

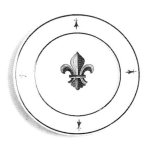

A set of 4 Quimper plates, decorated with fleurs-de-lys, c1900, 8in (20.5cm) diam.
£200–235 MLL

A Portuguese majolica charger, moulded and decorated in colours with motifs of fish and eels, late 19thC, 14½in (37cm) diam.
£500–550 GAK

A Palissy-type plate, applied with a pike among smaller fish, crayfish, a frog, lizard, shells and insects on leaves and a bed of extruded clay, typically coloured, the reverse in brown glazes, chipped and cracked, late 19thC, 17½in (44.5cm) wide.
£600–700 CSK

 ◀ A French Choisy-le-Roi majolica charger, c1900, 8in (20.5cm) diam.
£50–60 MofC

A Belleek earthenware meat plate, transfer-printed in blue and white with a thorn branch, First Period, 1865–90, 23in (58.5cm) wide.
£250–300 MLa

A Royal Doulton Nursery Rhyme Series Ware plate, decorated by Savage Cooper, c1903–39, 7in (18cm) diam.
£80–90 HER

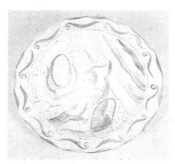

A Wedgwood creamware plate, designed by Elaine Thérèse Lessore, decorated with a figure before a dressing table mirror, artist's signature in lustre, impressed 'WEDGWOOD' and date code, c1920, 9¼in (23.5cm) diam.
£150–200 Bon

Elaine Thérèse Lessore (1883–1944), daughter of Jules Lessore and married to painter Walter Sickert, decorated ceramics for Wedgwood in the 1920s and '30s.

An American redware slip-decorated dish, 19thC, 9in (23cm) diam.
£200–220 A&A

A Longpark plate, decorated in shades of orange, brown and green, inscribed 'Du zummat, Du gude ef you ken, But du zummat', 1903–09, 5in (13cm) diam.
£15–20 ATQ

A Longpark plate, decorated with Scandy pattern, inscribed 'From Margate, may the hinges of friendship never grow rusty', 1910–24, 9in (23cm) diam.
£20–30 ATQ

The Scandy pattern was devised by Aller Vale and much used by other West Country firms. Inspired by Oriental pottery, the design was said to be based on the tail of a peacock.

A Royal Bonn charger, decorated with a girl smoking, within a brown rim, marked, c1900, 19¾in (50cm) diam.
£500–550 S(NY)

This decoration is after a design by Alphonse Mucha for Job cigarette papers, c1896.

A Gouda plate, decorated in a green and blue abstract pattern on an orange ground, with blue lined rim, restored, c1910, 12in (30.5cm) diam.
£65–75 RAC

A Wood & Sons plate, designed by Frederick Rhead, decorated with Benaris pattern in shades of red, blue and orange, c1918, 10in (25.5cm) diam.
£65–85 PC

A pair of Quimper plates, with yellow rims, c1920, 9½in (24cm) diam.
£90–100 each MofC

A pair of Quimper plates, marked 'Henriot Quimper', c1920, 9½in (24cm) diam.
£125–150 MofC

A Royal Doulton plate, decorated in underglaze blue with William Shakespeare encircled by characters from his plays, 1920, 10½in (26.5cm) diam.
£60–70 BRU

A Wedgwood lustre plate, hand-painted in brown and green, c1920, 10½in (26.5cm) diam.
£60–70 PGA

A Gouda Zuid-Holland earthenware wall plate, by H. L. A. Breetvelt, in blue, yellow and brown, factory mark, 1920–23, 18¾in (47.5cm) diam.
£1,700–2,000 S(Am)

A Gouda pottery charger, decorated by H. L. A. Breetvelt, c1925, 16¾in (42.5cm) diam.
£450–500 OO

A Carter, Stabler & Adams red earthenware fruit plate, shape No. 495, designed by Truda Adams, decorated by Ann Hatchard, impressed 'Carter Stabler & Adams, Poole England', 1924–30, 11¼in (28.5cm) diam.
£250–300 PP

A Carter, Stabler & Adams charger, entitled 'Leipzig Girl', slight damage, initials in black, monogam, 1926–27, 17½in (44.5cm) diam.
£800–900 AAV

◀ An Italian maiolica *istoriato* plate, painted in Florentine style within a scrolling panel, the blue border painted with scrolling foliage below a gadrooned rim, damaged, 20thC, 20in (51cm) diam.
£300–350 CSK

Did you know?

Introduced in the early 16thC, *istoriato* is tin-glazed earthenware, particularly Italian maiolica, decorated with a historical, mythological or biblical scene. The literal translation is 'with a story in it', and it represented a departure from practical wares to pieces designed for display.

◀ An asparagus plate, c1930, 13½in (34.5cm) long.
£140–160 MofC

A Gray's Pottery plate, hand-decorated by Susie Cooper, pattern No. 8034, c1928, 9in (23cm) diam.
£160–180 BKK

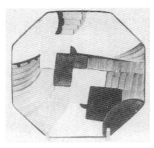

A Susie Cooper sandwich plate, decorated with Cubist pattern, c1929, 5in (12.5cm) wide.
£90–100 SCA

A Corona ware plate, by S. Hancock & Son, decorated with Lagoon pattern, c1930s, 10in (25.5cm) diam.
£85–95 HEM

A Crown Ducal wall plate, by A. G. Richardson, designed by Charlotte Rhead, decorated in green, yellow, blue and turquoise, pattern No. 3652, 1930s, 12in (30.5cm) diam.
£220–260 PC

Chintz ware

Ceramics with chintz decoration were first produced in the 19thC, when transfer-printing became popular. During the mid-1860s a cheaper process was discovered that would produce designs by means of lithographic printing. Introduced initially for the export market, chintzware became a major part of Grimwade's production under the Royal Winton name, and from the 1930s to the 1960s over 50 chintz patterns were produced.

A Royal Winton Chintz ware sandwich set, decorated in Marguerite pattern, 1930s, plate 5½in (14cm) diam.
£140–160 MLa

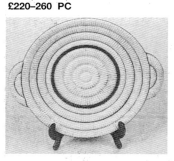

A pair of two-handled cake plates, the ribbed and fluted bands decorated with green and gold stripes, 1930s, 11in (28cm) wide.
£120–140 PSA

A Clews Tunstall Chameleon ware hand-painted charger, c1930, 12in (30.5cm) diam.
£100–150 YY

A Burleigh Ware plate, designed by Harold Bennett, decorated with Dawn pattern, 1930s, 8in (20.5cm) diam.
£22–25 BDA

A Royal Doulton Series Ware 'George and the Dragon' plate, decorated in orange and brown on a blue ground, c1931, 10½in (27cm) diam.
£80–100 BKK

A cream ground and bordered charger, decorated with leaves in autumnal colours, signed 'Charlotte Rhead', 1930s, 13in (33cm) diam.
£280–300 PCh

A Burleigh Ware charger, designed by Charlotte Rhead, tube-lined and painted in pale green, lemon, pink and blue, printed marks, 1930s, 14¼in (36cm) diam.
£230–250 WL

A Royal Winton Chintz ware plate, decorated with Sweet Pea pattern 1930s, 10in (25.5cm) square.
£95–100 BEV

A Maling ware green wall plate, with primrose border, c1936, 11½in (29cm) diam.
£100–120 CSA

A Royal Winton Chintz ware plate, decorated with Cheadle pattern, 1930s, 9¾in (25cm) diam.
£80–90 BEV

A Crown Ducal charger, designed by Charlotte Rhead, decorated in blue and mauve on a mottled grey ground within a blue border, printed mark, signed, c1935, 14½in (37cm) diam.
£280–320 GAK

A Royal Winton Chintz ware plate, decorated with Bedale pattern, 1930s, 7in (18cm) diam.
£40–45 BEV

▶ A set of 8 Sarreguemines fish plates and a dish, c1930, dish 21¼in (54cm) long.
£150–175 MLL

A Crown Ducal charger, designed by Charlotte Rhead, decorated with Hydrangea pattern, c1935, 14½in (37cm) diam.
£320–350 BDA

◀ A Wedgwood Queensware Travel series Windsor grey plate, with Train design by Eric Ravilious, c1936, 10in (25.5cm) diam.
£120–150 YY

▶ A Crown Ducal pottery plaque, designed by Charlotte Rhead, with Autumn Leaf pattern in orange and green on a caramel ground, printed mark, No. 4921, signed, 1930s, 14¼in (36cm) diam.
£200–240 Mit

◀ A Royal Winton Chintz ware plate and knife, decorated with Somerset pattern, c1936, plate 4in (10cm) square.
£80–100 BKK

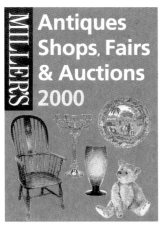

A charger, designed by
Charlotte Rhead, decorated
with Persian Rose pattern,
c1935, 12in (30.5cm) diam.
£100–120 HEA

A charger, designed by Charlotte
Rhead, decorated with Apples
pattern, c1938, 12in (30.5cm) diam.
£130–150 HEA

A Crown Ducal wall plaque,
designed by Charlotte Rhead,
decorated in shades of pink, blue
and brown, pattern No. 5803,
c1938, 14in (35.5cm) diam.
£250–300 PC

A charger, designed by
Charlotte Rhead, decorated
with leaves, unmarked, c1939,
12in (30.5cm) diam.
£100–120 HEA

A Crown Ducal charger, designed
by Charlotte Rhead, decorated
with a central vase of flowers and
foliage, pattern No. 6198, c1940,
14in (35.5cm) diam.
£130–150 HEA

A Royal Venton cake plate,
decorated with the Star Inn,
Alfriston, Sussex, in brown, red,
green and yellow, c1940,
9in (23cm) diam, on a stand.
£16–18 UTP

A set of 6 plates, designed by
Susie Cooper, each painted with
a geometric pattern in dark blue
against a light blue ground,
signed 'Susie Cooper 545',
c1940, 9in (23cm) diam.
£700–800 P

A charger, designed by Charlotte
Rhead, design No. TL 40, c1940,
12in (30.5cm) diam.
£125–150 YY

A Poole Pottery plate,
decorated with a ship, entitled
'The Ship of Harry Paye, Hoo',
drawn by Arthur Bradbury,
painted by Ruth Pavely, dated
'1948', 15in (38cm) diam.
£450–500 Bea

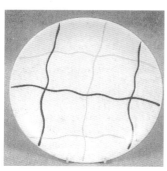

An Alfred Meakin dinner plate,
decorated with wavy lines, 1950s,
9½in (24cm) diam.
£8–10 GFR

A Midwinter side plate, designed by
Jessie Tait, decorated with Zambesi
pattern, 1950s, 6½in (16.5cm) diam.
£12–15 JR

An Eric Leaper charger, decorated
with the Bull, 1950s, 7in (18cm) diam.
£25–30 JR

A Ridgways plate, decorated with Homemaker pattern, 1950s, 7in (18cm) diam.
£8–10 PC

The Homemaker pattern was designed by Enid Seeney for Ridgways in 1955, and retailed through Woolworths until the 1960s. An archetypal image of 1950s style, Homemaker tableware was decorated with examples of contemporary taste, such as the boomerang-shaped table and two-seater sofa.

A Midwinter Stylecraft plate, designed by Jessie Tait, decorated with Red Domino pattern, c1953, 8½in (21.5cm) diam.
£12–15 AND

A Rye Pottery studio plate, decorated with a black, white, brown and green pattern, c1955, 9in (23cm) diam.
£150–180 NCA

A Rye Pottery studio plate, designed by John Cole, decorated with a black, white and blue pattern, c1951, 10in (25.5cm) diam.
£150–180 NCA

Two Midwinter Stylecraft plates, designed by Jessie Tait, decorated with Fiesta and Fantasy patterns, c1954, largest 9½in (24cm) diam.
£10–15 each AND

A Denby plate, with cloisonné decoration, c1955, 6½in (16.5cm) diam.
£45–55 PC

A Midwinter plate, designed by Sir Terence Conran, decorated with Nature Study pattern, c1955, 9½in (24cm) diam.
£15–20 DgC

◄ A Rye Pottery studio plate, decorated with a red, black and white pattern, c1955, 11in (28cm) diam.
£110–130 NCA

A Midwinter Stylecraft platter, designed by Jessie Tate, decorated with Ming Tree pattern, c1953, 13½in (34.5cm) wide.
£35–40 AND

A Denby Tigo ware plate, c1955, 10¼in (26cm) diam.
£90–100 PC

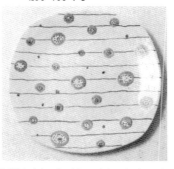

A Midwinter Fashion plate, designed by Jessie Tait, decorated with Festival pattern, c1955, 8¾in (22cm) diam.
£18–20 AND

Two Midwinter plates, designed by Jessie Tait, decorated with Toadstools pattern and Cuban Fantasy pattern, c1956, largest 12in (30.5cm) wide.
£35–45 each AND

Two Midwinter Fashion plates, designed by Sir Terence Conran, decorated with Plant Life pattern, c1956, largest 9¾in (25cm) wide.
£20–30 each AND

POTS

A Wedgwood encaustic decorated black basalt bough pot, with flower holder, c1770, 7in (18cm) diam.
£520–600 PC

A Sarreguemines cachepot, c1875, 8in (20.5cm) diam.
£140–160 MLL

A majolica planter, c1880, 10½in (26.5cm) high.
£450–465 MofC

A Sarreguemines cachepot, c1880, 11½in (29cm) high.
£450–500 MofC

A pair of moss ware square pots, late 19thC, 2½in (6.5cm) high.
£18–20 JMC

An Orchies majolica cachepot, decorated with pink orchids on a green ground, c1900, 8in (20.5cm) diam.
£115–125 MLL

A Moorcroft copper lustre three-handled pot, c1916, 6½in (16.5cm) wide.
£270–300 CEX

A Doulton Lambeth pot, with wavy edge, decorated with blue flowers on a brown ground, initialled 'SC', 1918–20, 12in (30.5cm) diam.
£25–35 SnA

A Denby two-handled decorative pot and cover, with running glazes, c1925, 5½in (14cm) high.
£70–80 PC

A Walter Moorcroft pot, decorated with Anemone pattern, in shades of blue, green and pink on an ink blue ground, c1930, 4in (10cm) high.
£180–220 CEX

Doulton Lambeth

Influenced by John Sparkes, head of the Lambeth School of Art, Henry Doulton set up an art pottery studio in the late 1860s to develop a new range of art stonewares. By the 1880s the company was employing more than 200 staff, with designers such as Hannah Barlow and George Tinworth, producing highly individual work.

In 1877, Henry took over a Burslem manufacturer of domestic earthenwares which, under his leadership, established a reputation for high-quality tableware and ornaments.

A Rye Pottery pot, decorated in white, grey and yellow, c1950, 6½in (16.5cm) high.
£30–40 NCA

PRESERVE POTS

A William Moorcroft mustard pot and lid, decorated with Claremont pattern, with red, purple and green toadstools against a green ground, slight damage, stamped 'Moorcroft Burslem 1914', 2½in (6.5cm) high.
£550–650 P(Ba)

A Losol ware preserve jar, decorated with Rushton pattern, c1915, 4¾in (12cm) high.
£40–45 CSA

A bellied pot and cover, printed in sepia, the reverse and cover with heraldic shields on a buff ground, with gilt and black lining, c1918, 4½in (11.5cm) high.
£100–110 SAS

A Shorter & Sons beehive honey pot, 1920s, 6in (15cm) high.
£30–40 PC

A Marutomo ware jam pot, in the form of a thatched cottage, Japanese, 1920s, 3½in (9cm) wide.
£15–20 PC

A Carlton Ware jam pot, in the form of a cottage, 1920s, 5in (12.5cm) high.
£55–65 PC

A jam pot, in the form of Anne Hathaway's cottage, 1920s, 4½in (11.5cm) high.
£15–20 PC

A Burlington Ware Devon cob jam pot, 1920s, 5in (12.5cm) high.
£25–30 PC

A Shorter & Sons jam pot, with a pagoda roof, 1920s, 6½in (16.5cm) high.
£25–30 PC

A Carlton Ware green lustre preserve pot and cover, on a silver-plated stand, slight damage, black crown mark, 1920s, 2½in (6.5cm) high.
£20–25 StC

A Shorter & Sons jam pot, 1920s, 6½in (16.5cm) wide.
£25–30 PC

A Marutomo ware jam pot, Japanese, discoloured, 1920s, 3½in (9cm) wide.
£15–20 PC

Shorter & Son

Founded in 1878 in Staffordshire, Shorter & Son made majolica and earthenware products until 1927. From c1917, the company produced Toby jugs, Toby teapots and character jugs. In the early 1930s the company became renowned for its decorative wares and ornaments, in both traditional and contemporary styles, aimed at the popular market. In 1933, Mabel Leigh joined the company, and designed traditional cottage ware.

A Royal Winton Chintz ware preserve jar, with silver-plated cover, decorated with Summertime pattern in shades of pink, yellow and blue on a white ground, 1930s, 4½in (11.5cm) high.
£80–100 BEV

A Crown Devon preserve jar and cover, entitled 'Berry Inn', c1930, 4in (10cm) high.
£40–50 CSA

A Carlton Ware Anemone preserve pot, c1930, 5in (13cm) high.
£50–60 CSA

A Poole Pottery jam pot and cover, c1930, 4½in (11.5cm) high.
£40–50 JO

A Royal Winton jam pot and cover, 1930s, 4¼in (11cm) high.
£20–25 BEV

A Westminster Pottery jam pot, with circular thatched roof cover, 1930s, 6in (15cm) wide.
£25–30 PC

A Denby buff-coloured preserve pot and cover, with 2 birds forming the finial, c1930, 4in (10cm) high.
£80–100 KES

A Torquay Pottery jam pot, in the form of a cottage with a thatched roof, 1930s, 5½in (14cm) high.
£25–30 PC

A Price of Kensington jam pot and cover, 1930s, 4in (10cm) high.
£15–20 PC

Denby Pottery

Denby was founded in Denby, Derbyshire, as Bourne's Pottery in 1809, and is famous for its leadless glazed stoneware. In the 1920s many lines had become outmoded, but in 1931 Norman Wood joined the company and modernized production. It was during this period that Cottage Blue tableware was introduced, followed by the Epic and Manor Green ranges, both of which were still being made in the 1980s.

A James Kent Chintz ware jam pot and cover, decorated with Du Barry pattern, 1930s, 4¾in (12cm) high.
£70–80 BEV

▶ A Shorter & Sons dish and preserve jar, decorated with Anemone pattern, c1935, dish 5in (12.5cm) wide.
£15–20 CSA

A Shorter & Sons beehive-shaped honey jar, depicting a brown bee on a pale blue hive, c1935, 4½in (11.5cm) high.
£25–30 CSA

Clarice Cliff designed and decorated some Shorter wares in the 1930s.

A Quimper jam pot, decorated with trees and figures on a cream ground, 1950s, 3in (7.5cm) high.
£20–25 RAC

A Moorcroft jar and cover, decorated with Clematis pattern in shades of blue and pink on a pale green ground, 1930s, 7in (18cm) diam.
£400–450 PGA

SAUCE BOATS

A Staffordshire salt-glazed stoneware sauce boat, on 3 lion mask and paw feet, restored, c1750, 6¼in (16cm) long.
£250–300 DN

A salt-glazed stoneware scratch blue sauce boat, enriched in blue, restored, c1750, 6in (15cm) long.
£400–450 DN

A Staffordshire salt-glazed stoneware sauce boat, with C-scroll handle, brightly painted in coloured enamels with sprays of flowers and leaves, the handle, gadrooned rim and foot picked out in green, c1760, 7¾in (19.5cm) long.
£600–700 DN

A creamware sauce boat, with figure handle, moulded with the fable of the fox and the stork, c1790, 8in (20.5cm) wide.
£900–1,000 JHo

A Staffordshire gravy boat, possibly by J. Meir and Sons, star crack, late 19thC, 5in (12.5cm) high.
£18–25 MEG

A Crown Devon yellow sauce boat and stand, c1928, 5in (12.5cm) wide.
£15–20 CSA

▶ Two Royal Winton green sauce boats and stands, with yellow floral handles, c1930, 5in (12.5cm) long.
£30–35 each CSA

SERVICES

A Wedgwood dessert service, comprising
41 pieces, decorated with Shell and Seaweed
pattern, c1785.
£4,000–4,500 RIT

A Wedgwood composite Queensware part dinner
service, comprising 68 pieces, the borders painted
in green with oak leaves and acorns, minor damage,
impressed marks and painted pattern No. 819,
late 18th/early 19thC.
£3,000–3,500 C

A Wedgwood creamware miniature
tea service, comprising 15 pieces,
marked, c1790, tea kettle
4¾in (12cm) high.
£900–1,000 P

A Wedgwood creamware tea set,
comprising 8 pieces, each piece
decorated with a broad salmon-
coloured border bearing repeated
barley ears, impressed 'WEDGWOOD'
and other marks, late 18thC.
£750–850 Bon

A Neal & Bailey creamware part
dessert service, comprising 24 pieces,
painted with green, black and brown
to the rims, the centres with blue
flowers, c1800.
£1,300–1,500 Bon

A Wedgwood composite Queensware part dinner
service, comprising 53 pieces, the borders painted
with a band of blue daisies, extensive damage,
impressed marks and painted pattern No. 937,
late 18th/early 19thC.
£1,500–1,800 C

A Giustiniani part dessert service, comprising 7 pieces,
decorated in Greek 'black figure' style with warriors
and attendants, on a pale terracotta background, the
rims with various borders of leaves in black and white,
incised script marks, restored, early 19thC.
£1,450–1,650 P

◄ A Wedgwood Queensware
miniature cabaret, comprising
11 pieces, damaged, some pieces
with impressed upper case mark
and/or painter's marks, c1800.
£1,000–1,500 CNY

**A cabaret is a tray with matching
tea or coffee set.**

► A Spode part
dessert service,
comprising 16 pieces,
printed and brightly
painted with flowers
and foliage within
a gilt-decorated
orange rim, pattern
No. 1690, c1810.
£950–1,100 Bea(E)

A Wedgwood Drabware part
dessert service, comprising
17 pieces, pale green with gilt
rims, impressed marks, c1810.
£800–900 Bon

A Ridgway pearlware dessert service, comprising 18 pieces, painted in green and puce with sprays of flowers and leaves, within orange and pale green bands and vine-moulded borders, marked with pattern No. 779 in orange, damaged, c1815.
£550–650 DN

A Wedgwood creamware part dessert service, comprising a pair of ice pails, 3 oval dishes, 5 lobed dishes and 25 plates, each piece bearing a crest within a band of flowers and grasses and a gold rim, slight damage, 19thC, plates 8½in (21.5cm) diam.
£1,300–1,500 Bea

A stone china dinner service, comprising 105 pieces, each piece printed in Chinese style in blue with sprays of flowers and emblems, picked out in iron-red and gilt, probably Charles Meigh, slight damage, printed Chinese-style mark, pattern No. 147, c1835.
£950–1,100 DN

A Herculaneum pottery part dinner service, comprising 27 pieces, each printed in sepia and enamelled with flowers and shells, minor damage, impressed Liverbird mark, pattern No. 1917, c1830.
£1,100–1,250 S(S)

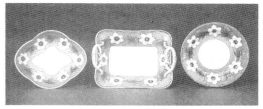

A Wedgwood pearlware part dessert service, comprising 26 pieces, each piece decorated with a band of passion flowers and leaves, on a buff border, some damage, impressed marks and pattern No. 1145, early 19thC.
£950–1,100 DN

A stone china part dessert service, probably Spode, comprising 14 pieces, printed in underglaze blue and enamelled with an Oriental landscape, the border with scattered flowers, slight damage, printed mark, c1820.
£600–700 S(S)

◀ An ironstone dessert service, by T. & J. Carey, comprising 15 pieces, decorated in purple and green with flowers and foliage, within a waved border, printed mark 'Saxon china', c1825, plates 8½in (21.5cm) diam.
£300–350 Hal

An earthenware dinner service, comprising 44 pieces, printed and painted with flowers and leaves within an arcaded scale border picked out in brown and gilt, pattern No. 3/651, c1880.
£600–675 DN

A Wedgwood part tea service, printed in iron-red within gilt line rims, comprising 2 shaped square bread and butter plates, an oval milk jug, 12 teacups and saucers, and 12 side plates, damaged, impressed marks, blue printed Portland vase marks, c1885.
£800–1,000 C

A French majolica fruit set, comprising 15 pieces, c1890, largest dish 10in (25.5cm) diam.
£800–900 MofC

A Minton stone china part dinner service, comprising 24 pieces, decorated in underglaze blue enamels and gilt with the Hindostan Japan pattern, with a central spray of flowers inside a complex border, minor damage, impressed and blue printed marks, pattern No. 5150, mid–19thC.
£520–620 S(S)

A Bishop & Stonier Bisto ware part dinner service, comprising 61 pieces, printed and painted in underglaze blue, iron-red and gilt with flowers and scrolls inside a gadroon-moulded border, minor repair and damage, printed marks, c1900.
£1,000–1,100 S(S)

A Limoges miniature tea set, with gilt edges, early 20thC, tray 2¾in (7cm) wide.
£40–45 TAC

A Susie Cooper dinner service, by Gray's Pottery, comprising 70 pieces, c1925.
£500–600 P(G)

Susie Cooper was employed as a painter for Gray's Pottery from 1922 to 1929, before establishing her own company.

A Staffordshire child's tea set, comprising 6 pieces, painted with the Noah's Ark pattern, late 1920s, teapot 5in (12.5cm) high.
£100–120 P(B)

A Shelley three-piece Boo Boo tea set, designed by Mabel Lucie Attwell, in the form of mushrooms, 1926–45, teapot 5½in (14cm) high.
£450–500 WWY

A Royal Cauldon hand-painted dinner service, 1920s, small plate 8in (20.5cm) diam.
£150–200 SnA

A Denby green-glazed Queen Anne tea set, some restoration, c1920, teapot 5¼in (13.5cm) wide.
£100–120 KES

A Susie Cooper tea-for-two, by Gray's Pottery, c1928, teapot 6in (15cm) high.
£130–160 GH

A Crown Ducal Orange Tree pattern tea set, c1928, teapot 6in (15cm) high.
£180–200 BKK

◄ A Carter, Stabler & Adams coffee pot, cups and saucers, decorated in shades of yellow, brown and blue on a cream ground, impressed backstamp, 1920s, coffee pot 9in (23cm) high.
Cups   £40–50 each
Coffee pot £65–75 HarC

An Art Deco Crown Devon coffee service, decorated in gilt with zigzag bands on a powder blue ground, printed marks in black and pattern No. 2614, c1930.
£580–650 DN

A Susie Cooper coffee service, comprising 16 pieces, printed marks in brown, coffee pot repaired, 1930s.
£200–220 DN

◄ A Carlton Ware coffee service, 1930s, coffee pot 11¾in (30cm) high.
£130–150 BSA

A Crown Ducal part tea and breakfast service, decorated with Orange Tree pattern, printed marks, c1930.
£350–400 WL

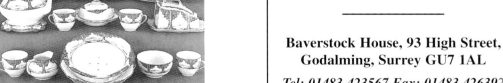

A Royal Winton tea service, comprising 23 pieces, decorated with Somerset pattern, 1930s.
£850–1,000 P(O)

A Royal Winton tea set for 2 persons, decorated with Oriental pattern, 1930s.
£220–250 HCC

A Midwinter Windmill design meat dish, sandwich plates and a jug, 1930s, meat dish 10in (25.5cm) long.
£70–90 DgC

A Burleigh Ware dinner service, decorated with Golden Days pattern, comprising 4 tureens, covers and stands, 3 oval dishes, and 3 sets of various sized plates, 1930s.
£350–400 E

An Empire Ware Tudor design three-piece tea set, 1930s, teapot 7½in (19cm) wide.
£100–120 LA

A Carlton Ware coffee service, comprising 15 pieces, decorated with Pagoda pattern, 1930–35, coffee pot 7in (18cm) high.
£400–500 PAC

A Midwinter coffee set, comprising 15 pieces, designed by Jessie Tait, decorated in Zambesi pattern in black, white and red, c1956, coffee pot 8in (20.5cm) high.
£200–220 AND

A Midwinter tea set, comprising 22 pieces, designed by Jessie Tait, decorated with Hollywood pattern in yellow and grey, c1956, teapot 6½in (16.5cm) high.
£250–300 AND

◄ A Poole Pottery tea-for-two, mid–1950s, tray 12¾in (32.5cm) wide.
£65–75 GRo

A selection of Midwinter Saladware, designed by Sir Terence Conran, decorated in yellow, green and red, c1956, largest plate 9½in (24cm) diam.
£40–50 each AND

A pair of Doulton Lambeth stoneware vases, decorated by Hannah Barlow, c1885, 35in (89cm) high.
£1,250–1,400 HAM

A pair of Doulton Lambeth tube-lined stoneware vases, c1890, 12½in (32cm) high.
£170–200 P(B)

A Royal Doulton flambé vase, possibly by Arthur Eaton, c1925, 18½in (47cm) high.
£4,000–4,500 S

A Doulton Lambeth stoneware vase, by Francis C. Pope, c1900, 15in (38cm) high.
£650–700 DSG

A Royal Doulton Chrysanthemum pattern trio, c1908, cup 2in (5cm) high.
£40–50 HEI

A Royal Doulton vase, decorated by Mark V. Marshall, c1902, 16in (40.5cm) high.
£2,200–2,400 POW

A Moorcroft Fish pattern vase, impressed mark, c1930, 9¼in (23.5cm) high.
£1,500–1,700 P

A Royal Doulton Chang ware vase, with thick crackled glaze, signed 'Noke', dated '9.27', 12in (30.5cm) high.
£1,300–1,500 CDC

A Moorcroft Flambé vase, decorated with irises, c1925, 8in (20.5cm) high.
£280–320 CDC

A Moorcroft vase, signed, c1920, 6½in (16.5cm) high.
£400–500 CEX

A Moorcroft salt-glazed vase, c1915, 6½in (16.5cm) high.
£1,000–1,250 DSG

A Moorcroft plate, c1930, 8in (20.5cm) diam.
£260–280 NP

A Staffordshire Prattware-type Toby jug, modelled as a corpulent gentleman holding a jug of foaming ale, c1820, 10½in (26.5cm) high.
£550–600 HYD

A Staffordshire Toby jug, decorated with underglaze Prattware-type colours, c1820, 10in (25.5cm) high.
£400–450 RWB

A copper lustre pottery mug, with raised flower decoration, c1835, 3in (7.5cm) high.
£40–50 GLN

A north country pottery jug, modelled with a satyr's face mask, c1830, 4½in (11.5cm) high.
£80–90 RWB

A Thomas Rathbone two-handled frog mug, decorated with Milkmaid pattern, c1820, 5in (12.5cm) high.
£400–450 GN

A Staffordshire Toby jug, modelled as a gentleman holding a flagon of ale, with figural modelled handle, mid-19thC, 10in (25.5cm) high.
£100–120 HYD

A Staffordshire two-handled mug, painted in Imari colours, c1835, 4½in (11.5cm) high.
£130–150 BSA

A Staffordshire pearlware mug, printed and painted overglaze, c1825, 4¾in (12cm) high.
£250–280 DAN

A Mason's Ironstone mug, painted with Japan pattern, c1825, 5¼in (13.5cm) high.
£350–400 JP

A Wemyss three-handled mug, painted with mallard ducks, c1900, 9½in (24cm) high.
£1,800–2,000 RdeR

A Wemyss mug, decorated with lilac blossoms, c1900, 5¾in (14.5cm) high.
£450–500 RdeR

A London delft tile, c1740,
6in (15cm) square.
£400–450 JHo

London delft tiles of this size are
very rare.

A Liverpool delft tile, c1760,
5¼in (13.5cm) square.
£1,500–1,650 JHo

The design and colours of this tile
are unusual.

A Liverpool delft tile, polychrome
decorated with a pot of flowers,
c1760, 5¼in (13.5cm) square.
£330–365 JHo

A pair of Dutch Delft tile pictures, painted in manganese with Biblical
scenes, some damage, late 18thC, 19½ x 14½in (49.5 x 37cm), framed.
£1,350–1,500 Bri

A Minton transfer-printed tile,
hand-coloured design by
L. T. Swetnam, c1886,
6in (15cm) square.
£45–50 HIG

A hand-painted tile,
by W. B. Simpson, c1890,
8in (20.5cm) square.
£45–50 HIG

A Carter & Co Dutch series
tile, hand-painted design
by J. Roelants, c1930,
5in (12.5cm) square.
£30–35 HIG

A Wemyss comb tray,
decorated with bunches
of violets, c1900,
10in (25.5cm) wide.
£350–400 RdeR

A Wemyss plaque,
decorated with a sprig
of purple plums, 1920,
5¾in (14.5cm) wide.
£150–200 RdeR

A Rouen faïence tray, decorated
with chinoiserie figures in a
landsape, slight damage,
c1730, 19in (48.5cm) wide.
£3,200–3,500 S

A Cantagalli 'Della Robbia' wall plaque,
decorated with the Virgin Mary and
Child between winged putti, and vines,
marked, late 19thC, 31in (78.5cm) diam.
£2,000–2,200 CSK

A Moorcroft MacIntyre jardinière, rim restored, c1900, 7in (18cm) high.
£375–450 IW

A Moorcroft MacIntyre vase, c1907, 8in (20.5cm) high.
£800–1,000 HEA

A Moorcroft Flamminian Ware vase, for Liberty & Co, c1910, 5in (12.5cm) high.
£150–180 YY

A Moorcroft Pomegranate pattern vase, c1910, 6½in (16.5cm) high.
£350–400 WN

A Moorcroft Leaf and Berry Flambé vase, c1930, 9½in (24cm) high.
£700–800 HEA

A Moorcroft Pomegranate pattern vase, c1910, 16¼in (41.5cm) high.
£250–300 GOO

A Moorcroft Flamminian Ware vase, 1906–30, 8½in (21.5cm) high.
£350–400 YY

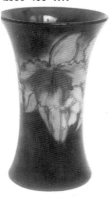

A Moorcroft Orchid pattern vase, c1940, 6in (15cm) high.
£125–150 WN

A Moorcroft bowl and cover, c1914, 8in (20.5cm) high.
£750–900 HEA

A Moorcroft Clematis pattern vase, c1950, 5in (12.5cm) high.
£120–140 YY

A Moorcroft Wisteria pattern vase, c1920, 7in (18cm) high.
£260–320 HEA

A Moorcroft Pomegranate pattern bowl, c1916, 8in (20.5cm) diam.
£200–240 HEA

A Moorcroft Leaf and Berry pattern jug, c1928, 5in (12.5cm) high.
£400–450 HEA

A Moorcroft Fruit and Leaves pattern vase, c1930, 6½in (16.5cm) high.
£275–300 WN

A William de Morgan glazed earthenware vase, decorated in Isnik palette with flowers, possibly an experimental piece, c1885, 15in (38cm) high.
£800–900 C

A Doulton Lambeth vase, c1890, 7½in (19cm) high.
£85–95 WAC

A Doulton Lambeth bottle, with silver stopper, 1920s, 9in (23cm) high.
£200–220 GAZE

A French silver-gilt and enamelled porcelain vase, late 19thC, 10in (25.5cm) high.
£4,000–4,500 SHa

A Gebrüder Heubach *pâte-sur-pâte* porcelain vase, with silver overlay, decorated with figures, c1890, 6¾in (17cm) high.
£400–450 ANO

An Austrian porcelain vase, by Amphora, decorated with a bird, c1900, 12½in (32cm) high.
£300–330 SUC

A Clement Massier lustre vase, c1900, 11in (28cm) high.
£600–675 SUC

A Martin Brothers vase, washed ground incised with lizards, marked, c1898, 11½in (29cm) high.
£2,000–2,200 HYD

A Doulton stoneware vase, by Hannah Barlow, c1900, 27in (68.5cm) high.
£600–700 GAZE

An Austrian Art Nouveau-style pottery vase, decorated with flowers, c1900, 16in (40.5cm) high.
£2,700–3,000 SHa

A Clement Massier lustre vase, with stylized flower, c1900, 6¾in (17cm) high.
£500–550 SUC

A Longwy vase, c1925,
10½in (26.5cm) high.
£600–660 SUC

A Myott waisted square-shaped
vase, 1920s, 8½in (21.5cm) high.
£85–95 BEV

A French Primavera vase,
c1925, 12⅛in (32cm) high.
£400–450 SUC

A pair of Royal Doulton stoneware vases,
designed by Nicki Webb, impressed mark,
1926, 16in (40.5cm) high.
£4,600–5,000 HYD

A Shelley Chintz ware vase, 1930s,
8in (20.5cm) high.
£80–100 BEV

A Ginori glazed earthenware
vase, designed by Gio Ponti,
c1925, 10½in (26.5cm) high.
£6,000–6,500 C

A Myott diamond-shaped graduated and
stepped vase, 1920s, 10¾in (27.5cm) high.
£55–65 BEV

A French pottery double vase, designed by Jean Lurçat,
St Vincent, 1940s, 10½in (26.5cm) high.
£1,000–1,200 SUC

A James Kent hand-painted vase,
1930s, 6¼in (16cm) high.
£70–80 WAC

A Crown Ducal vase, by Charlotte
Rhead, c1935, 7in (18cm) high.
£100–120 WAC

A Shelley vase, c1935,
6in (15cm) high.
£25–30 WAC

A Belleek earthenware plate, First Period, 1865–90, 10¾in (27.5cm) diam.
£150–200 MLa

A Staffordshire salt-glazed plate, with moulded edge, the centre decorated with a flower spray, c1750, 10in (25.5cm) diam.
£200–250 BRU

A Dutch Delft dish, painted in blue, green and yellow, with the initials 'WR', damaged and repaired, c1690, 11½in (29cm) diam.
£680–750 SAS

A Davenport stone china oval platter, with shaped rim, decorated with sprays of flowers, pattern No. 145, c1825, 11in (28cm) wide.
£100–125 BSA

A Mason's Ironstone plate, transfer-printed with blue and white Bird and Peony pattern, initialled 'G.P.', impressed circle mark, c1820, 9½in (24cm) diam.
£90–100 JP

A Mason's Ironstone soup plate, decorated with Mogul pattern, impressed mark, c1815, 9½in (24cm) diam.
£115–130 JP

A pearlware plate, the centre depicting Queen Caroline, enamel colouring faded, c1820, 6½in (16.5cm) diam.
£100–120 SAS

A pottery platter, by Charles Meigh, printed and painted with central spray of flowers, edged with single flowers within quatrefoil vignettes, c1840, 11in (28cm) wide.
£100–110 BRU

A Staffordshire Indian Ironstone plate, by Samuel Alcock, decorated with central spray of flowers, edged with vignettes, c1840, 10in (25.5cm) diam.
£40–50 BRU

A Staffordshire Prattware plate, inscribed 'The Queen – God Bless Her', c1860, 7in (18cm) diam.
£50–60 SER

A pair of Quimper faïence plates, one hand-decorated with a bagpiper, the other with his companion, signed 'Henriot Quimper', early 20thC, 10in (25.5cm) diam.
£150–165 BRU

A Wemyss plate, decorated with oranges and with a green rim, c1930, 8½in (21.5cm) diam.
£150–200 RdeR

A Dutch Delft jug, mark for Adriaan Koecks, c1700, later gilt-metal mount, 10in (25.5cm) high.
£8,000–9,000 C

A Sunderland pink lustre jug, decorated with a ship and a verse, c1810, 8¼in (21cm) high.
£300–340 IW

A Swansea Bonaparte jug, the figures with speech bubbles, c1815, 6¾in (17cm) high.
£1,250–1,400 TVM

A Prattware jug, decorated with Admiral Lord Nelson, c1790, 6in (15cm) high.
£500–560 TVM

A Mason's Ironstone jug, decorated in Japan pattern, c1820, 9¼in (23.5cm) high.
£450–500 JP

A Staffordshire copper lustre jug, with a blue band decorated with raised cherubs, c1830, 7in (18cm) high.
£75–85 SER

A Scottish commemorative jug, by Bell & Co, 1863, 8¾in (22cm) high.
£120–140 SAS

A Staffordshire jug, decorated in red and green enamel on a yellow ground, c1820, 4½in (11.5cm) high.
£200–250 HOW

A pottery commemorative jug, depicting Queen Victoria and Prince Albert, damaged and restored, 1840, 5¾in (14.5cm) high.
£130–150 SAS

A Wedgwood jasper vase, with snake handles, minor restoration, c1790, 15¾in (40cm) high.
£4,000–4,500 C

A Mason's Ironstone vase, enamelled and gilt, lid missing, c1820, 7¾in (19.5cm) high.
£350–400 JP

A pair of Mason's Ironstone vases and covers, marked, restored, c1830, 8¾in (22cm) high.
£360–400 JP

A Mason's Ironstone vase, probably by Samuel Bourne, slight damage, marked, c1820, 27¼in (69cm) high.
£6,400–7,000 C

A Van Briggle Pottery vase, entitled 'Lorelei', c1901, 11in (28cm) high.
£750–850 EKK

A Minton Secessionist vase, designed by L. V. Solon and J. W. Wadsworth, c1902, 17½in (44.5cm) high.
£600–675 DSG

A Zsolnay faïence lustre vase, painted with a bird of prey, impressed mark, c1905, 9¾in (24.5cm) high.
£2,500–3,000 DORO

A Martin Brothers stoneware model of a bird, dated '1911', 8in (20.5cm) high.
£4,000–4,500 P

A Zuid-Holland pottery rose bowl, with a pierced metal cover, c1905, 6in (15cm) diam.
£350–380 OO

A Longwy painted pottery sandwich dish, decorated with stylized daffodils and clematis, France, c1910, 15in (38cm) wide.
£145–175 DSG

A K. K. Fachschule Znaim floor vase, decorated with grapes, marked, c1905, 15¼in (38.5cm) high.
£800–900 DORO

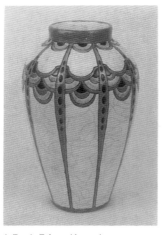

A Boch Frères Keramis vase, decorated in orange and black on an ivory ground, c1920, 14in (35.5cm) high
£100–120 GOO

A Boch Frères Keramis vase, decorated in orange and black on a grey ground, c1920, 9in (23cm) high.
£100–120 GOO

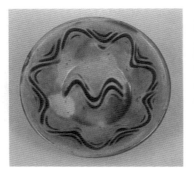

A Winchcombe pottery bowl, with finger-combed decoration, probably by Michael Cardew, 6¼in (16cm) diam.
£60–70 IW

A female head, designed by Lotte Calm for the Wiener Werkstätte, with black hair, and blue, yellow and green decoration, c1930, 9in (23cm) high.
£2,500–3,000 SUC

A Myott jug, c1930, 9¾in (25cm) high.
£40–45 CSA

A Carter Stabler & Adams ship plate, with the brig General Wolf, produced at Poole Pottery, 1939, 15in (38cm) diam.
£600–700 PP

A Winchcombe pottery vase, by Raymond Finch, with yellow/green ground, c1939, 9½in (24cm) high.
£200–220 IW

A Crown Devon charger, c1930, 18in (45.5cm) diam.
£500–600 WTA

A Boch Frères Keramis vase, decorated in blue and yellow, c1920, 13½in (34.5cm) high.
£100–120 GOO

A pair of ceramic book-ends, in the form of Pierrot and Pierrette, possibly Limoges, c1930, 7¼in (19cm) high.
£125–150 WTA

A Crown Ducal charger, designed by Charlotte Rhead, pattern No. 6016, c1939, 12in (30.5cm) diam.
£300–350 PC

A Shelley salad drainer and saucer, c1935, 7½in (19cm) diam.
£35–40 WAC

A Gouda pottery jug, c1920, 9½in (24cm) high.
£90–100 WAC

A Gray's Pottery jug, hand-painted with a flower, 1930s, 4in (10cm) high.
£35–40 WAC

A Wadeheath pottery jug, 1930s, 6¾in (17cm) high.
£45–50 WAC

A Myott jug, c1930, 7¾in (20cm) high.
£25–30 CSA

A Royal Lancastrian double-handled lustre vase, c1920, 6½in (16.5cm) high.
£500–600 ASA

A Beswick jug, c1935, 7½in (19cm) high.
£70–80 WTA

A Wilkinson charger, designed by Frank Brangwyn, painted with a jungle scene, c1933, 17¼in (44cm) high.
£2,000–2,500 C

A Burleigh ware tea set, decorated with orange flowers, c1930s, teapot 5in (12.5cm) high.
£70–75 WAC

A Gouda pottery vase, Ivora factory, c1910, 9in (23cm) high.
£250–300 OO

A Gouda pottery vase, with butterfly design, c1920, 11¼in (28.5cm) high.
£300–350 OO

A Gouda pottery vase, Regina factory, c1920, 13in (33cm) high.
£250–300 OO

A Villeroy & Boch vase, c1923, 12¾in (32.5cm) high.
£300–350 SUC

A Spode cream tureen, decorated with Tiber pattern, on fixed base, with original pierced ladle, c1815, 7in (18cm) long.
£400–500 GN

A Don Pottery blue and white transfer-printed platter, decorated with Italian Fountain pattern, c1830, 17½in (44.5cm) wide.
£400–500 IW

A J. & R. Clews blue and white transfer-printed plate, c1810, 10in (25.5cm) diam.
£120–150 GN

A blue and white transfer-printed platter, attributed to Ridgway, British Scenery Series, Leamington Baths, c1820, 18½in (47cm) wide.
£700–800 GN

A Swansea pottery pearlware plate, transfer decorated from a copper plate engraved by Thomas Rothwell, c1800, 9in (23cm) diam.
£180–220 RP

A Minton transfer-printed puzzle jug, with serpent handle, c1825, 14in (35.5cm) high.
£1,300–1,500 GN

A two-handled tureen, by Jones & Son, printed all over in blue with a coronation scene, small chip and minor restoration, the base with printed mark of Knowledge and Britannia, c1821, 15in (38cm) wide.
£350–400 SAS

A blue and white transfer-printed jug, some damage, c1820, 8½in (21.5cm) high.
£100–120 IW

A blue and white transfer printed tankard, perhaps Turner & Co, c1795, 4¾in (12cm) high.
£100–150 IW

A blue transfer printed proclamation jug, the base marked 'VR' in a star, c1837, 11in (28cm) high.
£650–750 SAS

A Robert Hamilton blue and white transfer-printed platter, Ruined Castle pattern, c1820, 19in (48.5cm) wide.
£450–500 IW

A Ridgway College Series platter, showing Trinity College, c1820, 10in (25.5cm) wide.
£450–500 SCO

A Carey blue and white transfer-printed dessert plate, with a view of Woburn Abbey, c1820, 9in (23cm) diam.
£250–300 GN

A Spode blue and white foot bath, transfer-printed with the Tower pattern, c1820, 18in (45.5cm) diam.
£1,700–2,000 GN

A Durlach fluted two-handled tureen, cover and stand, damaged, c1750, stand 15½in (39.5cm) wide.
£8,500–9,500 C

A Spode platter, transfer-printed with The Grasshopper pattern, c1812, 19in (48cm) wide.
£350–400 GN

A Spode blue and white transfer-printed plate, decorated with view of the Bridge of Lucano, c1820, 10in (25.5cm) diam.
£100–120 GN

A delft-ware blue and white charger, decorated with a bird, c1720, 13½in (34.5cm) diam.
£250–300 AnE

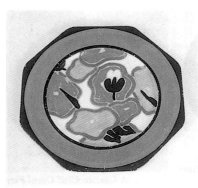

A Clarice Cliff Orange Chintz pattern plate, 1930s, 8in (20.5cm) diam.
£450–500 RIC

A Clarice Cliff Applique Lugano vase, c1930, 8in (20.5cm) high.
£5,500–6,000 BKK

A Clarice Cliff Clouvre pattern vase, Inspiration range, c1930, 6in (15cm) high.
£3,500–4,000 BKK

A Clarice Cliff Alton pattern sabot, printed factory marks, c1933, 5¾in (14.5cm) long.
£250–275 WTA

A Clarice Cliff Athens jug, brown Café-au-Lait pattern, 1930s, 8in (20.5cm) high.
£400–450 RIC

A Clarice Cliff Bizarre plate, decorated with Orange Roof Cottage design, c1932, 9in (23cm) high.
£500–550 WTA

A Clarice Cliff Conical sugar sifter, Poplar pattern, 1930s, 5½in (14cm) high.
£750–850 RIC

A Clarice Cliff Conical jug, Delecia pattern, c1930, 9½in (24cm) high.
£250–300 BKK

A Clarice Cliff Red Autumn pattern tea-for-two, c1931, teapot 5in (12.5cm) high.
£3,500–4,000 BKK

A Clarice Cliff Applique plate, decorated with Caravan pattern , c1934, 9in (23cm) diam.
£3,000–3,500 BKK

A Clarice Cliff Orange Chintz bomb sugar sifter, c1932, 6in (15cm) high.
£300–350 WTA

A Clarice Cliff Lotus jug, decorated with Applique Lucerne pattern, c1932, 11¾in (30cm) high.
£7,000–8,000 BKK

A Clarice Cliff Fantasque Bizarre Conical bowl, decorated with Trees and House pattern, c1930, 7½in (19cm) high.
£550–600 P

A Clarice Cliff pottery group, from the Age of Jazz series, c1930, 7in (18cm) high.
£9,000–10,000 MAV

A Clarice Cliff Autumn pattern jardinière, c1930, 6¾in (17cm) high.
£400–450 P(B)

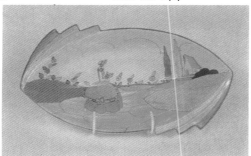

A Clarice Cliff Bizarre bowl, decorated with Gayday pattern, c1930, 8½in (21.5cm) diam.
£200–250 GSP

A Clarice Cliff Fin dish, decorated with Idyll pattern, shape No. 475, c1931, 12¾in (32.5cm) wide.
£500–600 MAV

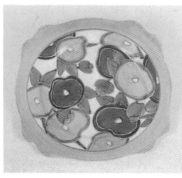

A Clarice Cliff Chintz
pattern plate, 1930s,
10½in (26.5cm) diam.
£350–400 RIC

A Clarice Cliff Inspiration Lily pattern
plate, c1929, 10in (25.5cm) diam.
£850–1,000 BKK

A Clarice Cliff Coral Firs pattern
charger, c1930, 13in (33cm) diam.
£500–600 YY

A Clarice Cliff Orange
House pattern lamp
base, c1930,
14in (35.5cm) high.
£800–900 RIC

A Clarice Cliff Circle Tree pattern jug,
1930s, 4in (10cm) high.
£450–500 RIC

A Clarice Cliff jug, c1930,
3½in (9cm) high.
£450–500 PC

A Clarice Cliff Conical shape coffee service,
decorated with Castelated Circle pattern,
cups and saucers from Tankard shape range,
c1929, coffee pot 7¼in (18.5cm) high.
£1,700–2,000 BKK

Three Clarice Cliff Bizarre Crown shape jugs,
decorated with Coral Firs pattern, 1930s,
largest 4¼in (11cm) high.
£575–675 TMA

A Clarice Cliff Gayday
pattern candlestick, 1930s,
3½in (9cm) square.
£250–300 RIC

A Clarice Cliff Sunrise
pattern candlestick,
1930s, 7in (18cm) high.
£700–800 RIC

A wall plate, painted by Clarice Cliff
to a design by Frank Brangwyn,
17in (43cm) diam.
£3,200–3,800 Bon

A Clarice Cliff biscuit barrel
and cover, Red Tree pattern,
c1930, 6½in (16.5cm) high.
£2,000–2,200 BKK

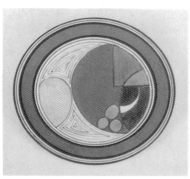

A Clarice Cliff wall plate, decorated
with Orange Melon pattern, c1929,
10in (25.5cm) diam.
£900–1,000 BKK

TEA & COFFEE POTS

A Staffordshire Jackfield black-glazed coffee pot, with traces of original oil gilding, c1750, 10in (25.5cm) high.
£380–420 JRe

A glazed redware teapot, with sprig decoration, c1750, 3½in (9cm) high.
£200–250 IW

A Staffordshire salt-glazed coffee pot and cover, enamelled in colours with a Chinese lady in a blue and green robe, the rim and cover with a turquoise diaper border separated by shaped panels enclosing single flower-heads, the spout and handle enriched with iron-red foliage, Jacobs Collection No. 527, cracked, c1755, 8in (20.5cm) high.
£1,200–1,400 CNY

▶ A Staffordshire red stoneware teapot and cover, the sides sprigged with 4 sheep in pasture, the reverse sprigged with flowers, c1760, 3in (7.5cm) high.
£550–600 S(S)

A Staffordshire salt-glazed stoneware teapot and cover, in the form of a recumbent camel, moulded with birds and leaf scrolls, the neck with profiles within rectangular panels, some damage, c1750, 4¼in (11cm) high.
£1,100–1,200 DN

A Staffordshire slip-cast teapot and cover, c1750, 4¼in (11cm) high.
£1,650–1,850 JHo

A solid agate ware teapot, cover replaced, c1755, 3½in (9cm) high.
£450–550 IW

A glazed redware teapot, with engine-turned decoration, c1760, 5½in (14cm) high.
£320–350 JRe

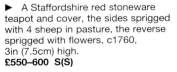

A Staffordshire Drab ware teapot, c1750, 4in (10cm) high.
£1,650–1,850 JHo

A Staffordshire agate ware teapot and cover, minor repairs, c1755, 4¾in (12cm) high.
£3,000–3,300 JHo

A Whieldon teapot, in the form of a house, some restoration, c1755, 5½in (14cm) high.
£550–650 IW

A Staffordshire or Liverpool transfer-printed teapot, c1755, 5in (12.5cm) high.
£750–900 JHo

A Staffordshire creamware teapot, c1765, 5in (12.5cm) high.
£1,500–1,800 JHo

A Staffordshire creamware pineapple-moulded coffee pot and cover, with a scrolling handle and leaf-moulded spout, decorated with yellow and green glazes, damaged and repaired, c1765, 9¼in (23.5cm) high.
£650–750 WW

A Staffordshire creamware globular teapot and cover, probably Wedgwood, with leaf-moulded handle, spout and ball knop, brightly decorated in the manner of David Rhodes with a shepherdess, buildings and trees, cracked, c1770, 4½in (11.5cm) high.
£850–1,000 DN

A creamware teapot, probably Yorkshire, with spattered decoration, cover replaced, c1780, 4in (10cm) high.
£200–250 IW

Items in the Pottery section have been arranged in date order within each sub-section.

A basalt teapot, with fine engine-turned fluting and spaniel finial, c1800, 3in (7.5cm) high.
£180–220 JRe

A Staffordshire salt-glazed teapot and cover, decorated in coloured enamels with flowers and utensils, cover damaged, c1765, 4¾in (12cm) high.
£400–500 DN

A William Greatbatch creamware teapot and cover, signed, c1770, 5in (13cm) high.
£750–850 DN

A creamware teapot and cover, with ear-shaped handle and flower knop, decorated in coloured enamels with flowers and leaves, the cover with a landscape, some damage, c1780, 5¼in (13.5cm) high.
£400–450 DN

A Wedgwood black basalt beehive-shaped teapot and cover, with all-over press-moulded body, impressed mark, c1810, 5½in (14cm) high.
£700–800 SK

▶ A Wedgwood black teapot, lid repaired, c1817, 4½in (11.5cm) high.
£200–250 GLN

A Leeds creamware teapot and cover, decorated in iron-red, green and black with roses and leaves, within iron-red bands, c1770, 6in (15cm) high.
£300–350 DN

A William Greatbatch teapot, in the form of a cauliflower, c1770, 5½in (14cm) high.
£2,000–2,200 JHo

A creamware teapot, painted with chinoiserie design in iron-red, blue and gilt, cover damaged, late 18thC, 4in (10cm) high.
£350–400 RBB

A Wedgwood three-colour jasper teapot and cover, on a white ground, impressed 'Wedgwood', damaged, restored, early 19thC, 4in (10cm) high, and a lilac jasper cup and saucer, the cup sprigged in white with putti and a dog on a lilac ground.
£1,000–1,200 S

A black basalt beehive-shaped teapot and cover, engine-turned around the body, cover and spout, the reeded loop handle with a foliate thumbpiece, the cover surmounted by a pierced concave knop, early 19thC, 4in (10cm) high.
£250–300 S(NY)

A treacle-glazed teapot and cover, moulded with 4 head and shoulder portraits of Admiral Lord Nelson in naval uniform, c1850, 10in (25.5cm) high.
£170–200 SAS

A Dixon & Austin, Sunderland, pearlware teapot, c1820, 6in (15cm) high.
£110–125 OCH

A majolica teapot, in Japanese style, c1880, 7½in (19cm) high.
£180–200 SSW

An Ashworths chocolate/coffee pot, with printed mark and pattern No. 2865, c1880, 9¾in (25cm) high.
£320–350 VH

An S. Fielding & Co majolica teapot and cover, decorated in yellow and blue on a brown ground, c1880, 9in (23cm) high.
£450–500 BRT

A French provincial yellow-glazed faïence teapot, c1880, 7in (17.5cm) high.
£80–100 RYA

A Bell pottery teapot and cover, c1880, 6½in (16.5cm) high.
£50–60 PC

A Measham ware teapot, the cover with acorn finial, cartouche to the side bearing the name of the original owners and date, 1882, 15in (38cm) high.
£250–300 JBL

A majolica teapot, in the form of a fish, decorated in shades of green, brown and yellow, c1885, 11in (28cm) wide.
£500–600 BRT

A bargeware teapot, c1887, 13½in (34.5cm) high.
£250–350 MSA

◀ A Carlton Ware tea kettle, white with gilt highlights, pattern No. 850, ribbon mark and 'Rd 149800', c1890–94, 6½in (16.5cm) high.
£65–80 StC

A Nove coffee pot and cover, with double scroll handle and flower finial, painted with 4 panels of brightly coloured flowers alternating with applied flower sprays, the acanthus-moulded foot and shell-moulded rim picked out in bright yellow, minor restoration, late 19thC, 9in (23cm) high.
£250–300 P

A Measham ware teapot and cover, applied with sprigs of flowers and a hand protruding from the neck, dark brown glaze, cover restored, late 19thC, 19¼in (49cm) high.
£600–700 S(S)

A George Jones Aesthetic period majolica teapot, in the form of a fish, complete with flat fish-shaped stand, late 19thC.
£750–850 L&E

A Staffordshire teapot, hand-painted with pink flowers and gilt foliage, on a black ground, c1890, 6in (15cm) high.
£60–70 CSA

Cottage ware

In the 19thC, the Staffordshire potteries produced many functional items such as spill holders, pastille burners and tea and coffee pots in the form of houses and cottages. These cottage designs reflected a romantic fascination with the rural past, as well as meeting contemporary demand for novelty shapes and reasonably-priced tableware. Many different makers produced cottage ware, including Price, Greens, Royal Winton and SylvaC, and some lines were also made in Japan. Condiment and tea sets are particularly sought-after today by collectors worldwide.

A Torquay pottery coffee pot, decorated with white flowers, 1908–15, 6½in (16.5cm) high.
£30–35 DSG

▶ A Kensington Pottery teapot and hot water jug, both in the form of The Huntsman's Inn, 1920s, 9in (23cm) wide.
£100–120 PC

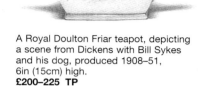

A Royal Doulton Friar teapot, depicting a scene from Dickens with Bill Sykes and his dog, produced 1908–51, 6in (15cm) high.
£200–225 TP

A beehive-shaped teapot, rim chipped, unmarked, 1920s, 5in (12.5cm) high.
£8–10 LA

A Japanese pottery beehive-shaped teapot, unmarked, 1920s, 5in (12.5cm) high.
£15–20 LA

A Burlington Devon Cob coffee pot, by John Shaw & Sons, Staffordshire, c1931–63, 7½in (19cm) wide.
£60–70 PC

A Beswick teapot, in the form of a circular thatched cottage, 1920s, 8in (20.5cm) wide.
£50–60 LA

A Burlington Devon Cob teapot and biscuit barrel, by John Shaw & Sons, Staffordshire, 1930s, teapot 7½in (19cm) high.
£50–60 each PC

A Denby Cottage Blue coffee filter, early 1930s, 9in (23cm) high.
£60–75 KES

A Carlton Ware coffee pot, with figurehead handle, pattern No. 3684, restored, black script mark, 1930s, 5½in (14cm) high.
£250–300 StC

A Burleigh Ware Zenith shape coffee pot, decorated with Meadowland pattern, 1930s, 7in (19cm) high.
£75–90 BUR

A Susie Cooper Kestrel coffee pot, decorated with apple-green polka dots, restored, unsigned, 1930s, 8in (20.5cm) high.
£30–35 DAC

A Continental teapot and butter dish, 1930s, teapot 6in (15cm) wide.
£15–20 each PC

A Carlton Ware coffee pot and cover, painted with red and brown banded decoration, c1935, 8½in (21.5cm) high.
£80–90 CSA

A Ye Olde Cottage teapot, unmarked, 1930s, 8in (20.5cm) wide.
£30–40 LA

A cut-sided stoneware teapot, by Shoji Hamada, with thrown handle, *tenmoku* glaze, small repair to spout, c1935, 10¾in (27cm) high.
£1,200–1,400 Bon

A Denby Cottage Blue teapot, with original 'Nevva-drip' patent spout, 1930s, 9¼in (23.5cm) high.
£25–30 KES

A Susie Cooper Kestrel shape hand-painted hot water pot, with banded decoration, 1930s, 5in (13cm) high.
£50–60 SCA

A Royal Winton teapot, decorated with Summertime pattern, 1930s, 6¼in (16cm) high.
£250–300 BEV

A SylvaC Ye Olde Cottage teapot, 1930s, 8½in (21.5cm) wide.
£40–50 PC

A teapot, in the form of a beige rabbit, marked 'Bunny', c1930, 8in (20.5cm) high.
£65–75 DKH

A Keele Street Pottery teapot, 1930s, 9in (23cm) wide.
£30–40 LA

► An Arthur Wood & Son teapot, in the form of Moreton Old Hall 1930s, 9in (23cm) wide.
£60–70 PC

◄ A Kensington coffee pot, with raised sunflower decoration, c1934, 8in (20.5cm) high.
£40–50 BKK

A Midwinter Stylecraft teapot and jug, designed by Jessie Tait, decorated with Fiesta pattern in yellow, green and black on a white ground, c1954, teapot 3½in (9cm) high.
£30–60 each AND

A Susie Cooper Rex shape teapot, decorated with Dresden Spray design, c1939, 5½in (14cm) high.
£100–120 CSA

A Winchcombe Pottery coffee jug, c1940, 8in (20.5cm) high.
£90–110 IW

A Royal Doulton Bunnykins teapot and cover, the ovoid body in the shape of a rabbit, the cover as its head, coloured in tones of brown, green and black, printed marks, c1940, 7¾in (20cm) wide.
£900–1,000 N

An Avonware teapot, by Avon Art Pottery, Staffordshire, with brown and green cover on a yellow body, c1940, 4in (10cm) high.
£20–25 CSA

An earthenware teapot, by Stig Lindberg, Sweden, for Gustavsberg, decorated in blues, purples, green and yellow with a hand-painted glazed bust of a woman, and other motifs, marked, c1952, 10in (25.5cm) high.
£230–260 Bon

A Torquay Pottery teapot, inscribed 'Lynmouth', decorated in shades of brown and blue on a cream ground, c1940, 4in (10cm) high.
£35–40 RAC

◄ A Crown Windsor cottage ware teapot, c1950, 5in (12.5cm) high.
£20–25 CSA

Torquay Pottery

Founded c1875 in Torquay, Devon, the Torquay Terracotta Co manufactured figures, busts animals, birds and a wide range of functional wares such as vases, jugs and tea wares. The firm became the Torquay Pottery Co in 1908, and continued to make glazed ware with printed landscapes and popular souvenir and novelty items until its closure c1939.

TILES

A Liverpool delft tile, c1765,
5in (12.5cm) square.
£65–75 JHo

A London delft tile, decorated with
Jacob's Ladder in manganese,
c1750, 5in (12.5cm) square.
£65–75 JHo

A Bristol delft tile, depicting
the Annunciation, c1750,
5in (12.5cm) square.
£65–75 JHo

A Dutch Delft tile, painted with
a fisherman and boats, c1750,
5¼in (13.5cm) square.
£35–45 IW

A Dutch tile, decorated in blue and
white with a swineherd and pigs,
c1750, 5in (12.5cm) square.
£30–40 IW

A Liverpool delft tile,
decorated in blue and white
with a basket of flowers, c1750,
5in (12.5cm) square.
£30–40 IW

A theatrical tile, depicting
Mr Lee Lewis in the character
of Harlequin, c1759,
5in (12.5cm) square.
£400–450 JHo

A London delft tile, with powdered
manganese ground, blue carnation
corners, c1760, 5in (12.5cm) high.
£75–85 JHo

A Bristol delft tile, painted in blue
with a horse amongst buildings and
trees, c1760, 5¼in (13.5cm) high.
£85–95 JHo

A panel of 12 delft polychrome tiles,
possibly Liverpool, each painted with
a bird in blue, yellow, manganese and
green, slight damage, c1760, each
5in (12.5cm) square, framed and glazed.
£1,400–1,600 Bon

An English delft blue and white
tile, c1760, 4in (10cm) square.
£55–65 PHA

A Liverpool tile, decorated in
manganese with a cow, c1765,
5in (12.5cm) square.
£130–150 JHo

A blue and white delft tile, painted with a flower, c1770, 3in (7.5cm) square.
£40–45 PHA

A tile depicting The Lark and Her Young Ones, from *Aesop's Fables,* c1770, 5in (12.5cm) square.
£180–200 JHo

An English delft blue and white tile, c1770, 4in (10cm) square.
£60–75 PHA

A theatrical tile of Mr Garrick playing Abel Drugger, from Johnson's *The Alchemist*, the print from Sayer's *Dramatic Characters*, published in 1770, 5in (12.5cm) square.
£400–450 JHo

Two Liverpool delft tiles, depicting 'The French Cook', and 'One lady in a chair accompanied by two gentlemen', printed in brick red, by Sadler, c1770, 5in (12.5cm) square, framed.
£350–400 DN

The French Cook tile has satirical references to the famine in France caused by the Seven Years of War, 1756–63, showing a French cook preparing cats and dogs. Both from the Hodgkin Collection.

A theatrical tile, depicting 'Mrs Barry in the character of Athenais', in Nathaniel Lee's *Theodosius*, dated '12th December 1776', probably printed by Green, restored, 5in (12.5cm) square.
£260–300 JHo

A Liverpool tile, depicting The Sheep Biter, from *Aesop's Fables*, Croxall's edition, c1770, 5in (12.5cm) square.
£150–180 JHo

▶ A Dutch Delft blue and white tile, late 18thC, 5in (12.5cm) square.
£35–45 IW

A Liverpool tile, depicting The Ape and the Fox, c1770, 5in (12.5cm) square.
£150–180 JHo

This design, printed in red with green enamelled borders, is also found on a set of creamware plates in the Victoria & Albert Museum.

A Liverpool tile, depicting The Sow and The Bitch, c1770, 5in (12.5cm) square.
£180–200 JHo

A set of 12 Dutch tiles, with puce weave basket and floral decoration, on a white ground, in a lacquered frame, 18thC, 20 x 16in (51 x 40.5cm).
£800–1,000 GH

A theatrical tile of Mr Lewis in Home's *Douglas*, the print from Lowndes' *New English Theatre* by Goldar after Dodd, dated '21st June 1777', 5in (12.5cm) square.
£350–400 JHo

A Dutch Delft polychrome tile, framed, early 19thC, 7½in (19cm) wide.
£50–60 SER

A Minton tile, decorated with a lady and white blossom, c1865, 9in (23cm) square.
£120–140 DSG

A set of Copeland tiles, designed by Lucien Besche, depicting the months of the year, c1870, 6in (15cm) square.
£85–110 each Nor

A Minton tile, designed by John Moyr Smith, c1875, 9in (23cm) square.
£100–120 DSG

A Minton & Hollins tile, corner chip, 1880s, 6in (15cm) square.
£6–8 GIN

A Makkum tile picture, consisting of 12 tiles, painted in colours, depicting a large galleon, late 19thC, 20 x 15¼in (51 x 38.5cm).
£850–950 S(Am)

A Maw & Co tile, Children's Pastimes series, c1890, 6in (15cm) square.
£45–50 HIG

A Minton transfer-printed tile, Idylls of the King series, designed by John Moyr Smith, c1890, 6in (15cm) square.
£27–30 HIG

A Minton & Hollins transfer-printed tile, Shakespeare series, c1890, 6in (15cm) square.
£18–20 HIG

A German earthenware tile, the design attributed to C. S. Luber, depicting a girl with a bouquet of daisies in a landscape, painted mark, c1902, 18in (45.5cm) wide.
£1,200–1,500 S(Am)

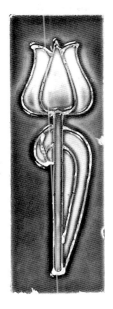

► An Art Nouveau tube-lined tile, depicting a stylized tulip and leaf, c1900, 6in (15cm) high.
£20–25 HIG

TOAST RACKS

A pair of Price of Kensington toast racks, 'His' and 'Hers', 1920s, 4in (10cm) wide.
£70–80 PC

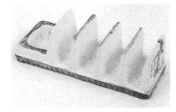

A Westminster Pottery toast rack, 1920s, 5¾in (14.5cm) wide.
£25–30 LA

A Carlton Ware toast rack, 1920s, 3¾in (9.5cm) wide.
£55–65 PC

A Susie Cooper toast rack, with sgraffito decoration, the space at either end for jam and butter, 1930s, 6in (15cm) wide.
£75–85 SCA

A Royal Winton toast rack, decorated with Sweet Pea pattern, 1930s, 4½in (11.5cm) wide.
£120–140 BEV

A Crown Ducal two-slice toast rack, decorated with Primrose pattern, 1930s, 4in (10cm) wide.
£70–80 BEV

TOBY & CHARACTER JUGS

A Staffordshire pearlware Toby jug, decorated in manganese, blue and yellow, c1780, 10in (25.5cm) high.
£800–900 S(NY)

A Staffordshire Toby jug, c1780, 10in (25.5cm) high.
£1,000–1,350 JHo

A Ralph Wood Toby jug, with black hat and green jacket, late 18thC, 9½in (24cm) high.
£2,500–2,800 Mit

A Staffordshire pearlware Toby jug, decorated in manganese, brown and yellow, slight damage, c1780, 10in (25.5cm) high.
£800–900 S(NY)

◄ A Staffordshire Toby jug, with sponged and underglaze decoration, c1790, 10½in (26.5cm) high.
£750–850 RWB

► A Ralph Wood Toby jug, depicting Admiral Lord Howe, decorated with running glazes, restored, c1790, 10in (25.5cm) high.
£900–1,000 JBL

Did you know?

Earthenware jugs in the form of a corpulent seated man wearing 18thC dress and a tricorn hat were made by Ralph Wood and his son from around 1760 at their Staffordshire pottery, and were widely copied by other potteries. The original Toby was probably Toby Philpot, about whom the song *The Brown Jug* was published in 1761. Many other jugs were made, depicting characters such as Martha Gunn. Following WWI, characters such as the first newspaper cartoonist, Sir Francis Carruthers-Gould, have also been commemorated in jug form.

A Collier Toby jug, decorated with blue running glazes, c1790, 10in (25.5cm) high.
£800–900 **JBL**

A Prattware Toby jug, decorated in mainly yellow underglaze colours, c1790, 10in (25.5cm) high.
£650–750 **JBL**

A Ralph Wood-type raised cup Toby jug, decorated with running glazes of blue and yellow, c1790, 10in (25.5cm) high.
£800–900 **JBL**

A Yorkshire-type pearlware Toby jug, decorated in brown, maroon and yellow, incised 'E. Wood, 1794', 9¼in (23.5cm) high.
£500–550 **S(NY)**

A creamware Toby jug, depicting a 'tipsy' man, wearing a frock coat and breeches, repaired, late 18thC, 10¼in (26cm) high.
£7,500–8,500 **S**

Items in the Pottery section have been arranged in date order within each sub-section.

A Ralph Wood-type Toby jug, with black hat, green jacket, brown leggings and black boots, late 18thC, 10in (25.5cm) high.
£700–800 **Mit**

A Ralph Wood-type Toby jug, with brown hat, green jacket and blue leggings, on a brown base, late 18thC, 9½in (24cm) high.
£600–700 **Mit**

A Prattware Toby jug, Gin Woman, her dress decorated with floral sprigs in underglaze blue, green and brown, slight damage, c1790, 10in (25.5cm) high.
£550–600 **DD**

A Toby jug, with ochre coat, brown breeches, wavy brown and white stockings and brown boots, early 19thC, 9in (23cm) high.
£110–130 **AP**

A Staffordshire pearlware Toby jug, decorated in underglaze colours and sponged base, c1800, 10in (25.5cm) high.
£750–850 **RWB**

A character jug, depicting a sailor seated on a money chest, with black hat and scarf, blue jacket with yellow buttons, blue striped trousers and black shoes with cream buckles, paintwork scuffed, c1800, 10in (25.5cm) high.
£500–600 **GAK**

A Toby jug, decorated in blues and greys, with running glaze, c1800, 10in (25.5cm) high.
£400–500 **JBL**

A Prattware Toby jug, decorated in shades of brown, ochre and orange, c1810, 9½in (24cm) high.
£350–400 S(NY)

A Walton 'Hearty Goodfellow' Toby jug, decorated in overglaze colours, with leaf design to small jug, c1820, 11in (28cm) high.
£700–800 JBL

A Staffordshire Toby jug, by Neale & Wilson, decorated in red, brown and green, 19thC, 10in (25.5cm) high.
£850–1,000 JBL

A Portobello Toby jug, depicting a snuff taker, c1830, 7in (18cm) high.
£300–350 RWB

A pearlware Toby jug, depicting a man seated wearing a blue coat and brown and yellow hat, a speckled jug on his knee, on a sponged octagonal base, some damage, possibly Scottish, c1830, 7¾in (19.5cm) high.
£320–350 CAG

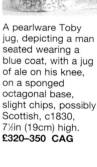

A pearlware Toby jug, depicting a man seated wearing a blue coat, with a jug of ale on his knee, on a sponged octagonal base, slight chips, possibly Scottish, c1830, 7½in (19cm) high.
£320–350 CAG

A stoneware Toby jug, the gentleman wearing a hat and taking snuff, with foliate handle and raised base, mid-19thC, 10in (25.5cm) high.
£100–120 AG

A Toby jug and cover, entitled 'The Landlord', decorated in underglaze blue, red and green, inscribed 'Home Brewed Ale', c1855, 11in (28cm) high.
£450–500 JBL

◄ A pearlware jug and cover, depicting a woman in a green and orange dress, white apron, and yellow hat, holding a bottle, on a vine-moulded base, damaged, c1830, 10in (25.5cm) high.
£600–700 DN

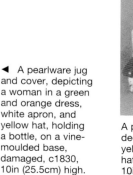

A pearlware Toby jug, decorated in blue, yellow, black and ochre, hat restored, 19thC, 10in (25.5cm) high.
£340–375 DN

A Staffordshire character jug, modelled as Admiral Lord Nelson, 19thC, 11½in (29cm) high.
£140–160 GAK

A pair of Punch and Judy character jugs, decorated in red and yellow, both characters seated, late 19thC, 11in (28cm) high.
£300–350 MAW

A pearlware character jug and cover, depicting Mr Punch, seated in an armchair and picked out in blue, green, yellow, black and puce, on green-glazed base, some restoration, c1870–80, 12¼in (31cm) high.
£550–600 DN

A Staffordshire Toby jug, c1885, 9in (23cm) high.
£120–130 JO

A Victorian Staffordshire jug, depicting Bacchus crowned with an ivy wreath, 8in (20.5cm) high.
£170–200 AnE

A Staffordshire Toby jug, c1890, 9in (23cm) high.
£100–130 JO

A Foley Intarsio Toby jug, designed by Frederick Rhead, decorated in shades of brown, green, yellow and red, c1890–1900, 7¼in (18.5cm) high.
£450–500 PGA

A Doulton Lambeth stoneware Toby jug, late 19thC, 10in (25.5cm) high.
£180–200 HYD

LOCATE THE SOURCE
The source of each illustration in Miller's can be found by checking the code letters below each caption with the Key to Illustrations, pages 376–379.

A Staffordshire Toby jug, entitled 'Hearty Good Fellow', modelled as a standing gentleman holding a clay pipe and mug of ale and wearing a tricorn hat, painted in enamelled colours, on a rustic base, inscribed, c1900, 11in (28cm) high.
£150–170 HYD

A Brannam green-glazed character jug, modelled from a cartoon of President Kruger, after designs by Sir Francis Carruthers-Gould, in the form of an elderly man smoking a pipe, the handle modelled as a boar's head, minor chips, incised marks for 1900, 6¼in (16cm) high.
£350–400 DN

A pair of Continental majolica character jugs, in the form of Industry and Liberty, decorated in coloured enamels, impressed marks, early 20thC, 10¼in (26cm) high.
£450–500 DN

A Sarreguemines advertising jug, No. 3181, overprinted in Australia, c1902, 8in (20.5cm) high.
£400–450 PC

A Wilkinson character jug, Marshal Foch, designed by Sir Francis Carruthers-Gould, inscribed 'Au Diable le Kaiser', black printed marks, 'FCG' monogram on side of base, c1914, 12¼in (31cm) high.
£950–1,100 C

A Onnaing jug, No. 784, shaped as a lady wearing a bonnet, with red interior, inscribed 'La Jupe-Culotte, c1904, 12in (30.5cm) high.
£350–400 PC

A Wilkinson Toby jug, designed by Sir Francis Carruthers-Gould, entitled 'Hell Fire Jack', printed marks, c1918, 10in (25.5cm) high.
£270–300 SK

A Beswick character jug, Old Bill, impressed mark, c1939–54, 4¾in (12cm) high.
£220–250 DN

A Royal Doulton character jug, Old King Cole, with yellow crown, registered No. 832354, c1939–60, 5½in (14cm) high.
£1,200–1,500 AG

A Johnnie Walker Toby jug, modelled as a huntsman wearing a red coat, boots, top hat and holding a monocle, inscribed, limited edition by Ashtead Potters, c1930, 14½in (37cm) high.
£130–150 HYD

A Royal Doulton character jug, designed by M. Henk, printed mark in brown, 1930s, 7in (18cm) high.
£475–550 DN

A Royal Doulton character jug, Jarge, c1950–60, 6½in (16.5cm) high.
£240–260 DA

A Royal Doulton character jug, 'arriet, designed by H. Fenton, printed mark in green, c1947–60, 6¼in (16cm) high.
£200–250 DN

◄ A Royal Doulton character jug, John Barleycorn, designed by C. J. Noke, D5327, printed mark in green, c1939–60, 7in (18cm) high.
£120–140 DN

TRAYS

A Watcombe pin/ashtray, depicting Shakespeare's house, 1920–45, 3½in (9cm) wide.
£10–15 PC

A pair of Carlton Ware ashtrays, depicting a bride and groom, black script mark, 1930s, 2½in (6.5cm) wide.
£150–200 StC

◀ A Doulton Lambeth slipcast pin tray, in the form of a kookaburra, 1920s, 2¾in (7cm) high.
£150–200 P

A Carter, Stabler & Adams ashtray, modelled as a boat, with vellum glaze and blue waves, probably designed by John Adams, 1930s, 7in (18cm) wide.
£65–75 HarC

A Royal Winton Chintz ware tray, decorated with Marguerite pattern, 1930s, 10in (25.5cm) wide.
£60–70 PAC

A Carlton Ware ashtray, with black transfer-printed hand-enamelled illustration and verse entitled 'Dreamer', shape No. 1755, black script mark, pattern No. 2831, 1930–40s, 3¾in (9.5cm) diam.
£20–30 StC

A Bursley Ware tray, designed by Charlotte Rhead, decorated in shades of green, orange and blue, pattern No. TL5, 1940s, 8¾in (22cm) long.
£100–120 PC

A Dartmouth pin tray, decorated with a group of figures riding a horse, inscribed 'Widecombe Fair', 1950s, 5¼in (13.5cm) high.
£10–15 PC

TUREENS & COVERED DISHES

A Dutch Delft butter dish and cover, the cover decorated with a Chinese lady and surmounted by a finial in the shape of a yellow apple surrounded by green leaves, glaze chipped, marked, 18thC, 5in (12.5cm) wide.
£800–900 S(Am)

A Leeds/Yorkshire creamware melon and leaf tureen and cover, the lobed fruit resting on its own fixed stand, a smaller fruit forming the bud finial, damaged, late 18thC, 8in (20.5cm) wide.
£700–800 Bon

A Swansea Pottery supper set, the decoration attributed to Thomas Pardoe, the borders in brown and green, finial of central dish restored, c1802, 20in (51cm) wide.
£800–900 PF

A Hicks & Meigh stone china tureen and cover, c1815, 12½in (31.5cm) wide.
£850–950 JP

A Stephen Folch stone china supper dish and cover, c1820, 12in (30.5cm) wide.
£300–330 VH

A Spode stone china muffin dish, decorated with Cabbage pattern No. 2061, printed mark, c1822, 8in (20.5cm) diam.
£100–120 JP

A Staffordshire pearlware tureen, modelled as a bird with pink plumage seated on her nest, with green-glazed and encrusted base, early 19thC, 8¾in (22cm) wide.
£450–550 Hal

A pink lustre double-handled pot and cover, slight damage, c1820, 4¼in (11cm) high.
£50–60 TAC

A Brameld vegetable tureen and cover, with leaf-moulded handles and knop, printed in blue and over-painted in bright colours with 'Twisted Tree' pattern, c1835, 14¼in (36cm) wide, and 3 plates.
£180–200 P

A pair of creamware sauce tureens and covers, with integral stands and scroll knops, each painted in iron-red and green, unmarked, one slightly cracked, early 19thC, 8¾in (22cm) high.
£650–700 WW

A stoneware game pie dish and cover, chips to lid, c1830, 10in (25.5cm) wide.
£100–120 OCH

A blue majolica sardine dish, with gilt decoration, the cover with a sardine finial, c1860, 8in (20.5cm) wide.
£270–300 SSW

A Harding miniature tureen and cover, transfer-printed in brown and white, c1840, 4in (10cm) high.
£70–80 OCH

A Wedgwood majolica game pie dish, with liner and lid, brown-glazed and applied with game and fruiting vine, hare finial, impressed date mark for 1864, slight damage, 9in (23cm) wide.
£500–600 TMA

◄ A Staffordshire pottery hen tureen and cover, c1860, 7½in (19cm) high.
£120–150 Ber

A Minton majolica two-handled game dish, the cover moulded with a hare and game birds, the basket-weave body moulded and decorated in green on a brown ground with foliage and acorns, damage to cover, impressed marks and date cypher for 1871, 12in (30.5cm) wide.
£500–550 GAK

A Staffordshire tureen, modelled as a dove, 19thC, 6in (15cm) high.
£400–475 ACA

A Savoie casserole and lid, decorated with brown on a yellow ground, c1880, 9in (23cm) diam.
£75–85 MLL

A Wedgwood buff-coloured game dish and liner, moulded with game and festoons of vines, the cover with hare finial, 19thC, 9in (23cm) wide.
£230–260 E

A French majolica tureen and lid, decorated in shades of green and yellow, unmarked, c1900, 13in (33cm) wide.
£180–200 MLL

A Midwinter tureen, designed by Jessie Tait, decorated with Zambesi pattern in black, white and red, c1956, 9in (23cm) wide, on original stand.
£75–90 AND

A George Jones majolica tureen, the cover with a fox finial, picked out in tones of green and brown the base with pendent trophies and game, with script mark '2262', c1875, 10½in (26.5cm) diam.
£2,000–2,500 N

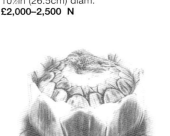

A majolica butter dish, in the form of an artichoke, decorated in green and yellow, the cover with a bird finial, c1880, 7½in (19cm) wide.
£130–150 SSW

A French rabbit tureen, c1900, 8in (20.5cm) wide.
£55–60 MLL

A Quimper tureen, decorated with stylized flowers and leaves in shades of orange and green with a blue rim, 1950s, 5in (12.5cm) high.
£40–50 RAC

A George Jones majolica game pie dish, relief-decorated in colours with geese, ducks and sporting trophies on a turquoise ground, the fern leaf strewn cover with a fox and a dead goose, cover repaired, No. 2267, c1875, 7½in (19cm) high.
£2,400–2,700 MCA

A Jackfield tureen, modelled as a hen, c1885, 7in (18cm) wide.
£200–220 JO

Game pie dishes

The liner of game pie dishes went into the oven and was then put into the dish/tureen to be brought to the table. Majolica tureens and game pie dishes are much sought-after by collectors. Price is greatly affected by the quality of moulding and brightness of decoration.

A Hulme & Christie sauce tureen on stand, c1900, 8½in (21.5cm) wide.
£35–45 TAC

A Denby Epic *petite marmite*, with fish handles, designed by Donald Gilbert, c1930, 5¼in (13cm) diam.
£12–15 KES

A pair of Wedgwood & Bentley vases and covers, the bodies moulded with grooves below an applied band of drapery, with circular Wedgwood & Bentley Etruria marks, some damage and repair, c1770, 11½in (29cm) wide.
£1,600–1,800 P

A Spode pearlware vase, decorated with blue fleurs-de-lys and coloured flowers, on a red ground of fish roe pattern, c1815, 5in (12.5cm) high.
£250–275 GAK

A Staffordshire copper lustre vase, decorated with a hand-painted cottage scene on a yellow ground, c1825, 5in (12.5cm) high.
£80–90 BRU

A Dutch Delft tulip vase, with 5 tubular openings to the arched shoulder, painted overall with floral sprays, with a floral bouquet to the front, and a branch issuing blossom to the reverse, set on a sloping base, restored, marked in underglaze blue 'Factory In De Klaauw', 18thC, 9in (23cm) high.
£1,300–1,500 S(Am)

A pair of pearlware pink lustre bough pots, c1820, 8½in (21.5cm) wide.
£1,000–1,200 RP

A Wedgwood jasper ware pot pourri vase, decorated with white Grecian figures and leaves on a blue ground, restored, mid–19thC, 12in (30.5cm) high.
£250–275 BRU

◄ A Swansea Pottery Dillwyn's Etruscan Ware vase, c1855, 13in (33cm) high.
£1,100–1,300 RP

A pair of Wedgwood *rosso antico* pot pourri vases and covers, each sprigged in black with stiff leaves interspersed with flowers above a similarly decorated foot, the covers pierced with holes, early 19thC, 7in (17.5cm) high.
£1,300–1,500 Bon

***Rosso antico* is a form of redware, ranging in colour from light red to chocolate brown.**

A pair of Staffordshire ironstone baluster-shaped vases, with flared necks, royal blue, moulded in relief with phoenix, fantastic rocks and chinoiseries picked out in gold, c1820, 22½in (57cm) high.
£1,300–1,500 J&L

A majolica two-handled vase and cover, moulded with a band of flowerhead roundels within stiff-leaf and laurel swag bands, decorated in bright colours, some damage, c1860, 23½in (59.5cm) high.
£900–1,100 DN

A Prattware vase, with trumpet-shaped neck, the shoulders set with twin loop handles, the black ground enamelled with a classical chariot scene and angels above a Greek key pattern in red, Pratt/Prince Albert stamp, rim restored, c1860, 17in (43cm) high.
£210–230 SAS

Prattware

The term Prattware is applied to two very different ceramic products. The first is a distinctive form of lead-glazed earthenware, often relief-moulded, and decorated in thick ochre, pale yellow, dull blue, green, purple and brown, often highlighting the moulding, and occasionally with a mottled or stippled effect. This type of ware is associated with the firm of William Pratt, founded c1775 at Lane Delph, Staffordshire, and was produced by the company c1785–1840.

The second and equally distinctive product, also known as Prattware, was made by F. & R. Pratt of Fenton. Established c1818, the firm developed a colour printing process which allowed pot lids and printed jugs to be made cheaply, and in great quantity, after about 1850.

A Wedgwood black basalt Portland vase, the dipped ground bearing a frieze of Thetis awaiting Peleus, 19thC, 9½in (24cm) high.
£1,500–1,700 Bon

A Minton majolica vase, in the form of a putto with a scythe, decorated in green and yellow, seated with a basket of grapes at his side, on a blue-bordered mound base, shape No. 1197, some restoration, impressed marks for 1868, 11¾in (30cm) high.
£2,000–2,200 DN

A Pilkington Royal Lancastrian vase, decorated in lustre by William S. Mycock, on a mottled blue ground, impressed marks and painted monogram, late 19thC, 5¾in (14.5cm) high.
£500–600 DN

A pair of Minton majolica vases, the bases on plinths modelled as wooden platforms, enriched in blue, yellow, green and ochre glazes, slight damage, impressed marks and date codes for 1868, 6¼in (16cm) high.
£1,100–1,300 CSK

A pair of Wedgwood faïence blue and white urns and covers, damaged and repaired, impressed marks, date codes for 1875, 13in (33cm) high.
£1,300–1,500 CSK

A Doulton Lambeth stoneware compressed baluster-shaped vase, decorated by Arthur B. Barlow, with a band of scrolling leaves within stiff-leaf bands, impressed mark, incised signature and dated '1872', 9½in (24cm) high.
£480–550 DN

A majolica urn and cover, by Brown-Westhead & Co, the twin handles applied with husking, on a square plinth base, enriched in blue, brown, yellow and green glazes, c1875, 20½in (52cm) high.
£500–550 WL

A Wedgwood black basalt crocus pot and tray, in the form of a hedgehog, slight damage, 19thC, 7in (18cm) high.
£500–550 TMA

A Doulton blue and white vase, c1880, 9in (30cm) high.
£180–200 RAC

A Linthorpe vase or oil lamp base, shape No. 652, designed by Christopher Dresser, c1880, 10in (25.5cm) high.
£500–600 NCA

A Linthorpe vase, shape No. 227, designed by Christopher Dresser, c1880, 6in (15cm) high.
£340–380 NCA

A Doulton Lambeth stoneware vase, decorated with stylized flowers and foliage in blue and green glazes on a buff-coloured ground, by Frank A. Butler, incised monogram 'FAB', impressed factory mark and '1877', 20½in (52cm) high.
£500–600 WW

A pair of Royal Doulton stoneware vases, decorated with scrolling stylized floral and foliate branches in yellow, brown and green on a mottled beige ground, by Mark V. Marshall, c1880, 11½in (29cm) high.
£600–700 HCH

A Linthorpe vase, with Christopher Dresser and Henry Tooth facsimile, c1880, 7in (17.5cm) high.
£550–600 NCA

A pair of Doulton Lambeth ovoid vases, with short necks, each incised with leaves and leaf scrolls on a pale blue ground, decorator's monogram 'W.W.', impressed marks for 1883, 7½in (19cm) high.
£500–600 HOLL

A Doulton Holbein green vase, decorated with yellow rabbits, c1880–90, 5½in (14cm) high.
£180–200 PGA

A Linthorpe two-handled vase, shape No. 958, c1883, 5in (12.5cm) high.
£80–100 NCA

Cross Reference
See Colour Review

A Doulton Lambeth stoneware vase, by Hannah Barlow, with incised decoration, rim restored, impressed date '1883', 16in (40.5cm) high.
£500–600 EH

An Ault vase, with Christopher Dresser signature, c1890, 9in (23cm) high.
£800–1,000 NCA

A pair of Doulton Lambeth stoneware baluster-shaped vases, by Hannah Barlow, incised with a wide band of donkeys and calves, within green and brown leaf pattern borders, impressed date '1884', and Nos. '631' and '656', 9½in (24cm) high.
£900–1,000 CAG

A Linthorpe pottery vase, shape No. 24, c1883, 9½in (24cm) high.
£250–300 NCA

Shape No. 24 is probably the most common of the Linthorpe shapes. It was designed by Christopher Dresser and has 3 or 4 'dimples' impressed into the vase. Only early pieces carry Dresser's facsimile, without which the value is reduced. Prices also depend upon the quality and brilliance of the glaze.

A pair of moss ware vases, late 19thC, 3¾in (9.5cm) high.
£20–30 JMC

A pair of moss ware vases, late 19thC, 4¼in (11cm) high.
£20–30 JMC

A Wedgwood Art Pottery vase, probably by George Marsden, of broad baluster shape, decorated in autumnal-coloured slips with scrolling foliage against black, restored, c1885, 11in (28cm) high.
£180–220 DSG

A Burmantofts dimpled blue vase, c1885, 7¾in (19.5cm) high.
£300–330 NCA

A Burmantofts red two-handled vase, c1885, 11in (28cm) high.
£120–140 NCA

Miller's is a price GUIDE not a price LIST

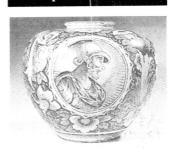

An Italian maiolica *vaso a palla*, probably Ginori factory, in the Venetian style, painted with a portrait of a bearded soldier and a lady, each within roundels on an *a foglie* ground, minor chips, 19thC, 13in (33cm) high.
£1,600–1,800 CSK

An Elton Ware eight-handled vase, with white, black and brown flowing glaze, c1885, 7½in (19cm) high.
£180–200 NCA

A Doulton Lambeth pottery vase, by Hannah Barlow, incised frieze of cattle and horses on moulded blue/green ground, impressed Art Union of London mark, late 19thC, 9½in (24cm) high.
£600–700 AH

▶ A pair of Quimper bud vases, monogrammed 'HB', c1885, 4½in (11.5cm) high.
£90–110 VH

A Wedgwood tricolour oviform urn and cover, applied in white with classically draped figures and trees, within moulded stiff-leaf paterae and anthemion borders, on a blue ground, enriched in gilt, damaged, impressed upper case mark, 19thC, 7in (17.5cm) high.
£400–500 CSK

A French faïence vase, decorated with flowers and butterflies on a white ground, 19thC, 9¾in (25cm) high.
£130–140 SER

A Martin Brothers two-handled vase, decorated with fish and seaweed, in brown, blue and green glaze, incised signature 'Martin Bros, London and Southall, 6–1888', 9in (23cm) high.
£1,600–1,800 RBB

A French lustreware vase, by Clement Massier, decorated with dense foliage, on a bronze mount, c1892, 11in (28cm) high.
£1,100–1,200 SUC

A Burmantofts faïence pottery vase, painted with a Persian-style design of flora and leaves in turquoise, brown, green and blue on a white ground, impressed mark, c1890, 9½in (24cm) high.
£360–400 P

A Doulton chiné vase, decorated with turquoise flowers, marked, 1885–1939, 3in (7.5cm) high.
£30–35 MAC

A Martin Brothers salt-glazed stoneware vase, incised with medallions enclosing masks and fruit-filled urns, in brown and pale blue, incised and dated '8–1894', 13½in (34.5cm) high.
£2,000–2,200 S(NY)

This and the item above are examples of the more conventional items made by the Martin Brothers.

A Carlton Ware two-handled vase, hand-painted with daisies, ribbon mark, c1890–94, 8¼in (21cm) high.
£70–80 StC

A Doulton Lambeth vase, by Rosina Harris, c1890, 7in (18cm) high.
£120–135 SnA

A pair of Doulton Lambeth stoneware vases, by Hannah B. Barlow and Florence E. Barlow, incised with ponies and trees, incised monogram, numbered '406' and '481', c1890, 27in (68.5cm) high.
£1,600–1,800 Bon

A pair of Carlton Ware vases, decorated with blue transfer-printed Petunia pattern, restored, blue crown mark, late 19thC, 9in (23cm) high.
£250–300 StC

A Carlton Ware vase, decorated with Marguerite pattern in red, blue and gilt Imari colours, restored, blue crown mark, late 19thC, 9in (23cm) high.
£150–200 StC

Further Reading

Miller's Art Nouveau & Art Deco Buyer's Guide, Miller's Publications, 1995

◄ A Doulton Burslem vase, painted with flowers on a white ground, signed by John Slater, c1890, 7½in (19cm) high.
£150–200 CSA

A pair of Sarreguemines stoneware vases, c1890, 9¼in (23.5cm) high.
£250–300 PC

◄ A Royal Doulton black and gold vase, c1890, 11in (28cm) high.
£85–100 RAC

A country slipware vase, with sgraffito decoration, c1890, 12in (30.5cm) high.
£130–160 IW

A Wedgwood gilt and bronzed black basalt vase and cover, moulded with festooned drapery between stiff-leaf, acanthus and bay leaf borders picked out in bronze gilding, impressed 'WEDGWOOD', late 19thC, 9in (23cm) high.
£2,300–2,500 Bon

An Ault two-handled vase, with Christopher Dresser signature, c1893, 8½in (21.5cm) high.
£800–1,000 NCA

An Ault vase, decorated with Chinese masks, designed by Christopher Dresser, c1893, 8in (20.5cm) high.
£1,000–1,200 NCA

A Brannam blue and green bulbous vase, with 3 swirling strap handles, incised fish-head decoration, monogrammed 'J D' for James Dewdney, c1890–1900, 12¾in (34.5cm) high.
£320–350 DA

A Burmantofts two-handled vase, with sunburst motifs, late 19thC, 9in (23cm) high.
£180–200 NCA

A Martin Brothers baluster-shaped vase, modelled in relief with starfish, on a matte blue ground, incised marks for January 1896, 11in (28cm) high.
£400–450 DN

A pair of Minton vases, with gilt rims, painted with lilac blossom on a pale green ground, by J. Hackley, signed, puce printed marks, c1891–1902, 9¾in (25cm) high.
£500–600 WL

A Burmantofts lime-green *solifleur* vase, late 19thC, 6in (15cm) high.
£85–100 NCA

A Baron vase, marked Barnstaple ware, c1894, 11in (28cm) high.
£130–150 NCA

► An Ault flower-holder, with Christopher Dresser facsimile signature, c1893, 4in (10cm) diam.
£180–200 NCA

A Martin Brothers vase, with buff and blue-washed ground, incised with aquatic creatures, the base incised 'Martin Bros, London and Southall', c1897, 9in (23cm) high.
£2,000–2,500 HYD

A Burmantofts lime-green vase, with a single handle, late 19thC, 11in (28cm) high.
£140–160 NCA

A Brannam vase, the neck with 3 scroll handles, incised and painted with a griffin, flowers and leaves, on a blue ground, incised mark and dated 1899, 12½in (31.5cm) high.
£300–350 DN

A Moorcroft Florian Ware vase, decorated with acanthus and floral scrolls, picked out in 2 tones of blue with white piping, signed, c1898, 3¼in (8.5cm) high.
£650–750 J&L

> Items in the Pottery section have been arranged in date order within each sub-section.

A Brannam pottery twin-handled vase, by James Dewdney, the body sgraffito-decorated with 2 panels each with a bird perched amid flora, in blue, green and brown, incised to base 'C. H. Brannam, Barum', and 'J. D. 1898', 16¾in (42.5cm) high.
£450–500 P

A stoneware vase, decorated with yellow flowers on a light green ground, marked to base 'DCS 1025', c1900, 19¼in (49cm) high.
£160–180 P(B)

A Moorcroft MacIntyre Florian ware vase, printed mark in brown and green, 1898–1905, 4in (10cm) high.
£400–500 RTo

A Martin Brothers salt-glazed stoneware vase, moulded as a ribbed six-sided pod with striations glazed in brown and black, set with 3 handles cast in the form of lizards with only hind legs, incised 'Martin Bros/London & Southall' and '11–1900', 11in (28cm) high.
£2,500–2,800 S(NY)

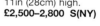

A Bretby Pottery vase, the base and collar simulating bronze, a central ivory-coloured band with Oriental-style mice and rabbits, c1900, 8½in (21.5cm) high.
£100–120 AAC

A Watcombe pottery oviform vase, with twin handles, painted in brown, black and pink with flowers and foliage on a white ground, c1900, 7¾in (19.5cm) high.
£60–70 DSG

A Brannam pottery vase, with loop handles, decorated in sgraffito with coloured slips in Art Nouveau style and with panels of fish, c1900, 19in (48.5cm) high.
£675–750 DSG

An Art Pottery vase, of double-gourd shape, decorated with streaked matte glaze with embossed floral mount on base, possibly French, c1900, 4in (10cm) high.
£140–160 SUC

An Art Nouveau vase, by Villeroy & Boch, with stylized orange and brown rose pattern, on a celadon ground, c1900, 19¾in (50cm) high.
£400–450 ANO

A Cantagalli lustre pottery vase, painted with a procession of Eastern figures on camels and people seated at a table in a rural setting, in purple, grey, yellow, blue and white, paper label to base, painter's cockerel monogram, c1900, 20in (51cm) high.
£1,300–1,500 P

An Amphora earthenware vase, the rim modelled in high relief with bats, glazed in shades of tan, yellow, green, brown and ivory heightened in gilt, impressed, c1900, 21in (53.5cm) high.
£4,000–4,500 S(NY)

An Amphora earthenware vase, applied with a large dragon with outspread wings, with a landscape of leafy trees glazed in shades of tan, ivory and gold on a lavender and white ground, impressed, c1900, 21in (53.5cm) high.
£3,200–3,600 S(NY)

A Moorcroft MacIntyre Peacock Feather pattern vase, c1900, 5in (12.5cm) high.
£700–800 HEA

A pair of Royal Doulton stoneware vases, each with a narrow neck and splayed rim, with a frieze of floral swags and blue lower band, c1900–10, 10¼in (26cm) high.
£160–200 P(B)

A pair of Bretby tall waisted vases, with Islamic-style frieze, decorated in green, yellow, red and blue overlaid with gilt, c1900, 12½in (32cm) high.
£100–120 P(B)

A pair of Doulton baluster vases, with everted rims, on a blue and treacle reserve, impressed marks, c1900, 13½in (34.5cm) high.
£320–360 GAK

A William Moorcroft Florian Ware vase, decorated with Narcissus pattern, in shades of yellow and blue, c1900, 9in (23cm) high.
£2,200–2,600 RUM

A Doulton Lambeth black vase, with blue and gold central band, c1900, 13½in (34.5cm) high.
£175–200 PAC

A Foley Intarsio vase, designed by Frederick Rhead, decorated with Watermill and Asparagus Trees pattern, in shades of blue, green and red, c1890–1900, 9in (23cm) high.
£450–500 PGA

A Moorcroft Florian Ware vase, c1900, 8½in (21.5cm) high.
£500–600 HEA

A Carlton Ware vase, enamelled with Old Wisteria transfer pattern, No. 2238, blue crown mark, early 20thC, 9¼in (23.5cm) high.
£80–100 StC

A Carlton Ware vase, enamelled with Parrots pattern, slight damage, black crown mark, early 20thC, 6½in (16.5cm) high.
£20–30 StC

A Zuid Holland pottery vase, the shoulders painted with mauve flowers and green leaves, marked, c1900, 6in (15cm) high.
£180–200 P

A vase, by N. S. A. Brantjes & Co, Holland, c1900, 8¼in (21cm) diam.
£500–600 OO

An Aller Vale tyg vase, decorated with Scandy pattern, inscribed 'Never say die', c1900, 4¼in (11cm) high.
£20–25 ATQ

A Mettlach pottery vase, designed by Hans Christiansen, decorated with the head of a maiden and pink, white and blue irises on a blue ground, maker's marks, c1900, 10in (25.5cm) high.
£1,300–1,500 P

A Moorcroft vase, decorated with vine leaves and grapes in cream, fawn and black on a mottled green and brown ground, early 20thC, 9¾in (25cm) high.
£550–650 DDM

◄ A Moorcroft Florian Ware vase, slight rim restoration, the base signed 'W. M. Des' in green, c1900, 8¼in (21.5cm) high.
£850–950 GAK

A Watcombe pottery udder vase, decorated with Sandringham pattern, slight damage, c1901–20, 4in (10cm) high.
£20–30 PC

This design was known as Sandringham, apparently in honour of Queen Alexandra, who liked the design so much that she commissioned a special order for her own use.

A William Moorcroft Florian Ware vase, decorated with Iris pattern in shades of pink and green, c1902, 8in (20.5cm) high.
£650–750 RUM

A Moorcroft MacIntyre Florian Ware vase, tube-lined with anemones and leaves on a shaded blue ground, rim chip, printed mark in brown and registration No. 326471, signed in green 'W. Moorcroft Dec', c1900, 8½in (21.5cm) high.
£200–250 DN

A Moorcroft MacIntyre Florian Ware vase, the bottle-shaped body tube-line decorated and painted in shades of blue with stylized iris and scrolling leaves, printed and painted marks, c1900, 8in (20.5cm) high.
£650–700 EH

A pair of Moorcroft MacIntyre Florian Ware spill vases, decorated in shades of cornflower blue with flowers and foliage, printed mark and signed 'W. Moorcroft Des' in green, c1900, 7in (18cm) high.
£1,300–1,500 GAK

A Weller 'Sicardo' lustre vase, by Jacques Sicard, American, c1901, 5in (12.5cm) high.
£500–550 YAN

This vase was retailed through Tiffany's in New York.

A Bernard Moore red lustre vase, with a dragon sketched in gold and black, c1901–05, 10in (25.5cm) high.
£500–600 NCA

A Bernard Moore red lustre vase, with sailing ship sketched in black, c1901–05, 9in (23cm) high.
£250–300 NCA

A Bernard Moore red lustre vase, with a dragon in gold, blue and ivory, c1901–05, 7in (17.5cm) high.
£550–650 NCA

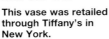

A Watcombe pinch vase, decorated with Wild Rose pattern in shades of pink and green on a white ground, c1901–20, 3¼in (8.5cm) high.
£20–30 BEV

A pair of Royal Doulton stoneware vases, decorated in muted colours with continuous landscape panels, on a dark blue ground, c1902–22, 7½in (19cm) high.
£225–250 POW

A Pilkington vase, with feathered blue, green and brown crystalline glaze effect, incised mark, c1903, 8in (20.5cm) high.
£550–600 PGA

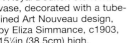

A Royal Doulton stoneware vase, decorated with a tube-lined Art Nouveau design, by Eliza Simmance, c1903, 15¼in (38.5cm) high.
£950–1,100 BWe

A Royal Doulton lobed baluster-shaped vase, with flared rim, decorated by Eliza Simmance in coloured enamels with stylized flowers and leaves, on a white ground, impressed and incised marks, c1903, 11¼in (28.5cm) high.
£600–700 DN

A Gouda pottery vase, made for Liberty's, c1903, 20in (51cm) high.
£350–400 OO

◄ A Longpark two-handled vase, with fluted rim, decorated with yellow daffodils on a green and brown ground, c1903–09, 5½in (14cm) high.
£60–70 PC

Vases & Urns • POTTERY 171

A Moorcroft vase, with floral and foliage moulded decoration in greens and blues in William Morris style, slight repair, c1902, 13in (33cm) high.
£450–500 RBB

A Pilkington bottle vase, designed by Walter Crane and decorated by Richard Joyce, c1907, 10in (25.5cm) high.
£1,800–2,000 SUC

A Moorcroft Claremont design vase, with a smoky blue ground, chipped, printed mark of Liberty and Co, green signature beneath, early 20thC, 7½in (19cm) high.
£800–900 WL

An Aller Vale udder vase, decorated with cream and blue scrolls, minor damage, c1891–1902, 4in (10cm) high.
£10–15 PC

A Della Robbia Persian-style vase, signed 'C.A.W.', c1903, 15in (38cm) high.
£270–300 ZEI

A Royal Doulton vase, decorated by Eliza Simmance, with impressed and incised mark, c1903, 13¾in (35cm) high.
£600–700 DN

A Martin Brothers vase, incised with birds on a buff ground, c1903, 5¾in (14.5cm) high.
£300–400 HYD

An Arts and Crafts pottery vase, possibly by Bernard Moore, with pewter mounts and hand-beaten finish, c1905, 7in (18cm) high.
£80–100 P(B)

A Poole Pottery moulded vase, designed by Owen Carter, the white stoneware covered with a red/gold lustre glaze, incised in script 'Carters Poole 1905', 12½in (32cm) high.
£400–480 PP

A bronze lustre vase, by Boch Frères, Keramis, decorated with irises, c1905, 15¾in (40cm) high.
£700–800 ANO

A Bernard Moore red lustre vase, with crab design by Edward R. Wilkes, c1905, 10in (25.5cm) high.
£250–300 NCA

A Gouda pottery two-handled vase, decorated by Van der Heydt, c1905, 18in (46cm) high.
£1,200–1,400 OO

A Doulton vase, with blue and brown glaze, early 20thC, 3½in (9cm) high.
£30–40 MAC

A Moorcroft globular vase, decorated with Claremont pattern, with red and yellow toadstools against a green ground, c1905, 11in (28cm) high.
£2,500–3,000 DSG

A Gouda Pottery vase, painted by P. Woerlee, signed, c1906, 8½in (21cm) high.
£600–700 OO

A Bernard Moore flambé vase, decorated with a Viking longship in turquoise and lustrous red against a dawn background, detailed with gilding, printed mark, numbered '1068', c1906, 7½in (19cm) high.
£500–600 C

A Royal Winton Grimwades green lustre vase, c1910, 7in (17.5cm) high.
£40–45 DSG

A Royal Doulton stoneware vase, the body decorated with heart-shaped cartouches filled with flowers and leaves on a dark blue ground, neck and foot in mottled green, c1910–20, 16in (41cm) high.
£85–100 P(B)

A Wood & Sons Korea ware vase, designed by Frederick Rhead, decorated with flowers and peacocks in yellow and white on a black ground, c1910, 6in (15cm) high.
£40–50 DSG

A Hele Cross vase, decorated with a parrot and trees, c1905–18, 5¼in (13.5cm) high.
£25–30 PC

A Royal Doulton Lambeth vase, with applied decoration, initialled 'BH', No. 2/58, c1910, 3in (7.5cm) high.
£100–120 TP

A Longpark tyg vase, decorated with pattern No. NI, inscribed 'Gude things be scarce', c1910–20, 4½in (11cm) high.
£20–25 ATQ

◄ A Royal Doulton stoneware oviform vase, decorated in relief with swags of fruit and flowers, picked out in amber, dark blue and pale blue glazes, c1910, 4¾in (12cm) high.
£45–55 RAC

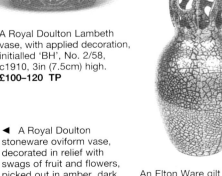

An Elton Ware gilt crackle ground vase, c1910, 13½in (34.5cm) high.
£800–900 NCA

A Lancastrian vase, with striated blue glaze effect, c1913, 11in (28cm) high.
£400–450 PGA

A Weller pottery vase, decorated in sunken relief with floral panels, picked out in colours, American, c1910, 8½in (21.5cm) high.
£145–165 DSG

A Rookwood pottery oviform vase, decorated in relief with daffodils beneath a matt and muted blue glaze, c1912, 9in (23cm) high.
£220–260 YAN

A Carter & Co oviform vase, covered overall with a tin glaze and painted in naturalistic colours, marked 'Carter & Co', c1915–21, 13in (33cm) high.
£280–350 HarC

A Chris Lanooij vase, signed, c1913, 6½in (16.5cm) high.
£150–180 OO

A Roseville pottery vase, decorated in shallow relief with wisteria, picked out in naturalistic colours against streaky brown, American, c1915, 6in (15cm) high.
£300–350 MSB

A Carter & Co pottery vase, decorated in underglaze blue with figures in panels, signed 'Carter & Co, Poole', c1915, 8in (20,5cm) high.
£400–450 P(B)

◄ A Moorcroft vase, decorated with Wisteria pattern, signed, c1918, 3½in (9cm) high.
£270–300 CEX

A Moorcroft vase, decorated with late Florian design, c1916, 8in (20.5cm) high.
£1,800–2,200 RUM

A Wood & Sons ovoid vase, designed by Frederick Rhead, decorated with Chung pattern in shades of blue on a red ground, c1918, 8in (20.5cm) high.
£100–120 PC

A Wood & Sons blue and white waisted vase, designed by Frederick Rhead, decorated with Prunus pattern, c1916, 8½in (22cm) high.
£65–80 PC

A Moorcroft Claremont vase, decorated with Toadstool pattern, on a shaded blue/green ground, maker's mark and initials, c1918, 7in (18cm) high.
£700–770 RIT

A pair of Doulton Slater's patent vases, with pink floral tube-lined decoration on a buff ground, c1920, 8¾in (22cm) high.
£180–220 P(B)

A William Moorcroft late Florian Ware vase, c1918, 12in (30.5cm) high.
£1,000–1,200 HEA

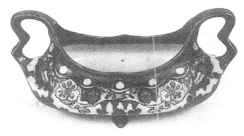

A Gouda vase, decorated with Corona pattern, on 3 feet, c1919, 12½in (32cm) wide.
£200–250 OO

A Carter, Stabler & Adams vase, painted by Nellie Bishton with Grape pattern in shades of purple, red and green with yellow rim, impressed backstamp, 1920s, 6in (15cm) high.
£80–100 HarC

A Wilton orange lustre vase, with geisha girl design and lustre interior, c1920, 10in (25.5cm) high.
£200–250 PGA

A Moorcroft two-handled vase, with Pomegranate design, green signature, repaired, c1920, 14in (35.5cm) high.
£1,000–1,200 RBB

Pomegranate became Moorcroft's most successful design, and remained in production until the late 1930s.

A Moorcroft Flambé vase, decorated with Ochre Poppy design on a blue/grey ground, c1920, 6½in (16.5cm) high.
£1,000–1,100 RBB

A Poole Pottery vase, 1920s, 7½in (19cm) high.
£45–50 WAC

A Longpark udder vase, decorated with yellow daffodils, black rubber stamp mark, 1918–25, 6in (15cm) high.
£40–50 PC

A ceramic vase, by Boch Frères, Kéramis Potteries, Belgium, decorated with orange and black, c1920, 10½in (26.5cm) high.
£100–120 GOO

Wares produced by Boch Frères at Keramis from the 1920s to the 1940s represent an important contribution to Belgian Art Deco. All pieces from this period are white-bodied.

▶ An Aller Vale vase, decorated in shades of blue and brown on an off-white ground, inscribed 'All's well that ends well', c1920, 4in (10cm) high.
£30–40 BEV

A Susie Cooper lustre vase, by Gray's Pottery, decorated in blue with orange, red and gold design, 1920s, 9in (23cm) high.
£450–500 PGA

A Susie Cooper lustre vase, by Gray's Pottery, decorated in red with blue, white and gold design, 1920s, 7in (18cm) high.
£500–600 PGA

A Moorcroft vase, tube-lined with pansies beneath a rich flambé glaze, impressed and painted marks, c1919–45, 13in (33cm) high.
£900–1,000 S(S)

A Barton Pottery vase, decorated with a seagull, c1920, 6in (15cm) high.
£40–50 AnE

A Susie Cooper lustre vase, by Gray's Pottery, decorated with a gold stag on a white ground, 1920s, 12in (30.5cm) high.
£600–650 PGA

A Quimper vase, marked 'HB Quimper', c1920, 10in (25.5cm) high.
£140–160 MofC

A William Moorcroft vase, decorated with purple grapes and vine leaves on a green ground, signed and inscribed, 1920s, 14½in (37cm) high.
£550–600 Mit

A Hancock's Rubens ware pomegranate vase, c1920, 9in (23cm) high.
£70–80 CSA

A Gouda vase, with Egyptian design c1924, 8¼in (21cm) high.
£220–250 OO

◄ A Gouda vase, decorated with Shinski design, c1924, 10½in (26.5cm) high.
£200–250 OO

A Carlton Ware vase, c1925, 4¼in (11cm) high.
£40–50 CSA

Gouda

Established in 1898, Gouda made hand-painted earthenware items, many of which were exported to Britain. Although good condition is important, restoration is acceptable on Gouda pieces.

A William Moorcroft vase, decorated with Pansy pattern c1925, 6in (15cm) high.
£300–350 HEA

A Carlton Ware vase and cover, c1925, 7½in (19cm) high.
£70–80 CSA

► A William Moorcroft two-handled vase, decorated with Wisteria pattern in shades of orange, yellow and brown on a blue ground, c1925, 8in (20.5cm) high.
£1,000–1,200 NP

A Lemon & Crute posy case, decorated with heather in shades of blue, green and mauve, c1925, 3in (7.5cm) high.
£10–15 TPCS

A Moorcroft vase, decorated with Wisteria pattern, c1925, 6in (15cm) high.
£350–400 RUM

A Moorcroft two-handled vase, decorated with Cornflower pattern, impressed mark, signed and dated '1927', 12¾in (32.5cm) high.
£3,000–3,500 SK

A Ruskin high-fired flambé vase, with 4 lug handles, decorated with a red and grey flecked glaze, dated '1927', 11½in (29cm) high.
£1,600–1,800 BWe

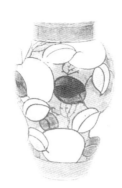

◀ A Bursley Ware vase, by Charlotte Rhead, pattern No. 735, c1926, 7in (18cm) high.
£150–180 HEA

A William Moorcroft vase, decorated with Chevron Landscape design in the Eventide palate, in shades of blue and orange, c1926, 9in (23cm) high.
£2,500–3,000 RUM

A Moorcroft vase, decorated with leaves and berries on a woodsmoke ground, signed, c1927, 6¼in (16cm) high.
£425–475 CEX

A Poole Pottery vase, painted with flowerheads, berries and scrolling foliage, impressed mark, c1927, 9½in (24cm) high.
£75–90 HYD

◀ A Moorcroft vase, decorated with Pomegranate pattern, signed, c1928, 3½in (9cm) high.
£250–285 CEX

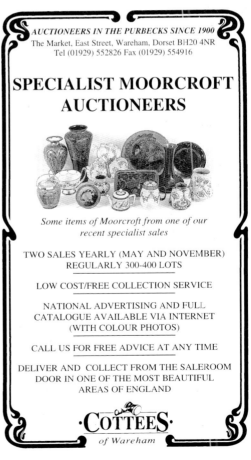

A Moorcroft baluster-shaped vase, decorated with orchid-type flowers on a blue ground, c1930, 11¾in (29.5cm) high.
£250–300 P(C)

A pair of Art Deco Carlton Ware vases, painted with abstract floral blooms and berry clusters in red, yellow, green, mauve and black against a blue ground, marked, c1930, 8in (20.5cm) high.
£200–240 P

A Carter, Stabler & Adams vase, c1930, 9in (23cm) high.
£80–100 GOO

A Gouda vase, decorated with yellow and green design, c1930, 8½in (21.5cm) high.
£60–70 CSA

A Royal Doulton vase, decorated in blue, orange and yellow, 1930s, 4¾in (12cm) high.
£40–50 TAC

A Crown Devon vase, decorated with trees and flowers on a brown ground, 1930s, 5¼in (13.5cm) high.
£130–145 WAC

A Wedgwood pottery vase, designed by Keith Murray, decorated with horizontal ribbing beneath a cream-coloured glaze, c1930, 6½in (16.5cm) high.
£400–450 PGA

A Moorcroft pale blue glazed vase, c1930, 6in (15cm) high.
£150–180 DAC

A Moorcroft vase, decorated with leaves and berries in yellow, red and green, full signature and inscribed 'Potter to the Queen', c1930, 7in (18cm) high.
£450–500 PGA

◄ A Carter, Stabler & Adams twin-handled vase, designed by Truda Carter, c1930, 7in (18cm) high.
£275–300 RDG

A SylvaC lustre vase, decorated with a parrot, in shades of green, blue, pink and yellow, 1930s, 11in (28cm) high.
£90–100 PAC

◄ A Carter, Stabler & Adams pottery vase, designed by Truda Carter, decorated by Marjorie Batt, 1928–34, 8¾in (22cm) high.
£350–400 ADE

A Carter, Stabler & Adams vase, designed by Truda Carter, decorated by Ann Hatchard, 1928–34, 8¾in (22cm) high.
£450–500 ADE

A Carter, Stabler & Adams vase, designed by Truda Carter, decorated by Ann Hatchard, 1928–34, 7½in (19cm) high.
£450–500 ADE

A Carter, Stabler & Adams vase, designed by Truda Carter, decorated by Vera Bridle with Blue Bird pattern, 1928–33, 8¾in (22cm) high.
£250–300 ADE

A Carter, Stabler & Adams vase, designed by Truda Adams, decorated with blue, orange, mauve and green stylized flowers, slight damage, c1930, 14½in (37cm) high.
£700–800 RDG

A pair of Crown Devon vases, 1930s, 9¼in (23.5cm) high.
£90–100 AAC

A Royal Cauldon vase, designed by Frederick Rhead, minor rim damage, c1930, 10in (25.5cm) high.
£50–60 DSG

▶ A Bretby globular vase, with trumpet-form neck, covered overall with a glaze resembling random splashes of blue, grey/brown and muted yellow, marked, c1930, 5¼in (13.5cm) high.
£40–50 DSG

A James Kent miniature vase, decorated with Hydrangea pattern, 1930s, 2½in (6.5cm) high.
£40–50 BEV

LOCATE THE SOURCE
The source of each illustration in Miller's can be found by checking the code letters below each caption with the Key to Illustrations, pages 376–379.

A Carter, Stabler & Adams vase, designed by Truda Adams, decorated with Persian deer pattern in shades of yellow, mauve and greeπn, c1930, 11in (28cm) high.
£450–500 RDG

A Carter, Stabler & Adams vase, designed by Truda Adams, decorated with Blue Bird pattern, 1930s, 6in (15cm) high.
£75–100 RDG

A Wedgwood vase, designed by Keith Murray, finished in Moonstone glaze, 1930s, 6½in (16.5cm) high.
£375–400 BEV

The white semi-matte Moonstone glaze was phased out from c1940, and was followed by the matte green and matte straw ranges.

A Wedgwood vase, designed by Keith Murray, finished in black matte glaze, 1930s, 4¼in (11cm) high.
£550–600 BEV

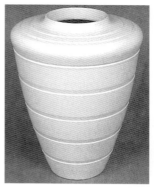

A Wedgwood vase, designed by Keith Murray, finished in white matte glaze, 1930s, 11in (28cm) high.
£225–250 BEV

A Wedgwood vase, designed by Keith Murray, finished in white matte glaze, 1930s, 6½in (16.5cm) high.
£175–200 BET

A Wedgwood vase, designed by Keith Murray, finished in straw-coloured matte glaze, 1930s, 7¼in (18.5cm) high.
£200–225 BEV

A Wedgwood vase, designed by Keith Murray, with green matte glaze, 1930s, 7in (18cm) high.
£175–200 BET

A William Moorcroft salt-glazed vase, decorated with Fish pattern in shades of beige and grey, c1930, 8in (20.5cm) high.
£1,200–1,400 RUM

Keith Murray

Having trained as an architect, Keith Murray's background is evident in the design of his ceramic wares during the 1930s and 1940s. Murray's work is recognizable for its simple geometric forms and lack of surface embellishment. He specialized in vases, which are often ribbed or fluted.

From 1932 to 1948, Murray worked for Wedgwood as an outside designer. He returned to architecture after 1948, but Wedgwood continued using his shapes for several years. His work was shown at many national and international exhibitions, and in 1936 he became one of Britain's first Royal Designers for Industry.

A Crown Ducal vase, designed by Charlotte Rhead, decorated with Persian Rose pattern, c1930, 8½in (21cm) high.
£250–280 YY

A William Moorcroft Fish and Waterweed pattern vase, with flambé glaze, 1930s, 9½in (24cm) high.
£1,500–1,800 HEA

A Denby Regent Pastel vase, designed by Donald Gilbert, decorated with penguins, 1930s, 10½in (26.5cm) high.
£300–330 KES

A Crown Ducal vase, by Charlotte Rhead, decorated in green, orange, red and gilt on a pale mottled green ground, with a dragon chasing an eternal pearl, printed factory marks and facsimile signature, c1930, 12¼in (31cm) high.
£75–90 P(E)

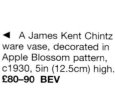

◄ A James Kent Chintz ware vase, decorated in Apple Blossom pattern, c1930, 5in (12.5cm) high.
£80–90 BEV

A Winchcombe Pottery vase, designed by Michael Cardew, some damage, c1930, 5½in (14cm) high.
£120–140 IW

A Winchcombe Pottery vase, 1930s, 11¾in (30cm) high.
£170–200 IW

A Poole Pottery vase, designed by Truda Carter, decorated with pattern BX, impressed and painted marks, c1930, 11in (28cm) high.
£650–750 DN

A Poole Pottery vase, c1930, 9in (23cm) high.
£70–80 JO

A Daison Torquay two-handled vase, after Linthorpe, c1930, 5in (7.5cm) high.
£180–220 NCA

A Reid & Co Roslyn hand-painted lustre vase, c1930, 10in (25.5cm) high.
£70–80 BKK

A Royal Stanley vase, decorated with clematis, c1930, 12in (30.5cm) high.
£135–160 DSG

A Royal Doulton flambé vase, decorated with a country landscape, c1930s, 11in (30cm) high.
£300–350 YY

Myott & Son

The company was founded in Stoke-on-Trent in 1898, moved to Cobridge, Staffordshire, in 1902 and to Hanley in 1947. Their distinctive vases, with bold geometric shapes and colourful decoration, were typical of the Art Deco style, and are very collectable today. Unfortunately, following a fire in 1947, all the early pattern records were lost.

A Hancock & Sons pottery vase, designed by Mollie Hancock, decorated with Waterlily pattern in shades of red, yellow, green and pink, c1930, 9in (23cm) high.
£120–140 CSA

▶ A Myott Castle vase, painted in brown, orange and black, c1930, 8½in (21.5cm) high.
£180–200 BKK

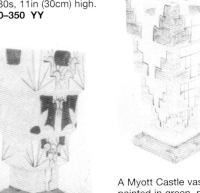

A Myott Castle vase, painted in green, pink, blue and mauve, c1930, 8½in (21.5cm) high.
£180–200 BKK

A Myott Torpedo shape vase, c1930, 8½in (21.5cm) high.
£280–300 BKK

A Myott Pyramid vase, decorated in orange, brown and green, c1934, 9in (23cm) high.
£140–160 BEV

A Myott Pyramid vase, with orange flowers, c1931, 8¾in (22cm) high.
£160–180 BKK

A Crown-Devon wall vase, hand-decorated in green and blue, pattern No. H422, c1934, 7½in (19cm) high.
£70–80 BKK

A Carter, Stabler & Adams Sylvan oviform vase, with horizontal banding beneath a muted green glaze with brown speckling, 1934–37, 9in (23cm) high.
£125–150 ADE

A Burleigh Ware vase, in the form of a sailing boat, c1932, 6in (15cm) high.
£75–90 BKK

A Burleigh Ware double vase, hand-painted in green and red on a yellow ground, c1933, 8in (20.5cm) high.
£100–120 BKK

A bulbous stoneware pot, by Charles Vyse, with red rust, black and green glaze, incised 'CV 1933', 5in (12.5cm) high.
£160–180 Bon

A Crown Devon enamelled vase, with gilt rims, c1935, 7in (18cm) high.
£40–50 CSA

A Crown Derby lustre vase, decorated with an enamelled Chinese landscape scene, c1935, 5in (12.5cm) high.
£30–40 CSA

A double-handled vase, with Manchu design, c1935, 5½in (13.5cm) high.
£100–120 HEA

A Crown Ducal vase, decorated with Green Patch pattern, c1935, 6½in (16cm) high.
£35–45 HEA

A Crown Ducal vase, decorated with pattern No. 5623, by Charlotte Rhead, c1935, 7½in (19cm) high.
£125–150 HEA

◄ A Byzantine vase, by Charlotte Rhead, c1935, 6in (15cm) high.
£125–150 HEA

► A Denby grey vase with handle, decorated with tubeline design in cobalt blue, mid-1930s, 7in (17.5cm) high.
£80–90 KES

A Thomas Forrest footed vase, decorated in Syrian pattern, 1930s, 7½in (19cm) high.
£150–180 BKK

A Manchu design vase, by Charlotte Rhead, c1935, 9½in (24cm) high.
£150–180 HEA

A Shorter tulip-shaped posy vase, in shades of yellow and green, c1935, 5in (12.5cm) high.
£25–30 CSA

A Carter, Stabler & Adams cylindrical-shaped vase, decorated with stylized flowers and leaves in an abstract design on an off-white ground, decorator's initials 'X & Y O', c1935, 12in (30.5cm) high.
£120–140 GAK

A Susie Cooper vase, with matte blue glaze, impressed decoration and incised signature, c1935, 7½in (19cm) high.
£80–90 CSA

A Wedgwood vase, designed by Keith Murray, decorated with horizontal banding beneath a straw-coloured glaze, c1935, 11¼in (28.5cm) high.
£400–450 ADE

A Crown Ducal vase, pattern No. 4521, c1936, 8½in (21cm) high.
£75–90 HEA

A Denby matte-glazed vase, designed by Alice Teichner, c1937, 8in (20.5cm) high.
£80–90 PC

A Crown Ducal ovoid vase, designed by Charlotte Rhead, decorated in shades of brown and orange on a speckled beige ground, pattern No. 4968, c1937, 7in (18cm) high.
£220–250 PC

A Burleigh Ware green vase, relief-moulded with flat-glazed Swan pattern, c1937, 7½in (19cm) high.
£100–120 BKK

A Crown Ducal vase, pattern No. 5411, designed by Charlotte Rhead, c1938, 5½in (13.5cm) high.
£80–100 HEA

► A Carter, Stabler & Adams vase, designed by Ruth Pavely, decorated in blues, browns, orange and grey with geometric flowers, foliage and chevrons, 1938–42, 10½in (26.5cm) high.
£800–900 ADE

Further Reading

Miller's Twentieth-Century Ceramics, Miller's Publications, 1999

◄ A Crown Ducal vase, pattern No. 5391, designed by Charlotte Rhead, c1938, 8in (20.5cm) high.
£180–220 HEA

A Crown Ducal vase,
by Charlotte Rhead,
pattern No. 6016, c1939,
7in (17.5cm) high.
£100–130 HEA

A Bursley Ware vase,
designed by Charlotte
Rhead, decorated in
shades of pink, blue and
beige, pattern No. TL 76,
1940s, 8½in (21cm) high.
£170–200 PC

A Moorcroft vase,
decorated with Anemone
pattern on a woodsmoke
ground, c1950,
4½in (11.5cm) high.
£200–220 CEX

Items in the Pottery
section have been
arranged in date order
within each sub-section.

A Moorcroft slender
baluster vase, decorated
with Pomegranate
pattern, c1940,
12½in (32cm) high.
£300–350 WW

A Bursley Ware vase,
designed by Charlotte
Rhead, decorated with
pink and blue flowers
on a white ground with
a brown rim, pattern
No. TL 4, 1940s,
12½in (32cm) high.
£350–400 PC

A Moorcroft vase,
decorated with Hibiscus
pattern, 1950s,
3¾in (9.5cm) high.
£160–175 CEX

A Maling ware vase,
with blue Rosine pattern,
c1940, 8in (20.5cm) high.
£80–100 CSA

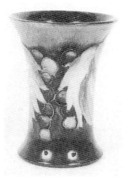

A Moorcroft vase, with
Leaf and Berry design,
c1946, 4in (10cm) high.
£300–350 HEA

A Midwinter vase,
brown with white
interior and wire
insert, impressed
mark, 1950s,
5in (12.5cm) high.
£40–50 GIN

A Bursley Ware vase,
designed by Charlotte
Rhead, decorated in
shades of yellow, brown
and orange, pattern
No. TL 5, 1940s,
6in (15cm) high.
£100–120 PC

A Moorcroft vase,
decorated with
Hibiscus pattern in
white and yellow on
a blue ground, c1949,
11in (28cm) high.
£425–475 DAC

A Crown Devon vase,
decorated in pale
turquoise with gilt rims,
c1950, 6in (15cm) high.
£15–20 CSA

◄ A Denby vase,
designed by Glyn
Colledge, c1950,
12½in (32cm) high.
£130–150 RAC

**Denby's most
important post-war
designer was Glyn
Colledge, and his
work is increasingly
sought after today.**

A Moorcroft Flambé vase, decorated in red tones with vine leaves and berries, c1950, 13in (33cm) high.
£1,850–2,200 DSG

A Denby vase, designed by Glyn Colledge, c1950, 10in (25.5cm) high.
£60–70 RAC

A Crown Devon lustre vase, decorated with enamelled Chinese landscape scene, c1950, 12in (30.5cm) high.
£150–170 CSA

A Walter Moorcroft vase, decorated with African Lily pattern, in shades of terracotta and yellow on a green ground, c1950, 5in (12.5cm) high.
£350–400 RUM

A stoneware pear-shaped pot, by Hans Coper, the buff textured base curving upwards to dark brown neck and flattened rim, impressed 'HC' seal, c1952, 13½in (34.5cm) high.
£3,000–3,300 Bon

A stoneware 'treacle' pot, by Hans Coper, with shiny amber-coloured glaze over a buff and brown tapering body, impressed 'HC' seal, early 1950s, 6in (15cm) high.
£4,500–5,000 Bon

Hans Coper

Renowned for his strong innovative forms and unusual glazes, Hans Coper was one of the best-known studio potters of the early 20thC, and worked closely with Lucie Rie. Unusual shapes with little additional decoration are hallmarks of many of his vases.

Hans Coper marked his wares with an impressed 'HC' cipher, resembling a potter's wheel on its side.

A Rye Pottery vase, 1950s, 4½in (11.5cm) high.
£50–60 NCA

A celadon crackle-glaze vase, by James Walford, c1950, 4¼in (11cm) high.
£80–100 IW

A 'tripot', by Hans Coper, with beige and brown geometric decoration and indications of carmine, c1956, 7¾in (19.5cm) high.
£5,500–6,500 Bon

► A Royal Copenhagen vase, with abstract design, 1950s–60s, 4⅛in (11.5cm) high.
£40–50 YY

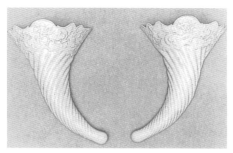

A pair of Staffordshire salt-glazed stoneware spirally moulded cornucopia-shaped wall pockets, restored, c1750, 9½in (24cm) high.
£500–600 DN

A Staffordshire wall pocket, c1765, 6½in (16.5cm) high.
£650–750 JHo

A pair of Pratt-type wall cornucopiae, each moulded with Cupid and a quiver of arrows, one depicting him drinking from a flask, the other holding a flaming vase, damaged and restored, probably Scottish, c1810, 12in (30.5cm) high.
£500–550 Bon

A pair of Royal Worcester majolica wall brackets, each supported by a pair of putti within a frieze of fruiting vines above a single cherub mask, restored, c1870, 9¾in (25cm) high.
£1,700–1,900 CSK

A Desvres wall pocket, c1880, 8in (20.5cm) high.
£100–120 PSA

A pair of William Brownfield majolica wall brackets, each modelled with a female mask above drapes, within scroll panels issuing oak leaves and swags of fruit, slight damage, impressed marks, date codes for 1882 and 1881, 9¾in (25cm) high.
£2,300–2,500 CSK

A pair of Cantagalli maiolica wall brackets, each supported on a putto astride a mythical sea creature, c1900, 17in (43cm) high.
£700–800 TMA

A Quimper wall horn, decorated with a figure on a cream ground, marked, c1885, 10in (25.5cm) high.
£180–200 VH

A Quimper posy holder, marked 'HB', c1920, 11in (28cm) high.
£100–120 MofC

An Arthur Wood hand-painted wall pocket, c1930, 9in (23cm) high.
£30–35 BKK

◄ A SylvaC wall pocket, depicting a rabbit, coloured in beige and green, 1930s, 7¾in (20cm) high.
£30–35 MEG

► A Burleigh Ware wall vase, the top decorated with a wreath, c1935, 7¾in (20cm) high.
£25–30 CSA

A Kensington Pottery wall vase, c1935, 7½in (19cm) high.
£20–30 CSA

A Crown Devon wall vase. c1935, 7½in (19cm) high.
£20–30 CSA

A Royal Winton wall vase, c1940, 3¾in (22cm) high.
£35–40 CSA

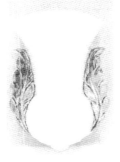

A Shorter wall pocket, c1940, 7in (18cm) high.
£15–20 CSA

WHISTLES

A Staffordshire whistle, in the form of an admiral, 19thC, 3¼in (8.5cm) high.
£170–200 TVM

▶ A Staffordshire whistle, in the form of a white bird on a green branch, 19thC, 2½in (6.5cm) high.
£120–150 TVM

A Staffordshire whistle, in the form of a white owl on a green branch, 19thC, 2¼in (6.5cm) high.
£150–180 TVM

▶ A Staffordshire whistle, in the form of a pierrot wearing an orange coat, on green moulded base, 19thC, 3½in (9cm) high.
£150–200 TVM

Pottery whistles were produced purely as decorative items.

A Yorkshire bird whistle, early 19thC, 5in (13cm) high.
£500–600 JHo

A Staffordshire whistle, The Cleric, wearing a blue robe, on a yellow base, 19thC, 2¼in (5.5cm) high.
£150–180 TVM

MISCELLANEOUS

A Rye Pottery model of a carpenter's bag, c1890, 5in (12.5cm) high.
£130–150 NCA

Two SylvaC pottery book ends, in the form of rabbits, coloured in beige and green, slight damage, 1930s, 5in (12.5cm) high.
£18–20 MEG

A Carter, Stabler & Adams white earthenware book end, designed by John Adams, shape No. 831, impressed marks, c1935, 8in (20.5cm) high.
£250–300 PP

A Bristol pottery barrel, painted with flowers and initialled 'JC', c1830, 4¾in (12cm) high.
£300–350 DAN

◄ A Carlton Ware bitters dispenser, with orange base, silver top and black transfer-printed figures, shape No. 304, black crown mark, 1920s, 7in (18cm) high.
£100–120 StC

A Royal Worcester majolica centrepiece, modelled by James Hadley, in the form of a merman and bulrushes supporting a shell, decorated in coloured enamels, the concave-sided triform base with a coral band, minor damage, c1870, 7¾in (19.5cm) high.
£1,400–1,600 DN

A French majolica base of a centre-piece, c1870, 12¾in (32.5cm) high.
£350–400 SSW

A Wedgwood majolica centrepiece, the pierced basket top glazed in mottled green, yellow, and brown, the pedestal surrounded by 3 putti, restored, impressed date code 'CBX' for 1869, 16in (40.5cm) high.
£1,000–1,200 MJB

A Shelley Pottery Nursery Ware child's chamber pot, decorated with children and pixies, beneath a blue line rim, after a design by Mabel Lucie Atwell, printed marks, 1930s, 7in (18cm) diam.
£350–400 DN

A pottery model of a brown rustic chair, Cumbria or north east England, c1890, 8¼in (21cm) high.
£120–140 IW

◄ A Halifax brown slipware miniature lambing chair, initialled and dated 'EC 1863', 8in (20.5cm) high.
£85–95 ANV

A clock face group of Daniel in the lion's den, painted in colours and gilt, on a gilt-lined base, slight wear, c1860, 10in (25.5cm) high.
£550–650 CSK

A Staffordshire pottery clock, depicting the Lion and the Unicorn, decorated in pale green, black and brown on a white ground, c1840, 10in (25.5cm) high.
£600–700 BHA

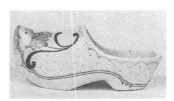

An Arnhem pottery clog, decorated in linear design, c1920, 6in (15cm) long.
£95–115 OO

A Carlton Ware cream and sugar set, on a silver-plated stand, decorated with Petunia pattern, brown transfer-printed blushware and hand-enamelled, pattern No. 945½, brown crown mark, 'Rd 258145', late 19thC, 7in (18cm) high.
£130–150 StC

A Scottish brown slipware bread crock, the handle and the edges in the form of bamboo, c1880, 17in (43cm) wide.
£425–475 B&R

A Carlton Ware tinted faïence cream and sugar set, on a silver-plated stand, pattern No. 605, c1890–94, 5in (12.5cm) high.
£50–60 StC

A Staffordshire cradle, c1800, 4½in (11.5cm) long.
£400–500 JHo

A Staffordshire cradle, c1800, 7½in (19cm) long.
£650–800 JHo

A Staffordshire cradle, c1800, 5in (12.5cm) long.
£450–500 JHo

A Copeland & Garrett footbath, the exterior printed in green, the interior rim with a similar band, mid-19thC, 21½in (54.5cm) diam, and a matching water jug.
£700–850 Bea

A Carlton Ware chocolate cup and cover, c1930, 5in (12.5cm) high.
£90–100 WN

A Midwinter blackbird pie funnel, c1950, 4½in (11.5cm) high.
£20–25 AND

◄ A Losol ware dressing table set, Blantyre pattern, c1915, tray 15in (38cm) wide.
£70–80 CSA

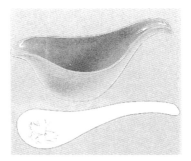

A Midwinter Cassandra pattern gravy boat and ladle, 1950s, 8½in (21.5cm) long.
£35–40 JR

A Gouda pottery humidor, decorated in Rhodian design, c1918, 8½in (21.5cm) high.
£220–250 OO
Sponge was kept in the lid to keep the tobacco moist.

A Spode pearlware eyebath, with scroll-moulded stem and oval foot, printed in blue with a version of the Tower pattern, within blue painted-line borders, hair crack, printed mark in blue, c1820, 2¾in (7cm) high.
£1,300–1,500 DN

A Poole Pottery table lamp, c1930, 6¾in (17cm) high.
£40–50 JO

A Bursley Ware lamp base, designed by Charlotte Rhead, decorated in shades of yellow and mauve, pattern No. TL30, 1940s, 7in (18cm) high.
£220–260 PC

A Denby table lamp, designed by Glyn Colledge, c1955, 7¼in (18.5cm) high.
£55–65 PC

A Derbyshire salt-glazed top hat, c1830, 3¼in (8.5cm) high.
£60–70 IW

A Rye Pottery green lamp base, decorated in a filament pattern, 1950s, 12in (30.5cm) diam.
£100–120 NCA

A Measham bargeware kettle, with a stand, 1893, 11in (28cm) high.
£300–350 JBL

A Carlton Ware match striker, marked, c1894–1900, 2½in (6.5cm) high.
£25–30 MAC

◄ A Wedgwood blue and white jasper portrait medallion of Admiral Lord Nelson, with a dipped bright blue ground, in a contemporary ebonized wood frame, damaged, impressed mark, c1798, 3½in (9cm) high.
£1,400–1,600 C

► A Staffordshire money box, modelled as a cottage, decorated with coloured enamels on a white ground, c1860, 4¾in (12cm) high.
£85–95 SER

A Yorkshire money box, modelled as a hen on her nest, c1860, 4¼in (11cm) wide.
£75–90 IW

An earthenware money box, possibly Sussex, late 19thC, 4in (10cm) high.
£60–80 IW

A money box, modelled as an owl, possibly Fremington, mid-19thC, 13in (33cm) high.
£850–1,000 BHa

A Derbyshire salt-glazed pipkin, c1840, 4in (10cm) high.
£50–60 IW

A Carlton Ware blue table bell, and yellow napkin ring, in the form of ladies in crinolines, c1930, largest 4in (10cm) high.
£30–40 each StC

An Obadiah Sherratt-type enamelled pearlware tablet, restored, c1830, 9½in (24cm) wide.
£600–700 Bon

A Carlton Ware pen holder, in the form of a tree stump and a brightly-coloured bird, c1925, 18in (45.5cm) wide.
£65–75 BSA

A Wedgwood creamware punch stand, on 3 scroll feet, restored, impressed mark, c1780, 7in (18cm) high.
£220–250 DN

A Minton majolica garden seat, set on lug feet, the top pierced with a medallion, glazed in typical colours on a turquoise ground, c1868, 17½in (44.5cm) high.
£1,500–1,800 S

A Susie Cooper punch bowl and 7 beakers, painted with a band of stylized leaves in shades of green and grey, crack to the rim of bowl, printed factory marks, 1930s, bowl 11in (28cm) diam, and 8 similar coasters.
£750–850 CSK

▶ A Wedgwood scent bottle, depicting 'Night Shedding Poppies' in white on a pale blue ground, with silver-gilt top and inner stopper, c1780, 4½in (11.5cm) high.
£1,600–1,800 BHa

A majolica shell, splashed in green, brown and ochre, on 3 dolphin supports, slight damage, 19thC, 9in (23cm) wide.
£90–110 HOLL

A sugar sifter, unmarked, 1950s, 5in (12.5cm) high.
£40–45 GFR

◄ A Royal Winton Chintz ware sugar bowl and lid, decorated with Sweet Pea pattern, in shades of pink, blue and green on a cream ground, 1930s, 3¼in (8.5cm) high.
£85–95 BET

Tea Canisters

Lidded jars for tea were made as early as the 1730s at Meissen, and were known as canisters. As tea was an expensive commodity, lockable boxes known as caddies were made into which the canisters fitted.

A Denby caddy spill holder, c1930s, 5in (12.5cm) high.
£140–160 KES

A Staffordshire slipware shoe warmer, early 19thC, 8in (20.5cm) high.
£235–265 TVM

A creamware tea canister, moulded with Oriental figures on cell diaper grounds, the rim with stiff-leaf bands, damaged, c1770, 4½in (11.5cm) high.
£250–300 DN

A Staffordshire agateware tea caddy, c1755, 4¾in (12cm) high.
£3,500–4,000 JHo

A Leeds tea caddy, c1800, 3½in (9cm) high.
£350–400 JHo

A Victorian toothbrush holder, registration number mark, c1891, 8in (20.5cm) wide.
£24–28 TAC

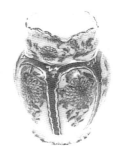

A Victorian toothbrush holder, by Salt Bros, Tunstall, with blue transfer-printed and gilt decoration, 5¼in (13.5cm) high.
£28–32 TAC

A Burleigh Ware toilet set, comprising 2 chamber pots, jug, basin, soap dish and liner, c1932, basin 15¾in (40cm) diam.
£350–400 BKK

▶ A Staffordshire watch holder, depicting 3 cherubs, c1860, 11in (28cm) high.
£170–200 JO

A lustre model of a yacht on waves, decorated in orange and green, 1920–30s, 4½in (11.5cm) high.
£10–12 JMC

A Staffordshire model of a church, c1835, 5in (12.5cm) high.
£400–450 RWB

A Wemyss Gordon plate, painted with raspberries, 8in (20.5cm) diam.
£300–400 RdeR

A pair of Wedgwood creamware chestnut baskets and stands, c1790.
£700–800 DAN

A Staffordshire pastille burner, c1840, 4½in (11.5cm) high.
£340–380 RWB

A pair of Quimper plates, 11in (28cm) diam. **£75–85 MofC**

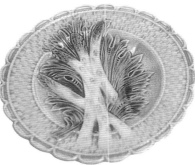

A set of 6 French asparagus plates, c1880, 9½in (24cm) diam.
£250–300 MofC

Two Staffordshire figures, 'The Lost Piece', from identical moulds, c1800.
£300–350 each DAN

A Staffordshire pastille burner, c1835, restored, 8in (20.5cm) high.
£300–340 RWB

A Staffordshire model of Shakespeare's house, repaired, c1850, 5in (12.5cm) high.
£200–220 RWB

A Staffordshire inkwell, restored, c1850, 4in (10cm) high.
£80–90 RWB

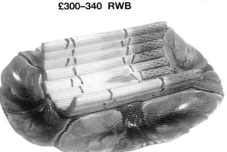

An asparagus cradle, c1880, 14½in (37cm) wide.
£150–200 MofC

A Staffordshire pastille burner, in the form of a house, chimney and flowers restored, c1835, 5½in (14cm) high.
£270–300 RWB

A Wemyss basket, decorated with cherries, c1900, 12in (30.5cm) wide.
£500–600 RdeR

A Wemyss commemorative mug, decorated with linked hearts, roses, thistles and shamrocks, inscribed 'Fear God, Honour The King', c1906, 5½in (14cm) high.
£500–600 RdeR

A Wemyss Gordon plate, decorated with brambles, c1890, 8in (20.5cm) diam.
£150–200 RdeR

A Wemyss Coomb pot, painted with roses, c1920, 10in (25.5cm) high.
£400–500 RdeR

A Wemyss plate, decorated with violets, c1900, 4in (10cm) diam.
£100–150 RdeR

A Wemyss plate, decorated with a beehive, c1890, 8in (20.5cm) diam.
£300–400 RdeR

A Wemyss mug, painted with daffodils, c1900, 5½in (14cm) high.
£300–400 RdeR

A Wemyss black and white pig, left ear restored, impressed Wemyss Ware R. H. & S. mark, c1910, 18in (45.5cm) wide.
£1,500–2,200 C(S)

A Wemyss plate, painted with irises, c1890, 8in (20.5cm) diam.
£200–250 RdeR

A Wemyss Bovey Tracey smiling cat, painted with pink roses, painted 'Wemyss Ware' and initials for Joseph Nekola, c1930, 12½in (32cm) high.
£2,000–2,200 CSK

A Wemyss quaiche, decorated with strawberries, c1900, 10½in (25.5cm) wide.
£200–300 RdeR

A quaiche was an early Scottish drinking bowl of staved wood with lug handles, and from the 17thC was made in silver and pewter.

Two Wemyss bowls, one inscribed and one decorated with crocuses, both impressed and with painted marks, c1900, largest 11in (28cm) diam.
top: £1,000–1,500
bottom: £700–900 C(S)

A Wemyss slop-pail lid, c1900,
10in (25.5cm) diam.
£130–150 RdeR

A Wemyss goose, 8in (20.5cm) high.
£450–500 RdeR

A Wemyss tyg, painted with roses,
c1900, 9½in (24cm) high.
£900–1,000 RdeR

A Wemyss honey pot, marked 'T.
Goode & Co', c1900, 7in (18cm) high.
£600–700 RdeR

A Wemyss teapot, chocolate pot, cream jug
and sugar bowl, c1900, jug 4in (10cm) high.
£150–445 each RdeR

A Wemyss box and stand, c1920,
3in (7.5cm) high.
£250–300 RdeR

A Wemyss forget-me-not inkwell,
c1900, 6in (15cm) wide.
£250–300 RdeR

A Wemyss pig, c1930,
8in (20.5cm) high.
£1,000–1,200 RdeR

A Wemyss Gorden plate, c1900,
8in (20.5cm) diam.
£250–300 RdeR

A Wemyss quaiche, painted with raspberries,
c1900, 8in (20.5cm) wide. **£250–300 RdeR**

A Wemyss jug and basin,
c1900, jug 10in (25.5cm) high.
£1,700–2,000 RdeR

A Wemyss pomade
pot, c1900,
3in (7.5cm) high.
£200–250 RdeR

A Wemyss matchbox, T. Goode & Co,
c1900,5in (12.5cm).
£350–400 RdeR

A Wemyss biscuit barrel, c1900,
4in (10cm) high.
£200–250 RdeR

A Wemyss pig, painted
with clover flowers, c1930,
11½in (29.5cm) high.
£2,500–3,000 RdeR

A Mason's Ironstone Bandana ware pot pourri vase, with pierced and solid covers, c1845, 14in (36cm) high.
£700–750 VH

A Mason's Ironstone card rack, impressed mark, c1815.
£800–850 VH

A C. J. Mason coffee can and saucer, pattern No. 878, c1815, saucer 5½in (14cm) diam.
£250–300 VH

A Mason's Ironstone soup plate, Japan pattern, impressed line mark, c1815, 9½in (24cm) diam.
£140–170 VH

A Mason's Ironstone vase and cover, c1815, 8in (20.5cm) high.
£400–450 VH

A hard paste porcelain teapot, by Miles Mason, slight damage, c1800, 6½in (16.5cm) high.
£750–800 VH

A C. J. Mason hand-painted plate, c1815, 8½in (21.5cm) diam.
£130–160 VH

A Mason's Ironstone dessert plate, c1813, 7½in (19cm) diam.
£120–140 VH

A Mason's Ironstone dessert dish, slight crack, c1815, 9½in (24cm) wide.
£350–390 VH

A bone china cup and saucer, c1808, saucer 5in (12.5cm) diam.
£200–250 VH

A Mason's Ironstone inkstand, impressed mark, c1815.
£850–950 VH

A relief moulded cup and saucer, by Miles Mason, c1818, saucer 5½in (14cm) diam.
£250–300 VH

A pair of Mason's Ironstone wine coolers, decorated with Japan pattern, 9½in (24cm) high.
£1,350–1,700 BEE

A pair of Mason's Ironstone sauce tureens, with stands, impressed mark, c1815, 8in (20.5cm) wide.
£850–950 BEE

A Mason's Ironstone dessert service, comprising 31 pieces, each piece moulded with cabbage leaf motifs, and hand-coloured in polychrome enamels, c1820.
£1,750–2,000 Bon

A Wemyss plate, painted with violets, c1890, 4¾in (12cm) diam.
£200–250 RdeR

A Mason's Ironstone drainer, with chinoiserie decoration, c1835, 12½in (32cm) wide.
£300–340 JP

A Wemyss mug, painted with daffodils, c1890, 5½in (14cm) high.
£350–400 RdeR

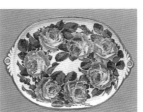

A Wemyss two-handled tray, with impressed mark by Karel Nekola, c1900, 17¾in (45cm) wide.
£850–1,000 HAR

A Mason's Ironstone inkstand, decorated with Bandana pattern, c1835, 8in (20.5cm) wide.
£1,000–1,250 JP

This inkstand is of a rare shape, also found in an even more rare variant on 6 feet.

A Wemyss cat, by J. Plichta, decorated with clover, c1930, 10¼in (26cm) high.
£200–250 RdeR

'Our Pets', No. 242, c1852, 3½in (9cm) diam.
£180–200 SAS

A Wemyss basket, painted with cherries, with fluted sides and twist handle, c1900, 8¾in (22cm) wide.
£500–600 RdeR

'Dublin Industrial Exhibition 1853', No. 143, 5in (12.5cm) diam.
£120–135 BHa

'Pegwell Bay', stamp for S. Banger, c1850, 4in (10cm) diam.
£600–650 SAS

'Golden Horn, Constantinople', c1854, No. 204, 4¼in (11cm) diam.
£150–180 SAS

A Meissen group of
Mezzetin and Columbine,
by J. J. Kändler, with a
dog at their feet, c1740,
7½in (19cm) high.
£9,500–10,000 C

A Meissen group of The Handkiss,
by J. J. Kändler, the lady with a pug on
her lap, minor damage and restoration,
c1740, 6in (15cm) high.
£32,000–35,000 C

A Meissen figure of
Columbine, by J. J.
Kändler and Reinicke,
c1744, 5½in (14cm) high.
£4,800–5,500 C

A Bow group of The Fortune
Teller, by the Muses
modeller, minor damage,
c1752, 7in (18cm) high.
£6,500–7,500 S

A Bow figure of Pierrot,
c1755, 6in (15cm) high.
£1,000–1,200 DMa

A Derby group, restored,
c1765, 11½in (29cm) high.
£2,500–3,000 DMa

A Bow figure of James
Quin as Falstaff, chipped
and repaired, c1750,
9in (23cm) high.
£2,000–2,200 S(NY)

A Meissen group of Augustus III and his wife,
by J. J. Kändler, c1744, 8½in (21.5cm) high.
£20,000–22,000 C

A Meissen group, by Paul
Scheurich, blue crossed
swords and dot mark,
incised signature, c1924,
11in (28cm) high.
£7,000–7,500 C

A pair of Derby figures, allegorical
of Liberty and Matrimony,
damaged and restored, c1765,
8½in (21.5cm) high.
£2,200–2,500 S(NY)

A Chelsea figure of Dr
Boloardo, after a model by
J. J. Kändler, damaged,
c1754, 6in (15cm) high.
£9,500–10,000 C

A pair of Derby figures, both with
flowers in their aprons, bocage behind,
on pink and gilt scroll bases, c1760,
7in (18cm) high.
£1,800–2,000 BHA

A Derby figure of Harlequin,
c1770, 6in (15cm) high.
£1,000–1,200 DMa

A Nymphenburg model of a
monkey, restored, impressed
shield, early 20thC,
11in (28cm) wide.
£500–600 C

A Meissen pagoda figure
pastille burner, by J. F.
Eberlein, damaged, marked,
c1735, 6in (15cm) high.
£5,000–6,000 C

A Meissen model of a
monkey, by J. G. Kirchner,
restored, marked, c1735,
10in (255.cm) high.
£5,500–6,500 C

A Chelsea model of a
seated hare, damaged,
c1755, 5in (12.5cm) high.
£12,000–14,000 S(NY)

A Meissen figure, by Acier, c1775,
6½in (16.5cm) high.
£1,300–1,500 BHA

A Meissen group of
Empress Catherine II,
damaged and restored,
marked, c1880,
10in (25.5cm) high.
£3,000–3,500 C

A Meissen figure of a
foot soldier, damaged
and restored, marked,
c1750, 9in (23cm) high.
£2,500–3,000 Bon

A pair of Chelsea groups of gallants and
companions, emblematic of the Seasons,
damaged and restored, gold anchor marks,
c1765, 13in (33cm) high.
£8,500–9,000 C

A Meissen model of Empress Catherine II
of Russia's favourite dog, damaged,
blue crossed swords mark, c1880,
17in (43cm) long.
£5,500–6,000 C

A Bow box and cover,
modelled as a duck, damaged,
c1756, 5in (12.5cm) long.
£18,500–22,000 S(NY)

A Bow box and cover,
modelled as a duck, damaged,
c1756, 5in (12.5cm) long.
£12,000–14,000 S(NY)

A pair of Meissen models of parakeets, after
J. J. Kändler, both perched on tree stumps, damaged
and restored, crossed swords mark in blue, incised
'63', impressed '34', 13in (33cm) high.
£2,000–3,000 CAG

A pair of Bow models of recumbent lions, both with one paw resting on a colourful globe, c1755, 4in (10cm) wide.
£11,000–12,000 P

A pair of Derby sheep, restored, c1815, 4in (10cm) high.
£450–550 SER

A pair of Derby figures of The Ranelagh Dancers, both on rococo bases with tree stumps and leafy bocage, damaged, c1765, largest 12in (30.5cm) high.
£520–600 TMA

A Duesbury Derby figure of a goddess, late 18thC, 7¼in (18.5cm) high.
£230–270 SER

A Bloor Derby group, c1820, 9½in (24cm) high.
£1,000–1,200 DAN

A pair of Meissen figures of a gentleman gardener and a lady with a basket of flowers, 19thC, 14in (35.5cm) high.
£2,250–2,500 Mit

A pair of Sitzendorf figures, c1900, 6¼in (16cm) high.
£170–200 P(B)

A Meissen figure of a map seller, c1750, 7in (18cm) high.
£2,800–3,200 BHA

A pair of French figures of a boy with a jug and a girl with a bowl, late 19thC, 9½in (24cm) high.
£280–320 MiA

A Meissen group of women, children and Cupid, restored, 19thC, 11in (28cm) high.
£1,000–1,200 SWO

A pair of Royal Worcester figures of Strephon and Phyllis, c1920, largest 6in (15cm) high.
£750–800 TH

A Rookwood Pottery, Ohio paperweight, in the form of an elephant, c1927, 3in (7.5cm) high.
£170–185 JMW

An oval baking dish with petal-shaped padded feet, 1850–1900, 10½in (26.5cm) long.
£120–140 NSA

A bowl, attributed to Yellow Rock, Philadelphia, coloured deep yellow, late 19thC, 12½in (32cm) diam.
£150–180 NSA

A Weller Pottery, Ohio bowl, painted with brown bands, 1920–30, 5in (12.5cm) diam.
£45–55 NSA

A Midwest pudding dish, mid-west, 1920–30, 4in (10cm) diam.
£65–75 NSA

A Weller Pottery, Ohio model of a kingfisher, c1918, 8¾in (22cm) high.
£340–370 JMW

A rectangular baking dish with padded feet, signed 'J. E. Jeffords, Philadelphia, Pennsylvania', 1868–1900, 8½in (21.5cm) long.
£270–300 NSA

A pudding dish, painted with blue Vining Flower pattern, with some stoneware in the clay body, 1900–20, 6in (15cm) diam.
£70–85 NSA

An Edwin and Mary Scheier, New Hampshire bowl, with incised pattern, 1940–50, 11¼in (28.5cm) diam.
£2,000–2,200 JMW

▶ A Hull Pottery, Ohio part set of canisters, with embossed wheat pattern, lids missing, 1920–30, largest 5½in (14cm) high.
£160–180 each NSA

A custard cup, painted with blue and peach bands, 1880–1920, 2¼in (5.5cm) high.
£50–60 NSA

A plain Yellowware colander with rolled rim, late 19thC, 9½in (24cm) diam.
£270–300 NSA

Two custard cups, one painted with blue band pattern, early 20thC, largest 2¾in (7cm) high.
£35–40 NSA

A bowl, decorated with white bands, 1920–30, 4¼in (11cm) diam.
£65–70 NSA

A Hull Pottery, Ohio spice jar, painted with blue bands, lid missing, 1905–17, 3½in (9cm) high.
£100–120 NSA

An Ohr Pottery, Mississippi puzzle mug, with moulded handle, 1902–07, 3in (7.5cm) high.
£460–500 JMW

A Polia Pillon, California hand-painted tray, c1950, 5in (12.5cm) long.
£85–95 JMW

A Shawsheen Pottery, Massachusetts teapot, with incised abstract floral pattern, 1906, 5in (12.5cm) high.
£820–920 JMW

▶ A mould, impressed with a pineapple, 19thC, 8½in (21.5in) long.
£180–200 NSA

The pineapple is a symbol of hospitality.

A Brush-McCoy, Ohio nutmeg jar, painted with bluebirds, lid missing, 1920–30, 3in (7.5cm) high.
£225–245 NSA

A Paul Revere Pottery, Massachusetts bowl, plate and mug set, Saturday Evening Girls series, hand-painted by Fannie Levine, with central rabbit pattern and inscribed 'Herbert', 'His Bowl', 'His Plate', 'His Mug', 1921, plate 5¾in (19cm) diam.
£1,000–1,200 JMW

A Grueby Pottery, Massachusetts trivet, with moulded geese pattern, 1900–08, 9½in (24cm) square.
£1,300–1,450 JMW

A Grueby Pottery, Massachusetts lamp base, with a Tiffany Studios shade, 1900–08, 27½in (70cm) high.
£6,200–6,800 JMW

A pair of Niloak Pottery, Arkansas Mission Ware candlesticks, 1910–47, 8in (20.5cm) high.
£460–500 JMW

An Ohr Pottery, Mississippi jug, 1902–07, 3¾in (9.5cm) high.
£820–920 JMW

A pair of Hull Pottery, Ohio Zane Grey jugs, painted with blue bands, early 20thC, largest 6in (15cm) high.
£100–120 NSA

A Dedham Pottery, Mass. pitcher, with 'Oak Block' pattern and crackleware glaze, 1896–1943, 6in (15cm) high.
£800–900 JMW

A Hull Pottery, Ohio jug, painted with blue bands, 1905–17, 4in (10cm) high.
£80–100 NSA

A Dorchester Pottery, Massachusetts jug, signed by N. Ricci, c1950, 6½in (16.5cm) high.
£200–220 JMW

A Dedham Pottery plate, painted with one-eared rabbit pattern, with crackle glaze, 1895, 8½in (21.5cm) diam.
£170–190 JMW

A Paul Revere Pottery, Massachusetts jug, Saturday Evening Girls series, painted with geese by Sarah Galner, 1913, 6¼in (16cm) high.
£1,750–2,000 JMW

A pitcher, mid-west, with pink and blue bands, 1900–30, 5¾in (14.5cm) high.
£120–140 NSA

A pie plate, 1860–1900, 8in (20.5cm) diam.
£80–100 NSA

A Dedham Pottery, Massachusetts plate, painted with crabs, designed by Maud Davenport, 1896–1943, 8½in (21.5cm) diam.
£280–320 JMW

▶ A Calco Pottery, California tile, with painted landscape pattern, 1923–33, 12¾in (32.5cm) wide, framed.
£1,125–1,225 JMW

A Paul Revere Pottery, Massachusetts plate, Saturday Evening Girls series, painted with running pigs, 1910, 8½in (21.5cm) diam.
£1,200–1,350 JMW

A Dedham Pottery plate, painted with dolphin pattern, with crackle glaze, 1896–1943, 8½in (21.5cm) diam.
£440–475 JMW

A Dedham Pottery, Massachusetts plate, painted with Tufted Duck pattern, c1895, 10in (25.5cm) diam.
£320–360 JMW

A Grueby Pottery, Massachusetts tile, with moulded and painted ship pattern, 1900–08, 6in (15.5cm) square.
£670–740 JMW

A Massachusetts pottery tile, late 19thC, 6in (15cm) square.
£125–145 MSB

Three Grueby Pottery, Massachusetts tiles, with various geometric designs, 1900–08, 3in (7.5cm) square.
£20–25 each JMW

A J. & J. G. Low Pottery, Massachusetts tile, with moulded portrait, c1881, 6in (15cm) square.
£90–110 JMW

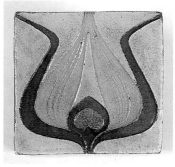

A Van Briggle Pottery, Colorado tile, with moulded stylized peacock feather pattern, 1905, 6in (15cm) square.
£250–280 JMW

A Dedham Pottery, Massachusetts Hugh Robertson vase, with experimental *sang de boeuf* glaze, 1895–1908, 9¾in (25cm) high.
£2,300–2,600 JMW

A Grueby Pottery, Massachusetts vase, with applied leaf and bud pattern, 1900–08, 10in (25.5cm) high.
£5,250–5,850 JMW

A William Walley, Massachusetts vase, with applied leaf pattern, 1898–1919, 7¾in (19.5cm) high.
£1,600–1,800 JMW

A William Walley vase, with applied leaf pattern, 1898, 6¼in (16cm) high.
£2,200–2,400 JMW

A Grueby Pottery vase, with applied leaf and tobacco flower pattern, 1900–08, 5¼in (13.5cm) high.
£6,500–7,500 JMW

A Grueby Pottery, Massachusetts vase, with three-colour daffodil pattern, 1900–08, 5¼in (14cm) high.
£5,000–5,500 JMW

A Chelsea Keramic Artworks, Massachusetts Pilgrim Flask vase, 1880–99, 10¾in (27.5cm) high.
£450–500 JMW

A Grueby Pottery, Massachusetts vase, with applied leaf and bud decoration, 1900–08, 6¾in (17cm) high.
£4,000–4,500 JMW

A Grueby Pottery, Massachusetts vase, with carved back panels, 1900–08, 3¾in (9.5cm) high.
£1,000–1,200 JMW

A William Walley, Mass. vase, with drip glaze, 1898, 4½in (11.5cm) high.
£220–250 JMW

◄ A Merrimac Pottery, Massachusetts vase, with applied leaf pattern, 1900–08, 7¾in (19.5cm) high.
£2,000–2,200 JMW

A Marblehead Pottery, Mass. vase, with pink glaze, 1904–36, 6½in (16.5) high.
£500–550 JMW

A Chelsea Keramic Art Works vase, with *sang de boeuf* glaze, c1895, 8in (20.5cm) high.
£2,100–2,200 JMW

A Van Briggle Pottery, Colorado vase, 1905, 13in (33cm) high.
£2,750–3,000 JMW

A Grueby Pottery, Massachusetts vase, with applied iris decoration, 1900–08, 12in (30.5cm) high.
£6,800–7,400 JMW

A Weller Pottery, Ohio matte green jardinière, with leaf motif, early 20thC, 10¼in (26cm) high.
£200–220 MSB

A Marblehead Pottery, Mass. vase, with floral pattern, 1909–20, 7in (18cm) high.
£2,000–2,200 JMW

A Marblehead Pottery, Massachusetts vase, with carved abstract pattern, c1909, 8½in (21.5cm) high.
£4,500–5,000 JMW

A Merrimac Pottery, Massachusetts vase, with applied leaf and floral pattern, 1900–08, 11¾in (30cm) high.
£1,750–2,000 JMW

A Marblehead Pottery vase, with abstract pattern, c1909, 9¼in (23.5cm) high.
£4,000–4,500 JMW

A Rookwood Pottery, Ohio vase, with Carved Matte pattern by Charles Todd, 1916, 10¼in (26cm) high.
£1,100–1,300 JMW

A Marblehead Pottery, Mass. vase, with incised and painted pattern, 1909–20, 4½in (11.5cm) high.
£1,100–1,200 JMW

A Marblehead Pottery, Mass. vase, with lavender matte glaze, 1909–20, 4¼in (11cm) high.
£170–190 JMW

A Rookwood Production, Ohio vase, with leaf pattern, 1910, 8¾in (22cm) high.
£250–280 JMW

A Teco Pottery, Illinois vase, designed by W. G. Dodd, shape No 85, c1910, 11½in (29cm) high.
£4,000–4,500 JMW

An Ohr Pottery, Mississippi vase, with everted rim, 1902–07, 3¾in (9.5cm) high.
£700–800 JMW

A Grueby Pottery vase, with applied leaf decoration, 1900–08, 3¾in (9.5cm) high.
£1,500–1,700 JMW

◀ A California faïence vase, signed 'California Porcelain', 1924, 3¼in (8.5cm) high.
£235–265 JMW

A Van Briggle Pottery, Colorado vase, with stylized peacock feather pattern, 1905, 5½in (14cm) high.
£1,325–1,475 JMW

A Grueby Pottery, Massachusetts vase, with applied leaf and bud pattern, 1900–08, 7½in (19cm) high.
£1,750–2,000 JMW

A Niloak Pottery, Arkansas Mission Ware vase, 1910–47, 6in (15cm) high.
£65–75 JMW

A Roseville Pine Cone vase, 1931, 6¼in (16cm) high.
£150–170 MSB

A Hampshire Pottery vase, 1904–18, 3¼in (8.5cm) high.
£180–200 JMW

A Roseville wisteria vase, 1933, 6½in (16.5cm) high.
£380–420 MSB

A Fulper Pottery, New Jersey vase, with cucumber crystaline glaze, c1910, 12¼in (31cm) high.
£1,200–1,400 JMW

A Marblehead Pottery, Massachusetts vase, with painted tree pattern, 1909–20, 3½in (9cm) high.
£1,600–1,800 JMW

A Clifton Pottery vase, with Homolobi pattern, c1906, 5¼in (13.5cm) diam.
£350–385 JMW

A Peters & Reed Pottery Moss Aztec jardinière, c1920, 4in (10cm) high.
£110–125 JMW

A Fulper Pottery, New Jersey vase, with drip glaze over mustard matte, 1909–16, 4¼in (11cm) high.
£385–425 JMW

A Weller Pottery, Ohio jardinière, decorated with Bedford Matte line pattern, 1915, 5¼in (13.5cm) high.
£225–250 JMW

A Newcombe Pottery, Louisiana vase, with abstract floral decoration by Sadie Irvine, 1913, 4¾in (12cm) high.
£1,500–1,850 JMW

A Weller Pottery, Ohio Blue Ware jardinière, decorated with Dancing Ladies pattern, c1920, 8½in (21.5cm) diam.
£320–360 JMW

A Roseville Cornucopia Water Lily vase, 1943, 6in (15cm) high.
£80–100 MSB

A Paul Revere Pottery, Massachusetts vase, Saturday Evening Girls series, with Daffodil pattern, 1914, 5¾in (15cm) high.
£1,400–1,550 JMW

A Paul Revere Pottery vase, Saturday Evening Girls series, with abstract pattern painted by Sarah Galner, 1916, 7¾in (20cm) high.
£2,200–2,500 JMW

A Roseville Pottery, Ohio jardinière and pedestal, decorated with Sunflower pattern, 1930, 28¾in (73cm) high.
£3,000–3,300 JMW

A Weller Pottery, Ohio vase, decorated with Cornish pattern, 1933, 8¼in (21cm) high.
£100–120 JMW

A Fulper Pottery, NJ vase, with mirror black and ivory flambé glaze, 1909–16, 9½in (24cm) high.
£275–325 JMW

A Teco Pottery, Illinois vase, c1910, 6¾in (17cm) high.
£400–450 JMW

A Clewell Pottery, Ohio vase, electroplated with copper on pottery blank, 1910–19, 7¼in (18cm) high.
£380–420 JMW

A Chicago Crucible vase, 1910–19, 6¾in (17cm) high.
£600–675 JMW

A Teco Pottery, Illinois vase, c1910, 9¼in (23.5cm) high.
£850–950 JMW

A Peters & Reed Pottery, Ohio vase, decorated with Shadow Ware line pattern, c1920, 8¾in (22cm) high.
£100–120 JMW

A Russell Crook, Massachusetts vase, with Moose pattern, 1915–25, 14¼in (36cm) high.
£3,300–3,700 JMW

A Russell Crook salt-glazed stoneware vase, decorated with Mammoth pattern, 1915–25, 11¾in (30cm) high.
£2,200–2,500 JMW

A Peters & Reed Pottery, Ohio vase, decorated with Mirror Ware line pattern, c1920, 12¼in (31cm) high.
£145–160 JMW

A Paul Revere Pottery vase, Saturday Evening Girls series, decorated with Lotus Flower pattern, 1926, 9in (23cm) high.
£1,200–1,400 JMW

A Shearwater Pottery, Mississippi vase, with decoration by James McConnell Anderson, c1930, 7¾in (19.5cm) high.
£1,000–1,200 JMW

A Roseville Pottery, Ohio vase, decorated with Luffa pattern, 1934, 8¼in (21cm) high.
£180–200 JMW

A Roseville Water Lily vase, 1943, 4in (10cm) diam.
£70–90 MSB

An Edwin and Mary Sheier, New Hampshire vase, 1940–50, 7in (18cm) high.
£270–300 JMW

A Roseville Zephyr Lily pillow vase, 1946, 7in (18cm) high.
£100–110 MSB

A Pisgah Forest Pottery, North Carolina vase, with applied decoration, 1958, 8¾in (22.5cm) high.
£500–550 JMW

Blue & White Ware

Inspired by Chinese ceramics, blue and white ware first made its appearance in Britain in the 17th century. The use of cobalt was developed on tin-glazed earthenware, and this came to be known as delft ware. Many factories then began to produce blue-painted wares, using cobalt-blue as it was the only colour that could be relied upon to withstand the high temperature required to fuse the glaze without changing colour.

In about 1770, underglaze blue transfer-printing was introduced in Britain. This was an inexpensive process whereby engraved copper plates were used to produce tissue prints, which were applied to a wide variety of pottery items before the glaze was added. Perfected by, amongst others, Sadler & Green and by potters such as Heath, Spode and Turner, the technique was soon taken up by many other companies.

Blue and white transfer-ware was produced in large quantities because, essentially, its purpose was utilitarian. All manner of domestic items were decorated by this process, although the most popular were dinner and tea services, and today the most common pieces found are plates. Many early patterns were copies of Chinese designs, or inspired by them (the most common being the well-known Willow pattern,

which was reproduced by several different manufacturers), and in the early part of the 19th century rural landscapes, botanical and animal subjects began to appear. All-over sheet patterns that cover an entire piece are sometimes found, as well as the more open, paler blue designs that permit much of the white pottery to show through.

Although many manufacturers made blue and white transfer-ware, much is not marked, and care is needed to distinguish original pieces from later reproductions. On the whole, antique pottery tends to be lighter than modern copies, the exceptions being ironstone and stone china. Older pieces tend to have softer, richer colouring and they also display a depth of perspective, particularly when the pattern is of a landscape or view. When held to the light any scratches or surface wear should be random and more obvious where wear would be expected.

The popularity of blue and white transfer-ware began to wane in the mid-19th century and by the end of the century it had given way completely to more colourful ceramics. Today, however, it is greatly sought after, (as are blue and white delft and porcelain wares), its range of patterns and wide variety of forms offering great scope for the collector. **Gillian Neale**

BASKETS

A Dublin delft blue and white basket, by Henry Delamain, decorated with a landscape beneath a border of pierced interlocking circles, the footrim pierced for suspension, slight damage, c1755, 6½in (16.5cm) diam.
£6,700–7,500 C

A Spode blue and white chestnut basket, decorated with Net pattern, c1810, 10½in (26.5cm) wide.
£250–300 GN

A Spode blue and white Italian pattern chestnut basket, c1820, 10in (25.5cm) wide.
£450–550 GN

◄ A Spode blue and white pierced basket, decorated in Tiber pattern, c1815, 8in (20.5cm) wide.
£300–350 GN

This basket would have formed part of a dessert service, and would originally have had a stand.

A Spode blue and white chestnut basket and stand, decorated with the Gothic Castle pattern, c1810, stand 9in (23cm) wide.
£450–500 GN

A blue and white two-handled basket, decorated with floral and scroll pattern border and pierced trelliswork body, mid-19thC, 8in (20.5cm) diam.
£300–350 TMA

BOWLS

A Liverpool delft blue and white bowl, decorated with a pair of exotic birds amid flowering shrubbery, the reverse with a bird in flight pursuing an insect, the interior with blossoms beneath a scroll-patterned blue band around the rim, c1765, 12in (30.5cm) diam.
£650–700 S(NY)

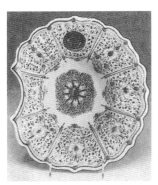

A Dutch Delft blue and white barber's bowl, with a soap depression, minor glaze chips, mid-18thC, 11½in (29cm) long.
£800–1,000 S(NY)

A London delft blue and white punchbowl, the interior inscribed 'Success to Trade', damaged, c1766, 10½in (26.5cm) diam.
£1,400–1,600 S(NY)

A London delft bowl inscribed 'Success to Trade No Stamps' provides proof that at least some of these delft punchbowls with 'Trade' inscriptions were made for the American market, or for British merchants involved in commerce with the American colonies.

A Davenport blue and white bowl, decorated with Bridgeless Willow pattern, damaged, c1820, 11½in (29cm) wide.
£230–260 P(G)

A pearlware blue and white commemorative bowl, decorated with portraits and inscriptions within a laurel-leaf border, the exterior with a Willow pattern scene, c1809, 10in (25.5cm) diam.
£160–180 SAS

A Hicks & Meigh blue and white bowl, British Views series, decorated with Wanstead House and Water Dog, c1820, 11in (28cm) diam.
£475–550 GN

A Davenport blue and white toilet bowl, decorated with Muleteer pattern with transfer-printed floral border, damaged and repaired, c1840, 13in (33cm) diam.
£80–100 MEG

A Spode blue and white dog bowl, decorated with Tower pattern, c1820, 8in (20.5cm) wide.
£750–850 GN

A blue and white bowl, the interior inscribed 'John Abrahams Commercial Inn, Newton', damaged, c1840, 11in (28cm) diam.
£100–110 PCh

A William Ridgway blue and white toilet bowl, decorated with Oriental Drama pattern, minor damage and repairs, c1840, 13in (33cm) diam.
£80–100 MEG

A blue and white bowl, decorated with Arcadian Chariots pattern, glaze repair, unmarked, mid-19thC, 8in (20.5cm) diam.
£70–80 MEG

A Copeland blue and white soup bowl and saucer, decorated with Italian pattern, 1920s, saucer 7in (18cm) diam.
£40–50 TAC

CHAMBER POTS

A child's blue and white chamber pot, decorated with Arcadian Chariots pattern, c1835, 6in (15cm) diam.
£250–300 GN

A Staffordshire blue and white vomit pot, c1840, 5in (12.5cm) diam.
£180–220 GN

A Davenport blue and white child's chamber pot/spittoon, decorated with Muleteer pattern, c1830, 5in (12.5cm) diam.
£145–165 OCH

CUPS & MUGS

An English delft blue and white coffee can, possibly Liverpool, mid-18thC, 2½in (6.5cm) high.
£2,000–2,500 S

A blue and white mug, extensive damage, c1800, 4¾in (12cm) high.
£25–30 MEG

A blue and white coffee can and saucer, decorated with Bullfinch pattern, c1820, saucer 5½in (14cm) diam.
£200–220 OCH

A blue and white sponge-decorated mug, with strap handle, c1830, 4in (10cm) high.
£120–140 RYA

A blue and white mug, inscribed 'imperial one pint', c1840, 4in (10cm) high.
£100–120 IW

A blue and white saucer, with gilt edge, unmarked, c1881, 5½in (14cm) diam.
£8–10 HEI

A George Jones blue and white trio, decorated with Casino pattern, c1907, plate 7½in (19cm) diam.
£20–25 TAC

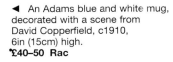

A Copeland blue and white breakfast cup and saucer, decorated with Italian pattern, 1920s, saucer 6½in (16.5cm) diam.
£22–28 TAC

◄ An Adams blue and white mug, decorated with a scene from David Copperfield, c1910, 6in (15cm) high.
£40–50 Rac

DISHES

A Dutch blue and white dish, decorated with a central tree, and a leaf and flower border, flaking to rim, 18thC, 14in (35.5cm) diam.
£300–350 BIG

A Dorotheenthal faïence blue and white dish, the centre painted with a concentric strapwork tassel and Cupid medallion, slight damage, c1735, 16¾in (42.5cm) wide.
£6,500–7,500 C

An English delft blue and white dish, cracked and chipped, c1760, 14in (35.5cm) diam.
£165–185 OCH

A Carey blue and white meat dish, decorated with Domestic Cattle pattern within a floral border, with grease reservoir, early 19thC, 21in (53.5cm) wide.
£750–900 GAK

A Wedgwood vegetable dish and cover, decorated with Hibiscus pattern, c1810, 18in (45.5cm) wide.
£300–350 GN

A Davenport dessert dish, decorated with Bisham Abbey, c1810, 9½in (24cm) wide.
£170–200 GN

A Job Ridgway dessert dish, decorated with Curling Palm pattern, c1810, 8in (20.5cm) wide.
£250–300 Nor

A blue and white meat dish, decorated with Long Bridge pattern, slight restoration, c1800, 21in (53cm) wide.
£100–120 P(B)

A blue and white meat dish, decorated with Oriental Sports pattern, c1809, 15½in (39.5cm) wide.
£750–850 P(B)

A John Meir blue and white meat dish, printed with River Fishing pattern, c1810, 21in (53.5cm) wide.
£450–550 P(B)

A Swansea Pottery meat dish, decorated with Ladies of Llangollen pattern, early 19thC, 21in (53.5cm) wide.
£900–1,100 PF

▶ A Rogers blue and white meat dish, decorated with Monopteros pattern, c1814–36, 21¼in (54cm) wide.
£350–400 P(B)

A Rogers game dish, decorated with Greek Statue pattern, c1810, 9½in (24cm) wide.
£275–350 GN

A Spode blue and white platter, decorated with Tower pattern, c1815, 21in (53.5cm) wide.
£350–550 GN

A Spode blue and white dessert comport, decorated with Lanje Lijsen pattern, c1820, 12in (30.5cm) diam.
£350–450 GN

A Joseph Stubbs blue and white dish, decorated with a pineapple and fruit, made for the American market, c1820, 20½in (52cm) wide.
£675–750 SCO

A Ridgway blue and white meat dish, British Scenery series decorated with Village Fisherman pattern, c1820s, 17in (43cm) wide.
£500–600 P(B)

A Don Pottery blue and white meat dish, decorated with a view of Corigliano, c1820, 20½in (52cm) wide.
£550–600 TMA

A Herculaneum pearlware meat dish, Indian series, decorated with the Gate of a Mosque built by Hafiz Ramit, within a broad band of vines and leaves, c1820, 20½in (52cm) wide.
£750–800 DN

A Spode pearlware dish, decorated with Lucano pattern, in original mahogany tray with scroll handles, c1820, 18½in (47cm) wide.
£1,300–1,500 DN

A Thomas Godwin blue and white meat platter, decorated with a view of London, c1820, 18½in (47cm) wide.
£750–900 GN

A Spode blue and white dessert dish, with Union Wreath border, the centre with the arms of Eton College, c1820, 8in (20.5cm) wide.
£160–200 SCO

An Andrew Stevenson blue and white dessert dish, c1820, 8in (20.5cm) high.
£200–250 Nor

An Enoch Wood blue and white pie dish, decorated with the Bank of England, c1820, 11¼in (29cm) wide.
£450–600 GN

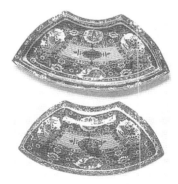

A Spode blue and white supper dish and cover, decorated with Net pattern, c1820, dish 14in (35.5cm) wide.
£250–300 GN

A blue and white dish, decorated with Nuneham Courtney, Wild Rose Border series, 19thC, 16in (40.5cm) wide.
£80–100 AP

A Rogers blue and white meat plate, decorated with Camel pattern, some cracks, impressed mark 'Rogers 16', c1825, 17in (43cm) wide.
£330–380 Hal

A blue and white platter, Antique Scenery series, decorated with Craig Miller Castle, c1825, 15in (38cm) wide.
£450–500 GN

A Middlesbro' Pottery blue and white meat dish, decorated with Nuneham Courtney, Wild Rose border, c1830, 17¾in (45cm) wide.
£140–170 Gam

A Copeland blue and white grape dish, decorated with Italian pattern, c1909, 6½in (16.5cm) diam.
£45–55 TAC

A Minton blue and white dish, decorated with Willow pattern, c1900, 5in (12.5cm) diam.
£12–16 TAC

► A blue and white potted beef dish, c1835, 3in (7.5cm) wide.
£70–80 SCO

A Spode blue and white comport, decorated with Jasmine pattern, with moulded shell and scroll handles, c1850, 14in (35.5cm) wide.
£320–380 TMA

A Staffordshire stoneware blue and white fish-shaped pickle dish, decorated with Willow pattern, mid-19thC, 6in (15cm) wide.
£40–50 MEG

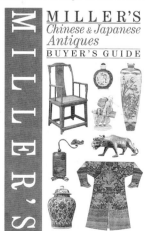
DRAINERS

► A Davenport blue and white drainer, decorated with Oxburgh Hall, impressed mark, c1810, 16½in (42cm) wide.
£220–260 P(B)

◄ A blue and white drainer, decorated with Grazing Rabbits pattern, c1820, 15in (38cm) wide.
£250–300 SCO

► A pair of Staffordshire blue and white pearlware milk strainers, decorated with Milsey pattern, 19thC, 3¾in (9.5cm) wide.
£400–500 Nor

FEEDERS

◄ A blue and white infant's feeding bottle, by Pountney & Allies, Bristol, decorated in Abbey pattern, c1825, 6in (15cm) wide.
£400–500 GN

A blue and white infant's feeding bottle, c1835, 7in (17.5cm) long.
£350–400 GN

A Minton blue and white invalid feeder, with Butterfly and Flowers pattern, c1825, 3in (7.5cm) high.
£175–250 GN

A Minton blue and white invalid feeder, decorated with Butterfly and Flowers pattern, c1830, 6in (15cm) wide.
£220–250 GN

A Minton blue and white invalid feeder, decorated with Moss Rose pattern, repaired, c1835, 2½in (6.5crn) high.
£80–100 GN

A Podmore & Walker blue and white pap feeder, decorated with an Italian scene, c1830, 4½in (11.5cm) long.
£170–220 GN

Pap Feeders

Pap feeders are small boat-shaped dishes with a lip at one end, used for feeding children and invalids. Many were made in Staffordshire and used from the early 18th to mid-19thC. Pap was a mixture of bread, chewed by the nurse, then soaked in wine and mixed with meal and sugar.

A Ridgway blue and white pap boat, from the Humphrey's Clock series Little Nell and her Grandfather, c1840, 4¾in (12cm) long.
£120–200 P(B)

FOOTBATHS

◄ A Wedgwood blue and white footbath, deorated with scenes of the Tower of London, Balmoral Castle and Windsor Castle, the base with a scene after Claude Lorraine from a series of prints In and Around Rome, c1825, 14in (35.5cm) high.
£3,500–4,000 GN

A Minton blue and white floral patterned footbath, restored, c1830, 19¾in (50cm) wide.
£1,600–1,800 DN

A pair of Spode blue and white footbaths, with Bridge of Locano pattern, one damaged, c1850, 20½in (52crn) wide.
£2,000–2,500 S(S)

A Copeland & Garrett blue and white footbath, decorated with a sheet pattern, c1840, 20in (50.5cm) long.
£1,200–1,500 GN

► A Minton blue and white footbath, decorated with a floral pattern, c1840, 19in (48cm) long.
£1,000–1,200 GN

A Herculaneum Pottery blue and white jug, printed with the Willow Pattern, impressed mark, spout chipped, c1810, 8¾in (22cm) high.
£90–110 P(B)

A blue and white floral mask jug, possibly Minton, c1820, 9in (23cm) high.
£230–260 Nor

A blue and white stoneware jug, c1820, 5¼in (13.5cm) high.
£60–70 MEG

A Davenport blue and white sauce boat on stand, decorated views of the River Rhine, c1830, 7½in (19cm) wide.
£110–130 Nor

A J. & W. Ridgway blue and white footbath jug, with Indian Temple design, c1825, 12in (30.5cm) high.
£1,000–1,100 GN

A blue and white pearlware jug, printed with a view of Washington, within a band of flowers and leaves, probably J. Tams & Co, c1825, 9½in (24cm) high.
£850–950 DN

A pair of Minton blue and white opaque punch, ale or cider jugs, printed with Florentine pattern, one impressed '6 quartz', blue printed marks within a scroll cartoche, damaged, c1840, 12in (31cm) high.
£1,800–2,200 C

A spongeware blue and white jug, c1840, 10in (25.5cm) high.
£180–220 Ber

Two Copeland blue and white cream jugs, decorated with Italian pattern, c1911, largest 4¾in (12cm) high.
£38–45 each TAC

A blue and white jug, by Dillwyn, Swansea, decorated in Women with Baskets pattern, c1820, 8in (20.5cm) high.
£350–450 RP

A Copeland jug, decorated with Italian pattern, c1919, 7in (18cm) high.
£62–72 TAC

A Victorian Trent blue and white jug, 5in (12.5cm) high.
£60–70 LUC

PLATES

An English delft plate, painted blue within arcaded and flowerhead bands, c1740, 9in (23cm) diam.
£360–400 DN

An English delft plate, decorated in blue and white on a manganese ground, c1740, 8¾in (22cm) diam.
£250–300 JHo

A delft plate, painted in blue on a manganese ground, probably Bristol, c1735, 8½in (21.5cm) diam.
£280–350 S(NY)

A Dutch Delft blue and white plate, decorated with a spray of wild flowers, c1760, 9¼in (23.5cm) diam.
£80–100 BRU

An English delft dish, decorated with flowers, damaged, c1760, 14in (35.5cm) high.
£100–150 OCH

A Joshua Heath blue and white plate, depicting George Washington and the Arms of the United States, restored, c1780, 10in (25.5cm) diam.
£3,300–3,700 SLN

◄ A Dutch Delft plate, decorated with a central vase of flowers and edged with Ming-style peonies, 1760, 9¾in (25cm) daim.
£100–120 BRU

► A blue and white soup plate, with The Piping Shepherd pattern, c1802, 9¾in (25cm) diam.
£120–160 HEI

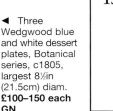

◄ Three Wedgwood blue and white dessert plates, Botanical series, c1805, largest 8½in (21.5cm) diam.
£100–150 each GN

A Brameld blue and white dinner plate, Returning Woodman pattern, c1806, 10in (25.5cm) wide.
£225–275 Nor

A Wedgwood blue and white plate, with floral border, c1810, 10in (25.5cm) diam.
£150–200 SCO

A Thomas Lakin blue and white soup plate, decorated with Classical Ruins pattern, c1810, 9½in (24cm) diam.
£80–90 GN

A William Mason blue and white plate, decorated with Furness Abbey pattern, 1811–23, 8in (20.5cm) diam.
£80–120 GN

A Rogers blue and white plate, decorated with Boston State House, c1815, 6½in (16.5cm) diam.
£150–200 Nor

A blue and white dinner plate, Shipping series, decorated with The Frigate, c1815, 10in (25.5cm) diam.
£250–350 Nor

A Rogers blue and white plate, decorated with Elephant pattern, c1815, 10in (25.5cm) diam.
£100–120 Nor

A Rogers blue and white plate, decorated with Boston State House, c1820, 18in (45.5cm) wide.
£750–850 A&A

A Brameld Rockingham blue and white plate, decorated with Castle of Rochefort pattern, c1820, 8½in (21.5cm) diam.
£120–150 GN

An Enoch Wood blue and white plate, Sporting series, decorated with a pointer, c1820, 8¼in (21.5cm) diam.
£200–245 SCO

This is a very rare series made for the American Market.

A Ralph Hall blue and white plate, decorated with Sheltered Peasants pattern, c1820, 10in (25.5cm) diam.
£180–275 GN

► A Ridgway blue and white plate, depicting Christchurch, Oxford, c1820, 10in (25.5cm) diam.
£120–140 SCO

A Spode blue and white plate, Indian Sporting series, decorated with Death of the Bear pattern, c1820, 10in (25.5cm) diam.
£150–180 GN

A blue and white plate, decorated with Durham Ox pattern within a floral border, c1820, 9¾in (25cm) diam.
£350–400 P(B)

A blue and white plate, decorated with the Piping Shepherd pattern, c1820, 9½in (24cm) diam.
£150–180 P(B)

A Bevington and Co, Swansea, blue and white oval plate, decorated with Monopteros pattern, c1820, 17in (43cm) wide.
£400–500 GN

A Turner blue and white plate, decorated with The Villagers pattern, c1830, 14½in (37cm) wide.
£350–400 GN

A Don Pottery blue and white plate, impressed mark, c1830, 8¼in (21cm) diam.
£115–130 JP

A Ridgway blue and white plate decorated with British Flowers pattern, c1830, 10in (25.5cm) diam.
£150–200 Nor

A Minton miniature plate decorated with De Gaunt Castle, c1830, 3in (7.5cm) diam.
£60–65 OCH

A child's blue and white plate, possibly Davenport, decorated with a view of Windsor Castle, c1840, 6¾in (17cm) diam.
£75–90 IW

A blue and white charger, British Marine series, c1835, 14½in (37cm) diam.
£400–500 GN

A pair of Spode blue and white plates, decorated with the Sarcophagi and Sepulchres at the Head of the Harbour at Cacamo, from the Caramanian series, 1815–20, 10in (25.5cm) diam.
£280–320 TMA

A W. Ridgway & Son blue and white platter, decorated with Catskill Moss, Boston and Bunker's Hill pattern, some damage, dated '1844', 19in (48cm) wide.
£400–450 SK(B)

A Podmore, Walker & Co blue and white platter, British America pattern, c1850, 21in (53cm) wide.
£500–600 RIT

◀ A blue and white plate, depicting Nuneham Courtney, Nr Oxford, with Wild Rose pattern border, c1880, 10in (25.5cm) diam.
£50–60 PBi

▶ A May blue and white platter, marked, c1920, 15¾in (40cm) wide.
£22–28 PSA

SERVICES

A child's Staffordshire blue and white dinner service, comprising 42 pieces, decorated with a country house in a landscape setting, early 19thC, largest tureen 4in (10cm) high.
£700–800 P(G)

A Whitehaven blue and white dinner service, decorated in Marseillaise pattern, early 19thC.
£1,500–2,000 Mit

A pearlware blue and white dessert service, comprising 13 pieces, the rims pierced and moulded with leaf and scroll design, the centres printed in blue with rural landscapes, 19thC, dish 9½in (24cm) wide.
£900–1,000 CAG

A Wedgwood blue and white dinner service, comprising 58 pieces, decorated with Ferrara pattern, early 19thC.
£900–1,100 JH

A Copeland blue and white combination 'lazy Susan' coffee urn and 14-piece coffee service, printed with Willow pattern within gilt line rims, damaged, c1860.
£800–900 CSK

Further Reading

The Dictionary of Blue and White Printed Pottery, 1780–1880, Antiques Collectors' Club, 1994

A Bristol Alkalon China blue and white dinner service, comprising 53 pieces, printed in flow blue in Chinese style with Mandarin pattern, impressed marks, c1900.
£1,200–1,350 HOLL

TEAPOTS & COFFEE POTS

A Spode blue and white miniature teapot, decorated with Daisy and Bead pattern, c1815, 3in (7.5cm) high.
£220–250 SCO

◄ A pearlware blue and white coffee pot, damaged, c1790, 11½in (29cm) high.
£180–200 OCH

A Spode blue and white vase-shaped coffee pot, decorated with Woodman design, c1850, 10½in (27cm) wide.
£500–600 GN

TUREENS & STANDS

A Spode pearlware blue and white egg tureen, cover and liner, with scroll handle, printed with Forest Landscape pattern, damaged and restored, c1810, 10¼in (26cm) wide.
£250–400 HOLL

This egg tureen would have formed the centre of a supper set.

A Rogers blue and white miniature tureen, decorated in Minopteros pattern, c1820, 2in (5cm) wide.
£180–200 AMH

A Riley blue and white sauce tureen and stand, decorated with Girl Musician pattern, c1820.
£350–400 GN

A Spode blue and white soup tureen, decorated in Net pattern, c1820, 11in (28cm) high.
£300–500 GN

A Spode blue and white miniature tureen, decorated with Tower pattern, 1820–30, tureen 3½in (9cm) high.
£125–145 OCH

A Henshaw and Co blue and white sauce tureen, decorated with Castle and Bridge pattern, hairline crack to base, 1820–30, 5½in (14cm) high.
£250–300 OCH

Two Booth's children's blue and white toy plates and a muffin dish, decorated with blue and gilt Willow pattern, 1930s, tureen ¾in (2cm) high.
£30–40 MRW

A Staffordshire blue and white Dr Syntax series sauce tureen stand, decorated with 'Dr Syntax copying the wit of the window', c1880, 9in (23cm) wide.
£130–150 Nor

VASES

A Dutch Delft blue and white four-piece garniture, comprising a pair of octagonal baluster-shaped vases and covers, and a pair of beakers, each moulded on the front with a cartouche with a bird perched on a flowering branch above a basket of flowers, damaged and repaired, c1775, largest 14in (35.5cm) high.
£2,700–3,000 S(NY)

An Adams blue and white vase, c1915, 12in (30.5cm) high.
£120–140 SSW

◄ A pair of blue and white vases and covers, decorated with river landscapes and figure panels, late 19thC, 13¾in (35cm) high.
£200–220 P(E)

MISCELLANEOUS

A blue and white toilet box, c1840, 8in (20.5cm) wide.
£150–220 Nor

A Ridgway blue and white female bed bottle, Humphrey's Clock series, decorated with tales from *The Old Curiosity Shop*, c1835, 12in (30.5cm) long.
£500–600 GN

◄ A set of 12 Wedgwood blue and white tiles, designed by Helen J A Miles with the months of the year, c1877, each tile 6in (15cm) square.
£500–550 SK

Patterns

Many English manufacturers produced their own versions of the famous Willow pattern, originally found on Chinese ceramics. Patterns such as views from foreign lands were taken from fashionable engravings. Unusual patterns can affect the value of a piece.

A Spode blue and white slop bucket, decorated with Italian pattern, c1820, 10in (25.5cm) wide.
£500–600 GN

A blue and white cheese cradle, attributed to Bathwell & Goodfellow, decorated in Palladian Porch pattern, c1820, 11in (28cm) wide.
£1,000–1,200 GN

A Spode blue and white egg cup holder, decorated with daisy pattern, 1820, 7½in (19cm) diam.
£220–250 SCO

An Adams blue and white cheese dish and cover, decorated with Cattle Scenery pattern, c1880, 9in (23cm) wide.
£220–300 Nor

◄ A pair of delft blue and white flower bricks, decorated with stylized flowers and foliage, London or Bristol, slight damage, c1745, 6in (15cm) wide.
£1,000–1,200 CSK

A Minton flow blue garden seat, dated '1878', 17in (43cm) high.
£900–1,200 GN

A Dutch Delft blue and white inkwell, decorated with trailing flowers and leaves, rim chips, 18thC, 4½in (11.5cm) wide.
£340–380 DN

A South Wales Pottery, Llanelly, blue and white jug and bowl set, decorated with Milan pattern, c1850, 12in (30.5cm) high.
£375–450 RP

Shapes

Many of the shapes used by English and French factories for the production of blue and white ware were derived from those used for silver. As a result of the fashion for Oriental imports from the late 17thC, Dutch potters in particular were inspired by chinoiserie shapes and designs.

A blue and white pottery model of a cow, on a green base, possibly Portobello, early 19thC, 4in (10cm) long.
£350–400 JHo

A blue and white pattern ladle, decorated with Spode's Italian pattern, maker unknown, c1820, 13in (33cm) long.
£100–120 SCO

A blue and white money box, on raised bun feet, c1880, 6½in (16.5cm) long.
£350–450 INC

This was used as an RSPCA charity collection box.

A Davenport blue and white mustard pot, decorated with the Family and Mule pattern, c1820, 3in (7.5cm) diam.
£120–150 GN

A blue and white spongeware salt, rim chipped, c1820, 3in (7.5cm) diam.
£30–40 RYA

A Spode blue and white spitoon, with fixed top, decorated in Tower pattern, c1820, 4in (10cm) high.
£400–475 GN

A delft blue and white tea caddy, with metal mount to rim, cover missing, damaged and restored, 18thC, 6in (15cm) high.
£250–300 CSK

A Copeland blue and white toast rack, decorated with Italian pattern, 1940s, 4½in (11.5cm) wide.
£70–85 TAC

Clarice Cliff

Clarice Cliff's name has become synonymous with Art Deco vibrantly-coloured jazzy ceramics. However, it was not until 1923 when she was 24 years old that Cliff got her first break, spending long hours at the A. J. Wilkinson factory in Burslem learning about manufacturing and decorating ceramics. Having established herself as a talented modeller, in 1927 she had the idea to add bright enamel colours in bold triangles to old stock from the adjoining Newport Pottery. This simple ware was given the memorable and outrageous name, Bizarre. Next Cliff issued her Crocus pattern, which remained in production until 1963.

Numerous abstract designs followed in just a few months, and by 1929 Newport Pottery was devoted to manufacturing Bizarre. By 1930 Cliff had 60 skilled paintresses producing her ware and was made Art Director, the first woman to attain this role in the Staffordshire Potteries.

During the 1930s Clarice Cliff became a household name, and her wares were exported around the Empire. The secret of her success was that she was able both to model her own shapes (which by 1935 totalled over 600), and control the patterns put on them. The result was a vast choice of ware in abstract, fruit, floral and landscape designs. The Bizarre name was phased out in 1936, as the vogue in Britain moved to more conservative ceramics, but Cliff still sold thousands of tableware sets until the outbreak of World War II. Just after this she married the factory owner Colley Shorter, and went into semi-retirement. After 1946 Cliff travelled extensively, helping promote traditional ware in the North American export markets.

Bizarre ware was rediscovered in the early 1970s by intrigued collectors and a price spiral began. Conical sugar dredgers that were valued at £10 ($16) in 1976 can now sell for between £800 and £3,000 ($1,300 and $5,000). Early Morning tea sets, with Stamford or Conical shape teapots, in designs such as Windbells or Trees and House, could be bought for under £100 ($160) in 1984, but today can command at least £3,000 ($5,000).

North American collectors will find a mass of traditional printed tableware with 'Clarice Cliff Royal Staffordshire Ceramics' backstamp. This was issued from 1946 to 1963, but is often mistaken as being Cliff's work before Bizarre.

By offering an ever-changing choice of shapes and patterns to help sell ware during the Depression, Clarice Cliff created a huge diverse range that nowadays challenges even the most knowledgeable. It is this that has made her one of the most popular and collectable British Art Deco ceramicists.   **Leonard Griffin**

BOWLS & DISHES

A Clarice Cliff Bizarre Double Conical bowl, decorated with Inspiration Persian pattern in shades of yellow, blue and purple on a turquoise ground, on stepped foot, restored chip to rim, printed factory marks, 1930s, 7in (18cm) high.
£1,200–1,500 CSK

Issued in June 1929, shape No 380 was called a Conical Double Deck in factory literature, and this evocative name describes the one-piece vessel which has 2 wells for water.

A Clarice Cliff Bizarre bowl, decorated with Rhodanthe pattern, with yellow-ground interior, 1930s, 9¾in (25cm) diam.
£200–220 MCA

A Clarice Cliff Bizarre sundae dish, shape No. 259, decorated with Nasturtium pattern, 1930s, 2in (5cm) high.
£180–220 BDA

▶ A Clarice Cliff Fantasque bowl, decorated with Comets pattern, c1930, 6½in (16.5cm) diam.
£650–750 WL

A Clarice Cliff comport, decorated with Original Bizarre pattern, c1930, 7in (18cm) diam.
£680–750 MAV

A Clarice Cliff Bizarre bowl, decorated with Swirls pattern, small chip, factory marks, c1930, 8¼in (21cm) diam.
£350–380 CSK

A Clarice Cliff Bizarre Havre bowl, decorated with Shark's Teeth pattern, factory marks, c1930, 8¼in (21cm) diam.
£280–320 Bon

A Clarice Cliff bowl, decorated with Yellow Autumn pattern, c1930, 4½in (11.5cm) diam.
£220–250 PC

A Clarice Cliff Dover jardinière, decorated with Branch and Square design, c1929–30, 3½in (9cm) high.
£375–425 MEG

A Clarice Cliff Havre bowl, decorated in Pastel Autumn pattern, c1932, 9in (23cm) diam.
£250–300 WTA

◀ A Clarice Cliff Havre bowl, decorated with Canterbury Bells pattern, c1932, 8in (20.5cm) diam.
£220–250 MEG

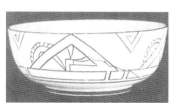

A Clarice Cliff Bizarre Holborn bowl, decorated with Orange V pattern, marked, 1930s, 9¼in (24cm) diam.
£340–400 Bon

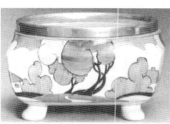

A Clarice Cliff Bizarre Fantasque square-shaped bowl, with electroplated rim, decorated with Blue Autumn pattern, Newport Pottery, c1935, 8in (20.5cm) square.
£450–500 AG

A Clarice Cliff sugar bowl, decorated with Coral Firs pattern, c1933, 3¼in (8.5cm) high.
£200–250 RIC

LOCATE THE SOURCE
The source of each illustration in Miller's can be found by checking the code letters below each caption with the Key to Illustrations, pages 376–379.

◀ A Clarice Cliff Biarritz shape bowl, decorated with Coral Firs pattern, c1934, 6in (15cm) wide.
£200–220 BKK

▶ A Clarice Cliff Newport Bizarre jardinière, decorated with Latona pattern, painted mark, 1930s, 10in (25.5cm) diam.
£480–520 GAK

◀ A Clarice Cliff Bizarre Holborn bowl, decorated with Aurea pattern, c1935, 8¼in (21cm) diam.
£270–300 GSP

CANDLESTICKS

A Clarice Cliff Bizarre candlestick, shape no 310, decorated in Geometric pattern, the base with hand-painted 'Bizarre' mark, 1928, 4½in (11.5cm) diam.
£320–350 RIC

► A Clarice Cliff Fantasque dwarf candlestick, decorated with Bobbins pattern, 1930s, 3in (7.5cm) high.
£220–250 P(B)

A Clarice Cliff candle holder, inverted 368 shape, Fern Pot, decorated with Pastel Autumn pattern, c1930, 3½in (9cm) high.
£820–900 DSG

A Clarice Cliff candlestick, shape no. 331, decorated with Delecia Citrus pattern, c1930, 3½in (9cm) diam.
£260–300 RIC

A Clarice Cliff Bizarre candlestick, in the form of a water nymph, 1930s, 6¾in (17.5cm) high.
£400–450 WL

JUGS

A Clarice Cliff Conical jug, decorated with Umbrellas and Rain pattern, c1929, 7in (18cm) high.
£600–700 RIC

► A set of 3 Clarice Cliff tankard jugs, decorated in Crocus pattern, 1930s, tallest 6¼in (16cm) high.
£500–550 DN

A Clarice Cliff Eton jug, decorated with Swirls pattern, c1930, 5in (12.5cm) high.
£550–600 BKK

A Clarice Cliff two-handled Lotus jug, decorated with Melon pattern, Fantasque mark, c1930, 11½in (29cm) high.
£950–1,100 Bon

A Clarice Cliff Lotus shape jug, decorated with Anemone pattern, late 1930s, 11½in (29cm) high.
£380–420 GH

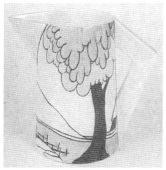

A Clarice Cliff conical jug, decorated with House and Bridge pattern, c1931, 7in (18cm) high.
£1,000–1,200 RIC

A Clarice Cliff Lotus jug, decorated with Idyll pattern, c1932, 5½in (14cm) high.
£550–600 WTA

A Clarice Cliff Bizarre beer pitcher, decorated with Idyll pattern, c1932, 11in (28cm) high.
£900–1,000 GH

A Clarice Cliff Athens shape jug, decorated with Honolulu pattern, c1933, 8in (20.5cm) high.
£600–700 RIC

A Clarice Cliff Celtic Harvest teapot and jug, decorated with embossed wheat and flowers, Newport Pottery, c1935, jug 7½in (19cm) high.
£250–300 MAR

A Clarice Cliff Lynton shape Bizarre jug, 1930s, 3in (7.5cm) high.
£135–155 DAC

◄ A Clarice Cliff Castellated Circle pattern jug, c1930, 4in (10cm) high.
£380–450 BKK

► A Clarice Cliff Dragon Fantasque jug, shape no 628, decorated in Secrets pattern, printed mark and facsimile signature, impressed no '3', early 1930s, 7in (18cm) high.
£300–350 TEN

◄ A Clarice Cliff Tolphin shape toilet jug, decorated with Applique Lugano pattern, rim damaged and repaired, black Bizarre mark to base, 1930s, 9¾in (25cm) high.
£1,200–1,400 CAG

PLATES

A Clarice Cliff plate, decorated with Original Bizarre pattern, c1928, 7in (18cm) diam.
£120–140 BKK

A Clarice Cliff plate, decorated in Broth pattern, early gilt mark, c1929, 6¼in (16cm) diam.
£250–280 BKK

A Clarice Cliff tea plate, decorated in Brown Lily pattern, c1929, 6in (15cm) diam.
£250–300 PC

A Clarice Cliff tea plate, decorated in blue Luxor pattern, c1929, 6in (15cm) diam.
£550–600 PC

A Clarice Cliff Fantasque oval meat platter, decorated with Umbrellas pattern, painted in colours, printed factory marks, c1929, 21in (53cm) wide.
£350–400 CSK

A Clarice Cliff tea plate, decorated in black and red Umbrellas pattern, c1929, 6in (15cm) diam.
£270–300 PC

A Clarice Cliff Bizarre octagonal plate, decorated with Blue W pattern, c1930, 6in (15cm) diam.
£360–400 WTA

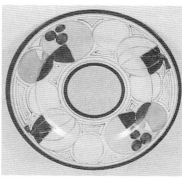

A Clarice Cliff plate, decorated with Melon pattern, c1930, 10in (25.5cm) diam.
£700–800 BKK

A Clarice Cliff plate, decorated around the rim in Secrets pattern, c1929, 9in (23cm) diam.
£80–100 YY

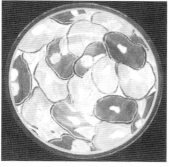

A Clarice Cliff charger, decorated with Blue Chintz pattern, lithograph Fantasque mark, c1930, 18in (45.5cm) diam.
£900–1,100 Bon

A Clarice Cliff tea plate, decorated in Red Flower pattern, c1930, 6in (15cm) diam.
£270–300 PC

A Clarice Cliff plate, decorated in Red Autumn pattern, c1931, 9in (23cm) diam.
£750–850 BKK

A Clarice Cliff tea plate, decorated in House and Bridge pattern, c1931, 6in (15cm) diam.
£450–500 PC

A Clarice Cliff tea plate, decorated in Farmhouse pattern, c1931, 6in (15cm) diam.
£270–300 PC

A Clarice Cliff plate, decorated in Farmhouse pattern, c1931, 10in (25.5cm) diam.
£630–700 BKK

A Clarice Cliff octagonal plate, decorated with Peter Pan Crocus pattern, c1931, 5½in (14cm) diam.
£280–320 BKK

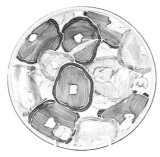

A Clarice Cliff Newport Bizarre Fantasque plate, decorated in Chintz pattern, printed marks, c1932, 9in (23cm) diam.
£300–350 GAK

A Clarice Cliff octagonal cake plate, decorated with Idyll pattern, c1932, 7½in (19cm) diam.
£270–300 CSA

A Clarice Cliff Biarritz plate, rim decorated with Blue Firs pattern, c1933, 10½in (26.5cm) wide.
£220–240 GH

A Newport Pottery Clarice Cliff Bizarre Fantasque octagonal plate, decorated with Secrets pattern, c1933, 10in (25.5cm) diam.
£220–250 MCA

A Clarice Cliff plate, decorated with brown and green lined pattern, c1933, 7in (18cm) diam.
£50–60 RAC

A Clarice Cliff tea plate, decorated in Goldstone pattern, c1933, 6in (15cm) diam.
£120–150 PC

Two Clarice Cliff tea plates, decorated in Cowslip pattern, one yellow, the other green, c1930, 6in (15cm) diam.
£150–200 each PC

◄ A Clarice Cliff tea plate, decorated in Trees and House pattern, c1930, 6in (15cm) diam.
£200–250 RIC

Fakes

During the past ten years, Clarice Cliff fakes have appeared on the market that have photographically-copied marks applied. They are identifiable by the inferior quality of the painting and by the fact that the marks look blurred.

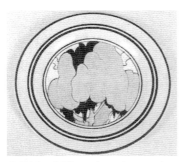

A Clarice Cliff tea plate, decorated with Solitude pattern, c1933, 6in (15cm) diam.
£450–500 PC

A Clarice Cliff Bizarre plate, decorated with Orange Secrets pattern, c1934, 9in (23cm) diam.
£450–500 WTA

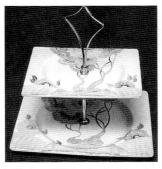

A Clarice Cliff Biarritz double cake plate, decorated with Pink Pearls pattern, c1935, 9½in (24cm) high.
£450–500 BKK

A Wilkinson's Pottery Clarice Cliff octagonal plate, decorated with Taormina pattern, c1936, 9in (23cm) diam.
£180–200 MCA

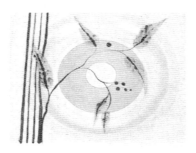

A Clarice Cliff Biarritz plate, decorated with Kelverne pattern, c1936, 9in (23cm) wide.
£100–120 PC

A set of 6 Clarice Cliff Original Bizarre tea plates, painted in orange, green and black with a star medallion on a yellow ground, printed marks in green and black and impressed marks, 1930s, 6¼in (16cm) square.
£1,000–1,200 DN

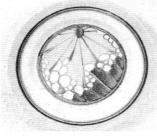

A Clarice Cliff plate, decorated with Broth pattern, 1930s, 6½in (16.5cm) diam.
£200–250 RIC

A Clarice Cliff Bizarre plate, designed by Dame Laura Knight, decorated with Circus Pattern, 1930s, 9in (23cm) diam.
£800–1,000 Bri

Laura Knight

Laura Knight was a Newlyn School artist who produced a series of circus paintings during the 1930s. These proved very popular and were translated into simplified dinnerware designs. John Armstrong produced similar designs for Foley.

PRESERVE JARS

A Clarice Cliff Fantasque beehive honey pot, 1930s, 3½in (9cm) high.
£150–200 WTA

A Clarice Cliff Daffodil shape conserve pot, decorated in Poplar pattern, c1932, 5in (13cm) high.
£350–400 WTA

A Clarice Cliff Bizarre jam pot and cover, decorated in House and Bridge pattern, c1931, 4in (10cm) high.
£200–250 WTA

A Clarice Cliff preserve pot and cover, shape No 527, painted with stylised lowers and foliage, 1930s, 4in (10cm) diam.
£70–90 GH

A Clarice Cliff Bizarre Conical preserve pot, decorated in Windbells pattern, rubber stamp mark, c1933, 4in (10cm) high.
£300–350 GAK

A Clarice Cliff jam pot and cover, shape No 527, decorated in Viscaria pattern, c1934, 4in (10cm) diam.
£160–200 RIC

SERVICES

A Clarice Cliff Tankard shape coffee service, comprising 21 pieces, decorated with Crocus pattern, 1928.
£1,250–1,450 HCC

A Clarice Cliff part dinner service, comprising 23 pieces, with Odilon shape tureens, decorated with Crocus pattern, 1930s.
£1,200–1,400 AH

A Clarice Cliff Conical tea-for-two set, decorated in Crocus pattern, c1932, plate 7in (18cm) diam.
£450–500 WTA

► A Clarice Cliff Fantasque Bizarre Conical part tea set, comprising teapot and cover, 2 cups and saucers and a side plate, painted in colours with Double V pattern, damaged, printed marks, 1930s.
£650–700 CSK

A Clarice Cliff Bizarre two-person tea set, with Stamford shape teapot, Bon Jour milk jug, decorated with Crocus pattern, facsimile signature in black and impressed date code for 1933.
£550–600 P(NE)

◄ A Clarice Cliff Bizarre tea set, comprising 29 pieces, decorated with Gayday pattern, with facsimile signature, c1930.
£2,200–2,500 P

Further Reading
Miller's Art Deco Antiques Checklist, Miller's Publications, 1991

► A Clarice Cliff Newport Pottery tête-a-tête, with Stamford teapot and Bon Jour milk jug, decorated in Gayday pattern, 1930s.
£450–500 W

A Clarice Cliff Bon Jour tea set, designed by Eva Crofts, decorated with Bizarre pattern in bright colours on a yellow ground, printed mark, c1933.
£2,200–2,600 RBB

A Clarice Cliff pottery Biarritz dinner and dessert service, comprising 2 tureens and covers, a gravy boat, a graduated set of 3 large rectangular plates, 6 dinner plates, 6 dessert plates and 6 smaller plates, each piece painted with a tree, a yellow trunk and pink and blue blossom, c1934, one tureen cover damaged.
£950–1,200 Bea

A Clarice Cliff Windsor shape tea-for-two, decorated with Gayday pattern, 1930s, plate 6in (15cm) diam.
£2,000–2,300 MAV

A Clarice Cliff Stamford shape tea-for-two, decorated with Sunshine pattern, marked, c1934, teapot 5in (12.5cm) high.
£550–600 AG

A Clarice Cliff Bon Jour bachelor tea set, comprising 7 pieces, designed by Eva Crofts, painted with a bird, trees and sun, in shades of red, green, black and yellow, factory marks, c1934, teapot 5¼in (13cm) high.
£1,500–1,650 CSK

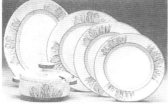

◄ A Clarice Cliff dinner service, comprising 48 pieces, decorated with Sungleam Crocus pattern, marked, 1930s.
£1,300–1,500 AG

► A Clarice Cliff Stamford shape tea-for-two, decorated with Gibraltar pattern, 1930s, plate 6in (15cm) diam.
£3,200–3,500 BKK

SUGAR SIFTERS

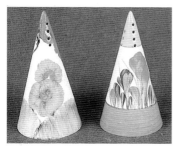

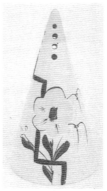

Two Clarice Cliff Bizarre Conical-shape sugar sifters, one decorated with Rhodanthe pattern, one with Crocus, 1930s, 5½in (14cm) high.
l. £250–300
r. £450–500 GH

> **Cross Reference**
> See Colour Review

A Clarice Cliff sugar shaker, decorated with Black Eye Marigold pattern, c1930, 5½in 14cm) high.
£250–300 TAC

A Clarice Cliff Bon Jour shape sugar shaker, decorated with Crocus pattern, c1933, 5in (13cm) high.
£220–250 WTA

A Clarice Cliff Conical sugar sifter, decorated with Orange Roof Cottage pattern, printed factory marks, c1932, 5in (13cm) high.
£1,000–1,200 WTA

A Clarice Cliff Bizarre sugar caster, decorated with My Garden pattern, printed and painted marks in black, 1930s, 5¾in (14.5cm) high.
£180–220 DN

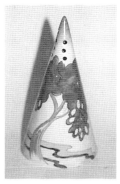

A Clarice Cliff Conical shape sugar sifter, c1935, 5½in (14cm) high.
£540–600 CSA

A Clarice Cliff Bon Jour shape sugar sifter, decorated with Secrets pattern, printed marks, 1930s, 5in (12.5cm) high.
£320–350 WL

A Clarice Cliff Conical sugar sifter, painted with Oasis pattern, blue foot rim, c1935, 5¼in (13.5cm) high.
£450–500 Bea(E)

TEAPOTS

A Clarice Cliff Bon Jour teapot, from Artists in Industry Series, 1930s, 5½in (14cm) high.
£300–350 RIC

A Clarice Cliff Conical shape teapot, decorated with Farmhouse pattern, c1931, 5¾in (14.5cm) high.
£900–1,000 CSA

A Clarice Cliff Windsor shape teapot, decorated with Sundew pattern, c1937, 5in (12.5cm) high.
£50–60 CSA

VASES

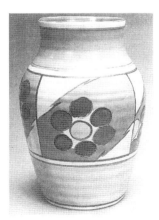

A Clarice Cliff Fantasque vase, shape No 355, decorated with Broth pattern, with Lawley's gold backstamp, c1930, 7in (18cm) high.
£550–650 GH

A Clarice Cliff vase, shape No 451, decorated in Limberlost pattern, c1930, 6in (15cm) high.
£350–450 RIC

A Clarice Cliff Fantasque vase, Isis shape, decorated with Pebbles pattern, restored, printed mark in black, 1929, 9¾in (24.5cm) high.
£720–800 DN

► A Clarice Cliff Lynton shape vase, decorated with Limberlost patern, c1932, 3¾in (9.5cm) high.
£250–300 RIC

A Clarice Cliff vase, shape No. 368, decorated with Summerhouse pattern, c1931, 3½in (9cm) high.
£420–460 BKK

A Clarice Cliff vase, shape No 369, decorated in Latona Knight Errant pattern, painted by John Butler, 1930, 10in (25.5cm) high.
£2,500–3,000 BKK

A Clarice Cliff reeded trumpet vase, decorated with My Garden pattern and a butterfly, c1930, 10in (25.5cm) high.
£160–180 GH

A Clarice Cliff Bizarre faceted baluster-shaped vase, shape No 342, decorated with Latona Tree pattern, printed and painted marks in black, c1931, 8in (20.5cm) high.
£580–650 DN

A Clarice Cliff vase, shape No 264, decorated with Applique Caravan pattern, c1931, 8in (20.5cm) high.
£2,700–3,000 WTA

A Clarice Cliff vase, shape No 265, decorated with Crocus pattern, c1931, 6in (15cm) high.
£300–350 BKK

A Clarice Cliff vase, shape No 362, decorated with Orange Chintz pattern, c1932, 8in (20.5cm) high.
£700–800 RIC

A Clarice Cliff vase, shape No 366, decorated with Apples pattern, c1931, 6in (15cm) high.
£1,200–1,500 RIC

A Clarice Cliff Isis vase, decorated in Orange Roof Cottage pattern, c1932, 12in (30.5cm) high.
£900–1,100 BKK

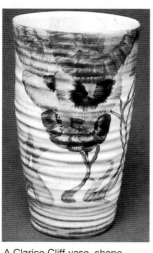

A Clarice Cliff vase, shape No 630, painted with Viscaria pattern, 7½in (19cm) high.
£480–520 BKK

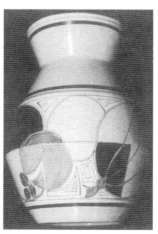

A Clarice Cliff Fantasque vase, shape no 360, decorated with Melon pattern, c1932, 8½in (21.5cm) high.
£800–1,000 WTA

A Clarice Cliff Newport Bizarre vase, decorated with Rudyard pattern, marked, 1930s, 3in (7.5cm) high.
£450–500 GAK

▶ A Clarice Cliff posy trough, decorated with My Garden pattern, c1935, 7¼in (18.5cm) diam.
£150–180 CSA

A Clarice Cliff Bizarre Fantasque vase, shape No 360, decorated with Solitude pattern, black printed mark, c1933, 8in (20.5cm) high.
£1,600–1,800 JM

A Clarice Cliff Bizarre vase, shape No 342, decorated with Sliced Fruit pattern, printed marks, 1930s, 7¾in (20cm) high.
£420–460 WL

A Clarice Cliff vase, shape No 386, decorated with Capri pattern, slight damage, c1935, 12¼in (31cm) high.
£280–320 Bea(E)

A Clarice Cliff spill jar, shape No. 196, decorated with Secrets pattern, 1930s, 9in (23cm) high.
£600–650 WTA

A Clarice Cliff Clouvre vase, brightly painted with orange, purple, blue and yellow flowers against a mottled purple ground, printed marks and script pattern name, c1930, 6in (15cm) high.
£450–550 N

A Clarice Cliff Bizarre vase, hairline crack, late 1930s, 6½in (16.5cm) high.
£80–100 MRW

A Clarice Cliff three-footed vase, decorated with My Garden pattern, c1937, 9in (23cm) high.
£100–120 BKK

A Clarice Cliff swan flower holder, with printed green factory marks, 1930s, 8in (20.5cm) high.
£250–300 WTA

A Clarice Cliff Fantasque Bizarre vase, shape No 341, decorated with Gibraltar pattern, printed factory marks to base, 1930s, 5½in (14cm) high.
£650–750 CAG

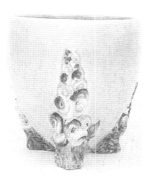

A Clarice Cliff vase, decorated with Forest Glen pattern, c1936, 12in (30.5cm) high.
£650–700 WTA

◄ A Clarice Cliff vase, shape No 370, decorated with Viscaria pattern, c1936, 5¾in (14.5cm) high.
£770–850 BKK

A Clarice Cliff posy vase, shaped as the gnarled base of a tree, decorated at each end in colours with groups of flowers amid grasses, late 1930s, 11in (28cm) long.
£70–80 RAC

WALL MASKS

A Clarice Cliff Bizarre wall mask, Flora, facsimile signature, c1935, 6¾in (17cm) high.
£250–280 P(Ba)
This pattern was made in several sizes.

A Clarice Cliff wall pocket, modelled as Pan with flowers and foliage in his hair, slight damage, factory marks, c1930, 8¼in (21cm) high.
£180–200 CSK

A Clarice Cliff wall mask, depicting Monique, the floral headband picked out in colours on a matte ground, blue printed mark, late 1930s, 7in (18cm) high.
£400–450 DN

MISCELLANEOUS

A Clarice Cliff ashtray, decorated with Umbrellas and Rain pattern, c1930, 4½in (11.5cm) diam.
£320–360 BKK

A Clarice Cliff ashtray, decorated with Orange Roof Cottage pattern, early 1930s, 5in (13cm) diam.
£150–200 RIC

A Clarice Cliff ashtray, decorated with Pastel Autumn pattern, c1931, 4½in (11.5cm) high.
£750–850 BKK

A Clarice Cliff smoker's set, decorated with Gibraltar pattern, 1931–32, tray 7½in (19cm) wide.
£5,500–6,000 MAV

A Clarice Cliff Bizarre biscuit barrel, shape No 478, decorated with Delecia pattern in coloured enamels, with silver-plated cover and handle, on tapering section feet, printed marks in black, c1930, 6¾in (17cm) high.
£400–450 DN

A Clarice Cliff Fantasque Bizarre biscuit barrel and cover, Hereford shape, decorated with Blue Chintz pattern, with swing handle, minor chips to rim, c1932, 6½in (16.5cm) high.
£230–260 GH

A Clarice Cliff Bizarre Fantasque tapered biscuit barrel, decorated with Blue Autumn pattern, electroplated mounts, c1935, 5in (12.5cm) diam.
£450–500 AG

◄ A Clarice Cliff Harvest biscuit barrel, c1938, 7¼in (18.5cm) high.
£170–200 CSA

► A Clarice Cliff Chester shape fern pot, decorated with Original Bizarre pattern, c1929, 3½in (9cm) high.
£370–400 BKK

Commemorative Ware

Commemorative items were often inexpensively made and, although they may be attractive to look at, their primary value lies in their historical significance and in whom or what they represent. Holding a coronation mug or a bust of a prominent personality can help bring history alive and provide a tangible link with events of the past.

Although commemorative wares were produced by delft potters in the 17th century, they did not reach the popular mass market until the late 18th and early 19th centuries, when transport and improved industrial techniques allowed their mass production and widespread distribution. Ceramics dominate the market, vast numbers having been produced during the Victorian era to celebrate both significant events and renowned individuals. That particular period also saw the beginning of a tradition in Britain for major exhibitions, the first being the Great Exhibition of 1851, the brainchild of Prince Albert and organized by Sir Henry Cole. Later came the International Exhibition of 1862, the British Empire Exhibition of 1924, the Empire Exhibition of 1938 in Scotland and, of course, the Festival of Britain in 1951. Each was a lavish celebration of its time, showcasing the most interesting and exciting aspects of the period and pointing the way to the future. In practically every case, the only physical reminders of these great exhibitions are the commemorative items made for their visitors, which are still collected today.

Demand for commemorative ware is strong, but whereas in the past interest centred on the most attractive items, today most collectors have a more academic interest in a particular subject and therefore collect related items. Items made for the nursery as instructional pieces are very collectable today. Commemorative ware with a royal connection lead the field, but the value of commemoratives linked to current royalty can be adversely affected by family crises or scandals. That said, there is a good, stable market for anything that refers to the Queen Mother owing to her continued popularity.

Commemorative wares with a political theme are popular too. Naturally, Winston Churchill figures prominently but, more recently, interest has grown in items that relate to Margaret Thatcher. Military themes also have a strong following, a large amount of material having been produced as a result of WWI. Lately, Crimean War commemoratives have made good prices. Of course, there is always a place for the unusual, and some collectors actively seek the rare and esoteric. **Andrew Hilton**

CUPS & MUGS

A Coalport commemorative loving cup, each side decorated with a head and shoulders silhouette of George III, inscribed in gilt 'Long May the King Live', the reverse with 'Token from Windsor', the rim gilt, 1810, 3¾in (9.5cm) high.
£900–1,000 SAS

A Staffordshire porcelain pink lustre banded cup and saucer, printed in black and inscribed 'HRH Princess Charlotte, died Nov 6 1817', 2¼in (5.5cm) high.
£110–120 SAS

A porcelain cup and saucer, each with a portrait of the Duke of York, within a band of brightly enamelled flowers and foliage, slight damage, 1827, saucer 5½in (14cm) diam.
£260–300 SAS

◀ A pottery mug, commemorating the coronation of King William IV and Queen Adelaide, the interior with union flowers and inscribed ribbons, c1831, 5in (12.5cm) high.
£175–200 SAS

A pottery mug, commemorating the coronation of King William IV and Queen Adelaide, printed in purple with portraits centred by a crown and flowers of the union, restored, inscribed and dated '1831', 4in (10cm) high.
£220–240 SAS

A pottery mug, printed in pink with named portraits of Earl Grey and Lord John Russell, centred by a spray of union flowers, crown and inscription 'Champions of Reform', 1832, 3¼in (8.5cm) high.
£170–200 SAS

A Swansea transfer-printed mug, commemorating the coronation of Queen Victoria, c1837, 2¼in (5.5cm) high.
£600–700 BCO

A Swansea mug, printed in purple with head and shoulder portraits of Queen Victoria centred by a floral bordered cartouche with crown, 'Victoria Regina' and dates of birth, proclamation and coronation, the interior rim with scrolling border, damaged, c1838, 3¼in (8.5cm) high.
£350–400 SAS

A Staffordshire mug, commemorating the coronation of Queen Victoria, the scroll handle with pinched decoration and printed in black with 2 portraits centred by a crown, the inner rim with trellis and floral panel border, inscribed, 1838, 3¼in (8.5cm) high.
£800–900 SAS

A pearlware mug, printed in blue with an inscription, commemorating the coronation of Queen Victoria, hairline cracks, c1838, 3in (7.5cm) high.
£500–600 Bon

A porcelain tea cup and saucer, printed and painted with Victoria and Albert, picked out in purple lustre, c1840, saucer 5½in (12.5cm) diam.
£45–55 SER

A porcelain mug, with scroll handle, printed in black with a named portrait of Sir Robert Peel, flanked by wheatears, gilt rims, slight damage, c1850, 3in (7.5cm) high.
£180–200 SAS

Sir Robert Peel died following a fall from his horse whilst riding in Hyde Park on 29 June 1850.

A pottery mug, printed in black with portraits centred by a crown and inscribed 'Victoria & Albert, married Feb 10th 1840', flanked by flowers of the union, c1840, 3½in (9cm) high.
£350–400 SAS

A loving cup, printed in black with portraits of Queen Victoria and Prince Albert, the reverse with scenes of agriculture, industry and trade above a ribboned inscription 'True blue principles Fear God and Honour the Queen', restored, dated '1844', 4¾in (12cm) high.
£240–270 SAS

Frog Mugs
A realistically modelled frog or toad was placed inside the mug, only to be seen by drinkers when they had finished their beverage. Some frogs were produced with hollow bodies and open mouths, so that they could spurt the drinker with liquid.

◄ A porcelain tea cup and saucer, printed in black to commemorate the Great Exhibition of 1851, within green and gilt borders, cup 3in (7.5cm) high.
£140–170 W&S

A lustre frog mug, commemorating the Crimean War, c1854, 5in (12.5cm) high.
£240–270 OCH

A pottery mug, commemorating the wedding of the Princess Royal, transfer-printed in black, lined in pink lustre, c1858, 2½in (6.5cm) high.
£160–180 SAS

A WIlliam of Orange commemorative mug, printed with red Orange Order decoration, mid-19thC, 4in (10cm) high.
£120–135 TVM

A pottery mug, commemorating the marriage of the Prince and Princess of Wales, the portraits surmounted by Prince of Wales feathers, inscribed, dated '1863', 4in (10cm) high.
£140–155 SAS

A Doulton Burslem pottery mug, commemorating Queen Victoria's Jubilee, printed in brown with young and old portrait medallions, inscribed ribbon and crown, 1887, 3¼in (8.5cm) high.
£95–110 SAS

A pottery mug, by WC & Co, commemorating the wedding of Edward VII to Princess Alexandra in 1863, printed in purple with an oval portrait panel depicting the Prince and Princess, inscribed and dated, printed mark, c1863, 3¼in (8.5cm) high.
£130–150 SAS

A mug, commemorating Queen Victoria's Jubilee, given by the Mayor of Gravesend, 1887, 3½in (9cm) high.
£80–100 CRO

◄ A pottery mug, commemorating the visit to Bournemouth by the Prince and Princess of Wales, printed in brown with oval portraits, centred by a view entitled 'Royal Victoria Hospital, Bournemouth', gilt rim, dated '1890', 2¾in (7cm) high.
£80–90 SAS

► A porcelain mug, by Wileman, commemorating the wedding of George V and Mary of Teck, enamelled with heraldic shield, flags and ribboned inscription, gilt rim, 1893, 2¾in (7cm) high.
£70–80 SAS

A pottery cup and saucer, by William Lowe, commemorating the Diamond Jubilee of Queen Victoria, printed in sepia with inscribed cartouche flanked by brightly coloured flags and flowers, gilt rims, 1897, saucer 8in (20.5cm) diam.
£70–80 SAS

A Carlton Ware beaker, commemorating Queen Victoria's Diamond Jubilee, brown transfer-printed and hand-enamelled, pattern No. 856, blue crown mark, 1897, 3½in (9cm) high.
£80–90 StC

A Staffordshire mug, commemorating the Boer War, in the form of Lord Kitchener, c1900, 6¼in (16cm) high.
£55–65 OD

A Copeland pottery tyg, commemorating the Transvaal War, decorated in colours with portraits, an allegory of Britannia, flags and inscriptions, with gilding, c1900, 5¼in (13.5cm) high.
£900–1,000 SAS

A Doulton two-handled loving cup, with moulded portrait of Admiral Lord Nelson, commemorating his centenary in 1905, 5¾in (14.5cm) high.
£600–680 TVM

A pottery tyg, printed in turquoise with portraits of the King and Queen, Bishop of Bath and Glastonbury Abbey, inscribed, dated '1909', 4in (10cm) high.
£35–40 SAS

An Aynsley porcelain commemorative mug, printed in sepia and enamelled in colours with portrait panels, ribbons, flowers of the union; scenes from the Empire and shield, gilt rim, 1911, 3in (7.5cm) high.
£45–50 SAS

A mug, commemorating the coronation of King George V and Queen Mary, presented to the Mayor of Rochester, June 22nd, 1911, 3in (7.5cm) high.
£30–35 COL

A pottery mug, commemorating the Prince of Wales' visit to Egremont, printed in black, inscribed for June 29th 1927, gilt rim, 2¾in (7cm) high.
£90–110 SAS

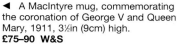

◄ A MacIntyre mug, commemorating the coronation of George V and Queen Mary, 1911, 3½in (9cm) high.
£75–90 W&S

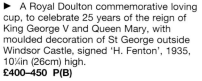

► A Royal Doulton commemorative loving cup, to celebrate 25 years of the reign of King George V and Queen Mary, with moulded decoration of St George outside Windsor Castle, signed 'H. Fenton', 1935, 10¼in (26cm) high.
£400–450 P(B)

A Hammersley mug, commemorating the Silver Jubilee of George V and Queen Mary, enamelled in red and green with a silver rim, c1935, 3½in (9cm) high.
£65–75 W&S

A Royal Doulton buff-coloured loving cup, commemorating the death of George V, printed with a sepia portrait within green foliate branches, inscribed and lined in silver, 1936, 4¾in (12cm) high.
£150–170 SAS

A Paragon loving cup, commemorating the Silver Jubilee of George V and Queen Mary, with floral handle, inscribed and lined in silver, 1935, 3½in (9cm) high.
£90–100 SAS

► A Bell china cup, saucer and plate, commemorating the coronation of King Edwards VIII, c1936, plate 5in (12.5cm) wide.
£80–100 CRO

A Burleigh Ware mug, designed by Dame Laura Knight, commemorating the coronation of George VI and Queen Elizabeth, printed marks, 1937, 3¼in (8.5cm) high.
£45–55 MAC

A cream-coloured mug, commemorating the accession of Edward VIII, moulded with monogram and inscription, c1936, 5in (12.5cm) high.
£65–75 SAS

A coronation cup and saucer, decorated with a photographic portrait of Princesses Elizabeth and Margaret, and a blue-lined rim, 1937, saucer 3in (7.5cm) diam.
£50–55 SAS

A CWS Windsor china mug, commemorating the coronation of Edward VIII, with red and blue 'ER' handle, c1936, 3in (7.5cm) high.
£60–70 W&S

A Royal Doulton loving cup, designed by Noke, with moulded portrait medallion of George VI and Queen Elizabeth, the reverse with view of Windsor Castle, the handles detailing the Dominions, dated '1937', 10½in (26.5cm) high.
£360–400 SAS

A Coronetware cup and saucer, by Parrot & Co, commemorating the coronation of George VI, 1937, saucer 3½in (9cm) diam.
£35–40 SAS

A Wedgwood blue pottery mug, depicting Sir Winston Churchill in white, and with inscription, c1941, 3in (7.5cm) high.
£85–95 W&S

Further Reading

Miller's Antiques Price Guide, Miller's Publications, 1999

JUGS

A jug, commemorating the coronation of George III and Queen Charlotte, c1780, 5in (12.5cm) high.
£1,200–1,350 JHo

A pottery jug, decorated with bands of pink lustre and printed in black with portraits, inscribed 'Queen Caroline', 1821, 4¾in (12cm) diam.
£180–200 SAS

A pearlware commemorative jug, printed in purple with Admiral Lord Nelson and his campaigns, c1810, 7in (18cm) high.
£550–600 TVM

A 'Green-Bag' jug, with pink lustre overglaze, with a picture and inscription 'God Save Queen Caroline!' on one side, 'Long Live Queen Caroline!' and a verse on the other side, c1821, 5½in (14cm) high.
£680–750 CRO

◄ A moulded pottery jug, commemorating the coronation of William IV, with an all-over trellis and daisy design, printed in blue with portraits beneath panels of coronation trophies within scrolling cartouches, c1831, 7¾in (19.5cm) high.
£340–380 SAS

A pearlware commemorative jug, printed in blue with a portrait of Admiral Lord Nelson, and with a view of HMS *Victory*, within military emblems, battle honours and leaf scrolls, inscribed, slight damage, c1810, 5½in (14cm) high.
£600–650 DN

A jug, transfer-printed in black, commemorating the coronation of William IV and Queen Adelaide, 1831, 5in (12.5cm) high.
£350–400 CRO

A brown stoneware jug, applied in white with portraits centred by superimposed profiles of Victoria and Albert beneath a border of oak leaves and acorns, c1890, 6in (15cm) high.
£125–150 SAS

A jug, by J. & M. P. Bell & Co, Glasgow Pottery, commemorating the wedding of the Prince of Wales and Princess Alexandra, 1863, 8in (20cm) high.
£125–175 CRO

A set of 3 Doulton Lambeth globular jugs, commemorating the Diamond Jubilee of Queen Victoria, each with young and old portrait medallions in green on a blue ground, the neck and foot rim coloured brown, inscribed and dated, 1897, largest 9½in (24cm) high.
£440–480 SAS

A porcelain jug, by Read & Clementson, printed in pink with 2 portraits, inscribed 'Victoria Regina, proclaimed 20th of June 1837', chip to top of handle, 5¼in (13.5cm) high.
£320–350 SAS

A Staffordshire copper lustre jug, with embossed portraits of Victoria and Albert, probably commemorating their wedding, c1840, 5in (12.5cm) high.
£160–200 RP

A Llanelly Pottery jug, commemorating the death of Prince Albert, c1863, 7¾in (19.5cm) high.
£250–300 RP

A Scottish pottery jug, commemorating the marriage of the Prince of Wales, later Edward VII, and named portrait of Princess Alexandra on reverse, by Bell & Co, 1863, 8¾in (22cm) high.
£140–160 SAS

A Doulton Lambeth brown stoneware jug, commemorating the Relief of Ladysmith, decorated with a sailor with rifle above, and inscribed scroll and portraits of Captain H. Lambton and Captain P. M. Scott, impressed marks, 1900, 8in (20.5cm) high.
£200–220 Oli

A Doulton jug, depicting Admiral Lord Nelson and his captains, c1905, 8½in (21.5cm) high.
£500–550 TVM

A Denby jug, commemorating the coming of age of Wilfred Hugh Julian Gough, Caer-Rhûn, inscribed in Welsh text, dated '1909', 7in (18cm) high.
£55–65 KES

◄ An Alfred Meakin Astoria shape mug, commemorating 'The Champions of Democracy', with printed colour portraits of Winston Churchill and Franklin D. Roosevelt, 1940s, 3½in (9cm) high.
£55–65 MSB

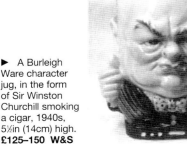

► A Burleigh Ware character jug, in the form of Sir Winston Churchill smoking a cigar, 1940s, 5½in (14cm) high.
£125–150 W&S

PLATES

A pearlware plate, entitled
'Her Majesty Caroline, Queen
of England', with blue-lined rim,
chipped, 1821, 6¾in (17cm) diam.
£170–200 SAS

A plate, commemorating the
coronation of William IV, inscribed,
1831, 7in (18cm) diam.
£350–400 MGC

A pottery plate, commemorating the
coronation of William IV, the border
moulded with animals and lined in
black, the centre printed in black,
restored, 1831, 7in (18cm) diam.
£150–170 SAS

A Staffordshire pottery miniature
plate, printed in dark brown with
the head and shoulders of Queen
Victoria, commemorating her
coronation, restored, 1838,
3¼in (8.5cm) diam.
£110–120 SAS

A pottery plate, commemorating the
wedding of Queen Victoria and Prince
Albert, with floral and scroll moulded
border, brown portraits and black
rim, inscribed and dated '1840',
5½in (14cm) diam.
£230–250 SAS

A Coalport plate, commemorating
the Golden Jubilee, printed in blue
with a portrait of Queen Victoria,
1887, 10½in (26.5cm) diam.
£125–150 W&S

An octagonal plate, by Wallis
Gimson & Co, commemorating
Queen Victoria's Golden Jubilee,
1887, 9½in (24cm) wide.
£85–100 MGC

A German plate, commemorating
Queen Victoria's Golden Jubilee,
1887, 7in (18cm) diam.
£80–100 CRO

A pottery plate, commemorating
Queen Victoria's Diamond Jubilee,
moulded with spiral-fluted border
and printed in dark blue with an
equestrian portrait, dated '1897',
7in (18cm) diam.
£150–180 SAS

 A Foley shell-moulded dish, in memory
of Queen Victoria, with sepia portrait
draped with a purple curtain surmounted
by flags and a crown, inscribed, by
Wileman, 1901, 4in (10cm) diam.
£100–120 SAS

▶ A porcelain plate, by S. Kepple,
commemorating the Coronation of Edward
VII, printed all over in blue with central oval
medallion, with gilded gadrooned border,
1902, 10in (25.5cm) diam.
£130–145 SAS

A memorial plaque, printed with a portrait of Queen Victoria in colours, inscribed and lined in black, minor chip to rear, c1901, 6in (15cm) high.
£180–200 SAS

A Paragon plate, decorated in bright colours, commemorating the Empire Exhibition, Scotland, 1938, inscribed on reverse, gilt rim, 10¾in (27.5cm) diam.
£200–220 SAS

A Tiffany brown and white plate, commemorating the New York World's Fair, 1939, 10in (25.5cm) diam.
£200–240 YAN

A J. & G. Meakin blue and white plate, commemorating the New York World's Fair, 1939, 10in (25.5cm) diam.
£150–170 YAN

A plate, by Homer Laughlin China Co, commemorating the 1939 San Francisco World's Fair, the blue border decorated with yellow sun and buff buildings, 10in (25.5cm) diam.
£145–165 YAN

A Coalport plate, commemorating the Coronation of George V, printed in blue with a border of naval vessels, inscribed and dated, the rim printed with the arms of the Dominions, 1911, 10¼in (26cm) diam.
£80–100 SAS

TEAPOTS

A Foley porcelain teapot and cover, commemorating Queen Victoria's Diamond Jubilee, the lobed body set with a gilded handle and spout, enamelled with royal coat-of-arms and inscription, by Wileman, 1897, 6¼in (16cm) high.
£130–150 SAS

A Jackfield teapot, commemorating Queen Victoria's Golden Jubilee, 1887, 6½in (16.5cm) high.
£120–140 MGC

Traditionally attributed to the factory in Shropshire, Jackfield ware was also made by several Staffordshire potteries. Jackfield is also a generic term, misused for almost any black and glossy ware.

◄ A General Household Utilities pottery teapot and cover, modelled in the form of a crown, printed in sepia with portraits and inscriptions commemorating the Coronation of King George VI and Queen Elizabeth, gilt lining, c1937, 5in (12.5cm) high.
£120–140 SAS

A German porcelain teapot and cover, commemorating the coronation of Edward VII, printed with portraits in colours on a ground of flags, inscribed and dated, the reverse with floral panel, gilt decoration, 1902, 7in (18cm) high.
£85–95 SAS

A Royal Doulton teapot, commemorating the coronation of King George and Queen Mary, 1911, 4in (10cm) high.
£180–200 CRO

Fairings

A fairing, entitled 'Our soldiers', c1870, 4in (10cm) wide.
£500–550 SAS

A fairing, entitled 'Our sisters of charity', c1870, 4in (10cm) wide.
£500–550 SAS

A fairing, entitled 'Please Sir, what would you charge to christen my doll?', c1875, 4in (10cm) wide.
£230–260 SAS

A fairing, entitled 'Cancan', c1875, 4in (10cm) wide.
£300–350 SAS

A fairing, entitled 'Come along these flowers don't smell very good', c1875, 4in (10cm) wide.
£100–120 SAS

A fairing, entitled 'Married for money', German, c1880, 3½in (9cm) wide.
£100–120 OD

A fairing, entitled 'Dangerous', restored, c1880, 4in (10cm) wide.
£450–500 SAS
This is a rare fairing.

A Victorian fairing, entitled 'Tea Party', German, 4in (10cm) high.
£140–160 LeB

A fairing match striker, modelled as a black and white cat, c1890, 4in (10cm) high.
£35–40 OD

A fairing, entitled 'You careless fool', late 19thC, 4in (10cm) high.
£85–100 SAS

A fairing, entitled 'Who is coming?', damaged, late 19thC, 3½in (9cm) wide.
£90–110 SAS

A fairing, entitled 'Who said Rats?', some damage, late 19thC, 3½in (9cm) wide.
£100–120 SAS

A fairing, entitled 'Twelve months after marriage', repaired, late 19thC, 3½in (9cm) wide.
£25–30 SAS

A fairing, entitled 'The Orphans', late 19thC, 4in (10cm) high.
£100–120 SAS

A fairing, entitled 'Shall we sleep first or how?', German, slight damage, late 19thC, 3½in (9cm) wide.
£25–30 SAS

A fairing, entitled 'Shamming sick', slight damage, late 19thC, 3½in (9cm) wide.
£160–180 SAS

A fairing, entitled 'Trespassing', restored, late 19thC, 4in (10cm) high.
£110–120 SAS

A fairing, entitled 'Now Ma-rm say when?', slight damage, late 19thC, 4in (10cm) high.
£100–120 SAS

A fairing, entitled 'If you please Sir', restored, late 19thC, 3½in (9cm) wide.
£100–120 SAS

A fairing, entitled 'Mr Jones, remove your Hat', late 19thC, 3½in (9cm) wide.
£100–120 SAS

A fairing, entitled 'He don't like his Pants', late 19thC, 3½in (9cm) wide.
£480–550 SAS

A fairing vase, in the form of a pink pig against a green tree, late 19thC, 6in (15cm) high.
£50–60 SAS

A Victorian fairing, entitled 'The last in bed to put out the light', 3in (7.5cm) wide.
£30–35 TAC

A fairing, entitled 'How happy could I be with either', late 19thC, 3½in (9cm) wide.
£120–140 SAS

A fairing, entitled 'Between two stools you fall to the ground', late 19thC, 3¼in (8.5cm) wide.
£200–240 SAS

A fairing, entitled 'Can you do this, grandma?', late 19thC, 3½in (9cm) wide.
£160–180 SAS

A fairing, entitled 'A Swell', repaired, late 19thC, 4in (10cm) wide.
£80–100 SAS

A fairing, entitled 'Looking Down upon his Luck', late 19thC, 3½in (9cm) wide.
£70–80 SAS

A fairing, entitled 'Five o'clock Tea', restored, late 19thC, 3½in (9cm) wide.
£90–100 SAS

A fairing, entitled 'Who is Coming?', late 19thC, 3½in (9cm) wide.
£65–70 SAS

A fairing, modelled as a green fallen fence with pigs playing, late 19thC, 4¼in (11cm) wide.
£70–80 SAS

A fairing, entitled 'To Epsom', restored, cycle frame detached in firing, late 19thC, 10in (25.5cm) wide.
£700–780 SAS

This is a very rare fairing.

A fairing, entitled 'Morning Prayer', German, 1900–20, 4in (10cm) high.
£200–220 LeB

A Continental fairing, in the form of an ashtray with a cat and monkey, c1900, 4½in (11.5cm) wide.
£30–40 OD

The items in the Fairings section have been arranged in date order.

A fairing, entitled 'An Awkward Interruption', late 19thC, 4in (10cm) wide.
£130–140 SAS

◀ A fairing, entitled 'God save the Queen', late 19thC, 3¼in (8.5cm) wide.
£140–160 SAS

A fairing, modelled as a car with 2 pig passengers, painted green, slight damage, early 20thC, 4¾in (12cm) wide.
£40–45 SAS

A fairing, entitled 'When a man is married his troubles begin', restored, German, c1910, 3in (7.5cm) high.
£25–35 OD

A fairing pepper pot, in the form of a top-hatted figure in a basket, 1920s, 3½in (9cm) high.
£18–22 JMC

A fairing, in the form of a boy in an orange cap with a dog in a wheelbarrow, 1920–30, 3¼in (8.5cm) high.
£20–25 JMC

A fairing, in the form of a boy with orange shoes on a green scooter, 1920–30, 3¼in (8.5cm) high.
£18–22 JMC

A fairing, in the form of a boy scout with a Scottie dog, 1920–30, 4¼in (11cm) high.
£25–35 JMC

A fairing tape measure holder, in the form of a Welsh lady, inscribed 'Cymru am Byth', 1920s, 3¾in (9.5cm) high.
£15–18 JMC

A fairing pintray, in the form of a goldfish, 1920–30, 3in (7.5cm) high.
£10–12 JMC

A fairing lustre model of a buff-coloured camel, German, 1920–30, 3½in (9cm) wide.
£15–20 JMC

A fairing group of 3 terrier dogs, 1920–30, 2¾in (7cm) wide.
£10–12 JMC

A fairing, in the form of an aeroplane and wedding bells within a horseshoe, inscribed 'A Present from Skegness', 1920–30, 2¾in (7cm) high.
£15–20 JMC

A fairing, in the form of a kitten in a boot, lined with orange, inscribed 'A Present from Southend-on-Sea', 1920s, 3½in (9cm) wide.
£12–15 JMC

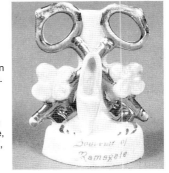

▶ A wedding fairing, in the form of gold coloured keys and a shoe, inscribed 'Souvenir of Ramsgate', 1920–30, 2¼in (5.5cm) high.
£15–20 JMC

A fairing, in the form of a yellow duckling on a boat, inscribed 'Souvenir of Westcliff-on-Sea', 1920–30, 2½in (6.5cm) high.
£10–15 JMC

A wedding fairing, in the form of a dove with a nest of eggs within a gold coloured horseshoe, inscribed 'Souvenir of Sheerness', 1920–30, 2½in (6.5cm) high.
£15–20 JMC

A fairing, in the form of a little devil with wedding rings, inscribed 'Souvenir from Paignton', 1920–30, 2¼in (5.5cm) high.
£12–16 JMC

A fairing, in the form of a dove and key on a horseshoe, with orange and green decoration, inscribed 'A Present from Brighton', 1920–30, 2¾in (7cm) high.
£15–20 JMC

Two fairings,
l. in the form of a clown with a ring, inscribed 'Souvenir of Felixstowe', c1920, 2½in (7cm) high.
r. in the form of a chef, inscribed 'A Present from Whitley Bay', c1920, 3in (7.5cm) high.
£20–30 each OD

A fairing, in the form of a gnome with a key in a horseshoe, inscribed 'Souvenir of Margate', 1920–30, 2¾in (7cm) high.
£12–18 JMC

A fairing pintray, depicting a teddy, inscribed 'A Present from Blackpool', 1920–30, 3in (7.5) wide.
£5–10 JMC

A fairing, in the form of a green and orange bucket with a bear, 1930s, 2¾in (7cm) high.
£15–20 JMC

A fairing, in the form of a bathing belle in a wicker chair, inscribed 'Souvenir of Southend-on-Sea', c1930, 2¾in (7cm) high.
£25–35 JMC

◀ A fairing ashtray, depicting Calico dog, entitled 'Snuffers', Japanese, 1930s, 3in (7.5cm) high.
£8–12 JMC

The items in the Fairings section have been arranged in date order.

▶ A fairing ashtray, with a bird, decorated in yellow, blue and orange, Japanese, 1930s, 4in (10cm) wide.
£10–12 JMC

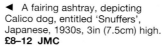

Goss & Crested China

Schools and colleges were among the first bodies for whom William Henry Goss (1833–1906) produced porcelain bearing heraldic crests. That was during the 1870s, but by 1887 towns and cities throughout Britain had agreed that he could reproduce their coats-of-arms on his products. In doing so, he generated an enthusiasm for collecting crested china that swept the country.

By the late 19th century, the development of the railways had led to a blossoming of tourism, seaside towns being particularly popular destinations for Victorian and Edwardian holidaymakers. Goss's son, Adolphus, realized that many of them would want souvenirs of their trips, and a small piece of china bearing a town's crest was ideal and affordable. Although his father was reluctant at first, Adolphus persevered with the idea, and before long W. H. Goss led the field in the manufacture of crested china. The company had agents for its wares in every town, and over 7,000 different heraldic devices appeared on Goss ceramics.

Goss porcelain was of high quality and intended for the middle classes. Frequently, pieces were conservatively styled and reproduced monuments, prominent buildings or classical works of art from museums in the areas in which they were to be sold. However, less serious subjects were also tackled and proved popular.

Before long, other potteries, such as Arcadian, Carlton, Shelley and Willow Art, saw the potential of crested china and rushed to follow Goss's lead. In general, their wares were not of such high quality and tended to be cheaper, but they provided a wide range of novelty designs that found a ready market. Since most factories marked the base of their products, they are easy to identify today.

Interest in collecting Goss and similar crested china reached its zenith during the Edwardian era, when, amazingly, it is estimated that nine out of ten homes in Britain contained at least one piece. After WWI, however, demand began to fall away, and production suffered a further serious blow during the Depression of the early 1930s. By the outbreak of WWII, it had come to an end completely.

Modern collectors often concentrate on a particular aspect of crested china, the most popular subjects being animals and military and comic novelty items. Some people prefer to collect the crests of particular towns or cities. As in their heyday, Goss pieces maintain the highest values today, cottages tending to be the most expensive.

Lynda Pine

ANIMALS & BIRDS

A model of an elephant, with Herne Bay crest, 1900–20, 2½in (6.5cm) wide.
£15–20 BCO

A Willow Art model of an Indian elephant, with Bagshot crest, 1920–25, 3in (7.5cm) wide.
£18–22 BCO

A Carlton model of a rabbit, with Poole crest, c1910, 2½in (6.5cm) wide.
£10–12 G&CC

A collection of crested china cats, c1900–20, largest 4in (10cm) high.
£15–75 each CCC

► A Willow Art model of a lion, with Great Yarmouth crest, 1910–25, 6in (15cm) wide.
£20–25 G&CC

◄ An Arcadian model of a peacock, with Harrogate crest, c1910, 5in (12.5cm) high.
£40–50 CCC

◄ An Arcadian model of a parrot, with Bristol crest, 1910–20, 3in (7.5cm) high.
£8–10 BCO

A Devonia China model of a Scottie dog, 1910–20, 2½in (6.5cm) high.
£15–18 G&CC

An Arcadian model of a Shetland pony, with Clacton-on-Sea crest, 1910–25, 4¼in (11cm) long.
£35–40 G&CC

An Arcadian model of Bill Sykes' dog, inscribed 'My word if you're not off', c1920, 2½in (6.5cm) long.
£25–30 G&CC

A Carlton Ware lustre model of a gramophone and dog, with Great Yarmouth crest, c1920, 3½in (9cm) wide.
£55–65 JMC

A Grafton model of a penguin, with Southsea crest, c1920, 3½in (9cm) high.
£24–28 BCO

A Grafton model of a cockerel, with Swindon crest, c1910, 4in (10cm) high.
£20–25 JMC

An Arcadian model of a hare, with Crowborough crest, c1920–25, 3in (7.5cm) wide.
£15–18 BCO

A Foley hare, with Bideford crest, c1920, 3in (7.5cm) wide.
£55–65 BCO

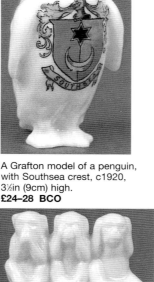

A Grafton model of a labrador puppy, with Isle of Wight crest, c1920, 2½in (6cm) high.
£18–20 G&CC

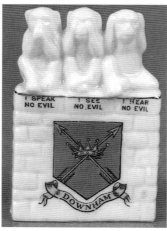

An Arcadian model of three wise monkeys, with Downham crest, c1920, 3in (7.5cm) high.
£15–18 JMC

A Grafton model of a mouse with green bead eyes, with Seaton, Devon crest, c1920, 1¾in (4.5cm) high.
£45–55 G&CC

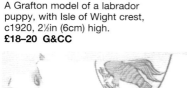

A Corona model of a pig, with Seaford crest, 1915–30, 3¼in (8.5cm) long.
£10–12 G&CC

l. to r. A Savoy model of a spaniel, a Gemma model of a dog, Arcadian models of a collie and a pup, and a Willow Art model of a Scottie dog in Glengarry, c1920, largest 3½in (8.5cm) high.
£8–35 each CCC

A Florentine model of a camel, with City of London crest, c1910, 2¼in (5.5cm) high.
£10–15 MGC

A Gemma model of a comical dog, with Southampton crest, c1920, 3½in (9cm) high.
£30–40 G&CC

A model of a Policeman Tortoise, possibly Arcadian, with Cleethorpes crest, c1915, 2½in (6.5cm) high.
£50–60 JMC

A model of a comical cat, with Jedburgh crest, c1915, 4in (10cm) high.
£12–15 MGC

A Willow Art model of a trumpeting elephant, c1910–20, 3¾in (9.5cm) wide.
£30–40 G&CC

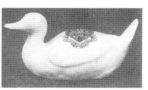

A Grafton model of a duck, with Newbury crest, 1910–20, 2½in (6.5cm) wide.
£15–18 BCO

A Florentine model of a kneeling elephant, with Durban crest, c1920, 2½in (6.5cm) high.
£30–35 MGC

An Arcadian model of a Scottie dog, with South Queensferry crest, c1910–20, 2½in (6.5cm) wide.
£12–15 G&CC

A Goss model of a pig, with Belfast crest. c1920, 2in (5cm) high.
£17–20 MLa

▶ A Grafton model of a fluffy rabbit, with Ryde crest, c1920, 3¾in (9.5cm) wide.
£20–25 BCO

◀ An Arcadian model of a black cat in a boot, with Ventnor crest, c1925, 2in (5cm) high.
£65–75 G&CC

l. A model of a cat, with Christchurch, Oxford, crest, c1920, 4in (10cm) high.
£10–15
r. An Arcadian sergeant major pepper pot, with Lulworth crest, c1920, 3¼in (8.5cm) high.
£50–60 G&CC

An Arcadian model of a pelican, with Lyndhurst crest, c1920, 3in (7.5cm) high.
£30–35 BCO

► A W. H. Goss model of the Trusty Servant, with City of Winchester crest, c1930, 5in (12.5cm) high.
£575–625 G&CC

A Carlton goose, with Corfe Castle crest, on a green base, c1920, 3in (7.5cm) wide.
£25–30 BCO

The Trusty Servant

The Trusty Servant was an ancient and emblematic figure painted on a wall adjoining the kitchen of Winchester College, accompanied by a verse. In 1839, William Savage opened a needlework shop in Winchester and when the tourist trade developed he introduced a range of souvenir china, including a figure of the Trusty Servant.

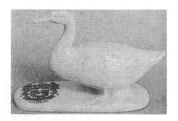

A W. H. Goss duck, with Aylesbury crest, c1925, 4in (10cm) wide.
£275–300 G&CC

Miller's is a price GUIDE not a price LIST

A foreign posy vase, in the form of a turkey, with Whitley Bay crest, c1930, 4in (10cm) high.
£45–55 CCC

A Swan china model, Black Cats on Seesaw, inscribed 'Ramsey Hunts', 1930s, 3¼in (8.5cm) wide.
£125–150 JMC

BASKETS & BOTTLES

An Arcadian basket of milk, with Bournemouth crest, the bottles with brown tops, c1925, 2½in (6.5cm) high.
£18–22 G&CC

A W. H. Goss Ostend Flemish bottle, inscribed Farnborough, c1910, 2½in (6.5cm) high.
£8–10 G&CC

A W. H. Goss Oriental water cooler, with Bexhill-on-Sea crest, c1925, 3in (7.5cm) high.
£20–25 G&CC

BOWLS

A Goss model of a witch's cauldron, inscribed 'Double double toyle and trouble, Fyer burne and caldrone bubble', c1900, 1¾in (4.5cm) high.
£20–30 MGC

A Goss sugar bowl, with Welsh Antiquities designs, c1880, 2½in (6.5cm) diam.
£45–60 MGC

A Goss Manx sugar basin, with yellow manx legs, commemorating the coronation of King George V and Queen Mary, 1911, 3¾in (9.5cm) diam.
£60–70 MGC

BUILDINGS

A W. H. Goss model of the Sandbach Crosses, c1880, 10¼in (26cm) high.
£1,300–1,500 G&CC

A Goss model of Ellen Terry's farmhouse at Smallhythe, Tenterden, Kent, chimneys restored, 1900, 2in (5cm) high.
£350–400 SAS

▶ A Goss model of Beachy Head lighthouse, with Sussex crest, c1912, 5in (12.5cm) high.
£80–100 CCC

This exact model also appears as the extremely rare Dungeness Lighthouse, only one example of which has been found.

A Goss night light, entitled 'Window in Thrums', c1880–1910, 4in (10cm) high.
£300–350 CCC

A Willow Art model of St Paul's Cathedral, coloured beige, c1910, 3½in (9cm) high.
£250–300 CCC

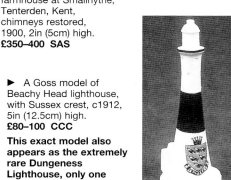

A Goss model of Samuel Johnson's house, Lichfield, c1890, 3in (7.5cm) high.
£150–170 SAS

A Willow Art model of Canterbury Cathedral, west front, with matching arms, c1910, 5in (12.5cm) high.
£35–40 CCC

◀ A Willow Art model of Ashington Boer War Memorial, with Ashington & Hirst crest, c1910–20, 5½in (14cm) high.
£70–80 BCO

A Goss model of Wordsworth's
birthplace, c1912, 2in (5cm) high.
£210–250 CCC

▶ A model of Captain Cook's
monument, with Whitby crest,
c1920–25, 5¼in (13cm) high.
£30–35 BCO

A Willow Art model of Gretna
Green Marriage Room, c1920,
3½in (9cm) high.
£30–35 MGC

A collection of models of crested buildings, 1920s,
3–5in (7.5–12.5cm) high.
l. to r.

Chatham Town Hall	**£60–70**
Shelley, Douglas Clock Tower	**£65–75**
Tuscan, Douglas Tower of Refuge	**£55–65**
Carlton Ware, Eddystone Lighthouse	**£10–12**
Willow Art, Flamborough Lighthouse	**£40–45 CCC**

A Goss model
of Portland
lighthouse, with
Blackpool crest,
1920–30,
4¾in (12cm) high.
£60–75 JMC

A Willow Art model
of Laceby Memorial,
with Leeds crest,
1920–25,
6in (15cm) high.
£25–30 BRT

A collection of models of crested buildings, 1920s,
largest 4in (10cm) high.
l. to r.

Carlton Ware, Deller's Café	**£110–125**
Savoy, Portsmouth Town Hall	**£55–65**
Arcadian, Rochester Castle	**£55–65**
Arcadian, Temple Bar	**£55–65 CCC**

A Goss model of
Lloyd George's early
home, c1913–30,
4¼in (10.5cm) wide.
£120–140 G&CC

A Willow Art model of
a fireplace, inscribed
'There's no place like home',
with Cheddar crest, c1920,
2½in (6.5cm) high.
£18–20 G&CC

l. A Goss model of an ancient kettle,
with Bettws-y-Coed crest, 1910–30,
4¼in (11cm) high.
£40–55
r. A Goss model of Portland lighthouse,
with Dorchester crest, 1914–30,
4¾in (12cm) high.
£60–75 G&CC

▶ A W. H. Goss nightlight, in the form
of Shakespeare's house, c1920,
7½in (19cm) wide.
£100–120 SAS

A Carlton model of Pit
Head, with Sunderland
crest, 1930s, 4¼in
(11cm) high.
£110–130 MGC

CANDLESTICKS & CANDLE EXTINGUISHERS

A Goss candle extinguisher, with Brugge crest, c1910–20, 2½in (6.5cm) high.
£10–12 G&CC

A Goss candle extinguisher, with Weston-super-Mare crest, c1910–20, 2½in (6.5cm) high.
£10–12 TAC

◄ A Shelley Notre Dame altar candlestick, with Montrose crest, c1920–25, 4¾in (12cm) high.
£15–18 BGA

► A Goss candle extinguisher, in the form of a nun, c1890, 3¾in (9.5cm) high.
£150–170 TH

Two Goss candle extinguishers, both in the form of a Welsh Lady, c1890, 4½in (11.5cm) high.
l. £100–120 r. £70–80 G&CC

A Goss candle extinguisher, with Worthing crest, c1910–20, 2½in (6.5cm) high.
£10–12 TAC

A Goss candlestick, with Tenterden crest, 1920s, 3½in (9cm) high.
£15–18 HEI

A Goss frilled candle holder, with Keswick crest, c1910–30, 4¼in (11cm) wide.
£15–20 G&CC

CUPS & MUGS

A Goss three-handled loving cup, with a portrait of W. H. Goss in high relief, c1900, 4in (10cm) high.
£160–180 CCC

A W. H. Goss mug, with colour transfer entitled 'Jackal', c1875, 2¾in (7cm) high.
£95–110 MAC

A Goss Durham Abbey Knocker cup, c1910, 3in (7.5cm) high.
£65–80 G&CC

Further Reading

Collecting Pottery & Porcelain, The Facts At Your Fingertips, Miller's, 1997

FIGURES

A Carlton Ware figure of a drunk leaning against a lamp post, entitled 'Show me the way to go home', with City of York crest, 1920–30, 4¼in (11cm) high.
£70–80 G&CC

A Willow Art statue, with St Alban's crest, 1910–25, 5½in (14cm) high.
£65–75 G&CC

A Grafton bust of Admiral Jellicoe, c1915, 6in (15cm) high.
£65–75 CCC

A Carlton Ware figure of a boy blowing bubbles, with Bournemouth crest, c1914, 4in (10cm) high.
£80–90 CCC

An Arcadian statue of St Winifred, with Holywell crest, c1910, 6in (15cm) high.
£90–110 CCC

A Savoy bust of John Travers Cornwall, hero of Jutland, with Sandwich crest, c1920, 4¼in (11cm) high.
£250–300 MGC

A Goss Churchill Toby jug, c1927, 6¼in (16cm) high.
£180–200 MGC

A Goss parian bust of Shakespeare, on a plinth in the form of 2 books, c1880–1900, 4in (10cm) high.
£80–90 MGC

A Goss Parian bust of Robert Southey, c1880, 7½in (19cm) high.
£125–150 CCC

A Goss Parian figure of Shakespeare leaning on a lectern, c1880–90, 7½in (18cm) high.
£200–250 CCC

A Goss Third Period figure, The Mother-in-Law, part of the Wedding Group, c1925–34, 4in (10cm) high.
£220–250 PAC

A Goss Third Period figure, The Bridesmaid, part of the Wedding Group, c1925–34, 4in (10cm) high.
£225–250 PAC

◄ An Arcadian model of a Welsh tea party group, with British Empire Exhibition decoration, 1924–25, 3¾in (9.5cm) high.
£60–70 G&CC

A Goss figure of Venus emerging from 2 shells, c1858–87, 7in (18cm) high.
£400–450 G&CC

A Goss parian bust of Lady Godiva, c1880, 4¼in (11cm) high.
£100–120 MLa

An Arcadian parian bust of George V, with City of London crest, c1910–20, 5½in (14cm) high.
£50–60 MGC

A Grafton figure of a soldier leaving a trench, inscribed 'Over the Top', and with Great Yarmouth crest, c1915, 4¼in (11cm) high.
£170–180 SAS

A selection of Goss figures of flower girls, 1930s, smallest 5½in (14cm) high.
£240–300 each G&CC

► A Carlton figure of a Scottish bagpiper, with Nairn crest, c1914–18, 5¾in (14.5cm) high.
£300–350 MGC

An Arcadian bust of John Bull, with Salford crest, c1910–20, 2¾in (7cm) high.
£15–20 MGC

► A Carlton figure of an Irish colleen, with Dublin crest, c1925, 5in (12.5cm) high.
£100–120 MLa

An Arcadian figure of a policeman, with Midhurst crest, c1920, 3¾in (9.5cm) high.
£35–45 G&CC

A Carlton group of the Biddenden Maids, with puzzle and Cranbrook crest, c1920, 4in (10cm) high.
£40–50 JMC

An Arcadian figure of a despatch rider, with crest, c1914–18, 3¼in (8cm) wide.
£85–95 G&CC

l. to r. Arcadian busts of Lord Roberts and King of the Belgians, a Savoy bust of Admiral Beatty, a Shelley bust of Sir John French, and an Arcadian bust of Sir John Jellicoe, c1914–18, tallest 6¾in (17cm) high.
£50–95 each CCC

A Carlton clown, with Bournemouth crest, c1920, 3in (7.5cm) high.
£30–40 MGC

◄ A Carlton figure of a Yorkshireman, with Bury St Edmunds crest, c1920–25, 5in (12.5cm) high.
£20–25 BCO

Three Goss flower girls, 1920–30, tallest 5½in (14cm) high.
l. to r. Bridesmaid   **£100–110**
Miss Prudence   **£150–170**
Joan   **£180–200 G&CC**

An Arcadian bust of Mr Punch, with Folkestone crest, c1920, 3¼in (8.5cm) high.
£65–75 G&CC

A Victoria boy on a scooter, with Colwyn Bay crest, 1910–30, 4in (10cm) high.
£20–25 G&CC

A Grafton WWI grenade thrower, with City of Bristol crest, 5½in (14cm) high.
£160–180 SAS

A Swan WW1 despatch rider, with Great Yarmouth crest, 3½in (9cm) long.
£85–95 SAS

► A Carlton figure with spinning wheel, with Dublin crest, 1910–30, 4in (10cm) high.
£40–65 G&CC

JUGS & EWERS

A Winchester flagon, with St Cross Hospital crest, c1890, 4½in (11.5cm) high.
£70–80 SAS

A Goss bagware jug, with Pembroke College, Oxford crest, c1860–80, 3in (7.5cm) high.
£30–40 MGC

A Goss York Roman Ewer, with Roman Armour design, c1880–1900, 5¼in (13cm) high.
£110–125 G&CC

A Goss jug, with Llangollen crest, c1880–1900, 3¼in (8.5cm) high.
£10–15 MGC

A Goss Shakespeare's jug, with matching arms, 1890–1900, 3¼in (8.5cm) high.
£30–40 G&CC

A Belleek cream jug, First Period, 1863–90, 3½in (9cm) high.
£200–220 MLa

A Goss Folkestone ewer, inscribed Burslem, c1900–20, 3¾in (9.5cm) high.
£12–16 G&CC

A Goss Maidstone Roman ewer, with Broadway crest, 1910–30, 3¼in (8.5cm) high.
£7–9 G&CC

A Goss Cambridge jug, commemorating the Coronation of Edward VII and Alexandra, 1902, 3¼in (8.5cm) high.
£80–90 MGC

▶ A Locke jug, with City of Bath crest, c1900, 1¾in (4.5cm) high.
£15–18 MLa

▶ A W. H. Goss Devon oak pitcher, with Bowness crest, c1910, 6in (15cm) high.
£5–6 G&CC

A Goss Glastonbury ancient ewer, with Oban crest, c1910, 3in (7.5cm) high.
£7–8 G&CC

A Goss Worcester jug, with Earl of Carlisle crest, c1910–30, 2½in (6.5cm) high.
£8–10 G&CC

A Belleek jug, with Earl of Antrim crest, Second Period, 1891–1926, 3¼in (8.5cm) high.
£100–150 MLa

SHOES

A Goss model of Queen Victoria's first shoe, c1880, 4in (10cm) long.
£25–30 MGC

A pair of shoes, with Portsmouth crest, 19thC, 6½in (16cm) long.
£25–30 TAR

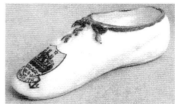

A Goss model of Queen Victoria's first shoe, c1880, 4in (10cm) long.
£25–30 G&CC

TRANSPORT

A Carlton model of HMS *Lion*, c1915, with City of London crest, 6½in (16.5cm) long.
£125–150 CCC

An Arcadian battleship, with Birmingham crest, 1914–18, 4¾in (12cm) long.
£25–30 G&CC

A Swan model of RMS *Lucitania*, with crest, c1914–18, 7½in (19cm) long.
£100–125 MGC

A Carlton warship, with Chester crest, 1914–18, 4¼in (11cm) long.
£40–45 SPU

Did you know?
The majority of Edwardian households owned Goss china. After WWI items such as ships, tanks and guns became particularly popular.

▶ An Arcadian ship, HMS *Queen Elizabeth*, with Brighton crest, 1920–30, 3½in (9cm) high.
£65–75 JMC

A Carlton model of a biplane, with Maidstone crest, 1914–18, 5¾in (14.5cm) wide.
£140–160 G&CC

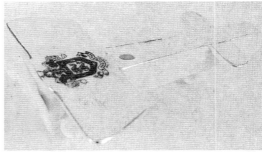

A Willow Art model of a WWI aeroplane, with Brighton crest, 1914–18, 6in (15cm) wide.
£60–70 SAS

A Willow Art model of a monoplane, with Hythe crest, c1918, 6in (15cm) wide.
£90–100 CCC

▶ An Arcadian model of an armoured car, with City of Nottingham crest, c1916, 3½in (9cm) wide.
£35–45 G&CC

A Shelley model of a charabanc, with Henry of Blois crest, c1910, 5in (12.5cm) wide.
£65–80 CCC

A Willow Art model of a British tank, with Bridlington crest, c1917, 4¾in (12cm) wide.
£30–35 JMC

An Arcadian model of a charabanc, with Brighton crest, 1920–30, 5¼in (13.5cm) wide.
£35–40 G&CC

A Florentine model of a charabanc, with Floreat Etona crest, c1920–25, 5in (12.5cm) wide.
£35–40 MGC

A Carlton model of a two-seater car, with Burton-on-Trent crest, c1925, 4in (10cm) wide.
£35–40 CCC

A Carlton model of a luggage trolley, with Wimborne crest and Luggage in Advance, c1920, 3¼in (8cm) wide.
£35–40 G&CC

A Limoges model of a French open car, with crest, c1910, 4in (10cm) wide.
£20–25 CCC

▶ A Shelley model of a steamroller, c1920–25, 5in (13cm) wide.
£400–450 CCC

VASES & URNS

A Goss Pompeiian centre-piece, with Ipswich crest, c1900, 5in (12.5cm) high.
£80–90 CCC

A Goss First Period vase, decorated with forget-me-nots, c1880, 4½in (11.5cm) high.
£90–100 CCC

A Goss flask, with knurled handles and multiple crests, c1900, 8in (20.5cm) high.
£100–120 CCC

A Goss & Peake terracotta vase, printed with classical equestrian subjects, c1870, 5½in (14cm) high.
£150–170 SAS

A Goss First Period vase, decorated with a floral spray in relief, c1880, 6½in (16.5cm) high.
£150–160 CCC

A Goss First Period vase, with butterfly handles, with Bridlington crest, c1890–1900, 4¾in (12cm) high.
£90–100 G&CC

A W. H. Goss Pompeiian centrepiece, with William the Conqueror crest, c1910, 5in (12.5cm) high.
£70–80 G&CC

A Goss Chichester Roman urn, commemorating the Golden Jubilee of Queen Victoria, with Garter Star decoration, dated '1887', 3¼in (8.5cm) high.
£80–90 MGC

A Goss urn, with Seaford crest, c1900–20, 2in (5cm) high.
£18–25 MGC

A Locke vase, with Durham City crest, c1900, 3in (7.5cm) high.
£15–18 MLa

A Goss urn and cover, with Saffron Waldron crest, 1900–20, 4¾in (12cm) high.
£60–70 G&CC

▶ A Goss Lincoln vase, with Badge of the City of Exeter emblem, c1900–20, 2½in (6.5cm) high.
£25–30 G&CC

A Goss bagware vase, with Edinburgh crest, 1900–30, 1¾in (4.5cm) high.
£10–12 G&CC

Bagware was the factory's longest running range. Items are in the form of a bag tied with a blue cord around the neck and handle.

A W. H. Goss Italian krater, made for the International League of Goss Collectors, c1922, 4in (10cm) high.
£125–150 G&CC

An Arcadian vase, with colour transfer of Market Cross, Devizes, 1910–30, 2½in (6.5cm) high.
£12–18 G&CC

A Belleek two-handled vase, with Ballymena crest, 1891–1926, 2in (5cm) high.
£100–150 MLa

A W. H. Goss Portland vase, with City of Nottingham crest, c1910, 2in (5cm) high.
£5–7 G&CC

A W. H. Goss Maltese *vase à canard*, with City of Wells crest, c1920, 1½in (4cm) high.
£15–20 G&CC

Goss Periods

First Period	1858–87
Second Period	1881–1934
Third Period	1929–39

MISCELLANEOUS

A Goss cylindrical pot and cover, with flower knop, c1890, 3in (7.5cm) high.
£180–200 CCC

A Gemma cheese dish, with Edinburgh crest, c1910, 3in (7.5cm) wide.
£6–8 G&CC

An Arcadian egg, with Boxford crest, inscribed 'A little Bird from Boxford', c1925, 2in (5.5cm) high.
£30–40 G&CC

A Goss ring tree, with Chichester crest, 1910–25, 2¼in (5.5cm) diam.
£30–35 G&CC

A Goss Peace plate, 1919, 8in (20.5cm) diam.
£250–300 G&CC

Two Goss preserve pots, decorated with cherries and blackberries, 1920s, 4in (10cm) high.
£85–100 each MGC

A Carlton model of a stick telephone, with Arundel crest, c1925, 7in (17.5cm) high.
£25–30 G&CC

A Corona model of a WWI cannon shell, with Margate crest, c1916, 2½in (6.5cm) high.
£10–12 G&CC

An Arcadian model of a WWI hand grenade, with City of Bristol crest, c1916, 2½in (6.5cm) high.
£15–20 G&CC

A Carlton model of a map of England, with Hastings crest and inscribed 'Blighty', c1915, 4½in (11.5cm) high.
£75–85 G&CC

l. to r. Goss models of a cenotaph, a Gloucester jug, a Welsh hat, a Whitstable patera and a Worcester jug, early 20thC, largest 2½in (6.5cm) high.
£20–75 each CCC

► A Goss bagware teapot, with Cambridge University crest, c1900, 6in (15cm) high.
£90–110 MLa

A Czechoslovakian model of a watering can, with Cork crest, c1940, 3in (7.5cm) high.
£4–5 MLa

◄ A Willow Art model of Teddy Tail cartoon character, with Great Yarmouth crest, 1920s, 5½in (14.5cm) high.
£95–100 BRT

An Arcadian Bathing Belle, reclining on a horseshoe base, with Stratford-upon-Avon crest, 1920–30, 4½in (11.5cm) wide.
£60–70 BCO

An Arcadian golfer's caddy and bag, with Melton Mowbray crest, 1920s, 3½in (9cm) high.
£90–100 JMC

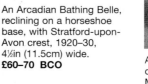

◄ A Carlton miniature teapot and cover, with Kingstown crest, c1900–20, 2in (5cm) high.
£10–12 MLa

Mason's & Other Ironstone

I ronstone wares are particularly attractive and are today avidly sought-after by collectors on both sides of the Atlantic. Its decorative quality and naive charm are admired by all. The vast array of patterns and shapes never fail to excite the imagination, and the chance of finding a rare and interesting piece keeps the collector ever vigilant. Identifying the factory can be interesting – Turner, Spode, Davenport, Hicks & Meigh, Ridgway, Stephen Folch and dozens of others, all making Ironstone-type wares in competition with Mason's and in some cases producing the same pattern.

The word Ironstone was introduced when the Mason family registered the patent name. Although other factories were already producing this type of ware, it was Miles Mason's youngest son, Charles James Mason who, at 21 years of age, took out patent No. 3724 on 31 July 1813 for 'a process for the Improvement of the Manufacture of English Porcelain, Ironstone Patent China'. The process, according to the specification, consisted of using 'Scoria Slag of Ironstone, pounded and ground in water in certain proportions with flint, Cornwall stone, clay and blue oxide of cobalt'. It was an extremely tough greyish, porcellaneous stoneware and, because of its strength and durability, was suitable both for domestic use and for export. The patent was granted for a period of fourteen years and was not renewed, probably because other major potters had perfected their own ironstone body recipes.

Mason's production of Ironstone reached extraordinary levels of technical and artistic excellence. The combination of rich colours such as mazarine blue, brick-red and bright gilding created a strong effect. By 1840 there were over 3,000 tableware patterns, and bisque porcelain, Bandana ware and White Ironstone were also introduced, the latter being made mainly for the American market. However, not all of these new products proved successful, and in 1848 Charles James Mason was declared bankrupt.

In the 1850s Francis Morley acquired the Mason's designs and moulds, and entered a partnership with Taylor Ashworth.

The dating of wares from the early 1900s is difficult, and it is best to seek professional advice when buying early 20th-century items. From 1922, many new patterns and glazes were introduced, thus setting the standard yet again for tableware throughout the world. It is from this period that today's collector might find affordable pieces and start to discover the interesting world of Mason's and other similar ironstone china. **Janice Paull**

DRAINERS

A Mason's Ironstone drainer, impressed mark, c1815, 14½in (37cm) wide.
£350–400 JP

A Mason's Ironstone drainer, decorated with Bamboo pattern, c1815, 14½in (37cm) wide.
£380–450 JP

A Mason's Ironstone drainer, decorated with Blue Pheasants pattern, impressed circle mark, c1813, 15in (38cm) wide.
£300–350 JP

INKSTANDS

A Mason's Ironstone inkstand, painted in black and enamelled with lakeside pavilions and Oriental flowers on a deep blue ground, restored, black printed mark, c1835, 13in (33cm) wide.
£700–800 S(S)

A Mason's Ironstone desk set, with a waisted plinth base, painted in the Imari palette with blue ground and gilt borders, covers restored, gilt worn, black printed mark, 19thC, 12in (30.5cm) wide.
£1,250–1,500 CSK

A Mason's Ironstone inkstand, with gilt loop handle, 2 wells with covers and a sander above a pen tray, decorated in blue, iron-red and gilt in Chinese style, damaged, c1815–20, 7¼in (18.5cm) wide.
£350–400 HOLL

JUGS

A Mason's Ironstone ewer and basin, decorated in mazarine blue, and painted with enamel flowers and gilding, circular impressed mark, c1815, 8½in (21.5cm) diam.
£550–600 VH

A Mason's Ironstone footbath jug, c1820, 13in (3cm) high.
£1,200–1,500 JP

A Mason's Ironstone jug, c1820, 9in (23cm) high.
£700–800 AnE

A Davenport ironstone jug, with bright Imari pattern, printed anchor mark, early 19thC, 8½in (21.5cm) high.
£250–280 GAK

A Mason's moulded jug, with vine stock handle, printed crown mark, c1835, 8in (20.5cm) high.
£300–350 JP

A pair of Mason's Ironstone octagonal-shaped jugs, each with serpent handle, printed in Chinese style with black figures on an iron-red 'Y' diaper ground, printed marks in black, c1830–40, 6½in (16.5cm) high.
£250–300 HOLL

A Mason's stoneware jug, moulded in relief and with vine-stock handle, printed crown mark and applied pad, impressed 'TOHO', c1835, 6¼in (16cm) high.
£350–400 JP

◄ A Mason's Ironstone jug, decorated in blue and orange, c1880, 7½in (19cm) high.
£150–175 SPU

► A Mason's Ironstone miniature wash jug, with blue neck, gilt handle and design, late 19thC, 1¾in 94.5cm) high.
£80–120 MRW

A Mason's Ironstone jug, decorated in blue, red and gilt, damaged, late 19thC, 10in (25.5cm) high.
£120–150 RAC

◄ A Mason's jug, decorated with Red Scale pattern, c1835, 5¼in (13.5cm) high.
£180–220 VH

PLATES

A Mason's platter, transfer-printed in underglaze blue with King's College Chapel, Cambridge, marked, c1815, 6½in (16.5cm) wide.
£180–200 JP

A Mason's Ironstone soup plate, decorated with Water Lily pattern, marked, c1815, 9½in (24cm) diam.
£140–160 VH

A Staffordshire ironstone platter, transfer-printed in black and colours, possibly Mason's, damaged, c1815, 21in (53.5cm) wide.
£550–600 S(NY)

An ironstone dessert plate, decorated with birds and flowers, marked, c1830, 8¼in (21cm) diam.
£100–120 JP

A Mason's plate, decorated with a prunus bush, pattern No. 2588, marked, c1830, 10in (25.5cm) diam.
£115–130 JP

A Mason's plate, decorated with Vase pattern, printed crown mark, c1835, 10in (25.5cm) diam.
£115–130 JP

◄ An Alcock Ironstone meat platter, decorated with Indian Tree pattern, c1840, 18in (45.5cm) wide.
£200–230 BRU

► A set of 6 Mason's Ironstone soup plates, with Flying Bird pattern, printed mark in blue, c1840, 8in (20.5cm) diam.
£350–400 MSW

◄ A Charles Meigh & Son ironstone plate, decorated with green flowers, c1850, 9in (23cm) diam.
£50–60 BRU

SERVICES

◄ A Mason's Ironstone part dinner service, comprising 80 pieces, decorated with Imari pattern, wear and slight damage, impressed upper case marks, c1815.
£8,500–10,000 CSK

A Mason's Ironstone part dinner service, comprising 50 pieces, decorated in iron-red and blue with orange lustre details, c1820.
£3,000–3,500 WW

A Mason's Ironstone dessert service, comprising 31 pieces, printed and coloured in green with a four-clawed dragon within panelled floral and pink diaper borders, gilt rims, damaged, tureens with impressed marks, plates and dishes with incised 'N', c1820, plates 9in (23cm) diam.
£3,250–3,750 S

A Mason's Ironstone dinner service, comprising 82 pieces, printed and painted in *famille verte* palette with figures and boats in a Chinese river landscape, picked out in gilt, pattern No. 1379, some damage, c1830.
£6,000–7,000 DN

A Mason's Ironstone dessert service, comprising 66 pieces, decorated with Chinese Mountain pattern, c1835.
£3,500–4,000 JP

A Mason's Ironstone part dinner service, comprising 17 pieces, decorated with Japan pattern, the covers surmounted by blue and gilt floral-sprigged knops, c1815.
£4,000–4,500 S(NY)

A Mason's Ironstone dinner service, comprising 52 pieces, decorated in iron-red and blue, c1860.
£3,300–3,600 PAD

TUREENS

A Davenport Ironstone soup tureen and cover, with scroll knop, decorated in Flying Bird pattern, printed mark, c1810, 12½in (32cm) wide.
£1,500–1,750 JP

A Mason's Ironstone sauce tureen and cover, with handles, decorated in Scroll pattern, c1815, 7½in (19cm) wide.
£250–300 JP

A Mason's Ironstone sauce tureen, cover and stand, with protruding scroll handles, decorated in chinoiserie pattern, c1815, 6¾in (17cm) high.
£260–290 VH

A Mason's Ironstone sauce tureen and stand, impressed mark, c1815, 7½in (19cm) high.
£450–500 JP

A Mason's Ironstone tureen, cover and stand, printed in blue and overpainted in colours, c1820, 8in (20.5cm) wide.
£400–450 JP

A Mason's Ironstone tureen and cover, printed in Peacock pattern, with a green border, printed mark, c1830, 8in (20.5cm) wide.
£250–300 GAZE

VASES

A pair of Mason's Ironstone vases, applied with birds, insects and flowers on mazarine blue ground, profusely gilded, c1815, 16¼in (41cm) high.
£3,200–4,000 JP

An ironstone vase and cover, with sepia-printed country scene over-painted in colours, c1815, 9¼in (23.5cm) high.
£750–850 JP

A Mason's Ironstone vase, in Japan Fence pattern, c1815, 4½in (11cm) high.
£350–400 JP

A pair of Mason's Ironstone two-handled vases, decorated in Imari style, c1815, 12in (30.5cm) high.
£3,000–3,300 Bri

An ironstone vase, gilded with chinoiserie figures, possibly Davenport, c1820, 25¼in (64cm) high.
£1,500–1,650 JP

A Staffordshire Ironstone pot pourri vase and cover, with 2 gilt loop handles, the body decorated in colours with chrysanthemums and Oriental flowers against a brick-red ground, c1820, 14in (35.5cm) high.
£850–950 Hal

A Mason's Ironstone pot pourri vase and domed cover, decorated and gilt in Imari palette damage, impressed mark, c1815, 11in (28cm) high.
£1,500–2,000 S

A pair of Mason's Ironstone pot pourris, with mazarine blue ground, painted and gilt with flowers, c1820, 8½in (21.5crn) high.
£1,500–1,800 JP

◀ An Ironstone lily vase, with flowers and butterflies, picked out in gilt on a lime green ground, probably Mason's, hairline crack to rim, c1830, 21¼in (54cm) high.
£1,100–1,300 DN

A Mason's vase, decorated in Imari palette, c1820, 14¾in (37.5cm) high.
£600–700 Bon

◀ A pair of Mason's Ironstone vases, c1830, 8in (20.5cm) high.
£800–900 JP

A Mason's Ironstone vase and cover, damaged and repaired, c1835, 41in (104cm) high.
£3,500–4,500 CSK

MISCELLANEOUS

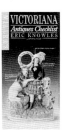

◀ A pair of Mason's Ironstone beaded candlesticks, decorated in iron-red and blue with Japan pattern, line impressed mark, c1815, 3½in (9cm) high.
£900–1,000 JP

A Mason's Ironstone mug, decorated with Japan pattern, with printed crown mark, c1825, 3in (7.5cm) high.
£260–310 JP

◀ A Mason's Ironstone flared base mug, crown mark, c1820, 4in (10cm) high.
£350–400 JP

▶ A Mason's Ironstone slop-bowl, transfer-printed in underglaze blue, inscribed 'Battle of Austerlitz', hairline crack, marked 'C. J. Mason', c1830, 6¾in (17cm) diam.
£130–160 JP

◀ A Mason's Ironstone footbath, with table and flowerpot pattern, damaged, printed mark, c1820, 19½in (49cm) wide.
£1,750–2,200 CSK

A Liverpool porcelain coffee pot and cover, by Richard Chaffers & Co, with Oriental decoration, c1760, 9½in (24cm) high.
£1,500–1,750 Hal

A Meissen flower-moulded part coffee service, comprising 12 pieces, c1840.
£2,000–2,200 S

A Lowestoft part tea service, comprising 19 pieces, decorated with a floral pattern in Chinese export style, some damage, c1780.
£2,500–3,000 Bon

A Royal Worcester miniature coffee pot, signed by Roberts, with black mark, c1950, 5in (12.5cm) high.
£320–350 DKH

A Lowestoft coffee pot, c1780, 10½in (26.5cm) high.
£2,400–2,800 DN

A Worcester porcelain teapot, the domed cover with flowerhead finial, decorated with an Oriental scene, c1765, 6in (15cm) high.
£460–500 CAG

A Russian porcelain tea service, comprising 19 pieces, probably Imperial Porcelain Factory, 19thC, teapot 10¼in (26cm) high.
£6,500–7,500 S

A Worcester porcelain teapot, repaired, c1770, 6¾in (17cm) high.
£400–450 CAG

A Worcester fluted tea service, comprising 34 pieces, decorated with the Jabberwocky pattern, the teapot with double interlaced handle, some damage, c1770, tray 7¼in (18.5cm) wide.
£7,000–8,000 P

A Coalport fluted cup and shaped saucer, decorated with green leaves on a white ground, gilt rims, green mark, c1900, cup 1¾in (4.5cm) high.
£120–150 MER

A Coalport cup and saucer, with graduated turquoise 'jewelling' on a gilt ground, green mark, c1900, cup 1¾in (4.5cm) high.
£500–550 MER

A Coalport cup and saucer, decorated with birds on a blue and gilt ground, green mark, cup 2in (5cm) high.
£110–130 MER

A Copeland Spode coffee cup and saucer, c1937, cup 2¼in (5.5cm) high.
£35–40 BEV

A Worcester tea bowl, coffee cup and saucer, painted in green, blue, iron-red and gilt, with Hop Trellis pattern, on a pink ground, c1775, saucer 4in (10cm) diam.
£820–900 DN

A Berlin coffee can and saucer, blue and gilt decorated with *en grisaille* portrait of Paul Petrowitz, late 18thC, saucer 4in (10cm) diam.
£2,000–2,200 E

A pair of Worcester flared beakers, Flight & Barr period, gilding worn, marked, c1800, 3¾in (9.5cm`) high.
£1,150–1,300 C

A Royal Doulton coffee cup and saucer, hand-painted with views of Kenilworth Castle, signed 'C. Hart', c1930, saucer 4in (10cm) diam.
£150–165 WAC

A Royal Worcester cup and saucer, decorated with the inside of a flower, puce mark, c1923, cup 1¾in (4.5cm) high.
£300–350 MER

A Meissen *hausmaler* tea bowl and saucer, decorated by Abraham Seuter, from the Berne service, restored, c1725, saucer 4in (10cm) diam.
£4,400–4,800 S

A Naples coffee can and saucer, painted with the 3 Muses, handle repaired, indistinct incised mark, c1790, saucer 5in (12.5cm) diam.
£2,200–2,400 C

A Vincennes tea bowl, painted in Meissen style with flower-sprays, chip to rim, marked, c1750, 2½in (6.5cm) high.
£950–1,100 S

A Meissen gold-mounted snuff box, the interior of the cover decorated with a scene from the Commedia dell'Arte, c1745, 3in (7.5cm) wide.
£4,600–5,000 C

A Doccia gilt-metal-mounted snuff box, inscribed with verses from Dante's *Inferno*, some damage, c1760, 3½in (9cm) wide.
£9,000–10,000 C

A Belleek jardinière, decorated with shamrocks, with fluted rim, Second Period, c1891–1926, 9½in (24cm) diam.
£1,700–2,000 MLa

A Sèvres jardinière, painted with rural scenes by André-Vincent Vieillard, minor restoration, marked, c1760, 7½in (19cm) high.
£9,000–10,000 S

During the 1750s and 1760s, Sèvres employed many of France's finest artists.

A Meissen box and cover, painted in the manner of J. G. Höroldt, marked, c1735, 4½in (11.5cm) diam.
£2,200–2,400 EH

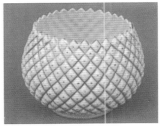

A Belleek Diamond flower pot, Third Period, green mark, c1965–81, 3in (7.5cm) diam.
£150–170 MLa

Founded at Belleek in County Fermanagh in 1863, the factory became famous for its pearly glazed translucent porcelain. When coloured, Belleek wares are in pastel tones. First and Second Period wares are particularly collectable today.

A Meissen gold-mounted letter box, inscribed, c1750, 3½in (9cm) wide.
£25,000–28,000 S

A Doccia gilt-metal-mounted box, in the form of a pug's head, c1770, 2in (5cm) high.
£4,500–5,500 S

A Meissen gold-mounted snuff box, c1740, 2in (5cm) high.
£30,000–32,000 S

A Meissen gold-mounted snuff box, minor damage, c1740, 2in (5cm) high.
£7,500–8,500 S

A Meissen silver-gilt-mounted snuff box, painted with battle scenes, minor damage, c1750, 2⅝in (6.5cm) wide.
£7,000–8,000 C

A Belleek shamrock biscuit barrel, Second Period, c1891–1926, 7½in (19cm) high.
£250–350 MLa

A Belleek Neptune cabaret set, Second Period, c1891–1926, jug 2½in (6.5cm) high.
£1,000–1,300 MLa

A Belleek blue and white earthenware tureen, First Period, c1865–90, 12in (30.5cm) wide.
£200–250 MLa

A Belleek earthenware transfer-printed and hand-painted dish, First Period, c1865–90, 19½in (49.5cm) wide.
£500–600 MLa

A Belleek plate, painted and gilded by Cyril Arnold, First Green Period, c1946–55, 9in (23cm) diam.
£2,000–2,500 MLa

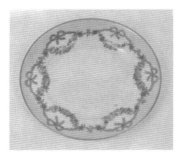

A Belleek plate, Third Period, c1926–46, 6¾in (17cm) diam.
£190–220 MLa

A Chelsea-Derby saucer dish, painted with neo-classical panels and swags on a pink ground, c1770, 7in (18cm) diam.
£450–550 DAN

A pair of John Ridgway dessert plates, pattern No. 8214, c1840, 9½in (24cm) diam.
£160–180 BSA

A Worcester saucer dish, Flight & Barr period, painted with blue flowers and gilt leaves, c1795, 8in (20.5cm) diam.
£75–85 BSA

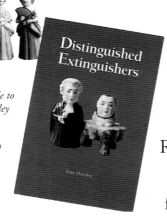

A Worcester dish, underglazed mark in blue, c1770, 11¼in (28.5cm) wide.
£900–1,000 CAG

A Worcester plate, Flight, Barr & Barr period, c1820, 8in (20.5cm) diam.
£400–500 DAN

A pair of Derby pastille burners, the pierced rims applied with bearded masks, marked 'S H', late 19thC, 5½in (14cm) high.
£350–500 Hal

A Minton floral encrusted inkstand, c1860, 11½in (29cm) wide.
£1,200–1,400 BHa

A Derby pot pourri bowl and pierced cover, crowned crossed baton mark in red, c1815, 11⅛in (29cm) high.
£1,200–1,600 DN

A Meissen *hausmaler* tankard, inscribed, c1745, 8in (20.5cm) high.
£10,000–11,000 S

A Meissen tankard, painted in the manner of J. G. Höroldt, c1733.
£13,500–15,000 Bon

Two Meissen silver-gilt-mounted pomade pots and covers, marked, *Pressnummer* 23, c1740, 5½in (14cm) high.
£14,000–16,000 C

A Derby Crown loving cup, painted by James Rouse Snr, marked and inscribed, date cipher for 1888, 5½in (14cm) high.
£1,700–2,000 MSW

A Meissen jar and cover, restored, marked, c1745, 7in (18cm) high.
£12,000–14,000 C

A Vienna gilt-metal-mounted casket, with monogram 'HDL', repaired, blue shield marks, c1785, 6in (15cm) wide.
£3,000–4,000 C

A Meissen ewer, emblematic of Air, after a model by J. J. Kändler, slight damage, marked, c1860, 25¾in (65.5cm) high.
£6,000–7,000 S

A Meissen ewer and basin, made for the Turkish market, blue crossed swords and star mark, c1790, ewer 13in (33cm) high.
£8,500–9,500 C

278 **COLOUR REVIEW • PORCELAIN**

A Meissen *famille verte* plate, the centre painted in underglaze blue with a flowering shrub within a flowerhead and zig-zig pattern, slight rubbing to well, blue crossed swords mark and 2 crossed lines to footrim, c1728, 8¾in (22cm) diam.
£7,000–8,000 C

A Chelsea Hans Sloane botanical plate, painted with a spray of puce specimen flowers, flowersprays, scattered foliage, butterflies and an insect, with shaped brown line rim, slight rubbing to enamels, red anchor mark, c1755, 12½in (32cm) diam.
£13,000–15,000 C

A Meissen dish, decorated in Imari pattern, slight rubbing, blue crossed swords and dot mark, c1730, 14¼in (36cm) diam.
£4,500–5,500 C

A pair of porcelain dessert plates, painted at the centre with flowers within a border painted with flower festoons, and moulded gilt scrolls, each impressed on the reverse 'Swansea', c1814, 8¾in (22cm) diam.
£350–400 Hal

A Nantgarw plate, London, decorated in coloured enamels, impressed mark, c1815, 9½in (24cm) diam.
£600–700 DN

A Worcester porcelain plate, from the Hope Service made for the Duke of Clarence, decorated by John Pennington, c1792, 9½in (24cm) diam.
£1,800–2,000 LHA

▶ A Worcester Sir Joshua Reynolds fluted dish, the centre decorated in Kakiemon style within a flower panelled gilt diaper band, c1770, 9in (23cm) diam.
£600–750 DN

A Minton bread plate, by A. W. Pugin, impressed shape No. '430', mid-19thC, 13¼in (33.5cm) diam.
£360–400 DN

A Worcester dish, decorated in enamels, blue seal mark, c1770, 7¼in (18.5cm) wide.
£300–320 DN

A pair of Bloor Derby pierced baskets, encrusted with flowers and gilt, on a yellow ground, c1825, 10in (25.5cm) wide.
£2,000–2,500 TK

A Meissen cream pot, cover and stand, painted with harbour scenes, crossed swords marks, c1735, stand 7in (18cm) diam.
£16,500–18,000 C

A Minton floral encrusted vase and cover, date mark for 1846, 12in (30.5cm) high.
£1,500–1,800 BHa

A Worcester First Period sweetmeat dish, with 'Blind Earl' moulding, painted in Sunburst pattern, c1758, 6in (15cm) diam.
£2,000–2,400 CHR

A Coalport vase, with painted flower panels and floral encrusted decoration, c1840, 12in (30.5cm) high.
£1,200–1,500 BHa

A pair of Spode ice pails, covers and liners, painted in pattern No. 2508, restored, c1820, 11½in (29cm) high.
£5,200–5,800 S

A Nymphenburg food warmer, cover and stand, painted by G. C. Lindemann, marked, c1765, 9in (23cm) high.
£40,000–45,000 S

A Naples two-handled soup tureen and cover, from the Fiordalisi service, restored, marked, c1790, 14¾in (37.5cm) wide.
£10,000–12,000 C

A Coalport two-handled vase and cover, marked, c1862, 21in (53.5cm) high.
£2,500–3,000 CSK

A pair of Chelsea sweetmeat figures, marked, c1760, 7½in (19cm) high.
£6,000–7,000 S

A pair of Meissen tureens and covers, modelled as partridges by J. J. Kändler, slight damage, marked, c1743, 6in (15cm) wide.
£15,000–18,000 C

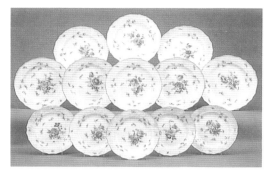

A Meissen part dinner service, comprising 71 pieces, painted with loose bouquets and scattered sprigs within gadroon moulded borders and gilt line rims, blue crossed swords mark, late 19thC.
£8,000–9,000 C

A Meissen part dinner service, comprising 75 pieces, painted with clusters of fruit, some chips, blue crossed swords mark, various Pressnummern and incised marks, c1870.
£9,000–10,000 C

A Derby pink ground part botanical dessert service, comprising 27 pieces, painted in rich colours in pattern No. 212 by William Pegg, blue crossed batons and 'D' mark, c1800.
£9,000–10,000 C(NY)

A New Hall porcelain part tea service, comprising 26 pieces, with gilded mazarine blue banding over-decorated with white leaves and harebells, pattern No. 540, 18thC.
£1,800–2,200 AH

A Höchst part tea and coffee service, comprising 13 pieces, chips and repairs, c1765, coffee pot 9½in (24cm) high.
£3,000–4,000 S

A Coalport composite part service for dinner and dessert, comprising 76 pieces, damaged, c1815.
£6,500–7,500 C

A Derby part dinner service, comprising 91 pieces, some damage, crowned crossed batons and 'D' marks in iron-red, various painter's numerals, tureen 14½in (37cm) wide.
£2,500–3,500 S(NY)

A Worcester Barr, Flight & Barr part dessert service, painted in the Imari palette, some rubbing to gilt rims, script, incised and impressed marks, c1815.
£12,000–14,000 C

A Minton bamboo moulded part washstand service, comprising 14 pieces, painted with leaves, impressed marks and date codes for 1866, chamber pot 5in (12.5cm) high.
£3,500–4,500 C

A Meissen cabinet plate, painted with a scene of Badagosse *(sic)*, crossed swords mark and 'I', c1814, 9in (23cm) diam.
£4,000–5,000 P

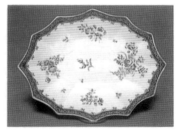

A Nymphenburg dish, from the Hof service, slight rubbing, blue star mark and impressed shield mark, c1765, 13½in (34.5cm) wide.
£3,500–4,000 C

A Sèvres plate, painted with a landscape, indistinct lustre signature, various marks, c1825, 9in (23cm) diam.
£9,000–10,000 C

A Chelsea sunflower dish, damaged, red anchor mark, c1755, 9in (23cm) wide.
£4,500–4,800 S(NY)

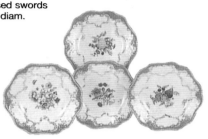

Twenty-four Meissen plates, painted with fruit, vegetables, flowers and insects within scroll borders and gilt cartouches, slight damage, blue crossed swords marks, Pressnummer '8', incised '13', c1880, 10½in (26.5cm) diam.
£6,500–7,500 C

A Meissen gilt-metal-mounted dish, blue crossed swords mark, c1890, 18in (45.5cm) diam.
£6,000–7,000 C

A Chelsea fable decorated plate, probably painted by Jefferyes Hamett O'Neale, small chips, c1755, 9in (23cm) diam.
£25,000–28,000 S(NY)

A Worcester dish, decorated in enamels with sprays of flowers and leaves, within blue and gilt borders, open crescent mark, c1775, 11in (28cm) wide.
£400–500 DN

A Worcester platter, some damage, gold crescent mark, c1775, 13½in (34.5cm) wide.
£26,000–28,000 S(NY)

A Vienna porcelain set of 5 chargers and a pair of urns, 'Antoinette and Famille', late 19thC, 12½in (32cm) diam.
£4,500–5,000 JHW

A Chelsea dish, painted in the manner of Jefferyes Hamett O'Neale, red anchor mark, c1752, 17in (43cm) diam.
£11,000–12,000 S

A Worcester plate, from the Duke of Gloucester service, painted with fruit, slight rubbing, gold crescent mark, c1770, 9in (23cm) diam.
£9,000–10,000 C

A Worcester cabbage-leaf-moulded jug, painted in the manner of N. van Bergham, c1760, 8in (20.5cm) high.
£1,200–1,400 Bon

A set of 7 Meissen wall sconces, marked, converted for electricity, damaged, c1880, 22½in (57cm) high.
£7,000–9,000 S

A Sèvres teapot and cover, minor chips, marked, c1757, 4½in (11.5cm) high.
£6,000–7,000 C

A Meissen gold-mounted snuff box, marked, c1723, 2½in (6.5cm) wide.
£38,000–45,000 S

A Meissen tea caddy and cover, blue crossed swords mark, c1730, 4in (10cm) high.
£8,000–9,000 C

A Caughley mug, painted by Fidelle Duvivier, c1792, 5½in (14cm) high.
£10,000–11,000 S(NY)

A Chelsea jug, some damage, incised mark, c1745, 4½in (11.5cm) high.
£13,000–14,000 C

A Dresden Meissen-style clock case, chipped, crossed swords mark, late 19thC, 28in (71cm) high.
£3,500–5,000 S

A Worcester 'Wigornia'-type cream boat, slight damage, c1752, 2½in (6.5cm) high.
£17,000–20,000 S(NY)

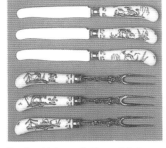

Twelve Meissen knife and fork handles, painted in the manner of A. F. von Löwenfinck, c1735, 3in (7.5cm) long, in velvet lined box.
£4,000–5,000 C

A Böttger bordaloue, crossed swords mark, c1725, 8in (20.5cm) wide.
£7,000–9,000 C

In 1708 the alchemist Johann Friedrich Böttger produced the first European formula for a true hard-paste porcelain. The following year Augustus the Strong opened a factory at Meissen for production. In 1710 they began to produce red stoneware and in 1713 exhibited Europe's first hard-paste porcelain. Böttger died in 1719 at the age of 37.

A Meissen cup and saucer, caduceus and pseudo Chinese mark, c1725.
£23,000–26,000 S

A Minton heavily decorated double inkstand, with floral-encrusted decoration, Meissen mark, c1830, 10in (25.5cm) wide.
£1,600–1,800 BHA

A Royal Worcester jug, with gilt handle, c1903, 4½in (11.5cm) high.
£150–180 QSA

A Worcester mug, painted with Dalhousie pattern, c1775, 4½in (11.5cm) high.
£1,200–1,400 AMH

A Minton pot pourri vase, c1867, 12¼in (31cm) high.
£900–1,000 AMH

A Royal Worcester reticulated vase and cover, by George Owen, dated '1913', 8in (20cm) high.
£15,000–16,000 P

A Copeland vase and cover, painted by C. F. Hurten, with turquoise, gilt and 'jewelled' borders, c1895, 12in (30.5cm) high.
£1,800–2,000 AMH

A pair of French porcelain campana-shaped vases, with beaded rims, painted with Napoleonic campaign scenes and landscapes, late 19thC, 8¼in (21cm) high.
£900–1,000 AH

A pair of French porcelain urn vases, painted with romantic scenes, signed 'F. Bellangon', 19thC, 34½in (87.5cm) high.
£12,000–14,000 M

A pair of Coalport flower-encrusted vases, c1840, 14in (35.5cm) high.
£2,500–3,000 BHa

A Derby vase, signed 'Gregory', c1907, 10½in (26.5cm) high.
£1,700–2,000 TH

A pair of Minton *pâte-sur-pâte* vases, c1885, 14in (35.5cm) high.
£1,800–2,000 Hal

A pair of German vases and covers, damaged and repaired, 19thC, 22in (56cm) high.
£1,800–2,000 Bon

A Coalport part dessert service, comprising 19 pieces, by Jabey Aston, painted with flowers on a pale grey ground, within a gilt border and foliate moulded rim, gilt pattern No. 3/421, c1836.
£6,500–7,200 S

A T. J. & J. Mayer Staffordshire enamelled parian dessert service, comprising 22 pieces, each piece moulded with fruiting vine and strawberry plants, minor rim chips, printed factory mark, c1851–55.
£3,800–4,200 S

A Royal Doulton part dessert service, comprising 10 pieces, painted with a spray of flowers, signed 'E.W.', c1904.
£460–520 Bea(E)

A Bloor Derby dinner service, comprising 74 pieces, painted with flowers within gadrooned borders, some damage, c1830.
£4,000–4,500 DN

A Derby Crown porcelain dessert service, comprising 16 pieces, painted with Japan floral pattern and segment borders in Imari colours, with gilt finish, impressed and printed marks, c1880.
£1,500–1,750 RBB

A Meissen part dinner, tea and dessert service, comprising 135 pieces, slight damage, late 19thC.
£4,800–5,200 S

A Flight & Barr armorial part dessert service, comprising 13 pieces, painted in iron-red, blue, black and gold with the arms of Somerville, Bart, inscribed 'Crains Dieu Tant Que Tu Viveras', with gilt-edged rim, damaged, c1801.
£6,500–7,200 S(NY)

A Frankenthal part service, comprising 14 pieces, painted with flowersprays, scattered flowers and a purple scrollwork, against a gilt striped ground, c1775.
£9,000–10,000 S

A pair of Ansbach soup plates, each painted with a central flowerspray, heightened with gilding, slight damage, c1767, 10in (25.5cm) diam.
£4,800–5,200 S

A Coalport cabinet plate, by Thomas Baxter, wear to gilding, signed and dated '1808', 9in (23cm) diam.
£3,500–3,800 P

A Chelsea Warren Hastings type plate, the border with rococo panels edged with gold, with lobed rim, slight chip, c1754, 11in (28cm) diam.
£2,000–2,250 P

A pair of Copeland blue ground cabinet plates, by J. Wallace, c1895, 9in (23cm) diam.
£2,200–2,500 AMH

An H. & R. Daniel comport, printed and painted with flowers on a green ground, c1835, 9in (23cm) diam.
£55–65 BSA

A Sèvres trembleuse saucer, c1780, 6½in (16.5cm) diam.
£130–150 ALB

A Swansea plate, marked, c1814–18, 8½in (21.5cm) diam.
£1,300–1,500 DN(H)

A pair of Royal Worcester plates, with turquoise, pink and 'jewelled' borders, c1886, 9¼in (23.5cm) diam.
£320–350 SLL

A Vienna porcelain tray, painted with Apollo on a gilt ground, signed 'Joh Ferstler', slight rubbing, c1811, 16½in (42cm) wide.
£5,000–6,000 DORO

A set of 17 Coalport dinner plates, painted in coloured enamels on a pale turquoise ground, c1820, 10¼in (26cm) diam.
£2,000–2,200 DN

A Wedgwood Fairyland lustre bowl, c1920, 8in (20.5cm) diam.
£2,800–3,200 P

A French porcelain box and cover, painted with landscapes, the cover with a mythological scene, late 19thC, 15¾in (40cm) wide.
£5,000–6,000 DORO

A Sèvres *bleu lapis* shaped jardinière, with all-over gilt decoration, date letter for 1763, 12¼in (31cm) wide.
£7,800–8,500 S(NY)

A Derby dish, painted in underglaze blue and coloured enamels in Imari style, with Chinese style six-character mark, c1780, 9in (23cm) wide.
£200–250 ALB

A Caughley kidney-shaped dish, decorated in underglaze blue with Weir pattern of a figure and pavilions in a landscape, c1785, 10½in (26.5cm) wide.
£200–250 AAV

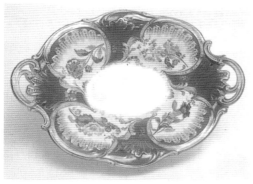

An H. & R. Daniel centrepiece, from a dessert service, the claret border with flowers and gilt decoration, pattern No. 8777, c1835, 12in (30.5cm) wide.
£120–135 BSA

A Royal Worcester stemmed dish, signed 'H. Stinton', c1919, 7in (18cm) high.
£1,800–2,000 TH

A pair of Chelsea bough pots, c1753, 7¼in (18.5cm) diam.
£1,500–1,750 S

A Royal Worcester jardinière, by W. Powell, signed, c1907, 13½in (34.5cm) high.
£5,750–6,500 S

A Meissen sugar box and cover, with rose knop finial, crossed swords mark in underglaze blue, c1745, 3¾in (9.5cm) high.
£1,200–1,400 S

A 53-piece part dinner service, by H. & R. Daniel, for the Earl of Shrewsbury, each piece with a central crest beneath the Earl's coronet, damaged, puce printed marks, c1827.
£7,000–10,000 C

A Derby 38-piece part dessert service, painted in the manner of Daniel Lucus with views of England, Italy and Germany, named in iron-red script on reverses, slight damage, marked, c1825.
£6,500–7,000 C

A Worcester 30-piece part tea and coffee service, each piece fluted and painted with a yellow urn within a gilt roundel surrounded by gilt 8-shaped scrolls and swags of husks, some damage and repairs, open crescent marks in underglaze blue, c1775.
£3,500–4,000 S(NY)

A Chamberlain's Worcester 28-piece part dessert service, the wells gilt with a band of foliage, the borders reserved and painted with specimen flowers within gilt foliate and C-scroll cartouches, some damage and repairs, printed iron-red crown and script marks, c1815.
£2,300–2,800 C

A Paris tête-à-tête, painted en grisaille with genre scenes in the style of J. B. Greuze, repaired, marked, c1785.
£10,000–11,000 S

A Sèvres bleu lapis 9-piece part tea service, painted with birds within gilt scroll and flower cartouches marked, c1757.
£13,000–15,000 C

A Nymphenburg 16-piece dessert service, each piece hand-painted with summer flowers, within a turquoise border filled with foliate reserves and pierced moulded rococo style scrolls, late 19thC.
£450–550 W

A Paris 7-piece solitaire, painted with warriors in classical dress, within gilt cartouches with richly gilt band and foliage borders, slop basin with incised 'D' mark, c1790, tray 12½in (32cm) wide.
£6,500–7,500 C

A Vienna 37-piece blue ground dinner service, later decorated, painted with a classical scene within a gilt frame within a gilt border, shield mark in underglaze blue, impressed numbers, porcelain early 19thC.
£30,000–32,000 S

Pot Lids

'The Outs', No. 16, 1850–90,
4in (10cm) diam.
£190–220 SAS

'Dangerous Skating',
No. 249, c1850,
4¾in (12cm) diam.
£110–120 SAS

'Derby Day', by F. & R. Pratt,
No. 257, c1850,
4in (10cm) diam.
£75–85 SER

'A False Move', No. 251, small chip,
c1850, 5¼in (13.5cm) diam.
£90–100 SAS

'Bear Hunting', No. 4, c1850,
3in (7.5cm) diam.
£200–220 SAS

'England's Pride', No. 149,
c1850, 4in (10cm) diam.
£220–250 SAS

'Alas! Poor Bruin', No. 1,
damaged and repaired,
c1850, 3½in (9cm) diam.
£40–45 BBR

'Brown Bears on a Rock',
No. 10, c1850, 3in (7.5cm) diam.
£90–100 BHa

'The Shrimpers', No. 63,
by F. & R. Pratt, minor damage,
c1850, 4in (10cm) diam.
£25–30 BBR

'The Late Duke of Wellington',
No. 161, c1852,
5in (12.5cm) diam.
£500–600 SAS

'The Great Exhibition 1851,
Closing Ceremony', No. 141,
c1851, 5¼in (13.5cm) diam.
£800–900 SAS

'Shrimping, Pegwell Bay',
No. 33, 1850, 3½in (9cm) diam.
£100–120 BHa

'Wellington', No. 160B, c1850,
5¼in (13.5cm) diam.
£80–120 SAS

'The Eastern Repast', No. 98,
c1850, 3in (7.5cm) diam.
£100–125 BHa

'The Allied Generals, FM Lord
Raglan, Gen. Canrobert', No. 168,
1854, 4¼in (10.5cm) diam.
£130–145 BHa

'The Listener', No. 363, with gold-
lined border, small chip, c1855,
4in (10cm) diam.
£70–80 SAS

'Lobster Fishing at Pegwell Bay', No.
24, restored, c1855, 4in (10cm) diam.
£80–90 SAS

'Belle Vue Tavern, Pegwell Bay',
No. 29, with white cliffs and with
base, c1855, 4in (10cm) diam.
£500–550 SAS

'A Letter from the Diggings',
No. 360, c1855, 4in (10cm) diam.
£90–100 BHa

'The Peasant Boys', after Murillo,
No. 348, 1855, 4in (10cm) diam.
£100–110 BHa

◄ 'The Waterfall', No. 365,
1855, 4in (10cm) diam.
£80–100 BHa

'The Village Wakes', No. 232,
1855, 3in (7.5cm) diam.
£165–180 BHa

Fakes

Fakes of rare pot lids exist, often
being made by sticking a print
on to an original, but blank, lid
and varnishing over. Tapping the
lid against your teeth is a good
test as the soft varnish feels
quite unlike the glassy glaze.

'Pegwell Bay Shrimpers', no ships, No.
31, chipped rim, c1855, 4¾in (12cm) diam.
£75–85 SAS

◄ 'Uncle Toby', No. 328, 1855,
4¼in (10.5cm) diam.
£30–35 SAS

'The Lovers', No. 119, 1855, 3in (7.5cm) diam.
£115–130 BHa

'Sebastopol', No. 208a, c1855, 4¼in (10.5cm) diam.
£80–90 SAS

'Church of the Holy Trinity, Stratford-on-Avon', No. 229, c1855, 4¾in (12cm) diam.
£90–100 SAS

'Osborne House', No. 182, c1860, 4¼in (11cm) diam.
£75–85 SAS

'Harbour of Hong Kong', No. 221, 1860, 4¼in (11cm) diam.
£60–70 BHa

'The Village Wedding', No. 240, third edition, 1857, 4in (10cm) diam.
£40–50 BHa

'On Guard', No. 340, 1860, 4¼in (11cm) diam.
£60–70 BHa

'May Day Dancers at the Swan Inn', No. 233, 1860, 4in (10cm) diam.
£75–85 BHa

'The Donkey's Foal', No. 386, 1865, 3½in (9cm) wide.
£95–110 BHa

'The Residence of Anne Hathaway', No. 228, 1860, 4in (10cm) diam.
£55–65 BHa

'The Wolf and the Lamb', No. 361, by F. & R. Pratt, c1860, 4¼in (11cm) diam.
£40–50 BBR

'The Old Watermill', No. 318, 1860, 2¾in (7cm) diam.
£90–110 BHa

◄ 'Autumn', No. 342b, 1850–90, 4in (10cm) diam.
£90–100 SAS

'Sandringham The Seat
of HRH The Prince of Wales',
No. 181, 1862,
4¼in (11cm) diam.
£90–110 BHa

'Bear Hunting',
No. 4, 1850–90,
3in (7.5cm) diam.
£230–250 SAS

'New Houses of Parliament',
No. 195, 1850–90,
4½in (11.4cm) diam.
£550–600 SAS

'The Late Prince Consort',
No. 153, 1862,
4in (10cm) diam.
£40–50 AnE

'Buckingham Palace',
No. 176, 1850–90,
5in (12.5cm) diam.
£320–360 SAS

'Old Jack', No. 215, 1850–90,
3in (7.5cm) diam.
£130–150 SAS

'Napirima, Trinidad',
No. 225, 1850–90,
5in (12.5cm) diam.
£220–250 SAS

'Tam-o'-Shanter and Souter
Johnny', No. 346, 1850–90,
4in (10cm) diam.
£100–120 SAS

'Tam-o'-Shanter',
No. 347, 1850–90,
4in (10cm) diam.
£130–150 SAS

A pot lid, inscribed
'Genuine Bears Grease',
by Patey & Co, c1880,
3in (7.5cm) diam.
£220–250 SAS

A pot lid, inscribed 'Otto of Rose
Cold Cream, prepared by
W. Charles Baker, Chemist,
Edinburgh', 1890–1900,
2¾in (7cm) diam.
£18–20 BBR

A pot lid, inscribed 'Rose
Lip Salve, Savory & Moore,
London', 1890–1900,
1½in (3cm) diam.
£60–70 BBR

Wemyss

In the early 1880s, the Fife Pottery at Gallatown, Kirkcaldy, Scotland, was run by the Heron family, producing a wide range of domestic wares either printed, sponged, painted, cream-coloured or in 'flowing' colours. They also sold a limited number of hand-painted teapots, kettles, cheese dishes and the like. With encouragement from the family at Wemyss Castle nearby, Robert Heron introduced a line of large and baronial pots, usually in yellow ochre or crimson glazes. He brought from central Europe a group of decorators that included Karel Nekola, who was soon put in charge of the painting shop at the Fife Pottery.

The advent of Wemyss ware in 1882 gave Nekola the chance to express his talent as a ceramic artist. The self-coloured wares gave way to imaginative decoration such as flowers, fruits, birds and bees. Thomas Goode of Mayfair had an exclusive arrangement with the Fife Pottery, and even had a Wemyss room where prospective buyers could browse through the latest offerings.

Karel Nekola worked for the Fife Pottery for 33 years, and trained eight or ten very competent people in the Wemyss painting style, the most artistic of these being James Sharp. After Nekola's death in 1915, the job of chief decorator went to Edwin Sandland. A superb and very rapid decorator from Stoke-on-Trent, he produced twice the number of pots in a day as any of his predecessors.

The Depression of the 1920s sealed the fate of the Fife Pottery. However, Karel Nekola's son, Joseph, gained employment with the Bovey Pottery Company in Devon in 1930, and continued to produce Wemyss ware. These products had a harder, whiter appearance due to the higher proportion of bone in the clay. Bovey Wemyss is never impressed, nor does it carry Thomas Goode's stamp. In the late 1930s the rights passed to Jan Plichta, a Czech, and prices for Plichta's items continue to rise.

The charm of Wemyss is in the quality of painting, strong colours, pleasing natural subjects and infinite variety. There are at least 250 different subjects depicted on Wemyss ware, from kittens to grasshoppers, and arum lilies to wisteria. Some 190 shapes range from umbrella stands to hatpin holders. New discoveries regularly come to light – a dark blue cat recently appeared at Sotheby's annual Wemyss sale at Gleneagles and sold for £12,650 ($20,500). Many of the styles and shapes look as 'modern' today as they did over a hundred years ago, and continue to be admired and collected for their natural charm and superb painting. **Victoria de Rin**

ANIMALS

A Wemyss model of a pig, impressed 'RH&S', c1895, 6¾in (17cm) wide.
£350–400 RdeR

A Wemyss model of a sleeping pig, painted with apples, c1900, 6¼in (16cm) wide.
£1,500–2,000 RdeR

A Wemyss flower-holder, in the form of a goose, restored, marked, c1900, 7¼in (18.5cm) high.
£220–250 HOLL

A Wemyss model of a piglet, painted with thistles, impressed 'Wemyss ware RH&S', c1900, 6¼in (16cm) wide.
£300–450 HAR

◄ A Wemyss model of a pig, with black and white sponged body, tail chipped, impressed mark, c1905, 6½in (16.5cm) wide.
£200–250 CAG

A Wemyss piglet money bank, painted with thistles, chipped, impressed and painted marks, c1900, 6in (15cm) wide.
£350–400 HAR

A Wemyss cat, by Plichta, painted with green shamrocks, c1930, 5¾in (14.5cm) high.
£50–60 RdeR

In the late 1930s Jan Plichta, a Czechoslovak, gained sole agency and under his name a popular series of small animals was produced, decorated with roses, clover and often flowers. These are greatly collected.

A Wemyss model of a pig, painted with shamrocks, impressed 'Wemyss Ware RH&S', 6in (15cm) wide.
£320–380 MJB

A Wemyss piglet money box, by Plichta, painted with a red flowering shamrock, c1930, 4in (10cm) high.
£200–300 RdeR

A Wemyss model of a cat, by Plichta, painted with red clover, c1930, 3¼in (8.5cm) high.
£35–50 RdeR

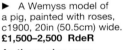

▶ A Wemyss model of a pig, painted with roses, c1900, 20in (50.5cm) wide.
£1,500–2,500 RdeR

As these pigs were made for the nursery, few have survived.

A Wemyss model of a pig, painted with clover, green painted marks, c1930, 6in (15cm) wide.
£270–300 MJB

A Wemyss model of a pig, with black markings on a white ground, impressed mark, 'T Goode' retailer's mark, early 20thC, 6¼in (16cm) high.
£350–400 TEN

Wemyss pigs in good condition are very sought-after today.

BOWLS & BASKETS

A Wemyss bulb bowl, painted with crocuses in shades of yellow, purple and green on a white ground, c1890, 8½in (21.5cm) wide.
£400–450 RdeR

A Wemyss miniature dog bowl, inscribed 'Every dog has his day', c1900, 4½in (11.5cm) diam.
£400–450 RdeR

◀ A Wemyss bowl, painted with black cockerels and hens on shaded green bands, minor chip, impressed 'Wemyss', printed retailer's mark, c1900, 15½in (39.5cm) high.
£400–450 WW

▶ A Wemyss bowl, painted with ducks, impressed marks, c1900, 5in (12.5cm) high.
£750–850 AG

A Wemyss basket, painted with sweet peas, c1900, 11¾in (30cm) wide.
£650–750 RdeR

CUPS & MUGS

A Wemyss commemorative loving cup, painted with pink ribbon-tied swags within loop rims, minor damage, impressed mark, c1897, 4¾in (12cm) high.
£120–150 HAR

A Wemyss loving cup, with green-painted borders, the sides painted with pink roses, impressed and green painted marks, c1900, 8in (20.5cm) wide.
£200–250 MJB

A Wemyss child's mug, painted with apples, c1900, 3½in (9cm) high.
£150–200 RdeR

A Wemyss mug, painted with a bee skep, minor staining, impressed 'Robert Heron & Son RH&S', c1900, 6in (15cm) high.
£350–400 PFK

A skep is a beehive made from straw.

A Wemyss mug, painted with black cockerels, c1900, 5½in (14cm) high.
£350–400 RdeR

A Wemyss three-handled loving cup, painted with wild roses, c1900, 9¼in (23.5cm) high.
£750–900 RdeR

A Wemyss cup and saucer, painted with roses, c1925, saucer 5in (12.5cm) diam.
£85–100 RdeR

A Wemyss mug, painted in pink, green and yellow with a band of growing tulips beneath a gren line band, impressed mark and printed retailer's mark 'T. Goode & Co', c1920, 5¾in (14.5cm) high.
£450–500 DN

A Wemyss Earlshall period mug, painted with a sampler design, handle restored, c1920, 5½in (14cm) high.
£850–1,000 RdeR

A Wemyss armorial frog mug, painted with a coat-of-arms and motto on a green-ground shield, impressed and painted marks by James Sharp, c1920, 5¾in (14.5cm) high.
£1,000–1,500 HAR

A Wemyss honey pot with lid, decorated with beehive pattern, c1890, 5in (12.5cm) high.
£300–350 RdeR

A Wemyss pomade pot and cover, painted with pink roses and foliage, impressed 'Wemyss', c1900, 4½in (11.5cm) diam.
£300–350 S

A Wemyss biscuit jar, painted with strawberries, c1920, 4in (10cm) high.
£200–250 RdeR

◄ A Wemyss preserve jar and cover, painted with strawberries and leaves with green painted scalloped borders, impressed mark and blue printed mark of T. Goode & Co, London, c1920, 6¼in (16cm) high.
£180–200 AG

A Wemyss Stuart flower pot, probably painted by J. Sharp, the flared sides with cabbage roses below a border of green spots, hair crack, c1900, 7in (18cm) high.
£200–250 S(S)

A Wemyss preserve jar, painted with greengages, c1900, 4in (10cm) high.
£200–250 RdeR

A Wemyss preserve pot, painted with raspberries, c1900, 5in (12.5cm) high.
£100–150 RdeR

► A Wemyss biscuit barrel, painted with purple plums and green foliage, impressed marks and printed label for T. Goode & Co, c1920, 4¾in (12cm) diam.
£130–160 AG

A Wemyss biscuit jar and cover, painted with oranges on a white ground, c1900, 5in (12.5cm) diam.
£180–200 RdeR

A Wemyss honey box, cover and stand, painted with beehive and bees, with thistle finial, early 20thC, 7½in (19cm) square.
£450–550 W

The original design was by the retailer Thomas Goode & Co, Mayfair, London.

A Wemyss jar and cover, painted with branches of purple damsons within dark green scalloped borders, chip to base, impressed 'Robert Heron & Son', c1920, 6¾in (17cm) high.
£150–200 P(EA)

PLATES

A Wemyss plate, painted with sprigs of red flowering clover, c1895, 5½in (14cm) diam.
£170–200 RdeR

A Wemyss plate, painted with buttercups and green foliage, c1895, 5½in (14cm) diam.
£250–300 RdeR

A Wemyss plate, painted with brambles, c1895, 5½in (14cm) diam.
£170–200 RdeR

Further Reading

Miller's Twentieth-Century Ceramics, Miller's Publications, 1999

A Wemyss plate, painted with deep purple plums on a white ground with green line rim, c1895, 6in (15cm) diam.
£150–180 RdeR

A Wemyss Gordon plate, painted with a beehive and a green rim, c1895, 8in (20.5cm) diam.
£250–300 RdeR

▶ A Wemyss Gordon plate, painted with hairy gooseberries, c1900, 8in (20.5cm) diam.
£450–550 RdeR

A Wemyss Gordon plate, painted with red gooseberries, 1890–1900, 8in (20.5cm) diam.
£300–350 RdeR

MISCELLANEOUS

A pair of Wemyss candlesticks, painted with wild roses, c1920, 11½in (29.5cm) high.
£500–550 RdeR

A Wemyss match striker, painted with pink and green flowers on a cream ground, c1900, 4in (10cm) high.
£200–250 RdeR

A pair of Wemyss candlesticks, painted with cherries, c1890, 12½in (32cm) high.
£250–300 RdeR

Only a few candlesticks were made after 1900, when electric light became popular in the home.

A Wemyss egg cup, painted with cherries, c1900, 2½in (6.5cm) high.
£100–150 RdeR

A Wemyss basin and jug painted with bands of black cockerels and hens on a green shaded grass band, the basin with hairline crack, the jug with small rim chip, impressed marks, c1900, basin 11in (28cm) diam.
£450–500 WW

◄ A Wemyss jug painted with green grass and a black cockerel, inscribed 'Bon Jour', c1900, 2¾in (7cm) high.
£175–200 RdeR

A Wemyss jug and basin, painted with yellow irises, c1910, 9in (23cm) high.
£900–1,000 RdeR

A Wemyss 12-piece toilet service, painted with cabbage roses, retailed by Thomas Goode & Co, damaged, c1900, jug 9in (23cm) high.
£700–800 WL

▶ A Wemyss heart-shaped tray, painted by Karel Nekola with a cockerel and a hen c1900, 10in (25.5cm) long.
£480–550 RdeR

◄ A Wemyss pin tray, inscribed 'Who Burnt the Table Cloth?', c1920, 5¼in (13.5cm) wide.
£120–150 RdeR

A Wemyss rectangular comb tray with canted corners, painted in coloured enamels with black cockerels within a green line border, damaged and repaired, impressed mark and printed retailer's mark in puce for T. Goode & Co, c1900, 10in (25.5cm) wide.
£140–160 HOLL

A Wemyss heart-shaped tray, painted with roses, c1895, 11½in (29cm) wide.
£250–300 RdeR

A Wemyss comb tray, painted with roses, c1895, 10in (25.5cm) wide.
£220–250 RdeR

A Wemyss pen tray, painted with cherries, c1895, 11¼in (28.5cm) wide.
£120–150 RdeR

A Wemyss plaque, painted with thistles and inscribed 'I looked for something Scotch to send you and the thistles asked if they would do', c1920, 5¾in (14.5cm) wide.
£250–300 RdeR

Marks

- Early Wemyss ware has an impressed mark and the words 'Wemyss Ware RH&S' in a semi-circle.
- Some pieces show the initials 'RH' for the Fife Pottery's owner, Robert Heron, as well as 'Wemyss'.
- The single word 'Wemyss' was used as a mark throughout the 19th and 20thC.
- On pieces executed by Karel Nekola, the 'y' of the word Wemyss is elongated. Karel's son, Joseph, marked his best pieces with the words 'Nekola pinxt'.
- Wemyss ware was retailed by Thomas Goode & Co, and the words 'Thos Goode' usually indicate an early production.
- In 1930 the factory moved to Bovey Tracey in Devon, after which the words 'Made in England' sometimes appear with the Wemyss mark.

A Wemyss plaque, painted by Karel Nekola, modelled as a birdcage enclosing a yellow canary, the base with a painted view of buildings, restored, signed in blue 'K N', early 20thC, 11in (28cm) high.
£2,500–3,000 S(Sc)

A Wemyss heart-shaped inkwell, painted with geese and green foliage, c1900, 6in (15cm) wide.
£550–600 RdeR

A Wemyss double inkstand, painted with green leaves and fifies in a sunset, c1900, 10in (25.5cm) wide.
£320–350 RdeR

This item is considered to be rare.

A Wemyss inkstand and inkwells, painted with leaves, a brown hen and a cockerel, c1920, 10in (25cm) wide.
£320–350 RdeR

▶ A Wemyss single Princess inkstand, with lid and integral stand, painted with mauve sweet peas with green and lemon detail, green script mark, c1910, 5in (12.5cm) diam.
£220–250 GAK

Porcelain

Thanks to the buoyant British economy, price levels in the most popular collecting areas are spiralling upwards. This is especially true for 18th-century English porcelain made from 1747 to 1765, particularly for rare examples of blue and white from Limehouse, Vauxhall, Worcester, Lund's Bristol, Chaffers, Gilbody and Lowestoft. When the chips are down it is still the earliest pieces from the Worcester factory that stimulate bidding to record levels. Longton Hall seems to have a smaller following, but a recent sale saw strong bidding from a Canadian dealer, which seems to emphasise the global nature of today's collecting, even for archetypal English factories. Wares from the Derby and Bow factories also have a strong following, especially for rare and perfect pieces.

Later Liverpool factories, such as those of Philip Christian, Pennington and Reid all have their followers, but price levels are far lower. There is still some sorting out to do before the surviving output of later wares is firmly attributed, and this area of collecting still offers excellent value and the chance to contribute to the ongoing debate. The newly-identified Isleworth wares from the late 18th and early 19th century are proof that discoveries are still there to be made.

English 19th-century porcelain remains a popular collecting field. Here the price differentiation between perfect and damaged pieces is, if anything, more sharply delineated than with 18th-century wares. Cracks, chips, rubbed decoration or gilding can all have a serious effect on value, and for many collectors restoration is not acceptable on fine porcelain such as Swansea, Nantgarw, Spode, Worcester and Minton.

German and French porcelain, with the exception of the finest Sèvres and Meissen, has been in the doldrums to some extent. Top quality Meissen was fetching very high prices in 1998 and this brought a flood of lesser pieces to the market place, much of which was rejected by collectors and dealers alike. The troubled German economy has made buyers very choosy. Dresden-style wares are very much out of fashion, as are the unmarked Paris-style porcelains.

Danish collectors have always provided a strong niche market for Royal Copenhagen porcelain, and there are signs that the superbly decorated wares of the late 19th and early 20th century are attracting a wider audience.

If I were starting a porcelain collection today I would be tempted to buy Continental and Japanese porcelain figures representing cartoon characters of the 1920s and '30s – Bonzo, Mickey Mouse, Felix and so on. There is a large range available – ashtrays, egg cups, tobacco jars, salt and pepper pots and so on. It would be a colourful and fun collection – in fact, I may have persuaded myself to start!

The rejection by many collectors of imperfect or incomplete 19th-century items, offers the new collector plenty of chance to build up a representative collection of damaged wares, from which much can be learned. This will stand the new collector in good stead to spot bargains and misidentified pieces. Unfortunately, these damaged examples, however useful, will never increase in value at the same rate as a perfect piece from the same factory. If collecting for investment then always buy the best items you can afford.

Where are the best places to buy? If my own experience is any guide, bargains and bad buys are found in all market places. I have found an 18th century Berlin plate in a boot sale for 50p and an early Meissen dish c1740 at my local church jumble sale. Sadly, such finds are rare and time consuming, and more often than not one leaves empty-handed having just missed a bargain. I have had most success from visits to specialist dealers who are usually only too pleased to help. Often a specialist dealer has stock which may not appeal to his or her usual collectors and you may well find a bargain. I remember buying 30 early 19th-century coffee cups that a Dallas dealer had left behind because he only wanted the saucers which, at the time, were in great demand as ashtrays! Auctions can also be sources of bargains.

Porcelain collecting gives great pleasure, combining the display of interesting and beautiful objects with the academic pleasures of research. I recommend that all new collectors read widely and attend some of the lectures which are available through museums and collectors' clubs (see page 372). A bargain is no use unless you can share your excitement with someone else.

Speaking to friends at a recent specialist porcelain sale in London, I was surprised to find how many of them used auction search services and the Internet. These services enable the collector to find items in auctions that they might not normally visit, and also to view and bid anywhere in the world from the comfort of their own homes. I have followed their example, and often view American and Australian porcelain sales on the Internet.

The auction search services have become ever more useful to the specialist. A few years ago I found it less than perfect, as the service constantly threw up false leads due to poor auction cataloguing. Expertise in identification is now rapidly improving, largely due to the widespread distribution of well-researched books and papers.

Chris Spencer

ANIMALS

A pair of Bow models of lions, painted in naturalistic polychrome enamels, on green washed bases, unmarked, c1750, 4in (10cm) wide.
£6,500–7,500 WW

A Bow white model of a lioness, with open jaws revealing 2 rows of pointed teeth, on an irregular shaped rocky base, c1752, 9in (23cm) wide.
£2,500–3,000 Bon

A Bow white model of a lion, with his right forepaw resting on a tree stump, on an irregular shaped rocky base, with applied mosswork, c1752, 8¾in (22cm) wide.
£2,500–3,000 Bon

A Meissen model of a Cavalier King Charles spaniel, with a brown/grey patched coat, brown eyes and open mouth, restored, blue crossed swords mark, mid-18thC, 8¼in (21cm) high.
£1,300–1,800 Bon

A Chelsea model of a hound, with light brown markings, wearing a black collar, red anchor mark, c1755, 2in (5cm) high.
£2,000–2,500 P

A Bow model of a brindle pug dog, resting on a yellow and brown cushion, wearing a collar with a flower, c1755, 4½in (11.5cm) wide.
£650–750 Bea(E)

A Chelsea model of a begging pug, after Meissen, naturalistically coloured, wearing a maroon collar applied with gilded bells and a flower, gold anchor mark, c1760, 3½in (9cm) high.
£1,000–1,200 P

A Capodimonte miniature group of a pug and her puppy, modelled by Guiseppe Gricci, with light-brown coat, black and grey ears and muzzle, wearing a blue collar and bow with gilt bells, on a dark-red cushion with gilt tassels at the angles, repaired, c1755, 2½in (6.5cm) high.
£6,500–7,000 C

▶ A Derby model of a cow and calf, with bocage behind, tips of horns restored, c1770, 5½in (14cm) high.
£550–650 DAN

◄ A Derby model of a retriever, decorated in shades of beige and cream on a green base, tail repaired, c1800, 5in (12.5cm) long.
£700–800 DAN

A pair of Staffordshire porcellaneous models of seated spaniels, each picked out in brown and wearing a gilt collar, one impressed 'CS', c1840, 7in (18cm) high.
£850–950 DN

A pair of Staffordshire porcellaneous models of seated spaniels, with both front legs separated, c1840, 4¾in (12cm) high.
£500–550 RWB

A pair of Staffordshire porcellaneous models of a cow and a bull, decorated with red, restored, c1840, 2¾in (7cm) high.
£450–550 DAN

A Staffordshire porcelain model of a white miniature poodle, c1840, 1¾in (4.5cm) wide.
£180–220 DAN

A pair of Royal supporters, modelled as a lion and a unicorn, their features picked out in iron-red and puce, probably Rockingham, c1840, 3½in (9cm) high.
£750–900 Bon

A Meissen group of a pug dog and 2 other dogs, one brown, one black, painted in colours throughout, on a gilt rococo scrolled base, some damage, crossed swords mark in underglaze blue, c1860, 7in (18cm) high.
£600–700 GAK

A Parian ware model of a group of dogs, after the painting by Landseer, restored, unmarked, c1860, 12½in (31.5cm) wide.
£320–350 SER

A Staffordshire model of a pointer, minor damage, c1850, 5in (12.5cm) high.
£120–175 SER

A pair of Meissen models of pug dogs, after models by J. J. Kändler, naturalistically painted in colours and gilt, some damage, blue crossed swords marks, incised numerals, late 19thC, largest 9½in (24cm) high.
£2,800–3,000 CSK

◄ Four Meissen monkey band models, wearing 18thC dress, painted and gilt, damaged and restored, blue crossed swords marks, 19thC, 5½in (14cm) high.
£1,000–1,200 CSK

A Meissen model of a heron, naturalistically modelled standing above rushes, the plumage painted in shades of grey and black, the foliage in green, on a mound base moulded with water lilies, extensively damaged and restored, marked, late 19thC, 20¼in (51.5cm) high.
£1,100–1,200 CSK

▶ A Meissen model of a pug, wearing a blue collar with gilt bells, sparsely coloured, minor chips, blue crossed swords mark, late 19thC, 10in (25.5cm) high.
£1,800–2,200 CSK

A pair of Meissen models of magpies, each perched on a tree trunk, on rockwork bases, late 19thC, 20in (51cm) high.
£1,200–1,350 AH

A Continental bisque model of a fish, incised 'G' on base, c1880, 9½in (24cm) long.
£30–35 SER

A Meissen model of a Bolognese terrier, after a model by J. J. Kändler, with brown fur, ear broken, crossed swords and incised numerals 'C76', c1880, 6½in (16.5cm) high.
£220–260 WL

A Meissen model of a turkey, after a model by J. J. Kändler, with blue head, orange neck and brown and cream plumage, on a rocky base, crossed swords mark, c1880, 23in (59cm) high.
£3,800–4,200 P

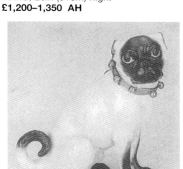

A pair of Meissen models of woodpeckers, each perched on a tree stump, naturalistically decorated in enamels, some damage, marks in blue and impressed and incised numerals, late 19thC, 10¾in (27.5cm) high.
£650–800 DN

A Royal Worcester model of a seated fox, early 20thC, 7in (18cm) high.
£220–250 BIG

Cross Reference
See Colour Review

A Royal Worcester model of a black and tan King Charles spaniel, on a turquoise cushion with gold tassels, c1910, 1½in (3.5cm) wide.
£450–500 TH

Two similar Samson models of Bolognese terriers, after Meissen models, enriched in shades of grey, minor chips and firing cracks, imitation blue crossed swords marks, c1900, 11¾in (30cm) high.
£1,300–1,500 CSK

A Royal Dux model of a horse, with green saddle and pink rug, on a rustic base, c1920, 7½in (19cm) wide.
£380–420 AH

Animals • PORCELAIN 303

BASKETS

A Bow pierced basket, the interior painted in underglaze blue with flowers and leaves, the exterior moulded with flowerheads picked out in blue, firing crack, c1765, 6¾in (17cm) diam.
£250–280 DN

A Bow pierced basket of garden flowers, applied with blue and yellow flowerheads, some damage and restoration, c1765, 3½in (9cm) wide.
£550–650 C

A Worcester pierced basket, printed in underglaze blue with the Pinecone pattern, painted border, c1775, 7¾in (19.5cm) diam.
£600–700 CHR

A Derby botanical basket, decorated in coloured enamels with angular stalked cranesbill within gilt borders, restored, inscribed verso, blue mark and pattern number '141', c1790, 10½in (26cm) wide.
£500–600 DN

Bow

The discovery of Bow's porcelain recipe resulted from years of experimentation by the potter Edward Heylyn and the artist Thomas Frye. They took out their first patent for a porcelain formula in 1744, but Bow porcelain was probably not on sale before 1748. It was coarser than hard-paste porcelain and the burnt animal bones used as a principal ingredient at Bow created a body that was liable to stain.

Early Bow is generally unmarked, but after c1765 an 'anchor and dagger' mark was painted in red enamel on colourful pieces that were possibly decorated outside the factory.

The Bow factory remained in production for nearly 30 years but fell victim to an economic recession in the mid-1770s, resulting in the closure of the factory in 1776.

A Worcester basket, the pierced border enamelled with yellow and green floral sprays, c1770, 7½in (19cm) diam.
£1,000–1,200 DN

A Worcester pierced quatrefoil two-handled stand for a chestnut basket, decorated in the atelier of James Giles, the centre with 2 exotic birds among trees, the handles applied with flowers and foliage, chips to flowers, c1770, 10in (25.5cm) wide.
£800–1,000 C

A Worcester two-handled basket, painted with flowers on a yellow ground, some wear, c1765, 7½in (19cm) wide.
£1,300–1,500 CNY

A Worcester basket, decorated in coloured enamels on a blue ground, with gilt scroll band and dentil rim, crescent mark, c1770, 8in (20.5cm) wide.
£750–850 DN

A Derby reticulated basket, painted in iron-red, purple, yellow, blue and green, with green rope-twist handles terminating in yellow, iron-red and green floral clusters, damaged and restored, c1765, 8½in (21cm) wide.
£450–500 S(NY)

A Worcester basket, printed in blue with the Pinecone pattern, cross-hatched crescent mark, c1770, 12in (30.5cm) diam.
£550–650 DN

Five Worcester Flight, Barr and Barr shallow baskets, with gilt rims, on pale green grounds, one restored, marked c1820, 5½in (14cm) wide.
£1,400–1,800 C

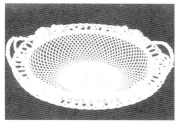

A Belleek three-strand basket, c1865–90, 12½in (32cm) long.
£2,000–2,500 MLa

Three-strand means the centre is woven from three-ply strands of porcelain. Later examples are four-ply or four-strand.

A Staffordshire porcelain basket, decorated with encrusted flowers and a blue bow, possibly by John Bevington, c1880, 10in (25.5cm) wide.
£100–120 AAC

A Belleek basket, with 2 twig handles, the border applied with roses and shamrock, marked, c1900, 9in (23cm) diam.
£750–825 HOLL

A Rockingham square basket, with an entwined rustic handle, the central gilded motif surrounded by colourful applied flowers and leaves, some damage, puce griffin mark, c1830, 7in (18cm) wide.
£520–600 P

A Belleek pierced basket, with central twig-shaped loop handle, the rim boldly encrusted with flowers and leaves, impressed mark 'Belleek' on a ribbon, c1870, 10¾in (27.5cm) wide.
£800–900 DN

A Belleek triple bird's nest basket, with glazed two-strand lattice bodies, c1880, 7in (18cm) wide.
£2,500–3,000 MLa

◄ Two Belleek baskets and covers, with crabstock handles:
l. after 1891, 12½in (32cm) wide.
£1,750–2,200
r. before 1891, 11in (28cm) wide.
£2,500–3,000 J&L

A Belleek four-strand heart-shaped basket, c1945, 5in (13cm) wide.
£250–300 MLa

A Derby two-handled basket, by Stevenson & Hancock, with blue mark, c1850, 6in (15cm) high.
£200–250 JHW

A Belleek pierced basket, with twig-shaped handles, the rim encrusted with sprays of lily of the valley, impressed 'Belleek Co Fermanah' on a ribbon, c1870, 11½in (29cm) diam.
£1,800–2,000 DN

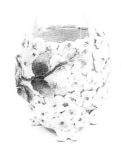

A Sitzendorf encrusted basket, c1880, 6¾in (17cm) high.
£70–80 VSt

A Belleek shamrock four-strand basket, c1930, 5½in (14cm) wide.
£350–375 MLa

On four-strand items, there is no period mark.

BOWLS

A Chelsea fluted bowl, in Meissen style, the exterior decorated in coloured enamels with a harbour scene depicting figures and boats, the interior with a spray of flowers and an insect, slight damage, stilt marks, c1752, 5¾in (14.5cm) diam.
£2,000–2,500 DN

A Worcester bowl, painted with 2 polychrome floral reserves within gilt scrollwork on flow-blue ground, with gilt dentil rim and central internal floral sprig, c1751–74, 6½in (16.5cm) high.
£320–350 RBB

A Worcester bowl, decorated in coloured enamels with a version of the Stag Hunt pattern, within flower and scroll-moulded cartouches, on a pleated ground, c1756, 6½in (16cm) diam.
£1,700–1,900 DN

A Dr Wall Worcester blue and white bowl, c1760, 8in (20.5cm) diam.
£400–450 ALB

Two Worcester junket bowls, printed in blue with the Pinecone pattern, wear and minor chips, hatched crescent marks, c1770, 10in (25.5cm) diam.
£700–800 CSK

A Worcester bowl, printed in blue with Marrow and Flower Sprays pattern, hatched crescent mark, c1780, 9in (23cm) diam.
£250–300 DN

A Wedgwood *sucrier*, enamelled with flowers, impressed, c1810, 3in (7.5cm) high.
£180–220 GLN

◄ A Minton punch bowl, c1810, 10½in (27cm) diam.
£1,400–1,750 AMH

A gilt metal and porcelain tazza, the dish decorated with a *fête de campagne* scene, mounted by shell-cast decoration with acanthus-cast handles, supported by 4 acanthus-cast feet linked by garlands, signed 'Pierrin', mid-19thC, 15½in (39cm) diam.
£1,100–1,300 P

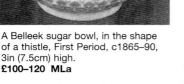

A Belleek sugar bowl, in the shape of a thistle, First Period, c1865–90, 3in (7.5cm) high.
£100–120 MLa

▶ A Samson Chinese export punch-bowl, decorated with flower sprays, c1890, 10¾in (27.5cm) diam.
£150–180 PC

A Belleek pink sugar dish, decorated with a shell pattern, Second Period, c1891–1926, 3¼in (8.5cm) diam.
£35–45 MLa

A Meissen bowl, later decorated within shaped green borders edged with gilt lines, minor glaze chips, blue crossed swords mark, gilt decorators crown mark, monogram, '32' and 3 stars, porcelain 18thC, decoration late 19thC, 8in (20.5cm) diam.
£1,500–1,800 C

A Wedgwood lustre footed bowl, the interior decorated with a gilt dragon on a pearly green ground, the exterior with 2 writhing dragons in pursuit of flaming pearls, restored, printed mark, pattern No. Z4829, early 20thC, 11in (28cm) diam.
£600–700 WW

A German porcelain figural bowl, painted and encrusted with flowers flanked by 4 standing putti, c1900, 7½in (19cm) diam.
£300–330 AH

A Wedgwood Fairyland lustre bowl, designed by Daisy Makeig-Jones, the interior decorated with the Ship and Mermaid pattern within arched panels, the exterior with the Fiddler in Tree pattern, c1920, 7¾in (19.5cm) wide.
£2,400–2,650 HOLL

A Worcester sugar bowl with cover, decorated in blue, iron-red and gilt pattern, c1770, 5in (12.5cm) high.
£550–650 DAN

A Sèvres *écuelle* and cover, painted in thick bright enamels with panels depicting figures on the shore, on a blue ground, painted mark in green with date code for 1770, 6¾in (17cm) wide.
£700–800 Bea

A Worcester reeded turquoise-ground sugar bowl and cover, with bud finial, the gilt borders within shaped bands with scallops and scrolls suspending swags of leaves and flowers, slight damage and wear, c1770–75, 5in (12.5cm) high.
£350–400 CSK

A Helena Wolfsohn bowl, cover and stand, in Meissen style, with puce ground, 'AR' monogram, late 19thC, 9in (23cm) diam.
£350–400 GAK

A Champion's Bristol porcelain covered bowl, with rose-form finial, the banded decoration of pink trellis and green leaves enclosed by gilding and interspersed with rose sprays, c1772, 5in (12.5cm) high.
£450–500 EL

A Crown Staffordshire miniature sugar bowl, decorated with purple flowers and gilt rims, c1906, 2in (5cm) wide.
£45–55 WAC

A Royal Worcester miniature sugar basin and cover, signed 'Roberts', black mark, c1950, 3in (7.5cm) high.
£160–200 DKH

A Belleek Celtic bowl and cover, Third Period, c1926–46, 3¾in (9.5cm) high.
£170–200 DeA

BUSTS

A Sèvres biscuit bust of Napoleon Bonaparte as First Consul, after the model by Boizot, inscribed marks, c1809, 11in (28cm) high.
£1,400–1,700 C

A Parian ware bust of John Sumner, by Robinson & Leadbeater, c1860–80, 12½in (32cm) high.
£275–325 JAK

A Copeland Parian ware bust of Nelson, c1850, 13¼in (33.5cm) high.
£1,500–1,650 TVM

A Kerr & Binns Worcester Parian ware bust of Prince Albert, by E. J. Jones, mid-19thC, 12½in (32cm) high.
£150–200 WW

A Copeland Parian ware bust of The Duke of Wellington, after the Comte d'Orsay, c1852, 11in (28cm) high.
£275–325 JAK

A Copeland bust of Milton, on a Parian base, c1860, 6in (15cm) high.
£70–80 SER

A Copeland Parian bust of Miranda, by W. Calder Marshall, c1860, 11in (28cm) high.
£250–300 JAK

A Parian ware bust of Shakespeare, probably by Wedgwood, c1860, 13½in (34.5cm) high.
£350–400 JAK

A Copeland Parian ware bust, entitled 'The Veiled Bride', by Rafaello Monti, c1861, 15½in (39.5cm) high.
£1,800–2,200 JAK

A Parian bust of Richard Cobden, by John Adams & Co, sculpted by E. W. Wyon, c1865, 16½in (42cm) high.
£250–300 JAK

A pair of Coalport Parian ware busts of Princess Alexandra and Edward, Prince of Wales, by John Rose, impressed and dated '18 February 1863', 13½in (34.5cm) high.
£650–750 AH

A Copeland Parian ware bust, entitled 'Lesbia', sculpted by W. G. Marshall RA for the Crystal Palace Art Union, inscribed and dated, c1870, 16½in (42cm) high.
£750–850 HAM

A Parian ware bust of Charles Dickens, by Turner & Co, c1870, 18½in (47cm) high.
£400–450 M

A Parian ware bust of Dr Kenealy MP, by George Ash, c1873, 11½in (29cm) high.
£140–160 JAK

Dr Kenealy was defender of the Tichborne Claimant which was the longest running trial of its day.

A Parian ware bust of Lord William Dargan, by Kerr & Binns, c1855, 9in (23cm) high.
£175–200 JAK

Lord Dargan was an Irish entrepreneur and railway builder. He financed the Dublin Exhibition in 1853.

A Parian ware bust of William Shakespeare, by Robinson & Leadbeater, c1880, 7½in (19cm) high.
£65–75 JAK

A Parian ware bust of Geothe, by Robinson & Leadbeater, c1880, 8in (20.5cm) high.
£100–120 JAK

A Parian ware bust of Handel, by Robinson & Leadbeater, c1880, 8in (20.5cm) high.
£100–120 JAK

A Parian ware tinted terracotta colour bust of Lord Salisbury, by Robinson & Leadbeater, c1880, 8in (20.5cm) high.
£100–120 JAK

A Parian ware bust of General Gordon, by W. H. Goss, c1885, 7¾in (19.5cm) high.
£200–250 MGC

A Parian ware bust of Clytie, by Robinson & Leadbeater, c1880, 13in (33cm) high.
£400–450 JAK

Clytie, a water nymph, was turned into a sun-flower by Apollo the sun god, so that she would always turn towards him in adoration!

Robinson & Leadbeater

Most Robinson & Leadbeater wares are unmarked. The firm is remarkable for the fact that its whole output was confined to Parian wares which they continued to produce long after other factories ceased production.

A Copeland Parian ware bust of Autumn, by Owen Hale, c1881, 18in (45.5cm) high.
£1,500–1,800 JAK

◀ A Parian ware bust of King Edward VII, by W. H. Goss, c1901, 6¼in (16cm) high.
£175–200 MGC

▶ A white bisque bust of Princess Mary, marked 'H. Tyler 1893', 10¾in (27.5cm) high.
£220–260 SAS

CANDLESTICKS & CANDLE EXTINGUISHERS

A pair of Derby figural candlesticks, each in the form of a kneeling cupid, in front of floral bocage, beside a pierced sconce, a quiver and arrows at their feet, the shell and scroll-moulded bases picked out in turquoise, puce and gilt, c1770, 7½in (19cm) high.
£700–800 DN

A pair of Chelsea Derby candlestick figures, modelled as scantily clad seated putti, each with one arm round the floral encrusted stick surmounted by tulip sconces, restored, marked with 'D' intersected by anchor mark in iron-red, c1780, 7½in (19cm) high.
£1,200–1,400 Bon

A Chamberlain's Worcester miniature chamber stick, with floral and gilt decoration on a white ground, slight damage, script mark in red, c1810, 2¼in (5.5cm) diam.
£300–350 MER

A pair of Meissen-style candlesticks, representing the four Seasons, detailed in colours and gilt, crossed swords mark in blue and incised script numerals, 19thC, 13in (33cm) high.
£1,000–1,200 RBB

A Kerr & Binns white glazed kneeling monk candle extinguisher, c1855, 4½in (11.5cm) high.
£500–600 TH

A pair of Sitzendorf figural three-branch candelabra, each in the form of a cherub supporting a cornucopia, on shaped bases painted with birds and insects, 19thC, 19¾in (50cm) high.
£460–520 P(B)

Sets/Pairs

Unless otherwise stated, any description which refers to 'a set' or 'a pair' includes a guide price for the entire set or the pair, even though the illustration may show only a single item.

A Chamberlain's Worcester chamberstick, the white ground painted with flowers, script mark, c1820, 1¾in (4.5cm) high.
£550–600 DIA

A Spode chamberstick, the dark blue ground enhanced with gilding, marked, c1820, 1¾in (4.5cm) high.
£550–600 DIA

A Chamberlain's Worcester chamberstick, decorated with the Finger and Thumb pattern, c1820, 1¾in (4.5cm) high.
£600–650 DIA

A Chamberlain's Worcester chamberstick, c1820.

◄ A Worcester Flight Barr & Barr chamberstick, the pale yellow ground painted with shells, painted script marks, c1820, 1¾in (4.5cm) high.
£730–800 DIA

A Spode taperstick, the claret ground decorated with raised gilding, marked 'Spode 3993', c1825, 2½in (6.5cm) high.
£375–425 DIA

A porcelain chamberstick, the base formed as a scallop shell, unmarked, c1830, 2in (5cm) high.
£400–450 DIA

A Belleek piano candlestick, Second Period, 9in (23cm) high.
£800–900 MLa

◀ A pair of Royal Worcester candle extinguishers, entitled 'Girl with Muff' and 'Boy with Boater', by Kate Greenaway, c1880, 4in (10cm) high.
£1,300–1,500 TH

A Grainger's Worcester chamberstick, decorated with roses and enhanced with gilding, painted script mark 'Grainger, Lee & Co, Worcester', c1825, 2in (5cm) high.
£400–450 DIA

A pair of Coalport candlesticks, with lime green ground, cracked and chipped, c1850, 12½in (32cm) high.
£450–500 C

A pair of Copeland white glazed candle extinguishers, entitled 'Normandy Maid and Man', c1860, 3in (7.5cm) high.
£200–220 TH

A Copeland Parian ware candlestick and extinguisher, depicting Elizabeth Fry, c1860, 5¼in (13.5cm) high.
£500–550 TH

A Minton chamberstick, in 'Dresden' shape, encrusted with flowers, standing on 4 shell feet, crossed swords mark, c1830, 7½in (19cm) wide.
£400–450 DIA

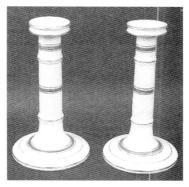

A pair of Belleek candlesticks, Second Period, 9½in (24cm) high.
£550–650 MLa

▶ A Meissen black candle extinguisher, depicting a priest, c1860, 3in (7.5cm) high.
£800–900 TH

A Staffordshire candle extinguisher, depicting a nun, c1870, 3in (7.5cm) high.
£50–60 TH

▶ A Royal Worcester candle extinguisher, depicting a monk, c1880, 6½in (16.5cm) high.
£300–350 TH

This character was also made as a freestanding figure.

A Royal Worcester candle extinguisher, entitled 'Mob Cap', decorated with gold edging, c1880, 3½in (9cm) high.
£500–600 TH

A Royal Worcester candle extinguisher, entitled 'Feathered Hat', c1880, 3¼in (8.5cm) high.
£800–900 TH

A Goss candle holder and extinguisher, decorated with forget-me-nots, c1890–1925, 2½in (6.5cm) high.
£75–100 G&CC

Cross Reference
See Goss & Crested China, page 251

A Goss white glazed Welsh lady candle extinguisher, c1890, 3¾in (9.5cm) high.
£100–125 TH

A Continental candle extinguisher, entitled 'Sairey Gamp' on base, c1890, 3½in (9cm) high.
£150–180 TH

A Grainger white glazed Tyrolean hat candle extinguisher, with a coloured feather decoration, c1895, 2¾in (7cm) high.
£110–130 TH

A pair of Derby candlesticks, modelled as a boy with fruit and a girl with flowers, the girl with crowned 'D' and baton mark in underglaze blue, late 19thC, 7in (18cm) high.
£280–340 Hal

A Royal Worcester candle extinguisher, entitled 'French Cook', c1898, 2½in (6.5cm) high.
£160–180 TH

A Royal Worcester candle extinguisher, in the form of a beige Japanese lady, c1901, 3in (7.5cm) high.
£200–220 TH

A Grainger's Worcester candle extinguisher, modelled as a lady's head, in white glazed parian with gilded highlights, shape 204, printed shield mark, c1900, 3½in (9cm) high.
£400–450 P

A Grainger monkey's head candle extinguisher, with blush decoration and gilt edges, 1901, 3¾in (9.5cm) high.
£350–400 TH

A pair of Nippon hand-painted candlesticks, Kinjo china, 1890s, 5½in (14cm) high.
£40–60 DgC

◀ A Royal Worcester full coloured Mandarin candle extinguisher, 1920, 3½in (9cm) high.
£200–225 TH

▶ A Royal Worcester candle extinguisher, depicting Monsieur Reynard, fully decorated 1955, 4¼in (10.5cm) high.
£425–475 TH

CENTREPIECES

A Bow six-shell sweetmeat stand, painted in *famille rose* style, mid-18thC, 8in (20.5cm) high.
£800–1,000 P

A Belleek tazza, c1865, 9in (23cm) high.
£1,800–2,000 MLa

A Minton centrepiece, modelled as an urn, turquoise with white and gilt Greek key design rim, a gilt stretcher carried by 2 putti with turquoise loincloths, gilt, white and turquoise base, crowned globe mark, factory mark and '1517' to base, mid-19thC, 12½in (32cm) high.
£2,000–2,200 RTo

A Dresden dessert comport, the bowl with pierced shaped rim with painted and encrusted sprays of flowers, 4 figures in 18thC costume encircling a central pedestal, marked, late 19thC, 13¾in (35cm) high.
£580–650 HYD

A Dresden centrepiece, the bowl raised on a scrolled stem set with a loving couple seated next to a pedestal, watched by a jealous gentleman, damaged, marked, mid-19thC, 21in (53.5cm) high.
£620–700 S(Am)

A pair of Minton dessert centrepieces, from the Abercromby service, designed by Albert Carrier-Belleuse, the composite columns supported by 2 mermaids, dated '1871', converted from candelabra, 26in (66cm) high.
£2,200–2,500 P(E)

A Potschappel centrepiece, the bowl raised on a foliate stem with a lady and gentleman dancing around a tree, on a waisted scroll-moulded openwork base, minor repairs, crossed lines and 'T' mark in underglaze blue, late 19thC, 18½in (47cm) high.
£300–350 S(Am)

A pair of Moore Brothers comports, each modelled as a bowl moulded from lily leaves, supported by 3 cherubs, partly enriched in colours within gilt borders, some damage, impressed marks and registration lozenge, late 19thC, 8in (20.5cm) high.
£800–900 CSK

A Sèvres-style gilt-metal mounted porcelain centrepiece, painted by Cantin, with foliate-cast feet each headed by a ram's mask and joined by a foliate swag, late 19thC, 18in (45.5cm) diam.
£1,100–1,300 C

◀ A pair of Continental porcelain comports, with rose encrusted pierced basket tops, the pillars with cherubs and climbing roses on rococo bases, late 19thC, 14½in (37cm) high.
£550–600 DA

A pair of Meissen figural comports, decorated in enamel and gilt with male and female figures, repaired, crossed swords marks, late 19thC, 10in (25.5cm) wide.
£700–800 SK

A pair of Moore Brothers fluted table ornaments, each modelled with flowerheads and leaves, picked out in green and gilt, on twig supports, some damage, printed marks in brown, c1885, 5½in (14cm) high.
£400–450 DN

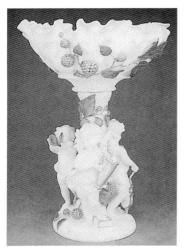

A porcelain centrepiece, in the form of putti playing musical instruments around a tree stump, supporting a fluted dish applied with fruiting vines and picked out in green and gilt, on mound base, probably by Moore Brothers, restored, c1890, 15in (38cm) high.
£700–800 DN

A German porcelain centrepiece, in the form of a young boy and girl flanking a flower encrusted tree stump, supporting a pierced basket painted and encrusted with flowers and leaves, on pierced domed base, late 19thC, 16¼in (41.5cm) high.
£500–550 DN(H)

A Meissen table centrepiece, with pierced panels printed with flowers in gilt foliated cartouches, on 4 encrusted floral scroll feet, underglazed blue crossed swords, 19thC, 21in (53.5cm) high.
£1,800–2,200 AG

> **Miller's is a price GUIDE not a price LIST**

CLOCK CASES

A Meissen clock case, the case with encrusted floral decoration, with a seated winged angelic figure, on a rectangular base with 4 pad feet, minor chips, crossed swords in underglaze blue, incised numerals, c1870, 12in (30.5cm) high, with brass key.
£3,300–3,800 S

A German porcelain clock case, the clock with French 8-day movement, the case encrusted with flowers, standing on 4 encrusted scroll feet, c1880, 39in (99cm) high.
£1,100–1,300 TPA

A Meissen porcelain rococo-scroll clock case, with enamel dial, brass movement striking on a bell, on a porcelain stand, both pieces decorated in colours and gilt, damaged and restored, blue crossed swords marks and incised marks, 19thC, 20in (51cm) high.
£3,000–3,500 CSK

CUPS & SAUCERS

A Limehouse blue and white cup, with a branch-moulded handle issuing flowering branches, enriched in cobalt, the interior with a band of flowers and foliage, damaged, c1745, cup 2in (5cm) high.
£2,000–2,500 CSK

A Chelsea tea bowl and saucer, each piece with scalloped edge, decorated with Tiger and Dragon pattern in the Kakiemon palette, chipped, c1755, saucer 4¾in (12cm) diam.
£1,100–1,200 Bon

A Worcester tea cup and saucer, c1755, saucer 5in (12.5cm) diam.
£450–500 BHA

A Worcester coffee cup, with grooved loop handle, painted in iron-red, green, puce and brown with a pheasant and flowering peony, enriched with gold, c1755, 2½in (6.5cm) high.
£1,800–2,200 P

A Vauxhall coffee cup, with simple loop handle, painted in underglaze blue with a Chinese woman and child in a continuous landscape, slight damage, c1756, 2¼in (5.5cm) high.
£900–1,100 DN

A Worcester tea bowl and saucer, decorated in black, with boys & riding bulls, workman's marks, slight damage, c1756, tea bowl 4in (10cm) diam.
£450–500 DN

◀ A Worcester bell-shaped coffee cup and saucer, decorated in coloured enamels with Putai and attendants, within iron-red and gilt spearhead borders, c1760, cup 2in (5cm) high.
£1,000–1,200 DN

A Worcester coffee cup and saucer, with turquoise border and pearl pattern, slight restoration, c1770, saucer 2¾in (7cm) diam.
£100–120 DAN

A Worcester blue-scale two-handled caudle cup, cover and stand, decorated with reserves of stylized chrysanthemums and insects within mirror-shaped cartouches, the interior with an insect and a flowerspray, interior of cup scratched, blue square seal marks, c1770, stand 5¾in (14.5cm) diam.
£400–450 CNY

A Liverpool transfer-printed coffee can, by Philip Christian, decorated in Fruit Sprigs pattern, c1770, 2½in (6.5cm) high.
£400–450 TVA

A Worcester tea bowl, coffee cup and saucer, decorated in iron-red and gilt within blue ground bands with flowerheads, blue seal marks, c1770, saucer 4in (10cm) diam.
£250–300 DN

◀ A Worcester large and small coffee cup and saucer, decorated in Kakiemon style with prunus, flowering branches and leaves, blue seal marks, c1770, saucer 3½in (9cm) diam.
£350–400 DN

◄ A Worcester tea cup and saucer, decorated in Kakiemon style, within blue ground fan-shaped bands, decorated with flower roundels and glit leaf scrolls, blue seal mark, c1770, 5in (12.5cm) diam.
£330–380 DN

A Worcester cup and cover, enamelled in colours with floral spray within royal blue and gilt panels, 2 pierced loop handles, the domed cover with flower pattern finial, lacking saucer, c1770, 4¼in (11cm) diam.
£360–400 CAG

A Chelsea-Derby two-handled cup, cover and saucer, painted in colours between turquoise geometric bands, slight wear, gilt mark, c1775, 5in (12.5cm) high.
£700–800 CSK

A Worcester fluted tea cup and saucer, decorated in shades of green and gilt, within gilt zig-zag borders, c1775, saucer 5in (12.5cm) diam.
£200–250 DN

A Worcester, Flight & Barr cup and saucer, decorated with gilt leaves and blue flowers, c1795, saucer 5½in (14cm) diam.
£115–125 BSA

A Sèvres cup and saucer, painted with pink roses within 2 concentric leaf and berry borders, painter's marks for Buteux and Fontaine, interlaced 'Ls' mark, date code for 1778, saucer 5in (12.5cm) diam.
£250–300 P

A Worcester fluted two-handled cup, cover and stand, with flower knop, the C-scroll handles moulded with patera, decorated *en grisaille* with an interlinked band, on a turquoise ground frieze and gilt borders, c1780, cup 5in (12.5cm) high.
£300–350 DN

A New Hall Imari pattern coffee can, blue and gold with fruiting trees and foliage, orange fruit, pattern No. 466, c1800, 2¼in (5.5cm) high.
£100–115 AnS

A Derby coffee can and saucer, the can painted by George Complin, pattern No. 207, with a still life of fruit reserved on a pale pink ground, puce painted crown, batons and 'D' mark, c1789, 2¼in (5.5cm) high.
£3,600–4,000 P(NE)

◄ A Pinxton coffee can and saucer, decorated in coloured enamels with a wooded river landscape, c1795, saucer 5in (12.5cm) diam.
£600–700 DN

Derby (1750–1848)

- Founded in 1750 by André Planché and John Heath.
- Planché bought out by John Heath and William Duesbury in 1756.
- In 1770 they bought the Chelsea factory, and for 14 years the company was known as Chelsea-Derby.
- Robert Bloor bought the company in 1811 and managed it until its closure in 1848.
- Crown Derby was established in the 19thC and is today the Royal Crown Derby Porcelain Co.

A Coalport spiral-fluted coffee can, c1805, 2½in (6.5cm) high.
£60–65 BSA

A Spode bat-printed coffee can, c1810, 2½in (6.5cm) high.
£50–55 BSA

A Spode coffee can, with cobalt ground, bat-printed in gold with a castellated building, from the Ancient Buildings series, pattern No. 1695, c1810, 2½in (6.5cm) high.
£350–400 AnS

A Chamberlain's Worcester tea cup and saucer, with gadrooned rim, painted in coloured enamels with roses, pansies and leaves, on gold ground bands, within gilt stiff leaf borders, painted mark in iron-red and pattern No. 924, c1816–20, cup 3½in (9cm) high.
£300–350 DN

A Miles Mason coffee can and saucer, moulded and painted with flowers on a pale blue ground, c1808, saucer 4in (10cm) diam.
£125–140 VH

A Miles Mason tea bowl and saucer, transfer-printed in underglaze blue with Veranda pattern, seal mark, c1810, 5in (12.5cm) diam.
£100–115 JP

Bat-printing

Bat-printing was used in Staffordshire in the early 19thC. Bat-printed wares had their decoration applied by transferring a print from a copper plate using a flat flexible sheet, or 'bat', of glue or gelatine. This overcame problems of printing on difficult shaped objects as the glue bat would stretch in a way that the normal process, using tissue to transfer the image, would not.

A Derby coffee can, decorated with blue, gilt and orange flowers with buds, c1815, 2½in (6.5cm) high.
£80–100 AnS

▶ A John and William Ridgway tea cup, coffee cup and saucer, decorated in coloured enamels, within gilt borders, pattern No. 2/974 in red, c1820, saucer 4in (10cm) diam.
£300–350 DN

A Miles Mason tea cup, coffee can and saucer, brightly decorated in Imari style, c1810, saucer 4in (10cm) diam.
£250–300 VH

A Derby coffee can, base inscribed 'On the coast of Sussex', c1810, 2½in (6.5cm) high.
£300–350 RA

A New Hall trio, decorated with a chinoiserie scene, c1815, saucer 5½in (14cm) diam.
£115–125 JP

A Swansea beaker, with a turned foot and everted rim, painted with blue flowers and gilt foliage, gilt line to rim and foot, c1820, 2½in (6.5cm) high.
£180–220 P

◄ A Charles Bourne trio, London shape, pattern No. 208, c1820, saucer 5½in (14cm) diam.
£350–400 TVA

A Nantgarw coffee can, attributed to Thomas Pardoe, decorated with a green woodpecker, the reverse with roses, convolvulus and a gilded moth, gilding to rim worn, c1821, 2¼in (5.5cm) high.
£750–850 P

A Bloor Derby covered chocolate cup and stand, by Leonard Lead, painted with flowers, c1825, 5½in (14cm) high.
£700–750 TK

A Hilditch & Sons cup and saucer, decorated in blue and white with an Oriental scene, c1825, 5½in (14cm) diam.
£70–80 OCH

A Belleek neptune cup and saucer, First Green Period, saucer 5¼in (13.5cm) diam.
£200–250 MLa

A Benjamin E. Goodwin cup and saucer, decorated in black with a peacock pattern, marked, c1834–41, saucer 4½in (11.5cm) diam.
£16–18 OCH

A Meissen blue ground cup and cover, painted in colours, within a shaped cartouche gilt with foliage, the rims gilt with scrolls, minor chip, blue crossed swords mark, 19thC, 5in (12.5cm) high.
£850–1,000 CSK

A Belleek Institute pattern cup and saucer, First Period, c1863–90, saucer 5¾in (14.5cm) diam.
£320–350 DeA

Miller's is a price GUIDE not a price LIST

A Sèvres cabinet cup and saucer, painted with classical devices in blue ground panels, between gilt bands, on a green ground, the interior, handle and rims richly gilt, printed marks, c1840.
£600–700 CSK

A Meissen yellow ground topographical cabinet cup, cover and stand, underglaze blue crossed swords mark, mid-19thC.
£700–800 Bon

A Sèvres-style coffee can and saucer, the can painted with a fisherman and companion, the saucer with a putto and dolphin, reserved on a blue, white and gilt design with turquoise 'jewelling' within borders of 'pearls' and 'rubies', marked, mid-19thC, saucer 5in (12.5cm) diam.
£950–1,100 P

A Worcester cup and saucer, c1876, saucer 5in (12.5cm) diam.
£100–120 YY

An unmarked Victorian cup and saucer, cup 2½in (6.5cm) high.
£13–16 PSA

A Royal Worcester tea cup and saucer, decorated in apricot, green and gold, etched 'ER' for Edward Raby, c1885, cup 2in (5cm) high.
£60–65 AnS

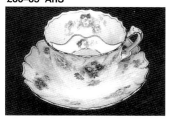

A Crescent China moustache cup and saucer, the spirally fluted bodies decorated with flowers and gilded, puce printed mark, c1890, saucer 6in (15cm) diam.
£55–65 SAS

A Grainger's Worcester coffee can and saucer, decorated with gold and black pattern, c1889–1902, saucer 4½in (11.5cm) diam.
£25–30 WAC

▶ A Coalport trio, hand-painted in gilt, mid-19thC, 3in (7.5cm) high.
£100–120 MRW

A Royal Crown Derby blue and white cup and saucer, c1883, saucer 5in (12.5cm) diam.
£24–28 PSA

A Spode hand-painted coffee can and saucer, c1889, saucer 4¼in (11cm) diam.
£45–55 WAC

A Belleek Sydney cup and saucer, Second Period, c1891–1926, 3¼in (8.5cm) diam.
£280–300 MLa

A Coalport cup and saucer, the cobalt-blue ground with heavy gilt decoration, gilded well to saucer and interior of cup, green mark, c1900, cup 1¾in (4.5cm) high.
£170–200 MER

A Royal Crown Derby cup and saucer, in cigar pattern No. 1128, c1887, saucer 5½in (14cm) diam.
£60–70 VSt

A Belleek Tridacna moustache cup and saucer, decorated in green with gilded rim, Second Period, c1891–1926, saucer 6in (15cm) diam.
£500–550 MLa

A Belleek Hexagon demi-tasse cup and saucer, the green tinted cup painted in gold with 'Baby', Second Period, c1891–1926, saucer 4¼in (11cm) diam.
£150–175 MLa

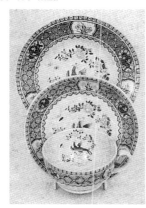

A Minton hand-coloured trio, c1900, plate 6½in (16.5cm) diam.
£20–24 TAC

A Royal Doulton trio, decorated with Hydrangea pattern, c1908, 7½in (19cm) diam.
£45–50 HEI

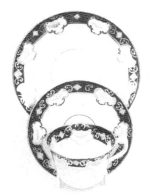

A Royal Albert trio, c1910, plate 7in (18cm) diam.
£15–18 TAC

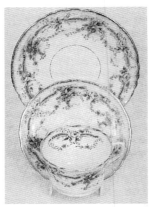

A Colclough & Co gilded trio, decorated with blue and lemon design, c1910, plate 6in (15cm) diam.
£12–14 TAC

The term 'trio', meaning a set of 3, can refer to either a matching coffee can, tea cup and saucer or cup, saucer and tea plate.

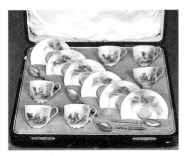

A set of 6 Royal Worcester coffee cups and saucers, by Harry Stinton, painted with Highland cattle, c1913.
£1,700–2,000 SWO

A Paragon/Star China Co coffee can and saucer, c1913, saucer 4½in (11.5cm) diam.
£30–35 WAC

Cross Reference
See Colour Review

A Royal Crown Derby cup and saucer, decorated with Witches pattern, c1914, saucer 5in (12.5cm) diam.
£60–70 YY

A Royal Worcester coffee can and saucer, decorated with black and gilt pattern, c1916, saucer 3¾in (9.5cm) diam.
£85–95 WAC

A Crown Staffordshire child's cup and saucer, decorated with golfing figures and gold rim, c1920, 2¼in (5.5cm) high.
£150–175 PGA

A Hammersley coffee cup and saucer, decorated with violets, 1920s, saucer 4¾in (12cm) diam.
£16–18 TAC

A Hammersley coffee cup and saucer, decorated with a pink and green festooned border, gilded, c1920, 2¼in (5.5cm) high.
£25–30 AnS

A Coalport trio, 1920s, plate 6½in (16.5cm) diam.
£30–35 PBi

A Belleek heart-shaped cup and saucer, painted with shamrock design, Third Period, c1926–46, 2¼in (5.5cm) high.
£100–120 MLa

A Belleek Celtic coffee cup and saucer, hand decorated, Third Period, saucer 5in (12.5cm) diam.
£200–220 MLa

A Belleek Limpet cup and saucer, decorated in pink with gilding, Third Period, c1926–46, 3¼in (8.5cm) diam.
£65–75 MLa

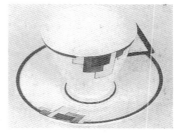

A Shelley Queen Anne shape coffee cup and saucer, c1928, saucer 4½in (11.5cm) diam.
£45–50 BEV

A Belleek Celtic trio, Third Period, c1926–46, cup 3in (7.5cm) high.
£220–245 MLa

A Royal Standard coffee can and saucer, c1929–40, saucer 4¾in (12cm) diam.
£25–30 WAC

A Shelley Vogue shape cup and saucer, c1930, saucer 4¾in (12cm) diam.
£85–95 BEV

A set of 6 Royal Crown Derby coffee cans and saucers, decorated in Imari style with flowers and leaves within flower panelled borders, in silk-lined fitted case, printed marks in red for 1931 and 1932, pattern No. 2712/2 in red, saucer 4in (10cm) diam.
£200–250 HOLL

A Shelley Chintz ware coffee cup and saucer, decorated with Regent pattern, in shades of yellow, blue and pink flowers, c1932, 2½in (6.5cm) high.
£35–40 BEV

A Paragon coffee cup and saucer, 1930s, saucer 4½in (11.5cm) diam.
£75–85 BEV

A Plant Tuscan China coffee cup and saucer, 1930s, saucer 4¼in (11cm) diam.
£30–35 BEV

A Royal China coffee cup and saucer, 1930s, saucer 4¾in (12cm) diam.
£30–35 BEV

A Noritake cup and saucer, green Komaru backstamp, c1930, 2¾in (7cm) high.
£15–20 DgC

A Gray's coffee cup and saucer, with silver lustre design, 1930s, saucer 4¾in (12cm) diam.
£30–35 BEV

A Susie Cooper coffee cup and saucer, decorated in Asterisk pattern, c1938, cup 2in (5cm) high.
£30–35 SCA

A Paragon trio, in Rockingham style, c1957, saucer 5½in (14cm) diam.
£10–15 VSt

DISHES

A Chelsea leaf dish, the stem handle with leaf and flower terminal, painted with flowersprays and a moth, with brown line rims, red anchor mark, 18thC, 10¾in (27.5cm) wide.
£200–220 P(Ch)

A Meissen leaf-shaped dish, moulded as 3 overlapping vine leaves with a stalk handle, painted in enamels, the leaves with green borders, marked, c1750, 10½in (26.5cm) wide.
£1,000–1,200 WW

A Chelsea fluted two-handled dish, decorated in coloured enamels with a spray of flowers, leaves and scattered flowers, within a brown line rim, red anchor mark, c1753, 8¼in (21cm) wide.
£700–800 DN

A Worcester dish, the interior painted in coloured enamels with flowers and leaves within a puce scroll band, the flared sides pierced with interlinked roundels and applied with flowerheads, small repair, c1760, 6½in (16.5cm) diam.
£600–700 DN

A Worcester blue and white pickle dish, painted with the Pickle Leaf Vine pattern, open crescent mark, c1760, 3in (7.5cm) wide.
£200–250 Bon

A Worcester fluted dish, painted in blue with the K'ang Hsi Lotus pattern, chips to rim, pseudo Chinese emblem mark, c1770, 9¾in (25cm) wide.
£350–400 DN

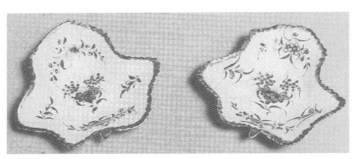

A pair of Worcester leaf-shaped pickle dishes, each painted in blue with the Pickle Leaf Vine pattern, within a blue line border, damaged, c1760, 4in (10cm) wide.
£350–400 DN

A Worcester kidney-shaped dish, decorated in the atelier of James Giles, in coloured enamels with a bold spray of flowers and fruits, scattered flowers and cherries, within a gilt line rim, damaged, c1770, 10¼in (26cm) wide.
£250–280 DN

◄ A Worcester lobed dish, decorated in the atelier of James Giles, with a central *grisaille* urn, garlanded in coloured enamels with flowers and leaves, within a gilt anthemion roundel, the blue ground decorated in gilt with a vine scroll band, blue crescent mark, c1770, 7¾in (20cm) square.
£650–750 DN

A Worcester cabbage leaf-shaped dish, printed in blue with the Wispy Chrysanthemum Spray pattern, chips to rim, hatched crescent mark, c1770, 10in (25.5cm) wide.
£350–400 DN

A Worcester junket dish, decorated in coloured enamels with 3 butterflies, within an underglazed blue flower and scroll band, the border with sprays of flowers and leaves within radiating blue and gilt flower panelled bands, blue seal mark, c1770, 10¼in (26cm) diam.
£2,000–2,200 DN

A Frankenthal lozenge-shaped dish, decorated in puce with a gentleman and companion in a wooded landscape, the rim with scattered flowers, painted mark in blue and incised repairer's marks, c1774, 11¼in (28.5cm) wide.
£650–700 DN

A Derby octagonal dish, decorated with leaves, c1780, 9in (23cm) wide.
£200–250 ALB

A Meissen dish, decorated with painted flowers, blue crossed swords mark, star and numeral '4', impressed 'I.33', Marcolini period, c1800, 11in (28cm) wide.
£180–220 Bon

A Spode child's dish, decorated in green, blue and yellow, pattern No. 2070, c1814, 4¼in (11cm) wide.
£55–60 OCH

A Charles Bourne stand and dessert dish, with loop handles, pattern No. 60, c1818, stand 4¾in (12cm) high.
£850–950 TVA

A pair of Derby shell-shaped dishes, each painted in coloured enamels, the borders picked out in gilt, crowned crossed baton marks in red, c1825, 9¾in (25cm) wide.
£480–530 DN

A Chamberlain's Worcester dish, with gadrooned rim, decorated in coloured enamels, with a named view of Hampton Court, Hereford, within a gilt stiff leaf roundel, on a puce ground, c1830, 9in (23cm) square.
£400–450 DN

A Staffordshire porcelain stand, with pieced border, painted in coloured enamels with a named view of 'Lambton Castle', within a gilt cartouche, on a turquoise ground, painted title in black, c1840, 9¾in (25cm) wide.
£300–350 DN

A Spode Imari pattern dish, c1880, 12in (30.5cm) wide.
£100–120 YY

A Taylor, Tunnicliffe & Co pickle dish, with raised gold and silver decoration, c1880, 6¼in (16cm) wide.
£140–160 GLN

A Copeland saucer dish, painted with a central sprig of mistletoe, the rim and well with a continuous band of holly, green printed mark, impressed crown, printed registration mark, 'No. 8275', late 19thC, 16¼in (41.5cm) diam.
£350–400 L

A Royal Worcester ice dish, decorated in the style of Edward Raby, with floral sprig bouquets on an ivory ground, shaped scalloped and gilded borders, c1892, 8in (20.5cm) wide.
£400–450 GAK

Edward Raby designed a series of etchings of flower subjects which were coloured in by juniors. Some etchings included his initials 'ER'.

▶ A Vienna dish, painted with a titled classical scene of 'Peles u. Thetis', on a claret ground, minor rubbing, shield mark and 'P.' in blue, signed 'Knoeller', late 19thC, 16in (40.5cm) diam.
£2,400–2,800 S

A Noritake lemon squeezer, with stylized flower design, red 'M' in wreath backstamp, 1920s, 6in (15cm) diam.
£15–20 DgC

A Noritake bonbon dish, decorated with a floral pattern, 1920s, 5in (12.5cm) diam.
£20–25 DgC

A Meissen dish, with a moulded Dulong pattern border, the centre painted in a muted autumnal palette, the border enriched in pink lustre and gilding, damaged, cancelled blue crossed swords and star mark, the porcelain late 18thC, the decoration late 19thC, 17½in (44.5cm) wide.
£700–800 C

A Royal Copenhagen Flora Danica dessert dish and cover, with dentate edge, the bell-shaped cover with pierced basketwork sides applied with gilded leaves and florets and painted with named botanical specimens, with bud knop, printed marks, early 20thC, 11½in (29cm) high.
£3,000–3,500 P

Noritake

In 1891, it was declared that all Japanese wares imported into the USA were to be marked with the word 'Nippon'. One of the most important factories to produce Nippon wares was the Noritake Company. Established in 1904 in Nagoya by Icizaemon Morimura, the company specialized in the production of hand-painted porcelain in competition with industrially printed ceramics.

During the 1920s, the American architect Frank Lloyd Wright was commissioned to supply designs reflecting the current vogue for Art Deco-style tea, coffee and dinner services.

After 1921 the Nippon mark was changed to 'Japan' or 'Made in Japan'.

Two Noritake bonbon dishes, decorated with central flower and leaf pattern, red 'M' in wreath backstamp, c1930, 7¾in (20cm) wide.
£18–25 each DgC

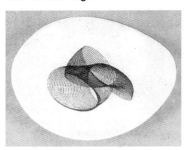

A Noritake boat-shaped bonbon dish, green 'M' in wreath backstamp, c1930, 7in (18cm) wide.
£18–25 DgC

◀ A Queensbury bone china ovoid dish, mid-1950s, 7in (18cm) wide.
£35–40 JR

A Shelley butter dish, decorated with Crocus pattern, in shades of pink and blue on a white ground, c1930, 4½in (11.5cm) wide.
£15–20 CSA

FIGURES

A pair of Bow figures depicting a nun and a monk, each seated and picked out in black and brown, on a flat base applied with coloured flowers and leaves, damaged, c1755, 4¾in (12cm) high.
£700–800 DN

A German porcelain figure of a putto, enriched in gilt, 18thC, 5in (12.5cm) high.
£300–350 CSK

A Bow figure of a flower seller, with pink skirt and blue hat, impressed mark, c1750, 6in (15cm) high.
£2,000–2,200 BHa

▶ A pair of Meissen figures of duellists, modelled by J. J. Kändler, in black, puce, white, turquoise and yellow, restored, blue crossed swords marks at back of base, c1755, 8in (20.5cm) high.
£4,500–5,000 C

A Bow group depicting The Fortune Teller, by the Muses Modeller, after a painting by Boucher entitled 'La Bonne Aventure', he wearing a yellow-trimmed brown coat, she in a yellow bodice and floral sprigged skirt, on a green base applied with colourful flowers, damaged, c1752, 7in (18cm) high.
£5,200–6,000 S

A Bow figure of a flautist, wearing a yellow jacket and flower-decorated breeches, seated on a mound, restored, c1756, 3¾in (9.5cm) high.
£500–600 DN

◀ A Meissen figure of Cupid, with a tricorn hat under his right arm and a sword tucked under his tailcoat, slight damage, c1755, 3¾in (9.5cm) high.
£400–500 Bon

Figures • PORCELAIN 325

A Derby figure of a shepherd, wearing a floral waistcoat, puce lined green jacket, floral breeches and white shoes with iron-red bows, chipped and restored, patch marks, c1760, 8¾in (22cm) high.
£280–350 N

A Sèvres biscuit figure of a boy seated on a tree stump, damaged, incised mark, c1760, 4¾in (12cm) high.
£600–700 C

A Frankenthal hunting group, modelled by Joh. Fr. Lück, with a hunter seated on a grassy mound with a hunting horn and a huntress loading a rifle, mounted on a marble plinth, cracked and restored, rampant lion and 'AB' monogram in underglaze blue, c1760, 10½in (26.5cm) high.
£4,000–5,000 S

A Derby figure of a child, wearing a pink and yellow jacket, sitting on a turquoise chair and stroking a cat, restored, patch marks beneath base, c1765, 5¾in (14.5cm) high.
£400–450 WW

A Bow figure of a woman, emblematic of Spring, restored, c1755, 4¾in (12cm) high.
£300–350 DN

A Meissen figure of a boy holding a staff and a cockerel, restored, c1760, 6in (15cm) high.
£1,400–1,600 DAN

A Bow figure of a hunter, in front of bocage, on a scroll base, slight restoration, c1765, 7¼in (18.5cm) high.
£700–800 DAN

A pair of Bow figures depicting Spring and Autumn, the man with a goblet and bunch of grapes, the lady with baskets and bunches of flowers, both seated among flowers on high rococo scroll bases picked out in gilding, marked, c1765, 6¾in (17cm) high.
£1,150–1,350 S

A Bow figure of a Turk, wearing a fur hat, blue jacket and floral pantaloons, standing on a pierced base surmounted by green and yellow glazed bocage, damaged and restored, painted anchor and dagger marks in red enamel, underglaze blue mark, c1765, 8in (20.5cm) high.
£220–260 Hal

A pair of Bow figures of a lady and gentleman, each holding bunches of grapes, on square shaped encrusted floral bases with scroll feet, c1765, 7in (18cm) high.
£2,000–2,200 AG

A pair of Bow figures of New Dancers, modelled on floral encrusted bases before floral bocages, raised on rococo scroll feet picked out in turquoise and gilt, damaged, restored, c1765, 9in (23cm) high.
£1,400–1,700 DN

A Sèvres group, modelled as a seated lady resisting the amorous advances of a courtly gentleman, minor damage, incised mark of Bachelier, mid-18thC, 8in (20.5cm) high.
£1,800–2,000 Bon

A pair of Derby floral encrusted figures of a lady and gentleman, patch marks to bases, c1765, 9in (23cm) high.
£1,500–1,800 AG

A Derby figure of a macaroni with a dog, c1765, 6in (15cm) high.
£850–950 BHA

A macaroni was an 18thC dandy who affected foreign manners.

◀ A pair of Derby figures, from the Piping Shepherds series, one with a dog at his feet, the other with a sheep, each before flowering bocage and on volute scroll-edge tricorn bases, c1770, 8¾in (22cm) high.
£600–700 Bon

A figure of a gladiator, probably Derby, picked out in yellow, turquoise, puce and gilding, patch marks, restored, late 18thC, 5in (12.5cm) high.
£400–500 Bon

A Derby figure of a girl, wearing a white bonnet and carrying a basket, the gilt scroll base surmounted by bocage, restored, incised numeral, c1770, 5in (12.5cm) high.
£100–120 Hal

◀ A Doccia figure group, depicting a man standing on a rocky mound leaning on a tree, wearing a blue jacket and breeches decorated with flowers, and a yellow and iron-red hat, a lady seated at his feet, chipped and restored, c1770, 9in (23cm) high.
£3,000–3,500 S

A Bow figure of a hussar, wearing a yellow cape, puce jacket enriched with gilding and iron-red trousers, the plinth enriched in turquoise and puce, damaged, c1765, 6in (15cm) high.
£650–750 C

A Derby figure group, entitled 'Time Clipping the Wings of Love', some damage, c1770, 12¾in (32.5cm) high.
£460–500 PCh

◄ A Wallendorf allegorical figure of Summer, modelled as a young woman holding a sheaf of wheat in her apron, wearing a yellow apron over a puce dress and a green hat lined in iron-red, the scroll-edged grassy base heightened in gilding, damaged and restored, c1775, 5¼in (13.5cm) high.
£500–600 S

A Höchst group of a boy with pet animals, modelled by J. P. Melchior, damaged and restored, incised wheel mark flanked by 'I' and 'SP', c1775, 6¾in (17cm) high.
£3,300–3,600 C

A Derby set of the French Seasons, after the Tournai models by N. J. F. Gauron, painted with bright polychrome enamels, rich gilt details, scrolling gilt leaf trails to the circular bases, late 18thC, 10in (25.5cm) high.
£3,000–3,500 WW

A Doccia group of peasants dancing back to back, he in a green jacket, white shirt, black breeches and shoes, she in a puce jacket, white apron, yellow skirt and red shoes, restored, c1775, 6½in (16.5cm) high.
£1,800–2,200 C

A pair of Sèvres figures, 'L'été' garlanded with wheat and carrying a large sheaf, 'L'hiver' pulling a cloak around himself, each on a slab base, damaged, incised mark of Bachelier, late 18thC, 6¼in (16cm) high.
£450–550 Bon

A Sèvres figure group, 'La Curiosité', modelled as a young boy opening a magic lantern to a girl holding a basket of fruit, a smaller boy at her side, firing cracks, late 18thC, 6¼in (16cm) high.
£2,100–2,500 Bon

Two Derby groups of Procris and Cephalus, and Renaldo and Armida, painted in colours and gilt, incised numerals 'N75' and 'No. 76', c1785, largest 8in (20.5cm) high.
£1,000–1,200 CSK

A set of 4 Derby figures modelled as children representing the Seasons, Autumn with corn sheafs, Spring with flowers, Winter with a brazier and Summer with baskets of flowers and fruit, restored, c1775, 5in (12.5cm) high.
£600–700 Bon

◄ A group of 3 Derby biscuit figures, modelled as Spring, Autumn and Winter, each on an integral plinth, minor damage, incised 'No. 5, G, S,' and other marks, c1790, 8in (20.5cm) high.
£400–500 Bon

A Meissen Marcolini group of the Three Graces, probably after a model by J. F. Eberlein, in white, scantily draped, with flowers in their hair, on a shaped base and pedestal with stepped foot, chipped and repaired, crossed swords and '+' in blue, incised 'No. 536', impressed numeral '50', c1780, 12¼in (31cm) high.
£1,500–1,800 S

A Derby figure of James Quinn as Falstaff, richly decorated in coloured enamels and gilt, on a scroll-moulded base, some damage, incised 'No. 291' and '3', c1780, 11½in (29cm) high.
£250–300 WW

A Derby figure of Britannia, decorated in pink, brown and green, chips to leaves, c1780, 14in (35.5cm) high.
£850–1,000 DAN

A miniature figure of Punchinello, holding a basket of pretzels, by Le Nove, restored, c1780, 2½in (6.5cm) high.
£1,400–1,700 C

A Derby figure, depicting Minerva in floral costume with red and green shawl, late 18thC, 14¾in (37.5cm) high.
£450–550 AH

A Derby figure of a putto, decorated in gilt, c1800, 5in (12.5cm) high.
£150–180 SER

A set of Derby biscuit figures of the French Seasons, after Pierre Stephan, slight damage, incised marks and 'No. 123', c1820, 7in (18cm) high.
£1,500–1,800 Hal

Bloor Derby

In 1811 the Derby factory was acquired from John Heath and William Duesbury's successors by Robert Bloor who, despite the fact that he went mad in 1826, continued to manage the ailing business. The quality of the figures declined – most were over-decorated with heavily rouged cheeks, sombre colours and square, octagonal, or even debased rococo-style bases. Owing to indiscriminate marketing of vast quantities of poor-quality goods, the factory finally closed in 1848.

▶ A pair of Bloor Derby figure groups, the Stocking Mender Group and the Shoe Mender Group, coloured in deep enamels on scroll bases, damaged and repaired, blue painted *faux* Meissen mark, c1820, 6½in (16.5cm) high.
£400–450 Bon

◀ A Paris gilt-metal mounted biscuit figure of Cupid, on a gilt-edged plinth, minor damage, stencilled mark in iron-red, c1810, 11½in (29cm) high.
£2,200–2,500 S

A set of 4 Derby figures, emblematic of the Continents, Asia, Africa, Europe and America, blue crossed swords and incised 'No. 200' marks, 'Robt. Bloor & Co', c1835, 8½in (21.5cm) high.
£1,400–1,600 C

A pair of Minton dancing figures, each brightly coloured, on scroll-moulded bases picked out in gilding, restored, c1840, 7¾in (19.5cm) high.
£280–320 Bon

A Copeland Parian figure of Narcissus, adapted by E. B. Stephens from Gibson's marble statue, c1847, 13in (33cm) high.
£600–700 JAK

A Chamberlain's Worcester figure of one of the Rainer brothers, c1828, 6in (15cm) high.
£500–600 DAN

A Belleek figure of Affection, First Period, 14½in (37cm) high.
£1,700–2,000 MLa

A Staffordshire porcellaneous figure of a Scotsman and a dog, c1845, 8½in (21.5cm) high.
£250–280 DAN

A Parian group by Bates, Brown-Westhead, Moore & Co, depicting Cupid and Psyche, designed by Gibson for the Art Union of London, c1858, 18in (45.5cm) high.
£1,000–1,200 JAK

A Copeland Parian figure of Storm, sculptor Brodie, minor faults to base, c1858, 18½in (47cm) high.
£450–550 JAK

A Minton Parian figure, Solitude, modelled as a semi-draped female seated on a rockwork plinth, with a stork or heron beneath, incised 'J. Lawlor, Sculp. – Art Union of London 1852', impressed marks under base rim, 20in (51cm) high.
£300–350 P(E)

A Parian ware figure of the muse of Art, slight chip, unmarked, c1854, 14¼in (36cm) high.
£150–220 SER

▶ A Parian figure of Princess Alice, her hands clasping a handkerchief, on a square plinth, base initialled 'A', slight damage, c1860, 14¼in (36cm) high.
£400–450 SAS

A Copeland Parian candle extinguisher and stand, in the form of a Bluecoat School boy, c1860, 4½in (11.5cm) high.
£270–300 TH

A Parian ware female figure with a harp, slight chip, unmarked, c1860, 24½in (62cm) high.
£300–350 SER

A Minton Parian figure of Dorothea, by John Bell, c1860, 13¼in (33.5cm) high.
£400–450 JAK

A Meissen figure of a child feeding a hen and chicks, c1860, 5in (12.5cm) high.
£700–800 BHA

Cross Reference
See Colour Review

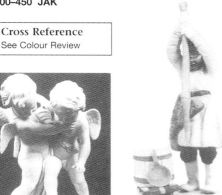

A Parian figure, entitled 'Cupids Contending', after Fiamingo for Copeland, c1860, 15in (38cm) high.
£900–1,100 JAK

A Gardner biscuit figure of a fisherman breaking a hole in the ice to fish, under mark and impressed, c1860–90, 11½in (29cm) high.
£550–650 PC

A pair of Meissen figures of a seated boy and girl, coloured in blue and gilt, crossed swords mark, 19thC, 5½in (14cm) high.
£700–850 P(B)

Parian

Developed by Copeland in the mid-19thC, Parian is fine white biscuit porcelain, mostly unglazed. The name derives from ancient Greek marble from the island of Paros.

► A Copeland Parian group, by J. Durham, entitled 'Go To Sleep', c1862, 18in (45.5cm) high.
£800–1,000 JAK

A Meissen musical group, depicting children, each playing an instrument and standing on rocks, pedestals and scrollwork, supported on a waisted circular base, the whole picked out in pastel colours and gilt, damaged, crossed swords in underglaze blue and impressed and incised numerals, c1860, 10¼in (26cm) high.
£1,100–1,200 N

A Meissen group of 2 cherubs, allegorical of Summer and Autumn, the base modelled with scrolls and coloured green, pink and blue, minor damage, crossed swords in underglaze blue, incised '1230', impressed '111', c1860, 10¾in (27.5cm) high.
£1,500–1,750 S(Am)

A Gardner figure of a wife with her drunken husband, marked and impressed in Cyrillic alphabet, c1860–90, 6in (15cm) high.
£500–600 PC

A Gardner figure of a woman with a child on her shoulders, marked and impressed, c1860–80, 12¼in (31cm) high.
£550–650 PC

A Parian ware group of 2 children, with a lamb lying at their feet, on an oval base, 19thC, 11½in (29cm) high.
£180–220 AH

A Gardner group of 2 boys playing by a broken wheel, impressed 'Gardner' in Russian Cyrillic alphabet, c1860–90, 4¼in (11cm) high.
£450–500 PC

A Parian ware figure, depicting Paul, c1865, 14in (35.5cm) high.
£180–220 HYD

Paul et Virginie **was a popular romance written by Bernadin de St Pierre in 1797.**

A Minton Parian figure of Miranda, by John Bell, c1865, 15½in (39.5cm) high.
£400–450 JAK

Miranda is the daughter of Prospero in Shakespeare's *The Tempest.*

A Nymphenburg figure of a cherub blacksmith, c1870, 4in (10cm) high.
£80–100 SER

A Parian group, probably Copeland, modelled as a naked female seated on a gnarled tree stump, with a doe and a fawn at her side, the base incised 'C. B. Birch Sc 1866', 20in (51cm) high.
£550–650 P(E)

A Copeland Parian figure of Musidora, by W. Theed, c1867, 17½in (44.5cm) high.
£550–650 JAK

A pair of Parian figures of girls, each wearing classical robes and standing on a fluted plinth, c1865, 14½in (37cm) high.
£250–300 Hal

A pair of Royal Worcester bone china figures, depicting a boy and a girl playing, each decorated in pink, blue, cream, green and brown on glazed Parian ground, models 'A 2/101' and '102', c1865, 12½in (32cm) high.
£1,600–1,800 QSA

A Meissen figure, The Woodcutter, c1880, 5½in (14cm) high.
£1,300–1,500 BHA

A Meissen figure, The Gardener, c1880, 5in (12.5cm) high.
£1,300–1,500 BHA

A Meissen figure of a lady card player, wearing a pale blue lined flowered pink open robe, a striped and flowered skirt and yellow shoes, damaged, blue crossed swords mark, incised 'F.64', painted number '10', c1880, 6½in (16.5cm) high.
£1,000–1,200 C

Two Royal Worcester blush porcelain figures, depicting a lady holding a bird's nest, wearing a hat and floral dress, and a man sharpening a scythe, wearing a hat, open-necked shirt and breeches, each on a rustic base, 19thC, largest 9½in (24cm) high.
£700–800 AH

A Royal Worcester group of a young boy and girl, modelled in Kate Greenaway style, by James Hadley, picked out in gilt, on an oval mound base, one hat with rim chip, printed mark in puce for 1884, applied registration mark for 1882, 8in (20.5cm) high.
£1,200–1,400 DN

A pair of Berlin Malabar figures, painted with sprays of flowers, the lady holding a parrot, on square bases, damaged, underglaze blue marks, 19thC, largest 16½in (42cm) high.
£1,400–1,700 CSK

A Royal Worcester figure of a Scotsman, seated wearing a beret and kilt, picked out in coloured enamels and gilt, on canted base, printed mark in puce for 1889 and registration mark for 1881, 6½in (16cm) high.
£400–500 DN

Cross Reference
See Colour Review

A Royal Worcester figure of John Bull, modelled by James Hadley, picked out in coloured enamels and gilt, on a canted base, slight damage, printed mark in puce for 1884 and registration mark for 1881, 7in (18cm) high.
£250–300 DN

A Royal Worcester figure from the London Cries series, after a model by James Hadley, entitled 'Water', on a circular base, shape No. 1002, damaged, printed and impressed marks, late 19thC, 7in (18cm) high.
£700–800 CSK

A set of 4 German figures of putti, depicting the elements, decorated in coloured enamels, damaged, pseudo crossed swords mark in blue, late 19thC, 9in (23cm) high.
£750–850 DN

A pair of Royal Worcester spill vase figures, after original models by James Hadley, with painted faces and gilded details, slight wear, printed puce and impressed marks, date codes for 1889 and 1890, 9½in (24cm) high.
£1,200–1,400 CSK

A Royal Worcester figure, in the form of a Beefeater, with green belt and brown shoes on a cream ground, c1890, 10in (25.5cm) high.
£325–350 TH

A pair of Royal Worcester figures of Moorish musicians, modelled by James Hadley, both dressed in long flowing robes standing beside obelisks, tinted ivory ground and gilt, signed, date ciphers for 1897, mould Nos. 1084, 13in (33cm) high.
£1,800–2,000 J&L

James Hadley was the senior modeller at Royal Worcester and established his own factory in 1896. Although he achieved little recognition for his work in his own lifetime, his figures maintained their popularity long after his death in 1903.

A pair of Robinson & Leadbeater Parian figures, depicting north Italian country musicians, decorated in green, red and sand coloured enamels, impressed 'R&L' mark and script marks to base, c1885, 16in (40.5cm) high.
£350–380 P(E)

A Berlin figure group of Paris and Helen, a dog and a lamb, late 19thC, 10in (25.5cm) high.
£260–300 AH

A figure of a young woman in 18thC dress, by Vion & Baury, Paris, entitled 'The Broken Pitcher', blue anchor printed mark, 19thC, 26in (66cm) high.
£400–450 CAG

A Continental Parian ware figure, 19thC, 8½in (21.5cm) high.
£45–55 MEG

A Copeland Parian ware figure, depicting a maiden, 19thC, 15in (38cm) high.
£250–300 HYD

A Meissen group depicting Cupid's chariot of love, glazed in pastel colours and gilding, the figures seated on a deep crimson cushion, damaged, blue underglaze crossed swords mark, late 19thC, 9in (23cm) high.
£1,600–1,800 MJB

A Dresden group, advertising Yardley's Old English Lavender, depicting a mother and 2 children carrying baskets of lavender, polychrome decorations, early 20thC, 12in (30.5cm) high.
£450–500 HCC

A Samson figure of Neptune, after a Derby original, a stylized dolphin at his feet, on a pierced scroll-moulded base applied with shells and leaves, gold anchor mark, c1900, 13½in (34.5cm) high.
£230–280 CSK

A Meissen figure of a young lady, holding a gold orb, wearing loose robes enriched in pale green, blue crossed swords mark, incised 'Q180', early 20thC, 11½in (29cm) high.
£1,500–1,600 CSK

A Royal Dux bust of a lady, dressed in a lace-trimmed décolleté dress, impressed tablet mark '454' and painted 'No. 15', applied pink triangle mark, c1900, 22in (56cm) high.
£1,700–2,000 WL

Royal Dux

The factory was founded in 1860 and became the most prolific of the three Bohemian firms. Their range included animals and classically-attired maidens.

◀ A collection of 7 bisque 'Frozen Charlotte' doll figures, including 4 nudes, 2 bathers and a mermaid, c1910, largest 5in (12.5cm) long.
£450–550 AH

A Royal Dux figure of a girl, semi-draped and seated on a rock, on a square base, c1910–20, 12in (30.5cm) high.
£1,000–1,200 HCC

Royal Dux figures and busts are highly sought after today.

A pair of Royal Worcester figures of Egyptian musicians, c1911, 12¾in (32.5cm) high.
£1,200–1,400 TH

A pair of Royal Dux figures, painted in pastel shades and highlighted with gilding, marked, early 20thC, 5in (12.5cm) high.
£240–265 HYD

A Royal Copenhagen figure of a milkmaid and cow, c1930, 6¼in (16cm) high.
£100–120 FrG

A Royal Copenhagen figure of Pan and his pipes, c1930, 5½in (14cm) high.
£200–220 FrG

Two Royal Worcester figures, Harlequin and Pierrot, painted in shades of blue, green, orange and red, c1931, 6½in (16.5cm) high.
£600–700 TH

A Shelley figure, in the form of a golfer, designed by Mabel Lucie Attwell, c1926–45, 6¼in (16cm) high.
£600–700 WWY

A Royal Doulton figure, 'The Bride', HN1600, holding a bouquet of yellow roses, signed, c1930s, 9in (23cm) high.
£300–350 CDC

◄ A Royal Doulton figure, 'Suzette', HN1696, c1935–49, 7in (18cm) high.
£250–300 P

A Royal Doulton figure, 'Victorian Lady', dressed in a mauve shawl, repair to head, c1932–45, 4in (10cm) high.
£60–70 MAC

A Royal Doulton figure, 'Pearly Boy', HN1547, c1933–49, 5½in (14cm) high.
£125–150 SnA

A pair of Shelley figures, in the form of a bride and groom, designed by Mabel Lucie Attwell, c1926–45, 6in (15cm) high.
£800–950 each WWY

A Royal Doulton group, 'The Flower Seller's Children', HN1206, modelled as a young boy and his sister on a bench with a large basket of flowers, printed and painted marks, c1926–49, 7¼in (18.5cm) high.
£250–300 HYD

A Royal Worcester figure, Thursday's Child, wearing a light blue tunic, modelled by Freda Doughty, c1940, 8in (20.5cm) high.
£150–170 VSt

A Royal Copenhagen figure of a Scandinavian child knitting, c1950, 5¾in (14.5cm) high.
£85–100 FrG

A Royal Worcester figure, entitled 'Magnolia Bud', shape No. 3144, printed marks and date cipher for 1936, 4½in (11.5cm) high.
£110–130 GAK

A Gzhel trial figure of Ivan Tsarevich and his princess on the magic grey wolf, c1940–55, 10¼in (26cm) high.
£400–500 PC

INKWELLS & INKSTANDS

A Derby inkstand, painted with scattered flowers and moulded with 3 wells set with baluster ink and pounce pots with covers, flanking a knopped column candlestick, the tray on 5 shell feet, restored, c1760, 10in (25.5cm) wide.
£1,400–1,600 S

A Caughley inkwell, with separate central well fitting with 4 holes for quill, printed in blue fruit and flower sprigs, traces of 'C' mark, c1785, 10in (25.5cm) diam.
£700–775 P

A Chamberlain's Worcester inkstand, with sarcophagus-shaped body, pierced heart-shaped handle, lift-out well and pounce pot with liner, on gilt paw feet, painted with a view of Worcester across the River Severn, on a blue ground, gilt borders and details, some damage, painted marks, early 19thC, 6in (15cm) wide.
£500–600 WW

A Derby inkstand, painted with panels of flowers on a cobalt blue ground, 1815, 11½in (29cm) wide.
£850–950 TK

A Staffordshire shell-shaped inkwell, with swan-neck handle, fitted with a well and 2 quill holders, decorated in coloured enamels with sprays of flowers and leaves, within gilt borders, rim chip restored, c1820, 5½in (14cm) wide.
£220–300 DN

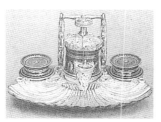

A ceramic and ormolu-mounted inkstand, the central drum-shaped receiver flanked by 2 turned circular receivers with shell-shaped pen tray, c1825, 12in (30.5cm) wide.
£1,800–2,000 P

A Chamberlain's Worcester flower encrusted inkstand, the base decorated with a floral spray, minor restoration, printed marks, c1830, 12in (30.5cm) wide.
£1,400–1,600 DIA

A Coalbrookdale-type two-handled quill stand and inkwell, with raised flower decoration, c1830, 4¾in (12cm) wide.
£250–300 ANT

A Coalport inkstand, the light blue and beige ground enhanced with bright gilding, minor restoration to base, c1840, 14in (35.5cm) wide.
£700–800 DIA

Items in the Porcelain section have been arranged in date order within each sub-section.

A Chamberlain's Worcester inkstand and cover, modelled after King John's tomb in Worcester Cathedral, with 3 internal covers and liners, restored, printed mark and historical account in puce, c1850, 8¼in (21cm) wide.
£400–500 Bon

A Samuel Alcock two-handled inkstand, fitted with a taperstick and 2 wells with covers, painted and encrusted with flowers and leaves, within green and gilt scroll-moulded borders, some damage, c1840, 14in (35.5cm) wide.
£550–600 DN

A Victorian porcelain inkwell on tray, unmarked, c1900, 9in (23cm) wide.
£180–220 JHW

JARDINIERES

A pair of Coalport cachepots, in Sèvres style, each painted with vignettes of Cupid, with leaf-moulded scroll handles, some wear, c1860, 4¼in (11cm) high.
£650–750 CSK

A Belleek low jardinière, decorated with naiads, First Period, 1863–90, 11in (28cm) high.
£1,000–1,200 MLa

A Meissen jardinière, with 2 shell and scroll handles, painted in underglaze blue with the Onion pattern, marked, late 19thC, 6¾in (17cm) high.
£200–220 HOLL

A Coalport jardinière, with rams-head handles, the reserve depicting exotic birds on a gilded deep blue ground, late 19thC, 7¾in (19.5cm) high.
£850–950 AH

A Dresden jardinière, painted with polychrome flowers on a gilt embellished trellis ground, c1900, 8¼in (21cm) high.
£450–500 AH

A Royal Worcester jardinière, with pierced flared rim, painted pink rose panels by Ethel Spilsbury, on gilt and ivory leaf and scroll-moulded ground, c1900, 8in (20.5cm) high,
£1,400–1,550 AH

JARS & COVERS

A Worcester jar and cover, decorated with Jabberwocky pattern c1765, 6in (15cm) high.
£1,250–1,450 BHA

Worcester is one of the most popular of the 18thC factories with collectors.

A Worcester tea canister, printed in underglaze blue with Obelisk and Vase pattern, the reverse with a European landscape group view, within gilt borders, hatched crescent mark, c1775, 5¼in (13.5cm) high.
£260–300 DN

A Worcester ribbed tea canister and domed cover, with flower knop, decorated in coloured enamels with an exotic bird in a branch and scattered flowers, c1775, 6¼in (16cm) high.
£450–550 DN

A Caughley tapering sided tea canister and cover, printed in blue with the Fenced Garden pattern, with monogram 'EW'. c1780, 5in (12.5cm) high.
£450–500 DN

A pair of Chamberlain's Worcester two-handled jars and covers, of baluster form, applied and painted with flowers and foliage, damaged, early 19thC, 12½in (32cm) high.
£450–500 Bea

A Belleek Beehive honey pot-on-stand, Second Period, 1891–1926, 6½in (16.5cm) high.
£100–110 DeA

A Wedgwood blue jasper ware pot and cover, applied with lions' masks and classical figure design, c1900, 6¼in (16cm) high.
£75–85 PSA

A pair of Royal Worcester Randolph Rose jars and covers, pierced covers with gilt speckled detail, the inner covers also with gilt detail, the lobed bases decorated with panels of coloured flowers, on a blush ground, printed marks and date cypher for 1897, shape No. 1314, 5in (12.5cm) high.
£600–700 GAK

A Royal Worcester blush ivory double lidded jar, with moulded wavy edge decoration, the lower base with a gilt border, registration No. 227399, printed puce mark dating from 1896, 8in (20.5cm) high.
£460–520 Mit

JUGS & EWERS

A Derby baluster-shaped jug, with scroll handle, decorated in coloured enamels with exotic birds, the reverse with a bold spray of flowers and leaves, within a brown line rim, restored, c1760, 8¼in (21cm) high.
£350–400 DN

A Worcester jug, with scroll handle and mask spout, painted in blue with the Dragon pattern, damaged, open crescent mark, c1760, 7½in (19cm) high.
£250–300 DN

▶ A Worcester jug, printed in black by Robert Hancock with The Tea Party and The Maid and Page, black line rim, c1770, 3¼in (8.5cm) high.
£280–320 DN

A Bow sparrowbeak jug, with loop handle, painted with polychrome floral sprays, slight damage, c1752, 7in (18cm) high.
£80–100 HYD

A Worcester cabbage leaf-moulded mask jug, with underglaze blue decoration, c1760, 8in (20.5cm) high.
£900–1,100 BHA

A Worcester jug, with scroll handle and mask spout, printed in blue with the Natural Sprays pattern, damaged, crescent mark, c1765, 6in (15cm) high.
£180–220 DN

A Worcester cabbage leaf-moulded mask jug, painted with exotic birds on an apple green ground within shaped gilt C-scroll cartouches, beneath a border of moulded gilt stiff leaves, restored, slight damage, c1770, 8in (20.5cm) high.
£2,500–2,800 C

A New Hall cream jug, printed with a Chinese landscape in underglaze blue, on 3 short feet, repaired, c1785, 5in (12.5cm) high.
£800–900 DN

A Liverpool cream jug, of Chelsea Ewer shape, by Pennington's, enamelled with sprays of flowers and leaves, above a stiff-leaf band picked out in green, yellow and puce, the interior with a puce band, c1775, 5in (12.5cm) high.
£400–450 DN

A Worcester jug, with scroll handle and mask spout, decorated in puce with an urn within a gilt scroll and flower cartouche, decorated in coloured enamels with flowers and leaves, beneath a blue and gilt band, marked, c1775, 5¾in (14.5cm) high.
£420–500 DN

A Worcester sparrow beak cream jug, c1775, 3½in (9cm) high.
£400–450 S

A Worcester blue and white mask jug, with cabbage leaf-moulded body, printed with floral sprays and butterflies, slight damage, c1780, 12in (30.5cm) high.
£300–350 RBB

A New Hall helmet-shaped cream jug, polychrome-decorated with a boy chasing a butterfly, pattern No. 421, c1795, 4½in (11.5cm) high.
£100–120 HYD

◄ A Vienna jug and cover, painted with flowersprays under a slanting black ribboned shoulder, on 3 scroll feet, date code, shield mark in underglaze blue, c1793, 6¼in (16cm) high.
£220–250 RTo

◄ A Worcester Sèvres-style cream jug, with pinched lip, decorated in coloured enamels with scattered cornflowers and gilt leaves, within gilt borders, script mark in puce, 1785–90, 2¾in (7cm) high.
£140–160 DN

A New Hall boat-shaped jug, painted with grapes and foliage on a mazarine blue ground, pattern No. 779, c1805, 4in (10cm) high.
£180–220 CHR

A Sèvres-style ewer and stand, painted with portraits of Louis XIV and members of the French court, within tooled gilt borders, the panels linked by gilt scrolls enriched with turquoise, white and red 'jewels', all within gilt dentil rims, slight damage and wear, script marks and titles to the base, 19thC, 6¾in (17cm) high.
£2,200–2,500 CSK

A Chamberlain's Worcester jug, painted in coloured enamels with The Chase, within a gilt panel, on a grey marble ground with gilt leaf and C-scroll bands, restored, painted mark, c1815, 6¼in (16cm) high.
£800–900 DN

A Copeland Parian ware jug, decorated with foliate scrolls and female masks, c1840, 11in (28cm) high.
£300–350 P(B)

◄ A large Sunderland lustre jug, inscribed with a verse 'The Sailor's Tear', also bearing transfers of the Bridge and 'Sailor's Farewell', with painted and pink lustre details, the presentation inscription dated '1841', 9in (23cm) high.
£350–400 RBB

◄ A Minton milk jug, decorated with gilt flowers, leaves and scrolls, pattern No. 4278, c1845, 7½in (19cm) high.
£60–65 BSA

► A Minton New Stone part washstand service, printed and coloured within green line rims, comprising a baluster jug, 2 circular bowls, a soap dish cover and liner, and a cover for a toothbrush holder, damaged, impressed marks and pattern 'A2534', date code for 1855, jug 12in (30.5cm) high.
£300–350 C

A Coalport white Goat and Bee jug, c1860, 4in (10cm) high.
£125–175 ALB

A Staffordshire porcellaneous Toby jug, the figure seated wearing a red coat with a black tricorn hat, the scroll handle moulded with a figure and acanthus leaves, mid-19thC, 9¼in (23.5cm) high.
£100–120 Hal

A Minton's part washstand service, printed with the Farley pattern, comprising a pear-shaped jug, 2 bowls, a sponge bowl and liner, and a toothbrush holder and cover, damaged, marked, pattern number 'A3735', date codes for 1885, jug 10½in (26.5cm) high.
£750–900 C

◀ A Worcester ewer, with scroll handle, decorated with a floral design, c1885, 10¼in (26cm) high.
£900–1,000 OBS

A Royal Worcester ewer, with gilt and rust floral decoration on an ivory ground, lizard handle with gilt jewel work, slight damage, c1889, 7in (18cm) high.
£160–175 GAK

A Belleek jug, with harp handle, First Period, 1863–90, 8¼in (21cm) high.
£700–800 MLa

▶ A Belleek urn jug, Second Period, 1891–1926, 7in (18cm) high.
£700–800 MLa

A Ridgway jug, decorated with Chinese Japan pattern, c1900, 4½in (11.5cm) high.
£40–50 CSA

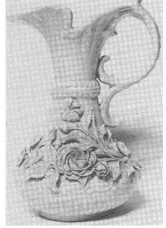

A Belleek jug, black transfer mark, c1890, 7½in (19cm) high.
£250–300 JHW

A Foley cream jug and sugar bowl, the lobed bodies enamelled with royal coat-of-arms, the reverse with flowers of the union and gilt rims, by Wileman, inscribed, c1897, jug 4in (10cm) high.
£50–60 SAS

▶ A Royal Crown Derby miniature cream jug, in the form of a milk churn, decorated in Old Derby Witches pattern, c1904, 2in (5cm) high.
£200–250 TVA

MUGS & TANKARDS

A Worcester blue and white mug, with a ribbed handle, painted with a fenced garden between an Oriental hut and a fisherman by an island below a crescent moon, small chip re-stuck to base, some firing faults, painter's mark, c1754, 2½in (6.5cm) high.
£2,200–2,400 CSK

A Worcester bell-shaped mug, with reeded loop handle, printed in black with a macaw perched on a fruiting branch, flanked by 4 butterflies, signed 'R. Hancock Fecit' concealed within the lower branch, c1757, 4¾in (12cm) high.
£1,350–1,500 DN

A Worcester baluster-shaped mug, with loop handle, printed in black by Robert Hancock with a portrait of the King of Prussia, titled on a ribbon beneath, the reverse with a figure emblematic of Fame and military trophies, signed 'R. H. Worcester', and with the anchor rebus of Holdship, c1757, 4¾in (12cm) high.
£720–800 DN

A Worcester bell-shaped tankard, with grooved strap handle, printed in black with a bust of George II, a ship in full sail and crowned martial trophies with a scroll inscribed 'Liberty', signed 'R. H. Worcester' with anchor rebus, c1760, 5½in (14cm) high.
£1,000–1,200 S

A Liverpool mug, Pennington's factory, with grooved loop handle, painted in blue with the Haymakers, misfired, c1760, 6in (15cm) high.
£1,800–2,200 S

There are 2 versions of the Haymakers pattern on porcelain. This example is the first version, taken from an engraving published by Robert Sayer in 1766.

A Lowestoft blue and white mug, with short cylindrical neck, decorated with a bird in flight between 2 flowering sprays, moulded leaf and lambrequin borders, painted numeral '5' to footrim, 1762–64, 3¾in (9.5cm) high.
£2,600–3,000 Bon

Lowestoft porcelain items often have a rusty discolouration on the base.

A Worcester mug, with reeded loop handle, printed in blue with the Plantation pattern, c1765, 6in (15cm) high.
£200–250 DN

▶ A Plymouth bell-shaped mug, painted with flowers below a gilded leaf border, red mark, c1768, 6in (15cm) high.
£250–300 P(Ch)

A Lowestoft blue and white tankard, decorated with a Chinese landscape and fence scene, the interior rim with a geometric pattern, marked '2' under base rim, c1765, 5in (12.5cm) high.
£2,600–3,000 JNic

A Lowestoft mug, with scroll handle, printed in underglaze blue with Chinese-style river landscape, the interior with a diaper band, slight damage, c1775, 5¾in (14.5cm) high.
£250–280 DN

A Worcester blue and white tankard, with transfer decoration, open crescent-form mark, c1776, 5in (12.5cm) high.
£175–200 EL

A Lowestoft mug, in the manner of 'Tulip painter', painted with bouquets of flowers among scattered sprigs, the interior rim painted in pink with a geometric pattern, applied with a strap handle, slight damage, c1775, 5½in (14cm) high.
£2,500–3,000 CSK

A Caughley blue and white coffee can, decorated with fence pattern, c1785, 2½in (6.5cm) high.
£110–120 DAN

A Worcester beaker, decorated in gilt with flowersprays and monogram 'E H', crescent mark and blue script mark, c1785, 3½in (9cm) high.
£160–180 DN

A Worcester coffee can, c1805, 2½in (6.5cm) high.
£70–80 BSA

A beaker, possibly by Worcester, with tapering sides, decorated in brown monochrome with figures in a continuous wooded landscape, within gilt bands, c1810, 3¼in (8.5cm) high.
£850–1,000 DN

A Spode coffee can, decorated with a band of orange flowers within a gilt background, pattern No. 984, c1810, 2½in (6.5cm) high.
£125–140 AnS

A Worcester Flight, Barr & Barr mug, painted with flowers, c1815, 3¼in (8.5cm) high.
£400–450 TVM

▶ A pair of Derby porter mugs, each painted with a rural scene within a gilded oval border, surrounded by bold acanthus leaf scrolling in orange and gilt, painted red marks and number '13', c1820, 4½in (11cm) high.
£1,000–1,200 P

A coffee can, decorated in blue, red, green and gilt, 19thC, 2¼in (5.5cm) high.
£50–60 PSA

A porcelain mug, decorated in coloured enamels with overlapping playing cards, c1860, 4¼in (11cm) high.
£275–325 DN

A Carlton Ware blue transfer-printed mug, some damage, ribbon mark, c1890–94, 3½in (9cm) high.
£30–40 StC

A Capo di Monte covered tankard, with relief figural design and finial, gilt-bronze eagle-form thumb latch, late 19thC, 12in (30.5cm) high.
£550–600 EL

A Royal Crown Derby miniature mug, decorated with pink flowers, blue upper border and gilt rims, c1907, 1¾in (4.5cm) diam.
£120–150 WAC

A Doulton stoneware three-handled tyg, sgraffito-decorated with blue foliage on a buff ground, silver-plated rim, repaired, signed 'Louisa Davis', date mark for 1880, 6¼in (16cm) high.
£70–80 WL

A tyg is a mug with 3 handles, used for communal drinking.

A Belleek mug, with black transfer-print of Blarney Castle, Second Period, 1891–1926, 4in (10cm) high.
£135–155 DeA

A Royal Worcester miniature two-handled mug, decorated with pink flowers on a buff ground, gilt rims, c1899, 1½in (4cm) diam.
£75–85 WAC

A Royal Worcester miniature mug, decorated with pink flowers on a buff ground, gilt rims, c1916, 1¼in (3cm) diam.
£75–85 WAC

A Belleek mug, inscribed 'Sligo' in a central cartouche, Second Period, 1891–1926, 2¾in (7cm) high.
£100–120 MLa

A Coalport miniature mug, depicting a robin on a central medallion with yellow ground and gilt rims, c1881–91, 1½in (4cm) diam.
£100–125 WAC

A Sèvres-style cabinet cup, with white enamel pique, 'jewelled' enamel decoration and gilt scrollwork, some damage, blue underglaze interlaced 'L' mark, initialled 'F' and impressed 'A', c1880, 3¾in (9.5cm) high.
£250–300 HCC

A Royal Worcester miniature tyg, decorated with gilt and hand-painted fruit in purple and orange on a white ground, monogrammed 'H. E.', c1930, 1½in (4cm) high.
£90–100 WAC

PASTILLE BURNERS

A pastille burner, modelled as a multi-roofed thatched villa, painted, heightened in gilt and decorated with shredded clay and floral encrustation, on a shaped base, early 19thC, 6in (15cm) high.
£1,700–2,000 P(EA)

A pastille burner and stand, perhaps Spode, modelled as a cottage, the interior of the base enriched in salmon pink, one pierced window with a face peering out, damaged, c1830, 5½in (14cm) high.
£600–700 S

A Staffordshire porcellaneous pastille burner, by Samuel Alcock, modelled as an octagonal cottage with umbrella roof, c1835, 5½in (14cm) high.
£350–400 RWB

A Staffordshire porcellaneous pastille burner, modelled as a house, c1835, 4½in (11.5cm) high.
£350–400 RWB

A Staffordshire pastille burner, modelled as a castle, gilt-decorated with pink and green foliage on a white ground, c1835, 4in (10cm) wide.
£170–200 JO

A pair of Staffordshire pastille burners, the windows detailed in gilt, applied with flowers and coloured granitic decoration, c1835, 3in (7.5cm) high.
£120–150 DN

A Staffordshire pastille burner, modelled as a cottage with a thatched roof, decorated in coloured enamels and gilt, c1835, 5½in (14cm) high.
£220–260 JO

A pastille burner, modelled as a cottage, damaged, c1840, 4½in (11.5cm) high.
£110–130 Bea

A Staffordshire pastille burner, modelled as a cottage, decorated in coloured enamels and gilt on a white ground, c1840, 4in (10cm) wide.
£170–200 ALB

◄ A Victorian Staffordshire pastille burner, modelled as a cottage, with red chimneys on a white ground, late 19thC, 4in (10cm) high.
£120–150 TVM

Did you know?
Popular in the 19thC, pastille burners were used for burning pastilles of compressed herbs as an air freshener. They were often in the form of a cottage or castle, with the smoke passing through the chimney.

PLAQUES

A plaque, probably Coalport, painted by J. Birbeck, Senior, with 4 trout on the bank of a mountain river, c1830, 10 x 11¾in (25.5 x 30cm).
£2,500–3,000 Bon

A pair of French bisque plaques, each moulded in bold relief, one with a mounted huntsman and deer, the other with a mounted huntswoman and hound, picked out in coloured enamels and gilt, minor damage, mid-19thC, 10in (25.5cm) diam.
£600–700 DN

A Berlin plaque, decorated with a scene of lovers, slight wear, impressed 'KPM', incised numerals, c1860, 8 x 13in (20.5 x 33cm).
£3,000–3,500 CSK

A Davenport plaque, painted by G. Evans, with 2 gold-finches perched on a wild rose bush, slight scratching, impressed mark Davenport patent, signed, c1850, 10 x 8in (25.5 x 20.5cm), framed and glazed.
£1,300–1,500 S

A German circular plaque, enamelled with the Madonna and Child with St. John looking on, after Raphael, 19thC, 4½in (11.5cm) diam, in a carved giltwood Florentine frame.
£300–350 DN

A Berlin plaque, with a head-and-shoulders portrait of an elderly lady, impressed 'KPM' and sceptre mark, 1860–80, 11 x 7in (28 x 18cm).
£1,800–2,000 N

A German plaque, painted with a portrait of a young woman, 19thC, 4½in (11.5cm) high.
£200–250 TMA

A Berlin plaque, impressed sceptre mark, 'KPM' and 'H', c1870, 12½ x 7½in (32 x 19cm), in a carved giltwood frame.
£4,000–5,500 P

A German plaque, painted with a three-quarter figure of Ruth, after Landelle, c1880, 8½ x 6in (21.5 x 15cm), unframed.
£650–800 P

◄ A Berlin plaque, painted in coloured enamels with Tannhauser and Venus, marked, 19thC, 11¼ x 9in (28.5 x 23cm), in a pierced giltwood Florentine frame.
£2,000–2,500 DN

PLATES

◀ A pair of Longton Hall strawberry-leaf moulded deep plates, the centres painted with flowers, the borders moulded with strawberries, chipped, c1755, 8¾in (22cm) diam.
£1,500–1,700 C

Longton Hall

Founded in 1750, Longton Hall was probably one of the first Staffordshire producers of soft-paste porcelain. Moulded patterns using floral, fruit and vegetable motifs were a particular speciality of the factory. Blue and white tablewares, copies of Chinese *famille rose* designs, tureens and pot pourri vases were also among their varied output. They also made what were known as 'Snowmen' figures, so named because of their poorly defined features and unpainted but thickly glazed bodies.

A Bow blue and white plate, c1760, 9in (23cm) diam.
£400–475 BHA

A Meissen plate, with pierced rim, painted with flowers, damaged, marked, c1760, 9in (23cm) diam.
£450–550 CSK

A Chelsea plate, painted within a red/brown lined border, red anchor mark, c1760, 8in (20.5cm) diam.
£170–200 HYD

A Chelsea dessert plate, decorated with fruit and leaves, on a blue ground, slight damage, gold anchor period, c1765, 9in (23cm) diam.
£250–300 GAK

A Worcester plate, decorated in enamels, the green-ground border with gilt scroll edge and puce floral garlands, c1770, 8in (20.5cm) diam.
£300–350 DN

A Sèvres plate, decorated with flowers, c1770, 9½in (24cm) diam.
£170–200 ALB

A Derby soup plate, centrally decorated *en grisaille* with an urn, the rim with laurel garlands, within blue and gilt flowerhead and anthemion borders, crowned 'D' mark in blue, c1775, 9in (23cm) diam.
£300–330 DN

A Doccia plate, with ozier-moulded border, brightly painted with an adaptation of a Japanese design of banded hedges, flowering peonies and a *ho-o* bird in thick enamels and gold, 18thC, 9in (23cm) diam.
£500–600 P

A Worcester plate, painted in blue with the Hundred Antiques pattern, seven-character Chinese-style marks, c1775, 8in (20.5cm) diam.
£250–300 DN

A Worcester plate, painted in blue with the Kangxi Lotus pattern, damaged, emblem mark, c1775, 7in (18cm) diam.
£170–200 DN

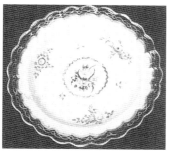

A Worcester plate, the scalloped border painted with puce and coloured flowers within a blue and gilt border, crescent mark, c1780, 8½in (21.5cm) diam.
£220–240 HYD

A Meissen plate, with gilt scalloped rim, c1780, 9½in (24cm) diam.
£175–200 ALB

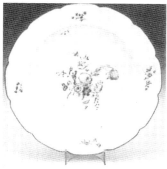

A Naples plate, painted with a spray of flowers within a border of sprigs and a lobed black-lined rim, late 18thC, 16¼in (41.5cm) diam.
£460–500 CSK

A Worcester plate, decorated in coloured enamels, within blue and gilt borders, c1780, 8½in (21.5cm) diam.
£350–400 DN

A Derby botanical dessert plate, possibly painted by John Brewer, decorated with 'Geranium Anemonefolium, Anemone-Leav'd Geranium' on a yellow ground, marked, c1795, 9in (23cm) diam.
£1,000–1,200 S

A Coalport plate, the centre painted in coloured enamels, the broad orange-ground border decorated in puce and gilt with panels and garlands of leaves and patera, c1810, 9½in (24cm) diam.
£250–300 DN

A Derby botanical plate, the centre painted with a single pink flower, within a blue ground border enriched in gilt, titled to the reverse 'Seringapatum Hollyhock', slight wear, iron-red marks, c1810, 9in (23cm) diam.
£350–400 CSK

A Derby plate, the centre painted with a rose in full bloom and a bud, within a gilt rim, slight wear, titled to the reverse 'Moss Rose', iron-red mark, c1810, 9in (23cm) diam.
£400–500 CSK

A Worcester Barr, Flight & Barr plate, decorated in Imari palette with flowers and leaves in shades of red, blue and gold, impressed and printed factory mark, 1807–13, 9½in (24cm) diam.
£200–220 WW

Nantgarw

The Nantgarw factory in Wales, founded in 1813, is renowned for the quality of its painting – usually beautiful floral designs. There are many fakes, both English and Continental, so advice should be sought when considering a purchase.

► A Nantgarw dessert plate, decorated in Sèvres style, within a posy of flowers within a wavy gilded and blue line border, impressed mark, c1818–22, 9½in (24cm) diam.
£300–350 HOLL

A Chamberlain's Worcester Regent China cabinet plate, painted with a view of the Government House and Council Chambers at Madras, within a pale lilac border, the rim moulded with gadroon shell and stiff-leaf edge, gilt highlight, marked, restored chip, c1811, 9½in (24cm) diam.
£900–1,000 Bon

In the early 19thC, Chamberlain developed a fine, hard, white and very translucent porcelain covered in a glassy Paris-type glaze. Known as Regent China, it was used almost exclusively for dinner and dessert services.

A Nantgarw plate, painted in coloured enamels with pink roses and a butterfly, with scroll, flower and ribbon-tie moulded border, impressed mark. c1820, 8½in (21.5cm) diam.
£500–550 DN

A Paris plate, with a printed panel of a mother and children, c1820, 9in (23cm) diam.
£80–100 DAN

A plate, decorated in blue, red, green and gilt, unmarked, early 19thC, 9in (23cm) diam.
£40–50 PSA

A Vienna plate, the black centre with honeysuckle design, 19thC, 9½in (24cm) diam.
£450–550 BHA

A plate, painted in sepia tones with a huntsman in a forest landscape shooting a woodcock, within florally-moulded borders painted with gilt muskets, shaped gilt edge, c1815, 10in (25.5cm) diam.
£200–220 Hal

▶ A set of 5 Derby plates, each boldly decorated in coloured enamel with sprays of flowers and leaves, within a gilt dentil border, stained, crowned crossed batons mark in red, c1820, 9¾in (25cm) diam.
£420–480 DN

A set of 6 Spode felspar plates, each decorated in enamels with flowers and leaves, the lime-green ground moulded in relief and picked out in gilt, printed marks, c1825, 9in (23cm) diam.
£500–550 DN

A pair of Berlin plates, one decorated with convolvulus, the other with bluebells, with gilt band rims, blue sceptre and printed double-headed eagle, 'KPM' marks, 1823–32, 9in (23cm) diam.
£400–500 CSK

A plate, the centre decorated in coloured enamels with flowers in a basket on a ledge, the rim decorated in gilt with bird masks and leaf scrolls, c1820, 8½in (21.5cm) diam.
£1,500–1,800 DN

▶ A set of 15 Berlin dessert plates, each centrally decorated in coloured enamels, the borders picked out in green, brown and gilt, damaged, marks in blue and stencilled mark in red, damaged, c1835, 9½in (24cm) diam.
£800–1,200 DN

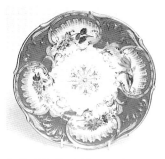

An H. & R. Daniel Savoy-shaped dessert plate, pattern No. 8777, c1840, 9½in (24cm) diam.
£80–100 BSA

A Wedgwood plate, decorated with flowers and insects on a white ground, mid-19thC, 5in (12.5cm) diam.
£10–12 BSA

A Minton bone china plate, painted to the centre with a kestrel perched on a leafy branch, the pierced and moulded border decorated with blue and orange enamel with gilded details and scalloped rim, probably by Joseph Smith, slight damage, impressed registration mark, mid-19thC, 9¼in (23.5cm) diam.
£80–100 WW

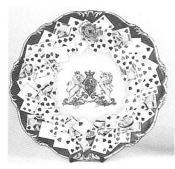

A plate, painted by James Copson with playing cards, one showing the reverse inscribed 'Duty One Shilling', on a deep green border encircling the royal arms, dated '1848', 8½in (21.5cm) diam.
£650–700 Bon

A Minton cabinet plate, the reticulated border with floral enamelled decoration, ermine mark, c1860, 10½in (26.5cm) diam.
£600–650 AMH

A Minton cabinet plate, the reticulated border with enamelled cherubs to the centre, painted by Thomas Kirkby, ermine mark, c1860, 10½in (26.5cm) diam.
£800–1,000 AMH

Two Berlin Schumann plates, with dark blue ground, both painted with views of Venice, each titled to the reverse 'Basilique de s. Marc. a Venise' and 'Pont de Rialto a Venise', underglaze blue and impressed marks, slight wear, c1860, 9¼in (23.5cm) diam.
£1,800–2,000 CSK

Eight Minton plates, each painted in shades of puce, with vignettes of Cupid at various pursuits including attending a cage, riding a goat, holding a bow and arrow and sitting by a basket of fruit, the borders gilt with a band of stylized leaves within gilt bands, slight wear, impressed marks, indistinct date codes, c1865, 9¼in (23.5cm) diam.
£800–900 CSK

A Copeland cabinet plate, the centre painted with a monogram in the form of roses, within pierced borders, with panels of fruit and flowers, printed mark, 1860s, 9in (23cm) diam.
£650–750 P(B)

A label on the reverse of this plate states that it is from the dessert service ordered by HRH the Prince of Wales before his marriage.

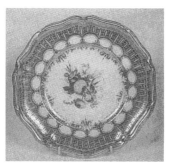

A Davenport cabinet plate, painted with a central floral spray within a heavily-gilded border, c1860, 9in (23cm) diam.
£300–350 BHA

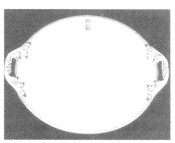

A Belleek ring-handled bread plate, with gilt family crest and decoration, First Period, 1863–90, 10¼ (26cm) diam.
£250–300 MLa

Further Reading

Miller's Pottery & Pottery Marks, Miller's Publications, 1995

A Belleek tray, the raised shaped rim with gold edging repeated to the central panel depicting a scaled dragon, with surrounding raised star and swirled patterns, First Period, 1863–90, 15in (38cm) diam.
£850–950 HCC

A Minton Albans dessert plate, the pierced shape with cloisonné decoration, c1875, 10in (25.5cm) diam.
£700–800 AMH

A Vienna plate, the centre painted with figures at an easel, on a gilded and 'jewelled' deep blue ground, signed, late 19thC, 9½in (24cm) diam.
£400–500 AH

A set of 4 plates, hand-painted with roses, gold leaves and trim, Rouen, France, c1870, 10in (25.5cm) diam.
£100–125 MSB

A Crown Derby plate, the centre painted with a stag in a mountain landscape within a pink border decorated with raised gilt ivy trails, printed and impressed marks, late 19thC, 9¼in (23.5cm) diam.
£80–100 WW

A Vienna plate, painted with a titled classical scene of Bacchus and Ariadne, flanked by panels of gilt scrolls on a red ground, signed 'Knoeller', shield mark in underglaze blue, c1880, 13in (33cm) diam.
£2,400–2,800 S

Vienna porcelain
Throughout the 19thC, the Vienna shield mark was much used by other factories copying the Vienna style. The use of inverted commas, 'Vienna' is widely used to denote the origin of such pieces when cataloguing.

◄ A Derby Crown Porcelain Co plate, painted by Rouse with a loose spray of garden flowers on a pink ground, enamelled and gilt border, slight wear, marked and inscribed to the reverse 'J. Rouse Senr Derby', c1880, 8½in (21.5cm) diam.
£450–500 CSK

A Minton plate, in the manner of Christopher Dresser, with blue border, c1872, 11in (28cm) diam.
£250–300 NCA

An Austrian cabinet plate, the centre painted with portraits of Peter the Great and Catherine the Great, the borders with portrait roundels, late 19thC, 14in (35.5cm) diam.
£1,300–1,500 SK

A set of 8 Limoges plates, by H. Mayet, each decorated with a different orchid and signed, within a scrolled gilt border, c1880, 8½in (21.5cm) diam.
£900–1,000 SLL

A Moore Brothers cabinet plate, painted with flowers on a crimson and gilt ground, c1892, 9in (23cm) diam.
£70–80 MiA

A plate, painted in the centre with a titled scene within a fluted pink ground, turquoise and gilt border, firing faults, slight wear, inscribed in iron-red to reverse, impressed '8', c1855, 9½in (24cm) diam.
£300–350 CSK

A Copeland Spode cabinet plate, decorated with figures in a landscape with blue and gilt panel of daisies, printed mark, late 19thC, 10in (25.5cm) square.
£80–100 P(B)

A French plate, painted with blackberries and spider *trompe l'oeil*, late 19thC, 9in (23cm) diam.
£250–300 BHA

A Stevenson & Hancock Derby plate, painted by W. Mosley, with tulips, pink roses and other summer flowers within two-tone burnished gilt scrolling foliate border, signed, crowned crossed batons 'S H' and 'D' marks in red, c1900, 8¾in (22cm) diam.
£420–500 N

A Minton *pâte-sur-pâte* plate, the centre with carved decoration depicting a winged cherub holding balanced scales, signed 'Birks', c1900, 9¾in (25cm) diam.
£800–950 RA

A German portrait plate, depicting the Countess of Harrington, signed 'Wagner', titled on reverse, raised gilt border with simulated jade medallions, c1900, 9½in (24cm) diam.
£350–400 SK

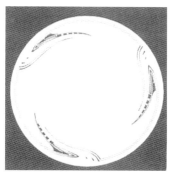

A Meissen porcelain plate, decorated by Henry van de Velde in underglaze blue, maker's mark, c1903, 10½in (26.5cm) diam.
£520–570 S

A set of 6 Royal Worcester plates, painted with game birds within gilt-edged borders with floral swags, slight damage, signed with monogram, date code for 1908, 9½in (24cm) diam.
£400–450 MCA

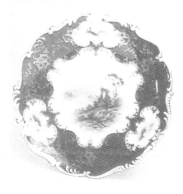

A Royal Crown Derby plate, decorated with Witches pattern, c1914, 9in (23cm) diam.
£70–80 YY

◄ A pair of Coalport plates, by P. Simpson, the cobalt blue ground rim decorated with gilt, printed marks in green, c1910, 9in (23cm) diam.
£300–350 EH

Cross Reference
See Colour Review

A pair of Copeland Sèvres-style plates, painted in coloured enamels, the turquoise border with flowers, printed marks in gilt, pattern No. C1237, c1900, 9½in (24cm) diam.
£340–380 DN

SAUCE & CREAM BOATS

A Worcester sauce boat, painted in colours within moulded circular cartouches, iron-red arrow and circle painter's mark, c1751, 7½in (19cm) wide.
£1,200–1,500 L

A Derby lobed sauce boat, with S-scroll handle, decorated in coloured enamels with sprays of flowers, leaves and scattered flowers, beneath a brown line rim, c1758, 8¼in (21cm) wide.
£320–350 DN

A Chaffer's Liverpool butter boat, decorated in coloured enamels with Chinese-style figures and a dog, with puce handle, c1760, 4½in (11.5cm) wide.
£500–700 DN

A Worcester cream boat, with stylized dolphins above a scallop, slight damage, c1760, 3¼in (8.5cm) high.
£280–320 CSK

A pair of Worcester lettuce-leaf-moulded sauce boats, painted in *famille rose* palette beneath a brown line rim, c1755, 7¼in (18.5cm) wide.
£1,000–1,200 DN

▶ A Longton Hall leaf-shaped sauce boat, with stalk loop handle, the exterior painted in blue with Chinese river landscapes, beneath a broad blue band, the interior with a river landscape, damaged, c1758, 7½in (19cm) wide.
£130–150 DN

A Worcester sauce boat, the pleat-moulded body with raised panels with puce scrolls and sprays of flowers, c1765, 6in (15cm) wide.
£850–900 P

A pair of Derby sauce boats, with gadrooned borders, moulded with fruit picked out in blue, the interiors decorated with sprays of flowers and leaves, some damage and repair, c1758, 7in (18cm) wide.
£280–320 DN

A pair of Derby leaf-moulded sauce boats, with stalk loop handles, enamelled with flowers and leaves within shaded green borders, the stalks picked out in puce, one handle restored, c1760, 7½in (19cm) wide.
£350–400 DN

Worcester

Founded by Dr Wall, William Davis and others in 1751, the factory has continued at Worcester to the present day. Early Worcester porcelain was the finest in England, and consisted mainly of tea and coffee sets and dinner ware. Transfer-printing was introduced by Hancock in 1756, at first in black with designs of buildings, celebrities etc. From the 1760s Oriental and European subjects became popular decoration, in a wide range of colours. In 1783 the factory was bought by Thomas Flight who, with Martin Barr, formed Flight & Barr. Owing to changes in partnership, the company became Barr, Flight & Barr (1804–13), and Flight, Barr & Barr (1813–40).

A Worcester fluted sauce boat, painted in blue Chinese style with buildings, trees and rockwork, the interior similarly decorated firing crack, crescent mark, c1765, 6in (15cm) wide.
£250–300 DN

A Worcester cream boat, the leaf-moulded and spiral-reeded body painted with flowers, c1768, 4¼in (11cm) wide.
£450–500 Bea(E)

A Derby shell-moulded sauce boat, painted in underglaze blue with scattered flower sprigs, cracked, chip to foot, c1770, 6in (15cm) wide.
£180–220 S

Ex-William A. Gurling collection.

A Worcester yellow-ground sauce boat, brightly decorated in coloured enamels, the fluted ground decorated in *famille verte* enamels with scattered flowers, restored, c1770, 7½in (19cm) wide.
£500–600 DN

A Worcester 'Chelsea Ewer' cream boat, decorated with blue convolvulus pattern over a wrythen-moulded fern foot, internally with cell diaper border enclosing a trefoil leaf spray, blue painted open crescent marks, slight damage, c1775, 4¼in (11cm) wide.
£450–500 Bon

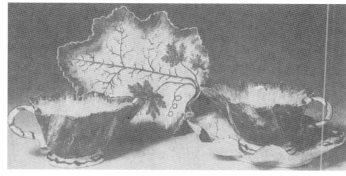

A pair of Bow sauce boats and stands, each with serrated green edges, with moulded veins and tendrils picked out in purple, the sauce boats moulded on the outside with overlapping leaves, c1770, stands 7½in (19cm) wide.
£3,500–4,000 P

A Lowestoft blue and white cream boat, of shell form, painted with scattered flower sprigs, incised cross mark, c1770, 3½in (9cm) wide.
£700–800 S

A Worcester fluted sauce boat, with loop handle, the interior painted in Chinese style in underglaze blue with boats in a wooded river landscape, the exterior with a broad band of flowers, scrolls and butterflies, c1775, 8in (20.5cm) wide.
£400–450 DN

A Worcester 'Chelsea Ewer' cream boat, the scroll handle with bird's head terminal, decorated in puce, purple, iron-red and gilt with scattered flowers and leaves, the interior with a pendant flower and puce diaper band, c1780, 2½in (6.5cm) high.
£400–500 DN

◄ A Worcester cream boat, with gadrooned edge and applied strap handle, painted in blue with the Narcissus pattern, crescent mark, c1776, 4¾in (12cm) wide.
£550–600 P

A Worcester sauce boat, of lobed form, with scroll handle, the interior painted in blue with the Sauceboat Peony pattern, within a cell diaper band, the exterior moulded with sprays of roses and leaves, crescent mark, c1770, 7in (18cm) wide.
£400–450 DN

A Worcester double-lipped sauce boat, with 2 C-scroll handles, the interior painted in blue with landscape design, the exterior painted in blue with Chinese landscapes, birds and flowers, within leaf-moulded roundels, decorator's mark, c1775, 7¼in (18.5cm) wide.
£950–1,100 DN

A Caughley lobed cream boat, with C-scroll handle, painted in coloured enamels with flowers and leaves, within gadrooned and iron-red line borders, c1785, 2¼in (5.5cm) wide.
£200–220 HOLL

A gold-mounted 'Girl-in-a-Swing' type scent bottle, decorated in yellow, white, puce, black and turquoise, the gold mount to the neck with chain attachment, slight damage, c1775, 4in (10cm) high.
£5,000–6,000 C

A 'Girl-in-a-Swing' scent bottle and cover, modelled as a bird, enamelled with bright polychrome plumage in tones of puce, green, yellow and manganese, with *deutsche Blumen* painted base, restored, c1760, 2¼in (5.5cm) high.
£850–950 Bon

'Girl-in-a-Swing' pieces are principally porcelain novelties, such as scent bottles and bonbonnières, produced in the mid-18thC by the London jeweller Charles Gouyn from his house in Bennet Street, St James's, London. The name derives from a figure group in the Victoria & Albert Museum by the same maker.

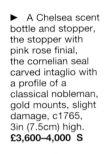

▶ A Chelsea scent bottle and stopper, the stopper with pink rose finial, the cornelian seal carved intaglio with a profile of a classical nobleman, gold mounts, slight damage, c1765, 3in (7.5cm) high.
£3,600–4,000 S

A Coalport double scent bottle, with stoppers, decorated with a country scene and gilt border, on a pink ground, c1860, 4in (10cm) high.
£600–700 BHa

A scent bottle in the form of a bird's egg, by MacIntyre, with silver screw top by Samson Mordan, c1880, 2in (5cm) high.
£450–500 BHa

A Fürstenburg scent flask, in the form of a pear, with a short chain attached, marked 'F' in under-glaze blue, c1770, 3in (7.5cm) high.
£1,600–1,800 S

A scent bottle, in the form of a Willow pattern plate, with silver top by Samson Mordan, c1889, 1¾in (4.5cm) diam.
£200–250 DIC

A Berlin scent bottle, with hinged cover, painted on both sides with Watteauesque figures, the ground picked out in celadon green, tsceptre mark in blue, 19thC, 3¼in (8.5cm) high.
£275–300 P

A Royal Worcester perfume flask, with a gilt-metal crown cover, printed mark in gilt 'Rd No. 56943', c1887, 2in (5cm) diam, with presentation box.
£800–1,000 Bon

◀ A scent bottle, with a silver top, commemorating the Royal Naval Exhibition in 1891, 2⅖in (6.5cm) diam.
£500–600 BHa

Further Reading

Miller's Perfume Bottles, Miller's Publications, 1999

SERVICES

A Sèvres *tête-à-tête*, painted with pink roses within gilt foliage garlands on a *bleu celeste* ground, comprising a milk jug, sugar bowl and cover, 2 cups and saucers and a tray, some damage and repair, painter's mark 'P', various incised marks, blue and green interlaced 'L' marks enclosing date letter 'P' for 1768.
£4,200–4,500 C

A Worcester Mansfield pattern part tea service, painted with a trellised rococo border, comprising teapot and cover, sparrowbeak jug, slop bowl, and 6 teabowls and saucers, some damage, open crescent marks, c1770.
£1,000–1,200 Bon

A Worcester fluted part tea and coffee service, comprising 23 pieces, finely gilt with husk swags suspended from rings and paterae in husk ovals and a band of Vitruvian scrolls around the base and inside the cups, the shaped pieces with floral finials, some damage, c1785, saucer 7¼in (18.5cm) diam.
£2,000–2,500 CNY

A Clignancourt cabaret service, comprising 8 pieces, with vignettes of putti bordered by flowerheads *en grisaille*, cobalt and gilt border, red stencilled monogram of 'protector' Louis-Stanislas-Xavier beneath crown, late 18thC, tray 8½in (21.5cm) wide.
£4,500–5,000 Bon

A Meissen ornithological part dinner service, comprising 17 pieces, the centres painted with exotic birds, *en camaieu bleu* borders with loose bouquets within gilt scroll-moulded cartouches on a *Dulong* pattern ground, waved gilt rims, blue crossed swords and dot marks, c1775, plate 9¾in (25cm) diam.
£5,000–6,000 C

A Meissen Marcolini part tea service, with flower bouquets and fruit within ribbon and flower borders and gilt dentil rims, comprising 11 tea cups and 10 saucers, slight damage, blue crossed swords and star marks, c1780.
£2,300–2,800 CSK

Spode

Josiah Spode founded the factory in Staffordshire in 1770, and it became famous for its bone china. Josiah II introduced New Stone China c1805. Spode traded as Copeland & Garrett from 1833 to 1848, then Copeland, until in 1970 the name Spode was once more revived.

◀ A Spode tea service, comprising 37 pieces, decorated in pink and gilt with roses, slight damage, painted mark in red, pattern No. 3886, early 19thC.
£300–350 CAG

A Coalport blue ground part dessert service, comprising 35 pieces, with still lifes of fruit and flowers within a gilt scallop surround intersected with a gilt zigzag, the rim gilt with foliate scrolls on the blue ground, some damage and wear, c1805.
£3,500–4,000 CNY

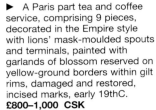

► A Paris part tea and coffee service, comprising 9 pieces, decorated in the Empire style with lions' mask-moulded spouts and terminals, painted with garlands of blossom reserved on yellow-ground borders within gilt rims, damaged and restored, incised marks, early 19thC.
£800–1,000 CSK

A Ridgway part dessert service, comprising 26 pieces, with loose sprays of flowers within similar scrolling gilt panels divided by beige shaped panels gilt with bouquets on a deep blue ground, with pale blue shaped gilt line rims, moulded with fruiting vines, some damage and wear, iron-red pattern No. 735, 1815–20.
£4,000–4,500 CSK

A Ridgway part tea and coffee service, with Imari floral pattern in iron-red, blue and green with gilt embellishments, comprising 8 tea cups, 4 coffee cups, 5 saucers, 2 saucer dishes, cream jug and sucrier, early 19thC.
£580–650 AH

Ridgway

Ridgway produced high-quality wares in porcelain, earthenware and stoneware, especially tea and dessert services. The porcelain of the 1802–40 period was rarely marked and its technical and artistic standards often lead to it being attributed to Worcester, Rockingham or Spode.

A Minton tea service, decorated in vivid colours and gilt, comprising a teapot, cover and stand, saucer dish, milk jug, 8 tea cups, and 7 coffee cans and 6 saucers, some damage, mark and pattern No. 539 in blue, c1810.
£4,700–5,200 S

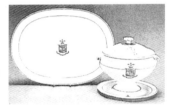

A Wedgwood pearlware part dinner service, comprising 12 pieces, each printed in black with a crest and armorial, inscribed with the motto 'Fide sed Cui Fede' picked out in green within green line borders, damage, impressed marks, c1815.
£600–700 DN

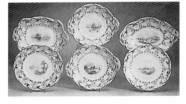

A Davenport part dessert service, comprising 10 pieces, decorated with landscapes within floral and vine borders, pattern No. 963, printed marks, slight damage, c1820.
£300–350 SK

A Derby ornithological part dessert service, Robert Bloor & Co, comprising 9 pieces, the centres painted in the manner of Richard Dodson, some damage, the dishes with crown, crossed batons and 'D' marks in gold, the plates with crown, crossed batons and 'D' marks in iron-red, c1815.
£1,800–2,200 C

A Wedgwood dessert service, comprising 10 pieces, each printed and painted with insects and botanical subjects on a cream ground, pierced Greek key border, some restoration, impressed marks, 19thC.
£1,000–1,200 WL

A Charles Bourne part dessert service, comprising 15 pieces, painted and gilt in the Imari palette with spray of peony branches, within shaped gilt line rims, some damage and wear, iron-red marks, pattern No. 62, c1820.
£700–800 CSK

A Rockingham part dessert service, comprising 5 pieces, painted with exotic birds within buff ground and gilt-scroll borders, some damage, one with puce printed mark, c1830.
£800–1,000 CSK

A Coalport dessert service, comprising 27 pieces, with gilt-decorated scrolling borders, brown printed foliage and polychrome enamel flowers, some pieces damaged, pattern No. 3/521, c1835.
£400–450 WW

◄ A Coalport dessert service, painted by S. Lawrence, comprising 25 pieces, each with a flowerspray in the centre, the border with floral bouquets within elaborate gilt cartouches on a deep blue ground, within yellow and gilt scroll-moulded rims, gilt fractional pattern No. 4/412, slight damage, c1840.
£4,200–4,600 S

► A Davenport botanical service, comprising 24 pieces, painted in colours with named botanical specimens, turquoise pearl border and gilt pierced rim, some damage, underglaze blue, printed mark, c1845, plate 9in (23cm) diam.
£2,200–2,800 S

A Staffordshire dinner service, comprising 77 pieces, decorated with Chinese Tree pattern No. 1959, some damage and repair, c1830.
£1,400–1,600 WL

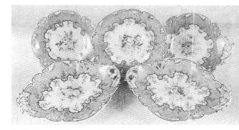

A Staffordshire apple-green and gilt-bordered dessert service, comprising 22 pieces, the centres painted in colours with floral sprays within shaped gilt reserves, the pierced rims with gilt leaf scroll pattern borders, pattern No. 8095, some damage, 19thC.
£300–350 CAG

A Samuel Alcock dessert service, each piece decorated in coloured enamels with flowers and leaves within green and gilt leaf scroll-decorated borders, comprising a pair of oval two-handled dishes, 3 low round stands and 12 plates, pattern No. 3/4749 in red, c1845.
£850–950 DN

► A Paris porcelain black-printed tea service, each piece decorated with figures in domestic settings or with characters in national costume, comprising teapot and cover, 2 sucriers and covers, slop basin, and 11 cups and saucers, minor cracks, mid-19thC.
£600–750 Bon

A Paris porcelain part dinner service, comprising 78 pieces, with sprays of multi-coloured flowers, slight wear, mid-19thC.
£800–1,000 SK(B)

► A Spode tea and coffee service, comprising 45 pieces, each decorated in Japan colours with wisteria and stylized flowers, slight damage, red capital Spode mark and pattern No. 2214, mid-19thC.
£2,500–3,000 P(S)

A Davenport botanical dessert service, comprising 28 pieces, finely painted with botanical specimens, within apple green borders with gilt enrichments, some damage, blue printed marks, c1860, plate 9in (23cm) diam.
£3,300–3,800 S

A Royal Worcester dessert service, comprising 18 pieces, painted in coloured enamels with a spray of flowers and leaves, the pink-ground borders decorated with stylized flowers and leaves within gilt dentil bands, some restoration, impressed marks, pattern No. 9035, c1870.
£700–800 DN

A Grainger & Co part dessert service, comprising 11 pieces, painted in coloured enamels with wild flowers, grasses and insects within blue and gilt borders, impressed marks and pattern No. 2443, c1875.
£550–600 DN

A Royal Crown Derby part dessert service, comprising 17 pieces, decorated in the Japan pattern, highlighted in gilding, some wear and repair, printed and impressed factory marks, 1878–90.
£600–700 S(S)

A Royal Worcester dessert service, comprising 15 pieces, painted with sprays of flowers within stylized borders, puce and gilt rim, slight damage, printed marks and date code for 1880.
£380–420 P(E)

A selection of Noritake porcelain, from a design by Frank Lloyd Wright, decorated with geometric forms in orange, yellow, green and grey, in production 1922–68.
£400–450 P

Frank Lloyd Wright designs are much sought-after today by American collectors.

◄ A William Brownfield dessert service, comprising 12 plates, 2 tall and 4 low stands, decorated in enamels with a bird on a branch within brown and gilt borders, on a puce ground, impressed marks for 1879 and pattern No. 1353.
£1,500–1,700 DN

A Worcester teapot and cover, decorated in bright enamels with flowers, beneath a stylized red border, c1770, 5¼in (13.5cm) high.
£250–300 P(E)

A Derby faceted teapot and cover, with hexagonal loop knop, decorated in coloured enamels with floral garlands, interlinked with gilt leaf scrolls, minor crack, crowned crossed baton mark in puce and pattern number, c1790, 6¾in (17cm) high,
£400–450 DN

A Royal Worcester teapot and cover, in Japanese style, with salamander handle and spout, moulded in relief with flowering branches and birds in flight, decorated in brown, green and gilt, chip to rim, moulded mark and registration mark for 1872, 8in (20.5cm) high.
£350–400 DN

A Crown Staffordshire miniature teapot and cover, decorated with violets, c1906, 1½in (4cm) high.
£55–65 WAC

A Pennington's baluster-shaped coffee pot and domed cover, decorated in enamels with sprays of flowers and leaves within puce diaper borders, the handle, knop and spout picked out in iron-red, c1775, 9½in (24cm) high.
£850–950 DN

A Spode miniature teapot, richly gilded, slight repair, c1820, 2in (5cm) high.
£350–400 JP

A Minton Amherst teapot, decorated with Japan pattern in shades of blue, red and gilt on a white ground, c1880, 4¼in (11cm) high.
£150–170 AMH

A Belleek dragon teapot, First Period, 1863–90, 6in (15cm) high.
£1,800–2,000 MLa

Inside the cover of this teapot is a recipe for tea-making.

A Lowestoft coffee pot and cover, painted with Oriental figures, on a geometric pattern ground reserved with monochrome cartouches of buildings on islands, damaged, firing faults, c1778, 10¼in (26cm) high.
£2,200–2,500 CSK

A Royal Worcester white reticulated teapot, by George Owen, double-walled and pierced with tracery, pale blue inner wall and bead highlights, impressed crown over standard round mark, c1862, 4½in (11.5cm) high.
£2,000–2,200 P(S)

A Belleek hexagonal teapot, Second Period, 1891–1926, 5½in (14cm) high.
£300–350 MLa

A Vezzi teapot, painted on each side in purple, blue, green, iron-red and yellow with a large flowerspray, spout restored, mark 'Va' in iron-red, incised 'A', c1725, 3in (7.5cm) high.
£4,500–5,000 S

A Chelsea hexagonal documentary teapot and cover, decorated in puce monochrome, attributed to Jefferyes Hamett O'Neale, damaged, replacement metal spout and finial, c1752, 6in (15cm) high.
£5,500–6,000 S

Miller's is a price GUIDE not a price LIST

A Worcester baluster-shaped coffee pot, with domed cover, printed in blue with the Fence pattern, hatched crescent mark, c1770, 10in (25.5cm) high.
£350–400 DN

A Worcester teapot and cover, painted in blue with the Mansfield pattern, chip to spout, crescent mark, c1770, 5in (12.5cm) high.
£150–180 DN

A Worcester teapot and cover, with flower knop, printed in blue with the Birds in Branches pattern, small chip to spout, hatched crescent mark, c1775, 5in (12.5cm) high.
£400–450 DN

A Lowestoft teapot, painted with flowers in underglaze blue, c1772, 5in (12.5cm) high.
£300–350 MSW

A Meissen rectangular chocolate pot, decorated with birds on a branch, the sides with columns, c1800, 4½in (11.5cm) high.
£650–750 RA

TEA & COFFEE SERVICES

A Worcester part tea service, decorated in Imari style, c1770.
£1,600–1,800 SK

A Lowestoft teapot, with rose design, c1770, 6in (15cm) high.
£800–1,000 BHA

A Pinxton 24-piece tea and coffee service, painted with a wide band of stylized flowers and gilt leaves, the letter 'R' inscribed in gold on each piece, some damage, pattern No. 312, c1805.
£1,400–1,600 P

A Spode 37-piece part tea and coffee service, printed in iron-red with a band of roses and gilt, minor damage, painted iron-red marks, pattern No. 786, early 19thC.
£1,200–1,400 C

A Staffordshire miniature tea service, each piece painted in coloured enamels with sprays of flowers and leaves, probably Hicks & Meigh, slight damage, 1825–30.
£400–450 DN

A teapot, sucrier and milk jug, painted with shaped panels of floral sprays in pink and red, within an elaborate gilt, buff and blue border, pattern No. 2/9271 in red, mid-19thC.
£500–550 P(NE)

A Copeland 33-piece part tea service, heavily gilt with stylized scrolling foliage, with deep blue detail on pale puce reserve, printed marks, c1860.
£450–500 GAK

A Gardner six-person tea service, marked with George and the Dragon and double-headed Imperial eagle in red, 1860–90, teapot 6¼in (16cm) high.
£350–400 PC

◄ A Sèvres-style 10-piece cased *tête-à-tête*, each piece painted with figures in a landscape and trophies within a tooled gilt frame on a turquoise-blue ground, with fitted leather-bound case, marked, slight damage, c1860–80.
£2,800–3,200 S

A Copeland Spode 36-piece part tea service, decorated with the Brompton pattern, printed and impressed marks, c1900.
£160–180 GAK

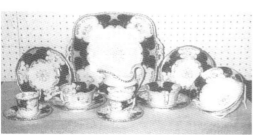

A Coalport 63-piece tea and coffee set, decorated with the Batwing pattern with cobalt blue floral panel and gilt decoration, early 20thC.
£500–560 PCh

A Coalport 7-piece miniature cabaret set, decorated all-over with graduated turquoise 'jewels' on solid gilt ground, c1912, tray 5in (12.5cm) diam.
£4,000–4,500 P

A Shelley 39-piece tea set, decorated with Cottage pattern, depicting a garden scene, on a white ground with blue banding, pattern No. 11604, c1927.
£550–650 AH

A Shelley part tea set, decorated with Blue Iris pattern on a white ground, pattern No. 11561, slight damage, c1927.
£700–800 Bea(E)

◄ An Art Deco New Chelsea Coraline 15-piece coffee service, decorated with floral sprays, c1930, coffee pot 9in (23cm) high.
£60–75 P(B)

A Rosenthal coffee service, designed by Roland Peynet, 1950s, coffee pot 8in (20.5cm) high.
£300–350 JES

TUREENS & COVERED DISHES

A Meissen soup tureen and cover, the knop modelled as a sliced lemon, the sides with entwined stem handles, the whole painted with *deutsche Blumen* and with a gilt line rim to the cover, marked, c1750, 13¾in (35cm) high.
£2,000–2,500 WW

A Meissen blue and white tureen and cover, with moulded strapwork handles and Frauenkopf terminals, damaged, blue crossed swords mark and 'K', mid-18thC, 9in (23cm) high.
£3,500–4,000 C

A Meissen two-handled tureen, cover and stand, with *Brühlsche Allerlei* moulding, painted in puce and green with flowers within gilt-edged moulded cartouches, slight damage, blue crossed swords marks to tureen and stand, c1750, stand 14in (35.5cm) diam.
£3,500–4,000 C

A pair of Worcester tureens, covers and stands, the rustic handles and finial with flower terminals, printed in blue with the Pinecone pattern and allied prints, gadroon moulded rims, hatched crescent marks, c1775.
£1,000–1,200 P

A Höchst quatrefoil tureen and cover, with green and yellow scroll and foliage handles and feet, painted with bouquets and flowersprays, the cover with artichoke and foliage finial, damaged, manganese wheel mark, 'PB' for Philipp Magnus Bechel, c1775, 13½in (34.5cm) wide.
£1,000–1,200 C

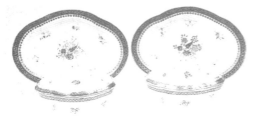

A pair of Caughley dessert tureens and stands, decorated in blue and gilt, c1785, stands 9¼in (23.5cm) wide.
£700–850 DAN

A Derby yellow-ground tureen, cover and stand, painted by Cuthbert Lawton in sepia with birds, c1805, 6½in (16.5cm) wide.
£750–850 TK

A Meissen tureen, cover and stand, the knop in the form of a putto, decorated in 17thC Dutch style in coloured enamels with figures and animals, one handle riveted, marked, late 18thC, 15¼in (38.5cm) wide.
£2,000–2,200 HOLL

▶ A pair of Minton sauce tureens, the covers with bud finials, with gadrooned rims, gilt mask loop handles, stylized sprig decoration in green and red with blue banding and gilt embellishment, each on spreading foot, 19thC, 7in (18cm) wide.
£400–450 AH

A Sèvres-style tureen and cover, painted with fruit and floral sprays within gilt and blue borders, date code for 1768, 13½in (34.5cm) diam.
£950–1,100 P(EA)

VASES & URNS

A Worcester Flight & Barr flared urn and stand, decorated in coloured enamels, within an oval gilt cartouche and titled 'Adelaide', on a bright yellow ground, the stand inscribed beneath in brown, painted marks in brown, c1800, 9in (23cm) high.
£800–1,000 DN

A pair of Derby flower pots and stands, Duesbury & Kean period, each with 2 gilded satyr handles and painted with large floral sprays within gilded borders and details, pattern No. 40, c1810, 7in (17.5cm) high.
£7,000–8,000 C

A pair of Paris porcelain vases, the gilt scroll handles with mask terminals, each painted with a panel of flowers and buildings on a *bleu de roi* ground with gilt flowerheads, repaired, printed mark, early 19thC, 12¼in (31cm) high.
£1,500–1,700 WW

A pair of Davenport D-shaped bough pots and covers, painted with floral panels, each on 4 gilt ball feet, slight damage and restoration, impressed marks, c1810, 6¾in (17cm) high.
£4,500–5,000 S

A garniture of Worcester Barr, Flight & Barr vases, painted with buildings in rural landscapes, with white beaded borders, the reverse with gilt foliate and scrollwork motifs, restored, impressed marks, c1810, largest 5½in (14cm) high.
£1,600–2,000 S

A pair of Sèvres-style urns, painted by H. Desprez with continuous scenes depicting Napoleon, within blue ground gilt borders with swans, crowned eagles, oak leaves with acorns, laurel garlands, gilt-metal mounts, damaged and repaired, signed, crowned 'N' marks and anthemion motifs, 19thC, 23½in (59.5cm) high.
£5,500–6,500 CSK

LOCATE THE SOURCE

The source of each illustration in Miller's can be found by checking the code letters below each caption with the Key to Illustrations, pages 376–379.

A Chamberlain's Worcester pierced flower vase and cover, decorated with a topographical view of Worcester, c1810, 8in (20.5cm) high.
£900–1,000 TK

A Derby campana vase, decorated with a view of a Continental city on an orange ground, c1810, 6¾in (17cm) high.
£1,000–1,250 TK

A Spode two-handled vase, decorated in Japan pattern within bead borders, lion mask gilt loop handles, marked in red and '967', c1810, 7½in (19cm) high.
£650–750 Hal

A Worcester two-handled urn and cover, decorated with flowers on a gilt trellis, the cover tightly encrusted with blossoms, early 19thC, 15in (38cm) high.
£4,000–5,000 CNY

A Coalport vase, with 2 scroll handles, the green ground encrusted and decorated in gilt with flowers and leaves, scroll-moulded foot, restored, painted mark in blue, c1825, 12¼in (31cm) high.
£520–600 HOLL

A garniture of Derby 'Long Tom' vases, decorated and gilt in a vivid Imari palette with a design of alternating panels of flowers and foliage, damaged and restored, red printed marks and '24', c1830, largest 24⅛in (62cm) high.
£5,000–5,500 S

A Minton vase and cover, with green rustic handles, one side painted with a view entitled 'Near Bagnall', the reverse with a flowerspray, gilt line borders and details, on a matched stand, unmarked, c1830, 9¾in (25cm) high.
£520–580 WW

A Worcester, Flight, Barr & Barr vase, with pierced cover, decorated with a view of Warwick Castle, restored, full script marks, c1830, 5½in (14cm) high.
£2,000–2,500 MER

A Sèvres vase, painted in the Japanese style, printed and incised marks in red and green, c1852, 12½in (32cm) high.
£1,000–1,200 S

▶ A pair of porcelain vases, with polychrome-painted summer flowers on a cobalt blue ground, the rim moulded with ivy leaves, picked out in gilt on an apricot ground, c1830, 9¼in (23.5cm) high.
£450–550 Bon

A pair of pot pourri vases and covers, of rococo form, probably H. & R. Daniel, enamelled in bold colours with sprays of exotic flowers within yellow and gilt borders and with leaf scroll handles and feet, the pierced covers with leaf finials, repaired, c1835, 17¼in (44cm) high.
£750–900 CAG

A pair of Dresden vases, painted in polychrome enamels with panels of figures and flowers, within gilt scrolling borders on turquoise grounds, 'AR' monograms, mid-19thC, 24in (61cm) high.
£1,750–2,000 WW

A pair of vases, with gilt rims, decorated with birds in a landscape within gilt foliate borders, on a blue ground, probably Coalport, 19thC, 3½in (9cm) high.
£250–300 GAK

A pair of Minton blue-ground 'Dresden scroll' vases and pierced covers, painted within leaf-moulded sections enriched in gilt, damaged and restored, c1835, 12½in (32cm) high.
£500–600 CSK

A Minton flower-encrusted vase and cover, design No. 219, the base heightened in turquoise and gilt, c1838, 12in (30.5cm) high.
£900–1,100 Bon

A pair of Sèvres-style *bleu celeste*-ground vases, with gilt-metal mounts, painted with figures wearing 18thC dress, damaged, 19thC, 12in (30.5cm) high.
£1,000–1,200 CSK

A Copeland & Garrett vase and cover, painted with flowers and fruit within scrolling enamel cartouches on a gilt leaf decorated beige ground, printed mark, mid-19thC, 11in (28cm) high.
£550–600 WW

A cornucopia vase, possibly by Jacob Petit, painted with flowers within gilt cartouches, on a blue ground, with eagle's head terminal, shaped rectangular base, gilt borders and highlights, mid-19thC, 9in (23cm) high.
£150–180 Hal

A French vase, with apple-green ground and Egyptian-revival polychrome-painted decoration, mounted as a lamp, c1860, 15½in (39.5cm) high.
£200–250 FBG

A pair of Coalbrookdale vases, with rustic loop handles, the white ground painted with exotic birds within flower-encrusted surrounds, mid-19thC, 9in (23cm) high.
£350–400 AH

A pair of Royal Worcester vases and covers, painted with hunting scenes, gilt and enamelled on a pink ground, late 19thC, 11⅛in (29cm) high.
£1,250–1,400 AH

A Belleek spill vase, decorated in Cleary pattern, First Period, 1863–90, 5in (12.5cm) high.
£150–200 MLa

A Dresden vase, with a painting of a stork, marked, c1880, 9in (23cm) high.
£150–180 VSt

A pair of Dresden vases and covers, with pink ground, gilt conical finials and each painted with 2 scenes of figures wearing 18thC-style dress, chipped and repaired, blue 'AR' monograms above stars, c1880, 13¾in (35cm) high.
£600–700 C

A Derby vase, with gilded decoration, c1887, 6½in (16.5cm) high.
£180–220 VSt

A Royal Worcester spill vase, formed as a hand clutching a Grecian urn, polychrome colouring with jewelled bracelet, c1890, 6in (15cm) high.
£400–450 GAK

This design is known as 'Mrs Hadley's Hand' and is said to be modelled by James Hadley after his wife's hand.

A Royal Worcester porcelain vase, with flared rim, pierced grotesque handles and applied masks, painted with clematis on an ivory-coloured ground with buff and gilt banding, 19thC, 13¼in (33.5cm) high.
£900–1,000 AH

A Minton *pâte-sur-pâte* decorated vase, c1891, 8½in (21.5cm) high.
£1,200–1,500 AMH

A pair of Copeland's 'jewelled' two-handled vases and covers, each painted with a lady, the reverse with a gilt geometric pattern between gilt fluting highlighted with gilt seeds, the domed cover with bud finial, some damage and repairs, signed 'S. Alcock', c1895, 10¾in (27.5cm) high.
£2,300–2,600 S

Samuel Alcock specialized in delicate figure subjects at Copeland's, and examples of his work are always in demand.

A Worcester Grainger & Co pot pourri vase, with pierced cover and inner cover, printed and painted with flowers and leaves within leaf and flowerhead-moulded borders picked out in gilt, on a blush ivory ground, printed mark in green, c1895, 10½in (26.5cm) high.
£600–700 DN

Sets/Pairs

Unless otherwise stated, any description which refers to 'a set' or 'a pair' includes a guide price for the entire set or the pair, even though the illustration may show only a single item.

A Royal Doulton vase, hand-decorated with garlands of flowers with gilt embellishments to the shaped rim, scrolled handles, signed 'C. B. Brough', late 19thC, 7½in (19cm) high.
£175–200 HCC

A Royal Worcester vase, decorated with flowers on a blush ivory ground, shape No. 1733, printed mark and date code for 1897, 7½in (19cm) high.
£200–240 P(B)

A pair of Royal Crown Derby vases and covers, with gilt rims, decorated with bellflowers on deep blue reserves, one cover missing and handles restored, signed 'Leroy', printed marks and date cypher for 1897, 6in (15cm) high.
£850–1,000 GAK

A pair of baluster vases and covers, by Carl Thieme, Potschappel, painted with hunting scenes, the finials formed as plumed helmets above rolled-up maps, the twin handles as warriors' heads, some damage, late 19thC, 18¼in (46.5cm) high.
£1,200–1,500 CSK

A pair of Bavarian baluster-form pot pourri vases, with encrusted flowers and amorini, painted in rich colours and gilt, late 19thC, 15in (38cm) high.
£450–550 RBB

An Austrian vase and cover, with gilt decoration on a blue ground, 19thC, 18½in (47cm) high.
£750–850 AH

A pair of Royal Worcester vases, decorated with flowers inside a gilt border on a red ground, c1900, 4in (10cm) high.
£700–800 TH

Further Reading

Miller's Collecting Pottery & Porcelain, The Facts At Your Fingertips, Miller's Publications, 1997

▶ A Royal Crown Derby vase, of campagna form, painted and signed by William Mosley, on a wide band reserved on a light apple-green ground with white and gilt leaf borders, mark in red and date code for 1903, 10½in (26.5cm) high.
£2,400–2,800 P

A Locke Worcester miniature vase, decorated with a mirror image pattern, c1900, 3¼in (8.5cm) high.
£40–50 TVA

A spill vase, with floral decoration, mid-19thC, 4in (10cm) high.
£220–270 DAN

▶ A pair of Royal Crown Derby vases, painted and gilt in the Imari palette, slight wear, printed and incised marks, date codes for 1904, 8½in (21.5cm) high.
£1,200–1,500 CSK

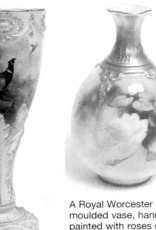

A pair of Royal Worcester spill vases, painted with pink roses on an ivory ground with gilt edging, one signed 'Spilsbury', c1905, 9in (23cm) high.
£600–700 AH

A Royal Worcester vase, by James Stinton, painted with a cock pheasant above a band of blush ivory stiff-leaves and flowers, on a circular foot, No. 1047, printed mark with date code for 1907, 9in (23cm) high.
£550–650 P(B)

A Royal Worcester moulded vase, hand-painted with roses on a shaded ground, with gilt highlights, c1910, 6in (15cm) high.
£200–250 QSA

A Meissen vase, the cobalt blue ground with gilt and floral decoration, 20thC, 6½in (16.5cm) high.
£375–450 BHA

Miller's is a price GUIDE not a price LIST

A pair of Royal Worcester vases and covers, shape No. 2425, painted and signed by Harry Stinton, some damage, printed mark in puce, date cypher for 1911, initialled 'CE' in burnt orange, 11in (28cm) high.
£3,000–3,500 HSS

A Royal Crown Derby 'jewelled' vase and cover, painted and signed by Albert Gregory, on a dark blue ground, with gilt handles, the cover with gilt pinecone finial, on a square base, marks in red and date code for 1911, 13½in (34.5cm) high.
£6,000–7,000 P

A Royal Worcester vase, with twin handles, hand-painted with flowers on a blush ivory ground, raised on a moulded gilded base with spreading foot, c1913, 6½in (16.5cm) high.
£550–600 QSA

A Royal Worcester vase and cover, shape No. 2247, painted with a basket of fruit on a table, on a dark blue ground gilt with *caillouté* design in French style, on a circular foot, signed 'R. Sebright', date code for 1921, 9in (23cm) high.
£2,800–3,000 P

A pair of New Chelsea vases, printed and painted with flowers within blue and gilt borders, c1919, 5in (12.5cm) high.
£110–130 WAC

New Chelsea is the trade name of a Staffordshire factory active from 1912–51.

A Belleek Princess vase, encrusted with flowers, Third Period, 1926–46, 9in (23cm) high.
£700–800 MLa

Index to Advertisers

Directory of Restorers

CERAMIC REPAIR AND RESTORATION,
Sevenoaks, Kent Tel: 01732 456695
Restoration sensitively undertaken on display antique and modern ceramics

CERAMICS RESCUE,
Ken Goodale, Westerham, Kent Tel: 01959 564188
Repair and restoration of china, porcelain and glass

CERAMIC RESTORATION,
40 Lower Street, Stansted, Essex CM24 8LR
Tel: 01279 812233

CERAMIC RESTORATION COURSES,
Roger Hawkins, 72 Derby Road, Nottingham NG1 5FD
Tel: 0115 950 7589
Inner-city workshop courses

JOHN CHARLES ANTIQUES,
Tale Manor, Tale, Devon EX14 0HJ Tel: 01884 277229
Porcelain restoration

ALAN FINNEY ANTIQUES,
Ceramic Restoration Studios, 3 John Street, Biddulph, Stoke-on-Trent, Staffs ST8 6BB Tel: 01782 517849
Restorer of pottery and porcelain

NIGHTINGALES CERAMIC CONSERVATION CENTRE,
Mrs Joy Harper, 58 Bredfield Road, Woodbridge, Suffolk IP12 1JE Tel: 01394 385609
Included in the Register of the Museums & Galleries Commission

NORTH DEVON CHINA RESTORATION,
Allen Pullen, Rosemary Cottage, South Healand, St Giles in the Wood, Torrington, Devon EX38 7JN
Tel/Fax: 01805 624936
email: nd.chinarestoration@btinternet.com
website: www.antiquesbulletin.com/ndcr
Courses available in china restoration

MILLSIDE ANTIQUE RESTORAION,
60 Hamels Drive, Hertford SG16 7SN
Tel: 01992 500507
Restorers of porcelain

THE MOWBRAY SCHOOL OF PORCELAIN RESTORATION,
Flint Barn, West End Lane, Essendon, Hatfield, Herts AL9 5RQ
Tel: 0181 367 1786 or 01707 270 158
Porcelain restoration courses in tranquil countryside

PORCELAIN RESTORERS,
240 Stockport Road, Cheadle Heath, Stockport SK3 0LX Tel: 0161 428 9599

SARAH THEAKSTON, BA WEST DEAN DIP,
The Battery House, Petworth House, Petworth, West Sussex GU28 0GDP
Tel/Fax: 01798 342763
Restoration of ceramics, glass and enamels

MONIQUE SHARP,
South Bucks Tel: 01494 678776
Full porcelain and china restoration service

Directory of Specialists

ART DECO ETC, 73 Upper Gloucester Road, Brighton, Sussex BN1 3LQ Tel: 01273 329268
Poole Pottery

BEVERLEY, 30 Church St, Marylebone, London NW8 8EP Tel: 020 7262 1576
19th & 20thC ceramics

BOTTLEBROOK ANTIQUES, Derby Tel: 01332 883363
English porcelain, specializing in Royal Crown Derby and Royal Worcester

DAVID BROWER, 113 Kensington Church Street, London W8 7LN Tel: 020 7221 4155
KPM, Meissen, and Oriental ceramics

ROY W. BUNN ANTIQUES, 34/36 Church Street, Barnoldswick, Colne, Cancs BB8 5UT Tel: 01282 813703
Staffordshire figures

CAMEO ANTIQUES, 19 Watergate Street, Chester, Cheshire CH1 2LB Tel/Fax: 01244 311467

CHURCH STREET ANTIQUES, 10 Church Street, Godalming, Surrey GU7 1EH Tel: 01483 860894
Art Deco ceramics

CLARICE CLIFF COLLECTORS CLUB, Fantasque House, Tennis Drive, The Park, Nottingham NG7 1AE

PADDY CLIFF'S CLARICE, 77 Coombe Valley Road, Preston, Weymouth DT3 6NS Tel: 01305 834945
Clarice Cliff

THE CRESTED CHINA COMPANY, The Station House, Driffield YO25 7PY Tel: 01377 257042
Goss and Crested China

ANDREW DANDO, 4 Wood Street, QueenSquare, Bath BA1 2JQ Tel: 01225 422702
English and Continental pottery and porcelain

DELF STREAM GALLERY, 14 New Street, Sandwich, Kent CT13 9AB Tel: 01304 617684
19th & 20tthC Art Pottery

JULIAN EADE, Tel: 020 8394 1515
Doulton stoneware, Royal Worcester, Minton and Royal Crown Derby

FAIR FINDS ANTIQUES, Rait, Perth PH2 7RT Tel: 01821 670379
Wemyss

ROY & DIANE GINNS, PO Box 129, East Grinstead, W Sussex
Toby jugs

GOSS & CRESTED CHINA LTD, 62 Murray Road, Horndean, Hants PO8 9JL Tel: 023 9259 7440
Goss & Crested China

JUDY & BRIAN HARDEN, PO Box 14, Bourton-on-the-Water, Glos GL54 2YR Tel: 01451 810684
Porcelain, especially Meissen

JONATHAN HORNE ANTIQUES, 66c Kensington Church Street, London W8 Tel: 020 7221 5658
Delftware, especially English

TONY HORSLEY ANTIQUES
Tel: 01273 550770 Fax: 01273 550855
Candle extinguishers, Royal Worcester

VALERIE HOWARD, 2 Campden Street (off Kensington Church St), London W8 7 EP Tel: 020 7792 9702
Mason's Ironstone, faïence of Quimper and Rouen

MARION LANGHAM, Tel: 020 7730 11002
Belleek

JACQUELINE OOSTHUIZEN, Unit 20 Bourbon-Hanby Antiques Centre, 151 Sydney Street, London SW3 Tel: 020 7352 6071
Staffordshire figures, animals, cottages, Toby jugs

PAULL'S OF KENILWORTH, Janice Paull, Beehive House, 125 Warwick Road, Old Kenilworth, Warwickshire CV8 1HY Tel: 01926 855253
email: janicepaull@btinternet.com
www.masonsironstone.com and janicepaull.ironstone.com
Large stock of English ironstone, general ceramics, glass, silver and jewellery

POTS AFFAIR, Stand S048/49 (Top Floor), Alfies Antique Market, 13–25 Church Street, London NW8 8DT Tel: 020 7402 0732
Torquay Pottery, British Art pottery

THE POSTHORN, Marshall Kennedy, 26/30 St Andrew Street, Castle Douglas, Kirkcudbrightshire, Scotland DG7 1DE Tel: 01556 502531
email: marshall@posthorn.co.uk www.posthorn.co.uk
Moorcroft pottery and member of Royal Crown Derby Collectors' Guild

POTTERIES ANTIQUES CENTRE & AUCTIONEERS, 271 Waterloo Road, Cobridge, Stoke-on-Trent, ST6 3HR Tel: 01782 201455
email:potteriesantiquecentre@compuserve.com
www.potteriesantiquecentre.com.
One of the largest centres in the North of England specialising in pottery

SYLVIA POWELL DECORATIVE ARTS, 18 The Mall, Camden Passage, London N1 OPD Tel: 020 7354 2977
www.sylvia-powell.com.
Doulton stoneware and other fine British and Continental art pottery

THE NEVILLE PUNDOLE GALLERY, 8a & 9 The Friars, Canterbury, Kent CT1 2AS Tel/Fax: 01227 453471
email pundole@globalnet.co.uk
www.cantweb.co.uk/pundole
Moorcroft pottery and other fine handmade wares

JOHN READ, 29 Lark Rise, Martlesham Heath, Ipswich IP5 7SA Tel: 01473 624897
Staffordshire

RICH DESIGNS, Unit 1, Grove Farm, Bromyard Road, Worcester WR2 5UG Tel: 01905 748214
All Clarice Cliff books and pots

ROGERS DE RIN, 76 Royal Hospital Road, London SW3 4HN Tel: 020 7352 9007
Wemyss

PETER SCOTT, Bartlett Street Antiques, 5/10 Bartlett Street, Bath, Avon BA1 2QZ Tel: 01225 310457
Early English pottery and rare and unusual transferware

SERENDIPITY, 168 High Street, Deal, Kent CT14 6BQ Tel: 01304 369165/366536
Staffordshire pottery

SPECIAL AUCTION SERVICES, The Coach House, Midgham Park, Reading RG7 5UG Tel: 0118 971 2949
Commemorative ware, pot lids, Prattware, fairings, Goss & Crested, Baxter and Le Blond Prints

STAFFORDSHIRE PRIDE, 3 Pierrepont Arcade, Camden Passage, London N1 8EF Tel: 020 8341 1943
Staffordshire

ISLWYN WATKINS, Offas Dyke Antiques Centre, Knighton, Powys, Wales LD7 1AT Tel: 01547 528635
18th & 19thC pottery and Studio pottery

RAY WALKER ANTIQUES
Burton Arcade, 296 Westbourne Grove, London W11 2PS Tel: 020 8464 7891
Staffordshire, and Sunderland lustre pottery

Glossary

acid etching technique involving treatment of glass with hydrofluoric acid, giving a matt or frosted finish.

agateware type of pottery resembling agate as a result of the partial blending of different-coloured clays.

applied decoration surface ornament made separately and applied to the body of an object.

basalt unglazed, very hard, fine-grained stoneware stained with cobalt and manganese oxides, developed by Wedgwood c1768.

biscuit (bisque) unglazed porcelain or earthenware fired once only. Popular for neoclassical porcelain figures because it suggests classical marble sculptures. Also used for making dolls' heads.

bocage encrustations of flowers, grass and moss generally used to decorate the supporting plinths of ceramic figures.

body the material from which a piece of pottery or porcelain is produced, although the term paste is more often used for porcelain. Also refers to the main part of a piece.

bone china a soft-paste porcelain consisting of petuntse (china stone), kaolin (china clay) and calcined bone.

brownware salt-glazed brown stoneware, especially that made in Nottingham, Derby and elsewhere in England.

cachepot ornamental container for flowerpots. A smaller form of jardiniére.

cameo a design in contrasting low relief, as found in **jasper ware**.

cartouche decorative frame in the form of a scroll of paper with rolled ends, usually surrounding an inscription or pictorial decoration.

celadon semi-opaque, green-tinted glaze used first on ware made during the Chinese Sung Dynasty (960–1280).

chinoiserie decoration consisting of Oriental-style figures and motifs, such as pagodas, pavilions, birds and lotus flowers, that permeated Europe from the Far East; prevalent from the late 17th century.

cloisonné enamel fired into compartments (cloisons) formed by metal wires.

cobalt basic blue colouring, originally imported from Saxony, Germany, extremely important in early ceramics as it stood up to the extreme heat of the glazing kiln.

cow creamer milk jugs modelled to resemble a cow. The tail would be the handle, the mouth the spout, and milk was poured into the body through an opening in its back.

crackleware (craquelure) deliberate cracked effect achieved by firing ceramics to a precise temperature.

crazing tiny, undesirable surface cracks caused by shrinking or other technical defects in a glaze.

creamware cream-coloured earthenware with a transparent lead glaze, developed by Wedgwood c1760.

Delftware tin-glazed earthenware from Delft, in the Netherlands, refers to British ware when it does not have a capital letter.

enamel form of decoration involving the application of metallic oxides to metal, ceramics, or glass in paste form or in an oil-based mixture, which is then usually fired for decorative effect.

faïence tin-glazed earthenware usually applied to France and Germany and also to later Italian ware. The name is derived from Faenza, one of the biggest pottery-making centres in Italy. (Similar to **mailolica** and delftware).

fairings mementoes of a visit to the fair, they were small porcelain items manufactured mainly in Germany in the last half of the last century and the early part of the 20th for the English market.

famille rose palette used on 18th-century Chinese porcelain, which includes a dominant opaque pink. Much copied in Europe.

feldspar porcelain a tough form of bone china which contains pure feldspar. Coalport were the first to sucessfully produce this type of porcelain.

flambé glaze made from copper, usually deep crimson, flecked with blue or purple, and often faintly crackled.

flatbacks pottery figures with flat, unmodelled and undecorated backs, designed to be viewed from the front only. They were intended as mantelpiece decorations and produced mainly in the 19thC by Staffordshire Potteries.

flow blue blurred blue transfer-printed decoration on Staffordshire earthenware.

fluting a pattern of concave grooves repeated in vertical, parallel lines. The inverse of **gadrooning**.

gadrooning decorative edging consisting of a series of convex, vertical or spiralling curves.

hard-paste porcelain pure white, translucent porcelain approximating to oriental 'china'. Has a metallic ring when struck and is immensely strong in spite of its apparent delicacy. It was first made in China using the combination of kaolin (china clay 50%), petuntse (china stone 25%) and quartz (25%). The strength is acquired by ageing the paste, kaolin and china stone before firing at high temperature.

Imari Japanese porcelain with dense decoration, based on brocade patterns, in a palette that is dominated by underglaze blue, iron-red, green, manganese, yellow and gold.

incised decoration decoration that is cut into the body of an object with a sharp metal point.

ironstone tough earthenware made from mineral base.

jasper ware hard, fine-grained, coloured stoneware developed by Wedgwood in the 1770s.

knop literally the bud of a flower, a term used to describe the decorative finial on teapot and vase lids.

lead glaze clear glaze generally composed of silicaceous sand, salt, soda and potash mixed with a lead component.

lustre ware pottery with an irridescent surface produced using metallic pigments, usually silver or copper.

maiolica tin-glazed earthenware produced in Italy from 15th–18thC.

majolica corruption of the term maiolica, which refers to a type of 19thC earthenware in elaborate forms with thick, brightly coloured glazes.

moulded tableware and figures made from pressing the body (stoneware, earthenware, porcelain etc.) between two moulds, allowing great freedom of shape and variety of decoration which could be repeated identically.

Parian semi-matt porcelain made with **feldspar** and therefore not requiring a separate glaze. Also called statuary porcelain, it became known as Parian because of its similarity to the white marble from the Greek island of Paros.

pâte-sur-pâte a kind of porcelain decoration involving low-relief designs carved in **slip** and applied in layers to a contrasting body.

redware stoneware, generally unglazed and often decorated with applied motifs in relief.

reeding a milled edge, or parallel pattern in the form of reeds.

relief decoration decoration that stands out from the surface of any object and is usually described, according to its depth, as low-relief or high-relief.

reserve a self-contained blank area within a pattern, reserved for other decoration.

saltglaze thin, glassy glaze applied to some stoneware and produced by throwing salt into the kiln at the height of firing. The glaze may show a pitted surface, known as 'orange peel'.

Satsuma type of Japanese pottery with elaborate decoration, crackle glaze and heavy gilding named after the Japanese port where it was made.

sgraffito form of ceramic decoration incised through a coloured slip, revealing the ground beneath.

slip smooth dilution of clay and water used in the making and decoration of pottery.

slipware type of red-bodied earthenware decorated largely with slip in contrasting colours.

spill vase or jar wide-mouthed, often straight-sided jar to hold strips of wood, paper, etc. to light pipes from the fire.

terracotta lightly fired red earthenware, usually unglazed.

tin glaze glassy glaze made opaque by the addition of tin oxide and commonly used on earthenware.

transfer-printing the process of transferring a single-colour image (a transfer), printed from an engraved copper plate on to tissue paper, on to the unglazed surface of a ceramic object.

tube-lining type of ceramic decoration in which thin trails of slip are applied as outlines to areas of coloured glaze.

tyg a drinking pot often with two or more handles.

underglaze colour or design painted before the application of the glaze on a ceramic object.

Key to Illustrations

Each illustration and descriptive caption is accompanied by a letter code. By referring to the following list of Auctioneers (denoted by *) and Dealers (•) the source of any item may immediately be determined. Inclusion in this edition in no way constitutes or implies a contract or binding offer on the part of any of our contributors to supply or sell the goods illustrated, or similar articles, at the prices stated. Advertisers are denoted by †.

If you require a valuation for an item, it is advisable to check whether the dealer or specialist will carry out this service and if there is a charge. Please mention Miller's when making an enquiry. Having found a specialist who will carry out your valuation it is best to send a photograph and description of the item to the specialist together with a stamped addressed envelope for the reply. A valuation by telephone is not possible.

Most dealers are only too happy to help with enquiries – however, they are very busy people and consideration of the above points would be welcomed.

A&A	•	Antiques & Art, 116 State Street, Portsmouth NH 03802 USA
AAC	•	No longer trading.
AAV	*	Academy Auctioneers & Valuers, Northcote House, Northcote Avenue, Ealing, London W5 3UR Tel: 020 8579 7466
ACA	•	Acorn Antiques, Durham House Antiques Centre, Stow-on-the-Wold, Gloucestershire GL54 1AA Tel: 01451 87040
ADE	•	Art Deco Etc, 73 Upper Gloucester Road, Brighton, East Sussex BN1 3LQ Tel: 01273 329268
AG	*	Anderson & Garland (Auctioneers), Marlborough House, Marlborough Crescent, Newcastle-upon-Tyne, Tyne & Wear NE1 4EE Tel: 0191 232 6278
AH	•	Andrew Hartley, Victoria Hall Salerooms, Little Lane, Ilkley, Yorkshire LS29 8EA Tel: 01943 816363
ALB	•	Albany Antiques, 8–10 London Road, Hindhead, Surrey GU26 6AF Tel: 01428 605528
AMH	•	Amherst Antiques, 23 London Road, Riverhead, Sevenoaks, Kent TN13 2BU Tel: 01732 455047
AND	•	Joan & Bob Anderson, Middlesex Tel: 020 8572 4328
AnE	•	Antiques Emporium, The Old Chapel, Long Street, Tetbury, Gloucestershire GL8 8AA Tel: 01666 505281
ANO	•	Art Nouveau Originals, Stamford Antiques Centre, The Exchange Hall, Broad Street, Stamford, Lincolnshire PE9 1PX Tel: 01780 762605
AnS	•	The Antique Shop, 30 Henley Street, Stratford-upon-Avon, Warwickshire CV37 6QW Tel: 01789 292485
ANT	•	Anthemion, Bridge Street, Cartmel, Grange-over-Sands, Cumbria LA11 7SH Tel: 015395 36295
ANV	•	Anvil Antiques, Cavendish Street, Cartmel, Cumbria AL11 6QA
AP	•	Andrew Pickford, The Hertford Saleroom, 42 St Andrew Street, Hertford, Hertfordshire SG14 1JA Tel: 01992 583508 Fax: 01992 501421
ARE	•	Arenski, 185 Westbourne Grove, London W11 2SB Tel: 020 7727 8599
ASA	•	A. S. Antiques, 26 Broad Street, Pendleton, Salford, Greater Manchester M6 5BY Tel: 0161 737 5938
ATQ	•	Antiquarius Antique Market, 131/141 King's Road, London SW3 5ST Tel: 020 7351 5353
B&R	•	Bread & Roses, Durham House Antique Centre, Sheep Street, Stow-on-the-Wold, Gloucestershire GL54 1SS Tel: 01451 870404
BBR	•	BBR, Elsecar, Barnsley, Yorkshire S74 8HJ Tel: 01226 745156
BCO	•	British Collectables, 1st Floor, 9 Georgian Village, Camden Passage, Islington, London N1 8EG Tel: 020 7359 4560
BDA	•	Briar's C20th Decorative Arts, Yorkshire Tel: 01756 798641
Bea	•	Bearnes Rainbow, Avenue Road, Torquay, Devon TQ2 5TG Tel: 01803 296277
Bea(E)	•	Bearnes, St Edmund's Court, Okehampton Street, Exeter, Devon EX4 1DU Tel: 01392 422800
BEE	•	Jonathan Beech, Westport, Co Mayo, Republic of Ireland Tel: 00353 98 28688
Ber	•	Berry Antiques, Berry House, 11–13 Stone Street, Cranbrook, Kent TN17 3HF Tel: 01580 712345
BET	•	Beth, GO43–44, Alfies Antique Market, 13–25 Church Street, Marylebone, London NW8 8DT Tel: 020 7723 5613
BEV	•	Beverley, 30 Church Street, Marylebone, London NW8 8EP Tel: 020 7262 1576
BHA	•	Bourbon Hanby Antiques & Jewellery, 151 Sydney Street, Chelsea, London SW3 6NT Tel: 020 7352 2106 Fax: 020 7365 0003
BHa	•†	Judy & Brian Harden Antiques, PO Box 14, Bourton-on-the-Water, Cheltenham, Gloucestershire GL54 2YR Tel: 01451 810684
BIG	•	Bigwood Auctioneers Ltd, The Old School, Tiddington, Stratford-upon-Avon, Warwickshire CV37 7AW Tel: 01789 269415
BKK	•	Bona Art Deco Store, The Hart Shopping Centre, Fleet, Hampshire GU13 8AZ Tel: 01252 616666
Bon	*	Bonhams, Montpelier Street, Knightsbridge, London SW7 1HH Tel: 020 7393 3994
BR	•	Bracketts, Auction Hall, Pantiles, Tunbridge Wells, Kent TN1 1UU Tel: 01892 544500
Bri	*	Bristol Auction Rooms, St John's Place, Apsley Road, Clifton, Bristol, Avon BS8 2ST Tel: 0117 973 7201
BRT	•	Britannia, Stand 101, Gray's Antique Market, 58 Davies Street, London W1Y 1AR Tel: 020 7629 6772
BRU	•	Brunel Antiques, Bartlett Street Antiques Centre, Bath, Somerset BA1 2QZ Tel: 01225 310457/446322
BSA	•	Bartlett Street Antique Centre, 5–10 Bartlett Street, Bath, Somerset BA1 2QZ Tel: 01225 446322/310457
BUR	•	House of Burleigh, The Old Shop Cottage, 2 Braunston Road, Knossington, Oakham, Rutland LE15 8LN Tel: 01664 454570/454114
BWA	•	Bow-Well Antiques, 103 West Bow, Edinburgh, Scotland EH1 2JP Tel: 0131 225 3335
BWe	*	Biddle & Webb Ltd, Ladywood Middleway, Birmingham, West Midlands B16 0PP Tel: 0121 455 8042
Byl	•	Bygones of Ireland, Westport Antiques Centre, Lodge Road, Westport, County Mayo Tel: 00 353 98 26132
C	*	Christie's Ltd, 8 King Street, St James's, London SW1Y 6QT Tel: 020 7839 9060
C(S)	*	Christie's Scotland Ltd, 164-166 Bath Street, Glasgow, Scotland G2 4TG Tel: 0141 332 8134
CaC	*	Cato Crane & Co, Liverpool Auction Rooms, 6 Stanhope Street, Liverpool, Merseyside L8 5RF Tel: 0151 709 5559
CAG	*	The Canterbury Auction Galleries, 40 Station Road West, Canterbury, Kent CT2 8AN Tel: 01227 763337
CCC	•†	Crested China Co, The Station House, Driffield, Yorkshire YO25 7PY Tel: 01377 257042
CDC	*	Capes Dunn & Co, The Auction Galleries, 38 Charles Street, Off Princess Street, Greater Manchester M1 7DB Tel: 0161 273 6060/1911

CEX • Corn Exchange Antiques Centre, 64 The Pantiles, Tunbridge Wells, Kent TN2 5TN Tel: 01892 539652

CGC * Cheffins Grain & Comins, 2 Clifton Road, Cambridge CB2 4BW Tel: 01223 358721/213343

CHR • No longer trading.

CHU • Church Street Antiques, 2 Church Street, Wells-next-the-Sea, Norfolk NR23 1JA Tel: 01328 711698

CNY * Christie's International Inc, 502 Park Avenue, (including Christie's East), New York, NY 10022 USA Tel: 00 1 212 546 1000

COL • Collectables, PO Box 130, Chatham, Kent ME5 0DZ Tel: 01634 828767

CPA • Cottage Pine Antiques, 19 Broad Street, Brinklow, Nr Rugby, Warwickshire CV23 0LS Tel: 01788 832673

CRO • No longer trading.

CSA • Church Street Antiques, 10 Church Street, Godalming, Surrey, GU7 1EH Tel: 01483 860894

CSK * Christie's South Kensington Ltd, 85 Old Brompton Road, London SW7 3LD Tel: 020 7581 7611

DA * Dee, Atkinson & Harrison, The Exchange Saleroom, Driffield, Yorkshire YO25 7LD Tel: 01377 253151

DAC • Didcot Antiques Centre, 220 Broadway, Didcot, Oxfordshire OX11 8RS

DAF • No longer trading.

DAN •† Andrew Dando, 4 Wood Street, Queen Square, Bath, Somerset BA1 2JQ Tel: 01225 422702

DD * David Duggleby, The Vine Street Salerooms, Scarborough, Yorkshire YO11 1XN Tel: 01723 507111

DDM * Dickinson Davy & Markham, Wrawby Street, Brigg, Humberside DN20 8JJ Tel: 01652 650172

DeA • Delphi Antiques, Powerscourt Townhouse Centre, South William Street, Dublin 2 Tel: 00 353 1 679 0331

DgC • Dragonlee Collectables, Kent Tel: 01622 729502

DIA • Mark Diamond Associates, Essex Tel: 020 8508 4479 Fax: 020 8508 1460

DIC • D. & B. Dickinson, The Antique Shop, 22 and 22a New Bond Street, Bath, Somerset BA1 1BA Tel: 01225 466502

DKH • David K. Hakeney, 400 Wincolmlee, Hull, Humberside HU2 0QL Tel: 01482 228190

DMa • David March, Abbots Leigh, Bristol, Gloucestershire Tel: 0117 937 2422

DN *† Dreweatt Neate, Donnington Priory, Donnington, Newbury, Berkshire, RG13 2JE Tel: 01635 553553

DN(H) *† Dreweatt Neate Holloways, 49 Parsons Street, Banbury, Oxfordshire OX16 8PF Tel: 01295 253197

Doc * Dockree's, Cheadle Hulme Business Centre, Clemence House, Mellor Road, Cheadle Hume, Cheshire SK8 5AT Tel: 0161 485 1258

DORO * Dorotheum, Palais Dorotheum, A-1010, Wein, Dorotheergasse 17, Austria Tel: 0043 1 515 600 Fax: 0043 1 515 474

DSG *† Delf Stream Gallery, 14 New Street, Sandwich, Kent CT13 9AB Tel: 01304 617684

E * Ewbank, Burnt Common Auction Room, London Road, Send, Woking, Surrey GU23 7LN Tel: 01483 223101

EH * Edgar Horn, 46–50 South Street, Eastbourne, Sussex BN21 4XB Tel: 01323 410419

EKK * Ekkehart, USA Tel: 001 415 571 9070

EL * Eldred's, Robert C. Eldred Co Inc, 1475 Route 6A, East Dennis, Massachusetts 02641 USA Tel: 001 508 385 3116

FBG • Frank H. Boos Gallery, 420 Enterprise Court, Bloomfield Hills, Michigan 48302 USA Tel: 001 248 332 1500

FrG • French Glasshouse, P14/16 Antiquarius, 135 King's Road, Chelsea, London SW3 4PW Tel: 020 7376 5394 Fax: 020 7376 5394

G&CC •† Goss & Crested China Centre & Museum, incorporating Milestone Publications, 62 Murray Road, Horndean, Hampshire PO8 9JL Tel: 023 9259 7440 Fax: 023 9259 1975

GAK * G. A. Key, 8 Market Place, Aylsham, Norfolk NR11 6EH Tel: 01263 733195

Gam * Clarke Gammon, Guildford Auction Rooms, Bedford Road, Guildford, Surrey GU1 4SJ Tel: 01483 572266

GAZE * Thomas Wm Gaze & Son, Diss Auction Rooms, Roydon Road, Diss, Norfolk IP22 3LN Tel: 01397 650306

GEM * Gem Antiques, 28 London Road, Sevenoaks, Kent TN13 1AP Tel: 01732 743540

GFR/ * Geoffrey Robinson, GO77–78 (Ground Floor),
GRo • Alfies Antique Market, 13–25 Church Street, Marylebone, London NW8 8DT Tel: 020 7723 0449 Fax: 020 7706 3254

GH * Gardiner Houlgate, The Old Malthouse, Comfortable Place, Upper Bristol Road, Bath, Somerset BA1 3AJ Tel: 01225 447933

GIN • Ginnell Gallery Antique Centre, 18–22 Lloyd Street, Greater Manchester M2 5WA Tel: 0161 833 9037

GLN • Glenville Antiques, 120 High Street, Yatton, Avon BS19 4DH Tel: 01934 832284

GN •† Gillian Neale Antiques, PO Box 247, Aylesbury, Buckinghamshire HP20 1JZ Tel: 01296 423754 Fax: 01296 334601

GOO * Gooday Gallery, 20 Richmond Hill, Richmond, Surrey TW10 6QX Tel: 020 8940 8652

GSP * Graves, Son & Pilcher, Hove Auction Rooms, Hove, Sussex BN3 2GL Tel: 01273 735266

GSW • Georg S. Wissinger Antiques, 21 & 44 West Street, Chipping Norton, Oxfordshire Tel: 01608 641369

Hal * Halls Fine Art Auctions, Welsh Bridge, Shrewsbury, Shropshire SY3 8LA Tel: 01743 231212

HAM *† Hamptons International, 93 High Street, Godalming, Surrey GU7 1AL Tel: 01483 423567 Fax: 01483 426392

HAR * William Hardy Ltd, 15a Blythswood Square, Glasgow, Scotland G2 4EW Tel: 0141 221 6780 Fax: 0141 248 6237

HarC • Hardy's Collectables, 862 & 874 Christchurch Road, Boscombe, Bournemouth, Dorset BH7 6DG Tel: 01202 422407/303030

HCC * H. C. Chapman & Son, The Auction Mart, North Street, Scarborough, Yorkshire YO11 1DL Tel: 01723 372424

HCH * No longer trading.

HEA • Peter Hearnden, Kent (appointment only) Tel: 01634 374132

HEI • Heirloom Antiques, 68 High Street, Tenterden, Kent TN30 6AU Tel: 01580 765535

HEM • The Hemswell Antiques Centre, Caenby Corner Estate, Hemswell Cliff, Gainsborough, Lincolnshire DN21 5TJ Tel: 01427 668389

HER • No longer trading.

HIG • Highcroft Antiques, Red Lion, 165 Portobello Road, London W11 2DY

HOLL *† Dreweatt Neate Holloways, 49 Parsons Street, Banbury, Oxfordshire OX16 8PF Tel: 01295 253197

HOW • No longer trading.

HSS * Phillips, 20 The Square, Retford, Nottinghamshire DN22 6BX Tel: 01777 708633

HYD * HY Duke & Son, Dorchester Fine Art Salerooms, Dorchester, Dorset DT1 1QS Tel: 01305 265080

INC • The Incurable Collector, Surrey Tel: 01932 860800

IS • Ian Sharp Antiques, 23 Front Street, Tynemouth, Tyne & Wear NE30 4DX Tel: 0191 296 0656

IW •† Islwyn Watkins, 1 High Street, Knighton, Powys, Wales LD7 1AT Tel: 01547 520145

J&L * No longer trading.

JAK •† Clive & Lynne Jackson, Gloucestershire Tel: 01242 254375 Fax: 01242 254375

JBL • Judi Bland, Durham House Antique Centre, Sheep Street, Stow-on-the-Wold, Gloucestershire GL54 1AA

JES • John Jesse, 160 Kensington Church Street, London W8 4BN Tel: 020 7229 0312

JH * Jacobs & Hunt, 26 Lavant Street, Petersfield, Hampshire GU32 3EF Tel: 01730 233933 Fax: 01730 231393

JHo •† Jonathan Horne, 66C Kensington Church Street, London W8 4BY Tel: 020 7221 5658

JHW • John Howkins, 1 Dereham Road, Norwich, Norfolk NR2 4HX Tel: 01603 627832 Fax: 01603 666626

JM • John Maxwell of Wilmslow, 133A Woodford Road, Woodford, Cheshire SK7 1QD Tel: 0161 439 5182

JMC • J. & M. Collectables, Kent Tel: 01580 891657

JNic * John Nicholson, The Auction Rooms, Longfield, Midhurst Road, Fernhurst, Surrey GU27 3HA Tel: 01428 653727

JO •† Jacqueline Oosthuizen, 23 Cale Street, Chelsea, London SW3 3QR Tel: 020 7352 6071

JP •† Janice Paull, Beehive House, 125 Warwick Road, Kenilworth, Warwickshire CV8 1HY Tel: 01926 851311

JR • No longer trading.

JRe •† John Read, 29 Lark Rise, Martlesham Heath, Ipswich, Suffolk IP5 7SA Tel: 01473 624897

JUN • Junktion, The Old Railway Station, New Bolingbroke, Boston, Lincolnshire PE22 7LB Tel: 01205 480068/480087

K * Kite, 15 Langton Street, London SW10 0JL Tel: 020 7351 2108 Mobile: 0411 887120

KES * Keystones, PO Box 387, Stafford, Staffordshire ST16 3FG Tel: 01785 256648

L * Lawrence Fine Art Auctioneers, South Street, Crewkerne, Somerset TA18 8AB Tel: 01460 73041

L&E * B. B. G. Locke & England, 18 Guy Street, Leamington Spa, Warwickshire CV32 4RT Tel: 01926 889100

LA • No longer trading.

LeB • Le Boudoir Collectables, Bartlett Street Antique Centre, Bath, Somerset BA1 2QZ Tel: 01225 311601

LHA * Lesley Hindman Auctioneers, 215 West Ohio Street, Chicago, Illinois USA IL60610 Tel: 001 312 670 0010 Fax: 001 312 670 4248

LT *† Louis Taylor Auctioneers & Valuers, Britannia House, 10 Town Road, Hanley, Stoke-on-Trent, Staffordshire ST1 1QG Tel: 01782 214111

LUC • R. K. Lucas & Son, The Tithe Exchange, 9 Victoria Place, Haverfordwest, Wales SA16 2JX Tel: 01437 762538

M * Morphets of Harrogate, 6 Albert Street, Harrogate, North Yorkshire HG1 1JL Tel: 01423 530030

MAC • Mall Antique Centre, 400 Wincolmlee, Hull East Yorkshire HU2 0QL Tel: 01482 327858

MAR * Frank R. Marshall & Co, Marshall House, Church Hill, Knutsford, Cheshire WA16 6DH Tel: 01565 653284

MAV • May Antiques, Antiquarius V13, 131–141 King's Road, Chelsea, London SW3 4PW Tel: 020 7351 5757

MAW * Thomas Mawer & Son, The Lincoln Saleroom, 63 Monks Road, Lincoln, Lincolnshire LN2 5HP Tel: 01522 524984

MCA *† Mervyn Carey, Twysden Cottage, Benenden, Cranbrook, Kent TN17 4LD Tel: 01580 240283

MEG • Megarry's and Forever Summer, Jericho Cottage, The Duckpond Green, Blackmore, Essex CM4 0RR Tel: 01277 821031/822170

MER • Mere Antiques, 13 Fore Street, Topsham, Exeter, Devon EX3 0HF Tel: 01392 874224 Fax: 01392 874224

MGC * Midlands Commemoratives, The Old Cornmarket Antique Centre, 70 Market Place, Warwick, Warwickshire, CV34 4SO Tel: 01926 419119

MiA • Old Mill Antiques Centre, Mill Street, Low Down, Bridgnorth, Shropshire WV15 5A Tel: 01746 768778

Mit * Mitchells, Fairfield House, Station Road, Cockermouth, Cumbria CA13 9PY Tel: 01900 827800

MJB • Michael J. Bowman, 6 Haccombe House, Netherton, Newton Abbot, Devon TQ12 4SJ Tel: 01626 872890

MLa •† Marion Langham, London Tel: 020 7730 1002

MLL •† Millers Antiques Ltd, Netherbrook House, 86 Christchurch Road, Ringwood, Hampshire BH24 1DR Tel: 01425 472062

MofC • Millers of Chelsea Antiques Ltd, Netherbrook House, 86 Christchurch Road, Ringwood, Hampshire BH24 1DR Tel: 01425 472062

MR * Martyn Rowe, Truro Auction Centre, City Wharf, Malpas Road, Truro, Cornwall TR2 2QH Tel: 01872 260020 Fax: 01872 261794

MRW • Malcolm Russ-Welch, Wild Jebbett, Pudding Bag Lane, Thurlaston, Nr. Rugby, Warwickshire CV23 9JZ Tel: 01788 810616

MSA • No longer trading.

MSB • Marilynn & Sheila Brass, PO Box 380503, Cambridge, MA 02238–0503, USA Tel: 00 1 617 491 6064

MSW • Marilyn Swain Auctions, The Old Barracks, Sandon Road, Grantham, Lincolnshire NG31 9AS Tel: 01476 568861

MTa • Maggie Tallentire, Cousy 82160 Caylus, Tarn et Garonne, France Tel: 00 33 563 24 05 27

N * Neales, 192–104 Mansfield Road, Nottingham, Nottinghamshire, NG1 3HU Tel: 0115 962 4141

NCA • New Century, 69 Kensington Church Street, London W8 4DB Tel: 020 7937 2410

Nor •† Sue Norman, L4 Antiquarius, 135 King's Road, Chelsea, London SW3 5ST Tel: 020 7352 7217

NP • Neville Pundole, 8A & 9 The Friars, Canterbury, Kent CT1 2AS Tel: 01227 453471

OBS • Old Button Shop Antiques, Lytchett Minster, Poole, Dorset BH16 6JF Tel: 01202 622169

OCH • Gillian Shepherd, Old Corner House Antiques, 6 Poplar Road, Wittersham, Tenterden, Kent TN30 7PG Tel: 01797 270236

OD • Offa's Dyke Antique Centre, 4 High Street, Knighton, Powys, Wales LD7 1AT Tel: 01547 528635

Oli * Olivers, Olivers Rooms, Burkitts Lane, Sudbury, Suffolk CO10 1HB Tel: 01787 880305

ONS * Onslow's, The Depot, 2 Michael Road, London SW6 2AD Tel: 020 7371 0505

OO • Peter Oosthuizen, Unit 4 Bourbon Hanby Antiques Centre, 151 Sydney Street, London SW3 6NT Tel: 020 7460 3078

P * Phillips, Blenstock House, 101 New Bond Street, London W1Y OAS Tel: 020 7629 6602/468 8233

P(B) * Phillips, 1 Old King Street, Bath, Somerset BA1 2JT Tel: 01225 310609

P(Ba) * Phillips Bayswater, 10 Salem Road, Bayswater, London W2 4DL Tel: 020 7229 9090

P(C) * Phillips Cardiff, 9–10 Westgate Street, Cardiff, Wales CF1 1DA Tel: 029 2039 6453

P(Ch) * Phillips North West, New House, 150 Christleton Road, Chester, Cheshire Tel: 01244 313936

P(E) * Phillips, Alphin Brook Road, Alphington, Exeter, Devon EX2 8TH Tel: 01392 439025

P(EA) * Phillips, 32 Boss Hall Road, Ipswich, Suffolk IP1 59J Tel: 01473 740494

P(G) * Phillips Fine Art Auctioneers, Millmead, Guildford, Surrey GU2 5BE Tel: 01483 504030

P(NE) * Phillips North East, St Mary's, Oakwellgate, Gateshead, Tyne & Wear NE8 2AX Tel: 0191 477 6688

P(O) * Phillips, 39 Park End Street, Oxford, Oxfordshire OX1 1JD Tel: 01865 723524

P(S) * Phillips, 49 London Road, Sevenoaks, Kent TN13 1AR Tel: 01732 740310

PAC * Potteries Antique Centre, 271 Waterloo Road, Cobridge, Stoke-on-Trent, Staffordshire ST6 3HR Tel: 01782 201455

PAD * Padworth Auctions, 30 The Broadway, Thatcham, Berkshire RG19 3HX Tel: 01734 713772 Fax: 01633 867681

PBi • Peter Bird, 811 Christchurch Road, Boscombe, Dorset BH21 1TZ Tel: 01202 429111

PC Private Collection

PCh * Peter Cheney, Western Road Auction Rooms, Western Road, Littlehampton, Sussex Tel: 01903 722264 & 713428

PFK * Penrith Farmers' & Kidd's plc, Skirsgill Salerooms, Penrith, Cumbria CA11 0DN Tel: 01768 890781 Fax: 01768 895058

PF * Peter Francis, The Curiosity Saleroom, 19 King Street, Carmarthen, South Wales SA31 1BH Tel: 01267 233456

PGA • Paul Gibbs Antiques, 25 Castle Street, Conway, Gwynedd, Wales, LL32 8AY Tel: 01492 593429/596533

PHA • Paul Hopwell, 30 High Street, West Haddon, Northamptonshire NN6 7AP Tel: 01788 510636

PLY * The Plymouth Auction Rooms, Edwin House, St John's Road, Cattedown, Plymouth, Devon PL4 0NZ Tel: 01752 254740

POW • Sylvia Powell Decorative Arts, 18 The Mall, Camden Passage, London N12 0PD Tel: 020 7354 2977/020 8458 4543

PP • Poole Pottery, The Quay, Poole, Dorset BH15 1RF Tel: 01202 666200

PrB • Pretty Bizarre, 170 High Street, Deal, Kent CT14 6BQ Tel: 07973 794537

PSA • Pantiles Spa Antiques, 4, 5, 6 Union House, The Pantiles, Tunbridge Wells, Kent TV4 8HE Tel: 01892 541377

QSA • Quiet Street Antiques, 3 Quiet Street, Bath, Avon BA1 2JG Tel: 01225 315727

RA • Roberts Antiques, Lancashire Tel: 01253 827798

Rac/ • Rochester Antiques Centre, 93 High Street,
RAC Rochester, Kent ME1 1LX Tel: 01634 846144

RAT • No longer trading.

RBB *† Russell, Baldwin & Bright, Fine Art Salerooms, Ryelands Road, Leominster, Herefordshire HR6 8NZ Tel: 01568 611122

RCh • Rayner & Chamberlain, London Tel: 020 8293 9439

RdeR •† Rogers de Rin, 76 Hospital Road, London SW3 4HN Tel: 020 7352 9007

RDG • Richard Dennis Gallery, 144 Kensington Church Street, London W8 4BN Tel: 020 7727 2061

RIC • Rich Designs, Unit 1, Grove Farm, Bromyard Road, Worcester WR2 5UG Tel: 01905 748214

RIT * Ritchie Inc, 288 King Street East, Toronto, Ontario, Canada, M5A 1K4 Tel: 364 1864

RP • Robert Pugh, Avon Tel: 01225 314713

RTo * Rupert Toovey & Co Ltd, Star Road, Partridge Green, Sussex RH13 8RJ Tel: 01403 711744

RUM • Rumours, 10 The Mall, Upper Street, Camden Passage, Islington, London N1 OPD Tel: 01582 873561

RWB •† Roy W. Bunn Antiques, 34–36 Church Street, Barnoldswick, Colne, Lancashire BB8 5UT Tel: 01282 813703

RYA • Robert Young Antiques, 68 Battersea Bridge Road, London SW1 3AG Tel: 020 7228 7847

S * Sotheby's 34–35 New Bond Street, London W1A 2AA Tel: 020 7293 5000

S(Am) * Sotheby's Amsterdam, Rokin 102, Amsterdam, The Netherlands, 1012 KZ Tel: 0031 20 550 2200

S(NY) * Sotheby's, 1334 York Avenue, New York, NY10021 USA Tel: 001212 606 7000

S(S) * Sotheby's Sussex, Summers Place, Billingshurst, Sussex RH14 9AD Tel: 01403 833500

S(Sc) * Sotheby's, 112 George Street, Edinburgh, Scotland EH2 4LH Tel: 0131 226 7201

SAS *† Special Auction Services, The Coach House, Midgham Park, Reading, Berkshire RG7 5UG Tel: 0118 971 2949

SCA • Susie Cooper Ceramics (Art Deco), GO70–4 Alfies Antique Market, 13–25 Church Street, London NW8 8DT Tel: 020 7723 0449

SCO •† Peter Scott, Stand 39, Bartlett Street Antiques Centre, Bath, Somerset BA1 2QZ Tel: 01225 310457

SER •† Serendipity, 168 High Street, Deal, Kent CT14 6BQ Tel: 01304 369165/366536

SHa • Shapiro & Co, Stand 380, Grays Antique Market, 58 Davies Street, London W12Y 1LB Tel: 020 7491 2710

SK * Skinner Inc, The Heritage On The Garden, 63 Park Plaza, Boston, MA 02116, USA Tel: 001 617 350 5400

SK(B) * Skinner Inc, 357 Main Street, Bolton, MA 01740 USA Tel: 001 978 779 6241

SLL • Sylvanna Llewelyn Antiques, Unit 5, Bourbon-Hanby Antiques Centre, 151 Sydney Street, Chelsea, London SW3 6NY Tel: 020 7351 4981

SLN * Sloan's, 4920 Wyaconda Road, North Bethesda, MD 20852, USA Tel: 001 301 468 4911/669 5066

SMI • Janie Smithson, Lincolnshire Tel/Fax: 01754 810265 Mobile: 0831 399180

SnA • Snape Maltings Antique & Collectors Centre, Saxmundham, Suffolk IP17 1SR Tel: 01728 688038

SPU • Spurrier-Smith Antiques, 28, 39, 41 Church Street, Ashbourne, Derbyshire DE6 1AJ Tel: 01335 343669/342198

SRC • Soviet Russia Collectables, PO Box 6, Virginia Water, Surrey GU25 4YU Tel: 01344 843091

SSW • Spencer Swaffer, 30 High Street, Arundel, Sussex BN18 9AB Tel: 01903 882132

StC • St Clere Antiques, PO Box 161, Sevenoaks, Kent TN15 6GA

SUC • Succession, 18 Richmond Hill, Richmond, Surrey TW10 6QX Tel: 020 8940 6774

SWN • Swan Antiques, Stone Street, Cranbrook, Kent TN17 3HF Tel: 01580 712720

SWO * G. E. Sworder & Sons, 14 Cambridge Road, Stansted Mountfitchet, Essex CM24 8BZ

TAC • Tenterden Antiques Centre, 66–66A High Street, Tenterden, Kent TN30 6AU

TAR • Lorraine Tarrant Antiques, 7–11 Market Place, Ringwood, Hampshire BH24 1AN Tel: 01425 461123

TEN * Tennants, The Auction Centre, Harmby Road, Leyburn, Yorkshire DL8 5SG Tel: 01969 623780

TH •† Tony Horsley, Sussex Tel: 01273 550770

TK • Timothy Kendrew, Ravenshead, Nottinghamshire NG15 9AL Tel: 01623 798924

TMA *† Brown & Merry, Tring Market Auctions, Brook Street, Tring, Hertfordshire HP23 5EF Tel: 01442 826446

TP • The Collector, Tom Power, 4 Queens Parade Close, Friern Barnet, London N11 3FY Tel: 020 8361 6111

TPA • Times Past Antiques, 59 High Street, Eton, Windsor, Berkshire SL4 6BL Tel: 01753 857018

TPCS • Torquay Pottery Collectors' Society, Torre Abbey, Avenue Road, Torquay, Devon TQ2 5JX

TRL * Thomson, Roddick & Laurie, 60 Whitesands, Dumfries, Scotland DG1 2RS Tel: 01387 255366 and 24 Lowther Street, Carlisle, Cumbria CA3 8DA Tel: 01228 28939/39636

TVA • Teme Valley Antiques, 1 The Bull Ring, Ludlow, Shropshire SY8 1AD Tel: 01584 874686

TVM • No longer trading.

UTP • Utility Plus, 66 High Street, West Ham, Pevensey, Sussex BN24 5LP

VH • Valerie Howard, By appointment only, 2 Campden Street, Off Kensington Church Street, London W8 7EP Tel: 020 7792 9702

VSt • Vera Strange Antiques, 811 Christchurch Road, Boscombe, Bournemouth, Dorset BH7 6HP Tel: 01202 429111

W * Walter's, No. 1 Mint Lane, Lincoln, Lincolnshire LN1 1UD Tel: 01522 525454

W&S • Pat Woodward & Alma Shaw, Unit G43, Ground Floor, Gloucester Antiques Centre, In The Historic Docks, Severn Road, Gloucester, Gloucestershire GL1 2LE

WAB • Warboys Antiques, Old Church School, High Street, Warboys, Huntingdon, Cambridgeshire PE17 4DF Tel: 01905 610680

WAC • Worcester Antiques Centre, Reindeer Court, Mealcheapen Street, Worcester, Worcestershire WR1 4DF Tel: 01905 610680

WilP • B. B. G. Wilson Peacock, The Auction Centre, 26 Newnham Street, Bedford, Bedfordshire MK40 3JR Tel: 01234 266366

WL * Wintertons Ltd, Lichfield, Auction Centre, Wood End Lane, Fradley, Lichfield, Staffordshire WS13 8NF Tel: 01543 263256

WN • What Now, Cavendish Arcade, The Crescent, Buxton, Derbyshire SK17 6BQ Tel: 01298 27178/23417

WTA • No longer trading.

WW * Woolley & Wallis, 51–61 Castle Street, Salisbury, Wiltshire SP1 3SU Tel: 01722 424500

WWY • When We Were Young, The Old Forge, High Street, Harmondsworth Village, Middlesex UB7 0AQ Tel: 020 8897 3583

YAN • Yanni's Antiques, 538 San Anselmo Avenue, San Anselmo, CA 94960 USA Tel: 001 415 459 2996

YC • Yesterday Child, Angel Arcade, 118 Islington High Street, London N1 8EG Tel: 020 7354 1601

YY • No longer trading.

ZEI • Zeitgeist, 58 Kensington Church Street, London W8 4DB Tel/Fax: 020 7938 4817

Index

Italic page numbers denote colour pages; **bold** numbers refer to information and pointer boxes.